Securing U.S. Innovation

Securing U.S. Innovation

The Challenge of Preserving a Competitive Advantage in the Creation of Knowledge

Darren E. Tromblay and Robert G. Spelbrink

ROWMAN & LITTLEFIELD
Lanham • Boulder • New York • London

Published by Rowman & Littlefield
A wholly owned subsidiary of The Rowman & Littlefield Publishing Group, Inc.
4501 Forbes Boulevard, Suite 200, Lanham, Maryland 20706
www.rowman.com

Unit A, Whitacre Mews, 26-34 Stannary Street, London SE11 4AB

British Library Cataloguing in Publication Information Available

Library of Congress Cataloging-in-Publication Data Available

ISBN 978-1-4422-5634-7 (cloth : alk. paper)
ISBN 978-1-4422-5635-4 (pbk. : alk. paper)
ISBN 978-1-4422-5636-1 (electronic)

∞™ The paper used in this publication meets the minimum requirements of American National Standard for Information Sciences—Permanence of Paper for Printed Library Materials, ANSI/NISO Z39.48-1992.

Printed in the United States of America

To my dear Washington, D.C., family at Holy Trinity Catholic Church.
—Darren E. Tromblay

A special thanks to Judy, for her love and support.
—Robert G. Spelbrink

Contents

Acknowledgments

Many people have contributed to our thinking on the issues discussed in this book. We owe a debt to Frederick J. Buckley, the model of what an FBI special agent should be, with his blend of intelligence, common sense, and humanity. Another individual of significant influence is "Deborah" [name redacted], who humored our thinking out loud about a number of the intelligence problems discussed within this book. The oracular "Molly" [name redacted] has long been a fount of insights as well as humor. John F. Fox Jr., a good friend, was always willing to lend an ear and an idea whenever we barged into his office without invitation. Finally, many thanks to Marie-Claire Antoine, our editor at Rowman & Littlefield, who believed that this was a worthwhile book to write.

Introduction

The United States—as a country—is increasingly at a loss when it comes to marshaling innovation to support and strengthen the elements of national power that Washington needs in order to protect and promote its interests. The U.S. position is a case study of trends that have global implications. The country—government, industry, and academia—is targeted by traditional foreign intelligence activities, albeit sometimes in a twenty-first-century guise, such as the use of cyber means to exfiltrate proprietary data rather than having an operative abscond with hard copies of documents. Private industry and academia, meanwhile, are outpacing the government's technological capabilities and are not always willing to cooperate with it, leaving U.S. security and intelligence agencies behind on new developments in areas such as encryption, even as threat actors are free to exploit these advances for nefarious purposes. Finally, foreign direct investment has created new norms for distribution of knowledge. Inflows and outflows of money ultimately result in the movement of ideas and technology. FDI activities of "buying in" and "selling out," in addition to bringing out legitimate transfers of intellectual property, also create new opportunities for economic espionage.

Through most of the history of the United States, innovation has been a prevailing and defining characteristic of the country. U.S. innovation has been a dominant force in the world and enabled it to become a global superpower. However, in recent years, the United States has increasingly been at a loss as to how to utilize innovation to promote and protect its national interests. Foreign threat actors wishing to acquire U.S. innovation by any means possible are continually targeting the U.S. government, industry, and academic institutions, while domestically, the private sector, where much innovation now occurs, has been increasingly diverging from the country's interests—as epitomized by the recent impasse between Apple and the FBI. The U.S.

government's role in protecting—and leveraging—the country's innovation in furtherance of the national interest is changing. Even as the United States continues to navigate a geopolitical environment in which innovation is essential to elements of national power, private industry and academia—which are increasing responsible for innovation—operate with increasing independence from U.S. government interests (and may also have to account for the preferences held by the leadership of geopolitical competitors where markets are located). Private industry and academia are also in an unenviable situation because, as frontrunners outpacing U.S. government innovation efforts, they are now in the crosshairs of state actors that are wielding professional intelligence services directed at collecting proprietary information. This is an inflection point in the progress of U.S. innovation. The U.S. government is underpowered and industry/academia is overwhelmed.

This is not a book about counterintelligence as an arcane field, but rather as a practical exercise. It is an endeavor to understand the capability for successful innovation in the international environment. It treats the capability as a concept that underpins the ability to establish, maintain, and enhance elements of national power. Because of the geopolitical significance of innovation, governments and nonstate actors pursue it. Intelligence collection and efforts to counter it are one element of a broader game. The book, therefore, is not simply about securing the capability for innovation; it is also a study of why intelligence and counterintelligence should be integrated into an understanding of any geopolitical problem and not viewed merely as a technocratic discipline.

Innovation by its nature is a relative concept. The "cutting edge" is only as far as the horizon has been pushed. State and nonstate actors, therefore, do not simply want specific technologies, but the ability to continually generate new capabilities. China, for example, in 2007 made the country's "capacity for innovation" a high priority.[1] The ongoing nature of innovation means that it is a field fraught with perpetual competition. The competition may be manifest at any number of levels—ranging from individual scientists, to companies, to nation-states seeking the newest ways to project power. When cooperation does occur, it can be counted on to be temporary or parasitic, as both sides seek their own advantage. An example of the latter is the U.S.–China relationship on matters of science and technology. When this relationship was initiated in 1979, the U.S. objectives were geopolitical—the objective being to engage and influence the newly opened China (the broader context being to use this relationship as a means to pressure Moscow)—while Beijing's incentive was acquisition of expertise. Nearly four decades later, the United States has lost this point of reference. Diplomatic engagement has yielded decreasing benefits, as China becomes increasingly aggressive, whereas China has continued to acquire technological knowledge that it can use against U.S. systems.

The topic of engagement is at the heart of this book, with the concepts of "buying in" and "selling out" being the categories of organization. Buying in refers to state and nonstate actors, which take the initiative to acquire U.S. assets through engagement with U.S. government, private sector, and academic institutions. This may take the form of actual investment in the private sector (for example, Chinese purchases of U.S. technology companies), the purchase of services or education, and the acquisition of U.S. government–sponsored expertise through scientific exchanges. Selling out, on the other hand, focuses on U.S. companies taking the initiative to pursue opportunities abroad. There is admittedly a gray area between these two ends of the spectrum, given that as the old aphorism goes, "it takes two to tango."

Buying in/selling out provides a paradigm to demonstrate that the innovative edge can shift through a spectrum of activities that range from licit to illicit. State-sponsored companies may make legitimate investments or may sponsor the visits of individuals who come to the United States with the express purpose of stealing proprietary knowledge. Similarly, individuals with scientific expertise may travel internationally to attend professional events or they may surreptitiously go abroad for debriefings by foreign governments that are attempting to secretly obtain an unfair advantage. These spectrums of activity require a more holistic look at how the United States operates within the international environment to protect its proprietary knowledge and technology. Increases in foreign interactions create commensurate increases in vulnerabilities.

Several countries—Russia and China—have a prominent place in this book. This is not an arbitrary singling out of specific state actors. Instead, it is consistent with identified geostrategic threats. Both China and Russia view themselves as powers directly engaged in rivalry with the United States. In his 2014 testimony on "Current and Projected National Security Threats to the United States," James Clapper, the director of National Intelligence, highlighted Russia and China as the "leading state intelligence threats to US interests."[2] Furthermore, Russia and China have been identified as being particularly aggressive in the cyber theater of operations. Russia's Ministry of Defense, for instance, is establishing a cyber command that will engage in offensive cyber operations.[3] Furthermore, Clapper characterized China as "an advanced cyber actor in terms of capabilities" and yet "often able to succeed in establishing access to their targets using less sophisticated cyber tools and techniques."[4] This ability to operate at a lower-tech level is interestingly similar to China's HUMINT collection, which has consistently used nonintelligence-affiliated individuals to gather information.

However, the United States faces other challenges to its capability for innovation. Smaller, rogue states (for example, Iran) have attempted to circumvent sanctions—that have blocked their ability to innovate—by engaging in surreptitious acquisition of technology. Other states (for example, North Korea) have attempted to destroy U.S. capabilities for creating new knowledge. While the Sony hack was arguably an act of political pique, it is not beyond the realm of possibility that a foreign state or nonstate actor, if given the chance, would destroy U.S. intellectual property to set back development of military or civilian capabilities. Of course it is not just geopolitical rivals that attempt to compromise U.S. innovation. Multiple allied and friendly countries—including France and Israel—have directed resources at acquiring U.S. technology. As the old adage goes, there are friendly governments, but there are no friendly intelligence services.

The United States is a unique point of focus for a discussion of competition over the capabilities for innovation. For the latter half of the twentieth century and into the twenty-first it was the global leader in creating technology. However, competitor nation-states are putting a concerted effort into catching up, through increased investment in research and development.[5] This zeal is apparent in foreign entities' interest in acquiring access to U.S. resources—especially human capital that not only catches a country up but also allows it to move ahead with innovation. However, the U.S. government has displayed lethargy about this narrowing gap between the United States and the rest of the world. Not only has it seen its share of R&D spending slipping, but it has also made decisions that have given competitors—especially China—access to the raw elements of innovation through educational exchanges, purchases of U.S. technology companies, and more. Additionally, the benefit of innovation by the private sector to U.S. national security has been diminished and even harmed by companies that refuse to cooperate with the U.S. government. Entities working in the field of encryption, for instance, have been resistant to cooperation with federal law enforcement. Furthermore, companies in the private sector that are engaged in R&D often find themselves pitted against state-directed intelligence resources, whether in the form of traditional spies or infiltration of their cyber networks.

This is a moment of great vulnerability for a leader in innovation. Washington relies on its advantage of previous decades to continue. The 2016 budget of the U.S. government stated, "Technological superiority enables the United States to project power to dangerous environments, defend against threats in all domains, and continuously adapt, innovate and prevail as new threats arise." However, it also acknowledges that "maintaining this superiority is becoming increasingly challenging as potential adversaries have accelerated their investments in modernizing their militaries and as disruptive technologies have proliferated, resulting in growing threats where U.S. access had been formerly assured."[6] The U.S. ability to leverage innovation to support elements of national power not only requires the forward movement of innovation—which already occurs—but also taking competition from foreign actors seriously and making decisions accordingly.

The competition between countries does not occur in a vacuum. Instead, multiple entities—including U.S. private industry—contribute to the capabilities that support a government's elements of national power. Companies seeking to do business with the U.S. government must be aware of the impact risk taking may have on the integrity of what they provide to Washington. This is not simply a question of good corporate citizenship; it is also a commercial consideration as one can only expect the government to demand assurances from vendors in the wake of high-profile scandals such as the breach of the Office of Personnel Management information on twenty-one million individuals. Additionally, corporate cooperation with the government is a public relations consideration. Firms that develop cutting-edge technologies such as point-to-point encryption have found themselves squarely in the spotlight over accusations that their products have prevented law enforcement and intelligence agencies from being able to disrupt terrorist and criminal activities.

The private sector and academia must also be concerned about the threat from foreign governments or nonstate actors. Because both industry and academia are often the drivers of innovation, their proprietary knowledge and technology are a target of intelligence collection. This collection is often sponsored by foreign governments that have professional intelligence services on which to draw expertise. While defending against a foreign intelligence service may be an unfair matchup, it is a reality that has resulted in repeated compromises, as this book illustrates. At the least, potential targets should evaluate their business decisions, particularly those with an international nexus, through the lens of introduced vulnerabilities. This does not mean that isolationism is a wise strategy. Instead, it means that a new level of due diligence should be undertaken. Measures must be taken to mitigate the identified risks. In the private sector, this will not only protect a company's assets but also provide an assurance to shareholders.

The illicit transfer of intellectual property occurs on multiple interlocking planes. Traditional collection by human agents provides a vector not only for gathering information but also for supporting collection through technical means; for example, the introduction of malware onto an entity's network. Cyber is an operational environment in which traditional intelligence objectives are carried out through new tradecraft and tactics.

The illicit competition to develop engines of innovation occurs on multiple—sometimes intersecting—fronts. Common to all of these is the human factor: the decision makers who are responsible for the gamut of actions that range from setting a state or nonstate actor's strategic priorities to the individuals responsible for tactical implementation. These individuals must evaluate and act on information. This process shapes the use of collection methods, whether those methods are of the most traditional, low-tech nature (for example, recruitment of spies by foreign intelligence services) or high-tech cyber attacks.

Currently it is the latter end of spectrum—high-tech cyber-facilitated collection—that is the focus of significant security concerns. As former NSA director Keith Alexander noted, the cyber theft of U.S. companies' intellectual property is "the greatest transfer of wealth in history."[7] The mind-boggling quantities of data that are being extracted from U.S. systems and the ability to corrupt those systems to impair the capabilities of the United States and its allies and friends sometimes overshadows the reality that cyber activities are only as effective as the human factor that perpetrates them and exploits the information. In 2014, the FBI contributed to the indictment of five Chinese hackers who were working on behalf of China's Peoples' Liberation Army (PLA). The U.S. action was viewed in some quarters as futile and even laughable (the individuals were not in the United States, and it was improbable that China would hand over these state-sponsored operatives). However, it drove home an important point: cyber operations are only an extension of their perpetrators.

Human imperfections introduce vulnerabilities into the most foolproof technology. Supposedly unbreakable Soviet codes were cracked by U.S. code breakers because intelligence operatives reused one-time encryption. Current iterations of mistakes in operational security may result in telltale indicators associated with cyber attacks, which may allow public and private sector institutions to identify the originator of an attack. Once an adversary has made its intentions known, whether via a cyber attack, a traditional pitch by an intelligence officer, or something else, its interests can be used against it by introducing false information into what it is collecting. For instance, in the early 1980s, after learning what technologies the Soviet Union was targeting, the United States provided it with modified items designed to fail. Private industry has begun to explore the use of deceptions for their own purposes. For instance, "honey pots" can be used to intentionally attract attacks so that security firms that can study attackers' operations.[8]

The human factor also introduces imperfections on the security side of the equation. The best defenses can fail if not used properly or if they are intentionally compromised. The trusted insider—an individual with legitimate access to an organization's sensitive information—poses the most serious threat to innovation. The insider who intentionally damages an organization by providing proprietary information to an adversary or competitor is most commonly conjured as a security concern. It is important to recognize that insiders can also be unwitting agents that are unaware of how they have been manipulated by an adversary. Unwitting insiders can have equally deleterious effects on an organization's interests as those that intentionally betray the trust of the organization. According to Sergei Tretyakov, Russia's SVR, the foreign intelligence successor to the KGB, was not above manipulating diplomatic sources who never realized that they were being used for intelligence-gathering purposes.[9] In the cyber realm such unwitting actors may inadvertently compromise information by falling victim to a spear-phishing attack—taking inappropriate precautions before opening a suspect email attachment.

This book can be viewed as a case study—using the United States as an example—of a country that benefits from and counts on the continued integrity of innovation in the global geopolitical and commercial setting. It factors in the strategic considerations of what the government's objectives and capabilities are in terms of using innovation to maintain elements of national power. Within this context, federal, state, local, private, and academic institutions pursue the work of innovation. This work can be to both the benefit and detriment of national interest. International engagement can create complications for the United States, as foreign state and nonstate entities may exploit such activities to gain an advantage with which they may challenge the U.S. government, its industries, and its academic institutions.

Chapters 1 and 2 examine the existing U.S. posture toward securing innovation. Context is provided by Washington's understanding of how innovation supports elements of national power—the levers that the United States employs to pursue its geopolitical objectives. This understanding has been codified throughout the country's history in a number of laws that govern the transfer of sensitive knowledge and the actors entitled to receive such information. Multiple U.S. government policy, security, and intelligence agencies are responsible for overseeing and ensuring compliance with these statutes.

Chapter 3 examines the apparatuses and tactics directed at collecting knowledge as they pertain to innovation. Countries—particularly authoritarian states such as China and Russia—can strategically define their objectives for technology development across sectors. These countries and their predecessors established organizations responsible for implementing collection to achieve the governments' science and technology objectives. Collection was through both legal and illegal means, but the purpose on the customer was the same. At the level of implementation, intelligence collectors (whether affiliated with a formal intelligence service or not) used a variety of tradecraft to acquire information.

Chapters 4 through 7 are the heart of the book. They examine how foreign entities have used international engagement—"buying in" and "selling out"—to target knowledge of strategic value to the countries with which they are associated. Chapter 4 and chapter 6 provide a discussion of how information is legitimately transferred out of the United States and into the reach of foreign governments. The significance of such transfers is that, while they may make immediate market sense, they in aggregate represent a Pandora's Box, yielding a windfall to governments that do not always share Washington's interests. This warrants greater scrutiny by bodies such as the Committee on Foreign Investment in the United States (CFIUS). The dark side of international engagements is found in chapters 5 and 7, which illustrate how, time and again, U.S. competitors and adversaries have exploited inherent vulnerabilities in commerce to surreptitiously acquire proprietary information from its rightful owners. Consistent with the government-driven collection activities discussed in chapter 3, foreign state and nonstate actors use licit and illicit means interchangeably to obtain desired information.

Chapter 8 examines the changing relationship between innovation in the public and private sector and its implications for the United States' continued ability to remain on the global cutting edge. U.S innovation, in the international environment, took shape during World War II and the Cold War as the United States was forced to become less isolationist. Until the end of the Cold War, the military-industrial complex spun off advances that could be applied in the civilian world. However, as the need for countering Soviet programs faded, the private sector, which had answered U.S. government needs, found a different customer base. The current landscape is one in which the United States is an adopter and adapter of technology rather than a sponsor and originator. The geopolitical upshot is that U.S. industry has greater freedom to make short-term decisions oriented toward gaining access to foreign markets that may run counter to the national interest. The downside is that the U.S. government has less ability to maintain security with respect to innovation.

Chapter 9 provides an accounting of the current U.S. government programs in place to engage private industry and academia on securing its innovation and the proprietary knowledge. Such programs can no longer rely on stereotypical security-oriented approaches to cleared defense contractors that are bound by government rules. Instead, the government will need to legitimately partner and find shared interests with the many private sector entities that control access to cutting-edge technologies that have implications for U.S. strategic interests, but that are not contractually or legally obligated to the government.

It is neither possible nor desirable for the United States' engines of innovation to disengage from the world. However, the government, private sector, and academic enterprises that produce the cutting-edge knowledge in their respective fields must give greater consideration to what the implications are for their proprietary information when they partner with foreign state and nonstate actors. Legitimate transfers of knowledge, even when legal, may not be in the long-term interests of the United States or the originating entity. Furthermore, new relationships or adoption of new technologies may introduce unforeseen vulnerabilities that should be mitigated before they provide access for illicit collection. Counterintelligence—identifying the ways in which information can be exfiltrated by a competitor or adversary—should become a core part of due diligence.

NOTES

1. "Mixed Bag, Pros and Cons: SOE's Are Good at Infrastructure Projects, Not So Good at Innovation," *Economist*, January 21, 2012.

2. *Annual Open Hearing on Current and Projected National Security Threats to the United States: Hearings before the Select Committee on Intelligence of the United States Senate*, 113th Cong. 3 (2014).

3. U.S. Cybersecurity and Policy: Senate Armed Services Committee (September 29, 2015) (Statement for the Record, U.S. Cybersecurity and Policy, Senate Armed Services Committee, James R. Clapper, Director of National Intelligence).

4. Ibid.

5. Mark Muro, Jonathan Rothwell, Scott Andes, Kenan Fikri, and Siodharth Kulkarni, *America's Advanced Industries: What They Are, Where They Are, and Why They Matter* (Washington, D.C.: Brookings, 2015), 11.

6. Fiscal Year 2016 Budget of the U.S. Government 48.

7. *Today's Rising Terrorist Threat and the Danger to the United States: Reflections on the Tenth Anniversary of the 9/11 Commission Report* (Washington, D.C.: Bipartisan Policy Center, 2014), 19.

8. "Firewalls and Firefights; Business and Cyber Crime," *Economist*, August 10, 2013.

9. Pete Earley, *Comrade J: The Untold Secrets of Russia's Master Spy in America After the End of the Cold War* (New York: Penguin, 2007), 182–83.

Chapter One

Theoretical and Legal Framework for Understanding the Role of Intelligence in Securing Innovation

The process of innovation is integral to sustaining national power in all of its forms. Innovation refers to "an idea, embodied in a technology, product, or process which is new and created value. To be impactful, innovations must also be scalable, not merely one-off novelties."[1] Because innovation is so fundamental to nation-states' survival through military, economic, and other means, it is often at the center of intelligence (acquisition) and counterintelligence (protection) activities. This creates a complex enterprise, as intelligence services not only have to identify what they are targeting but also ascertain what adversaries are interested in acquiring. For the United States it is even more convoluted, as much of the country's most cutting-edge intellectual capital is in the private sector. The history of legislation intended to protect the assets associated with U.S. innovation from foreign government–affiliated actors has shifted from focusing strictly on direct threats to the U.S. government to disruption of foreign threats—both commercial and governmental.

NATIONAL POWER AND INNOVATION

Power is, broadly, the ability to influence the behavior of another party to achieve a desired outcome. Elements of national power (ENPs), the tools that a state can wield in furtherance of its international objectives, consist of diplomacy, information, military force, and economics. ENPs provide the context for clandestine competition over the capacities for and the benefits from innovation. Political scientist Ashley Tellis identified that understanding national power is not only an accounting of visible assets but also entails unpacking capabilities such as the aptitude for innovation and the quality of

1

the knowledge base.[2] Furthermore, ENPs are not static objects for display; they must be converted through national processes and employed toward goals.[3] These processes may result in the wielding of "hard" or "soft" power. Hard power is the use of carrots and sticks—offering incentives or threatening consequences—to achieve desired outcomes. Soft power, a concept championed by the political scientist Joseph Nye, is leadership via attractiveness—it is premised on the idea that state and nonstate actors will voluntarily opt into cooperation with U.S. policies based on a perception that these are legitimate and worth supporting.

Innovation is integral to maintaining ENPs and in conversion of these into specific results. Clearly power in the military and economic fields is contingent on the competitive edge provided by successful innovation. However, it is equally valuable in the context of information. While innovation certainly has ramifications for the infrastructure that facilitates communications, it also, far more broadly, represents the new information (and resulting knowledge) that is a crux of competition between international actors. From a diplomatic perspective, innovation is a topic that the United States has used to build bridges and demonstrate its leadership. Maintaining a competitive edge in this area means that the United States will have this card to play. Innovation is equally applicable in the contexts of "hard" and "soft" power. On one end of the spectrum, it is integral to the creation of new weapons, and on the other, it has been used as a testament to the creativity of American society vis-à-vis repressive societies.

THE ROLE OF INNOVATION IN U.S. STRATEGY

The U.S. government's National Security Strategy, issued in early 2015, articulates a vision in which innovation is essential to multiple objectives. Safeguarding our "science and technology base to keep our edge in the capabilities needed to prevail against any adversary" is a component of the strategy's proposal to strengthen national defense.[4] The strategy's consideration of economic matters also dwells on issues of innovation:

> Scientific discovery and technological innovation empower American leadership with a competitive edge that secures our military advantage, propels our economy, and improves the human condition. Sustaining that edge requires robust Federal investments in basic and applied research. We must also strengthen science technology, engineering, and mathematics (STEM) education to produce tomorrow's discoverers, inventors, entrepreneurs, and high-skills workforce. . . . We will also keep our edge by opening our national labs to more commercial partnerships while tapping research and development in the private

sector including a wide range of start-ups and firms at the leading edge of the America's innovation economy.[5]

Finally, the strategy addresses the need to preserve access to "shared spaces," specifically cyber space and air and maritime security. All of these environments remain unconquered to varying degrees, primarily because technology sufficient to sustain a constant human presence in these settings has yet to be developed. Geopolitics abhors a vacuum, as current competition focused on the Arctic illustrates.[6] This means that innovation is central to the geopolitical competition to establish and maintain a presence in these realms.

The National Intelligence Strategy—which outlines the programs that will provide policymakers with an information advantage—highlights the necessity of advanced technology. It cites "innovation" among its Enterprise Objectives, focusing on finding and deploying new scientific discoveries and technologies.[7] A critical aspect of innovation is the cyber milieu. Among the Strategy's mission objectives is detecting and understanding cyber threats so as to support national security decision making, cyber security, and cyber effects operations. As the Strategy indicates, the intelligence community must be familiar with the results of innovation, as it "provides needed expertise to defend U.S. government networks along with other critical communications networks and national infrastructure." U.S. innovation does not exist in a vacuum, but instead exists in the context of what competitors and adversaries are accomplishing. The Strategy acknowledges this, suggesting that "state and non-state actors use digital technologies to achieve economic and military advantages, foment instability, increase control over content in cyberspace, and achieve other strategic goals."[8]

Counterintelligence, especially in its efforts to prevent the compromise of public and private sector proprietary information, is essential to ensuring that the United States reaps the rewards of innovation. The 2007 National Counterintelligence Strategy (the most recent publicly available version) highlights the scope of concerns, stating that foreign intelligence activities are not limited to targeting the intelligence community and the U.S. government. Instead, the "private sector and academia are fertile breeding grounds for advanced scientific discovery, cutting-edge technology, and advanced research and development that make them irresistible 'soft targets' for foreign intelligence collectors."[9] The task of protecting U.S. entities from foreign exploitation is made even more difficult because the significance of assets may not even be known to those who control them.[10] For instance, certain technologies and research that are ultimately deemed restricted emerge from unclassified and accessible work.

The capability for innovation (as opposed to the outcomes of that capability) is integral to the United States' international interests. As noted by the

2015 Strategy for American Innovation from the National Economic Council and the Office of Science Technology Policy, "while many countries can grow by adopting existing technologies and business practices, America must continually innovate, because [its] workers and firms are generally already operating at the technological frontier." Furthermore, according to a 2015 Brookings Institution study, the advanced industrial sector, which benefits from and often contributes to innovation, "looms large in supporting such national and global objectives as national security, energy independence, food sustainability, health and rising standards of living."[11] U.S. interests are not just tied to the outcomes of innovation but rather to the viability of the process, which includes such hard-to-measure factors as human capital, integrity of academic institutions, exclusivity of technology, and more.

ROLE OF PRIVATE
INDUSTRY INNOVATION IN U.S. STRATEGY

Even though innovation is indisputably key to the national interest, the United States' innovative base has shifted since the end of the Cold War to independent private industry (as opposed to contractors working at the behest of federal agencies). According to a 2014 report produced by the Center for Strategic and International Studies, the U.S. Department of Defense, thirty years prior, was a net supplier of innovation to the global market, as its military technologies informed civilian products.[12] As of 2014, it had become a net consumer of global, commercial innovation. More broadly, federal funding of applied research was two times higher in 1964 than it was in 2013 and federal funding of applied development was three times higher in 1964 than it was in 2013.[13]

This shift means that, even though the United States, as a country, can continue to innovate, this capability, essential to the national interest, is increasingly in the hands of companies that are not beholden to the government. Private industry is, therefore, responsible for an essential aspect of ENPs. This also puts them in the crosshairs of international rivalry for access to innovation and resultant technology. As a 2015 study produced by the Bipartisan Policy Center noted, a large share of China's rapidly increasing investments in research and development will be directed at achieving a competitive edge over the United States.[14] As this book will discuss in greater detail, China and other countries have repeatedly employed clandestine intelligence activities as one means by which to close the gap in knowledge. Consequently, the private sector must develop a counterintelligence competency—a field normally occupied by U.S. government entities such as the Federal Bureau of Investigation.

There are two broad types of knowledge state or nonstate actors will seek to obtain. The first of these is *innovation*—the new development that represents a breakthrough in understanding a topic, applying a technology, and more. This will be of greatest value to actors already on a similar plane with the United States. The second concept is the idea of *accrued knowledge*—the cumulative result of an ongoing program of innovation that provides the foundation on which current work is being done. This will be targeted by states that lag significantly behind U.S. capabilities. For instance, John Fialka of the *Wall Street Journal* discussed how China pursued technology that the United States viewed as outmoded, but which was of great value to Beijing, which was still developing a modern military and economy.[15] Acquisition of accrued knowledge, while inevitable, is how an actor can ultimately catch up with the United States and be positioned to target proprietary information.

Foreign actors use two broad methodologies to acquire knowledge from U.S. government, academic, and commercial entities—migration and economic espionage. The first of these, migration, refers to the coaxing of U.S. organizations to move innovation overseas voluntarily. It occurs as a consequence of the internationalization of R&D. The first of these, transnational migration of information, is a consequence of the internationalization of research and development. While there are benefits to globalization, it leads to the enhancement of state actors' technological bottom line, which can then be leveraged for activities in direct contradiction to U.S. interests. For instance, the Russian Federation's efforts to entice U.S. companies to develop a presence in Skolkovo—Moscow's attempt to establish a "Silicon Valley" by fiat—in 2010 could be viewed, in retrospect, as an attempt to build up the country's ability to wield power and influence. In the context of events in successive years, including the annexation of Crimea, meddling in the Ukraine, and an increasingly aggressive military, exercises that seem to be directed at menacing Western powers, Skolkovo appears as simply another aspect of Russia's attempt to marshal national power. The second and more brazen transfer of knowledge occurs via economic espionage—the smash-and-grab actions, whether by human operatives or through cyber conduits, that target specific items of interest.

HISTORICAL CONTEXT FOR U.S. INNOVATION

This book starts its examination of protecting U.S. knowledge with the beginning of the Cold War. Prior to this, the United States, during peacetime, had been isolationist, and dealings with foreign powers that might target R&D were limited. Intelligence did seek to protect U.S. assets, but this was to secure militarily significant entities in the context of wartime. However, following World War II, the United States recognized that it could not revert to an isolationist footing and its planning was done with a global view. In 1947, the National Security Act established the Central Intelligence Agency to develop information for decision makers, the Marshall Plan demonstrated that the United States was willing to make significant investments outside of its borders to bolster the economies of non-Communist countries, and National Security Council directive 68 articulated a defense posture that recognized global interests.

The internationalization that gained momentum with the Cold War has continued up to the present day. Although it has significant value, the distribution of American assets, engaged in or having access to research and development abroad, creates vulnerabilities. Companies such as those with a presence in China have been subjected to coercive measures directed at effecting a transfer of proprietary information. Meanwhile, the revolving doors of higher education, industry, and even certain U.S. government programs permit foreign talent to become intelligence collectors, as they enter the country and gain exposure to ideas and information prior to returning to their home countries (sometimes in direct response to their governments' direction).

U.S. LEGAL AUTHORITIES FOR PROTECTING INNOVATION

Between the early twentieth century and the present day (2015), the U.S. government has developed several statutes of particular importance to protecting the process of innovation, pursued by government, commercial, and academic entities, from exploitation by foreign powers. These are, in chronological order, the Espionage Act, the Foreign Agents Registration Act, and the Economic Espionage Act.

The Espionage Act of 1917

Because innovation and accrued knowledge are so closely tied to American defense, they are targets of theft by foreign adversaries. Sabotage (the destruction of capabilities) and espionage (the theft of specific capabilities) directed against innovation are threat activities that can be catastrophic to national security. This danger was acutely felt as the United States became involved in World War I. After winning reelection based on his ability to keep the United States from entering the war, President Woodrow Wilson eventually decided to enter the war. This created much opposition among many segments of the population that opposed involvement. It was thought that many of these groups, such as socialists, pacifists, and various labor groups, were taking steps to undermine the war effort.

The Espionage Act of 1917 is a U.S. federal law passed on June 15, 1917, shortly before the United States entered World War I. It was originally found in Title 50 of the United States Code (War), but is now listed under Title 18 (Crime). It was intended to prohibit interference with military operations or recruitment, to prevent insubordination in the military, and to prevent the support of U.S. enemies during wartime. Anyone convicted under the act would be subject to a prison term of twenty years and fine of $10,000. Much of the act served to supersede existing espionage laws. It was based on the Defense Secrets Act of 1911, particularly the sections referring to information of "national defense" to individuals not "entitled to have it." Sections of the Espionage Act of 1917 cover the following: vessels in ports of the United States, interference with foreign commerce by violent means, seizure of arms and other articles intended for export, enforcement of neutrality, passports, counterfeiting government sales, and search warrants. It criminalized "obtaining information respecting the national defense with intent or reason to believe that the information to be obtained is to be used to the injury of the United States" or obtaining things such as code books, signal books, sketches, photographs, photographic negatives, and blueprints and passing them on to the enemy.

Amendments to the Espionage Act were used to extend the laws in 1918. The so-called Sedition Act of 1918 prohibited many forms of speech, including "any disloyal, profane, scurrilous, or abusive language about the form of government of the United States . . . or the flag of the United States, or the uniform of the Army or Navy."[16] President Wilson had pressured Congress to introduce the anti-immigrant, anti-anarchist Sedition Act to protect wartime morale by deporting putatively undesirable political people. The Sedition Act amendments were repealed on March 3, 1921, but many provisions of the Espionage Act remain, codified under Title 18, Part 1, Chapter 37 of the U.S.C.[17] Although there has been much controversy through the years about the impact of the Espionage Act on curtailing free speech, the bulk of the law dealt with hostile acts of treason.

There were two periods in U.S. history characterized by the fear of Communist influence and infiltration into American society. Both utilized the Espionage Act to prosecute individuals deemed a threat to national security. The first red scare began after the Bolshevik Russian Revolution of 1917, as anarchist and left-wing activists inflamed national tensions during the patriotic years of World War I. One of the major motivations for the scare occurred in 1919, when a plot was discovered to mail thirty-six bombs to prominent political and financial figures including J. P. Morgan, John D. Rockefeller,

Supreme Court Justice Oliver Wendell Holmes, and U.S. Attorney General Alexander Mitchell Palmer.

The second red scare occurred after World War II and was popularly known as "McCarthyism" after Senator Joseph McCarthy, who led the movement. The anti-Communist sentiment was fueled in part by the discovery that the United States' secret program to develop nuclear weapons, the Manhattan Project, was heavily infiltrated by Soviet spies. These "atomic spies" provided highly classified design and production information to the Soviets. The espionage activity was extremely damaging to U.S. national security in that many of the technical aspects to the atomic bomb as well as strategic plans enabled the Soviet Union to develop and test its own nuclear weapon in 1949—barely four years after the U.S. detonated two atomic bombs on Japan.

The value lost to Soviet espionage efforts was devastating to U.S. national security and represents a prime example of how espionage can lead to loss of innovation and accrued knowledge. The production of a nuclear weapon required vast amounts of resources. Much of the difficulty involved obtaining enough nuclear material to create a warhead. Purification of Uranium-235 from natural uranium ore was initially beyond the ability of the Soviet Union. The Soviets were able to solve the problem of purification with information stolen from the Manhattan Project.[18] Without this information, the Soviets would have taken much longer to develop a nuclear weapon of their own.

The depth of Soviet spying became apparent beginning in 1946 when the U.S. deciphered the code Moscow used to send its telegraph cables to and from the United States. The decryption project, code-named VENONA, was used to uncover many of the spies in the U.S. atomic weapons program. It is uncertain to this day the exact number of spies utilized by the Soviets, but U.S. investigations resulted in the imprisonment or execution of a dozen or more people accused of passing atomic secrets to the Soviets.

The Foreign Agents Registration Act

The Foreign Agents Registration Act (FARA) is the backbone (albeit a weak one) of U.S. government efforts to counter surreptitious foreign influence. FARA was originally focused on disrupting German propagandists (although in 1941 the FBI did attempt to use the act against a Soviet assigned to the state-run Amtorg trading company).[19] Its impetus was the House of Representatives' Special Committee on Un-American Activities. As originally written, FARA was extremely broad, in that the propaganda activities did not have to be for or on behalf of a foreign principal. It was first amended in 1942, when Congress broadened the law to include a preface that took into account protection of foreign policy, national defense, and internal security.[20]

In 1966, Congress significantly amended FARA to focus on the integrity of the U.S. government's decision-making process and to emphasize agents seeking economic or political advantage for their clients.[21] Senator William Fulbright was a driving figure in this process. In 1962, the senator began an inquiry into the "Non-Diplomatic Activities of Representatives of Foreign Governments" due to his concern about the number of incidents in which foreign governments and their agents attempted to influence the conduct of American foreign policy by techniques outside normal diplomatic channels.[22]

In recent decades, multiple legislators have identified loopholes in the law and have tried to amend or replace FARA accordingly. The legislation includes seven categories of activities exempt from registration. Among these are provisions that excluded foreign government officials acting within their legitimate duties and foreign commercial entities as well as religious, scholastic, academic, scientific, and fine arts entities.[23] However, as discussed in subsequent chapters, governments pursuing influence of U.S. policy have exploited many of these channels. In 1991, representatives Dan Glickman and Marcy Kaptur attempted to require written notification of all exception claims.[24] (Their interest was driven by concerns about foreign commercial lobbying.)

The persistent drumbeat for change has produced limited results. Congressman Dan Glickman proposed replacing FARA entirely in 1991 with new legislation that would eliminate loopholes such as lawyers being able to contact members of the executive branch on foreign clients' behalf.[25] As Glickman stated in a hearing that year, "With the end of the Cold War, we should be less worried about ideological indoctrination and focus our concern instead on the global economic competition that has seen some of our Nation's strongest industries overwhelmed and our finest economic and cultural assets sold to foreign purchasers."[26] In 1992, Senator Carl Levin, after sponsoring hearings the previous year, introduced a bill that would have replaced parts of FARA.[27] Another serious effort to reform FARA occurred in 2008, when senators Charles E. Schumer and Claire McCaskill introduced legislation that would require foreign agents to provide additional registration information.[28]

In 1995, the Lobbying Disclosure Act (LDA) amended aspects of FARA. LDA's amendments to FARA ultimately meant that FARA applied to instances including "political activities; acting as a public relations counsel; publicity agent; or political consultant, collecting or disbursing contributions for the foreign principal and representing the interests of the foreign principal before any agency or official of the Government of the United States."[29] However, despite the concerns about commerce stated above, private foreign entities would register under the LDA, not FARA.[30]

FARA's administrative history highlights the overlap between international affairs, domestic security, and intelligence collection. From FARA's passage until 1942, the State Department was responsible for its administration. When FBI Special Agents working in the field identified violations they could not investigate, they had to pass the information to FBIHQ where it was then referred to the State Department.[31] However, Secretary of State Cordell Hull viewed FARA as a policing rather a foreign policy function, and the State Department did not have investigative personnel of its own.[32] With the 1942 amendment, the Department of Justice assumed responsibility for FARA. The Counterespionage Section of the Department of Justice's National Security Division currently administers and enforces the registration of foreign agents, while the FBI has responsibility for FARA investigations.

Although FARA is usually used to disrupt influence activities conducted on behalf of foreign powers, it and the LDA (which amended it) have applicability to the topics of this book as state-run companies, which are components of a foreign government's elements of national power and attempts to acquire U.S. knowledge and associated technology. For instance, the U.S. House of Representatives Permanent Select Committee on Intelligence issued its *Investigative Report on the U.S. National Security Issues Posed by Chinese Telecommunications Companies Huawei and ZTE* in October 2012, which stated that the "Chinese government and the Chinese Communist Party . . . [could] exert influence over the corporate boards and management of private sector companies, either formally through personnel choices, or in more subtle ways." In 2012, Huawei increased its lobbying expenditures fourfold from the same period of time in 2011, hired six lobbying firms, and added its first in-house lobbyist.[33] Given China's ability to control Huawei, a company operating in the high-technology telecommunications sector, which is a tempting target for economic espionage, are the company's lobbyists simply working on behalf of a commercial entity or are they effectively agents of a foreign power?

Related to FARA is Title 18 U.S., Section 951. This is directed at nonpolitical activities and requires all agents operating under the control of foreign governments or foreign officials other than diplomats to notify the Attorney General before acting. Registration for these activities is done via the DOJ's FARA Unit. It is this statute that has allowed the U.S. government to disrupt collection (as opposed to influence) activities that provided unclassified information to hostile foreign governments.

Two cases within the past decade illustrate this aspect of disrupting foreign agents. In early 2015, the DOJ announced the indictment of Evgeny Buryakov, an officer of the Russian foreign intelligence service (SVR), who was working under nonofficial cover as an employee of the Manhattan office of a Russian bank.[34] Buryakov responded to intelligence taskings from Igor Sporyshev, a trade representative—who was also an SVR officer—for the Russian Federation assigned to New York, and also exploited his cover as a banker to proactively gather intelligence about matters of interest to the Russian Federation.[35] Buryakov also provided assistance to Sporyshev's intelligence collection by formulating questions, at Sporyshev's request, for intelligence-gathering purposes by a leading Russian state-owned news organization.[36] Topics for inquiry that Buryakov suggested were: how the New York Stock Exchange used exchange-traded funds; potential limits on the use of high-frequency automated trading systems; and the potential interest among NYSE members about products tied to Russia.[37] A previous case that focused on collection on behalf of an adversarial government was identified in 2006 and involved Florida International University professor Carlos Alvarez and his wife, Elsa Alvarez, who provided a variety of unclassified information about anti-Castro groups and American officials to Cuba's Directorate of Intelligence.[38] Both the Buryakov and the Alvarez cases emphasize that assistance to foreign governments need not include classified information to damage U.S. interests. The same principle can be applied in situations in which an individual provides information that could help a foreign government or proxy, through a state-owned company or research institute, develop an increased capacity for innovation.

The Economic Espionage Act

A country's power is dependent, in part, on its economic viability. Even its military power is intertwined with the development of dual-use technology with both commercial and military application. Much of the innovation and competitiveness of U.S. companies depends upon proprietary information, know-how, and intangible assets. A "trade secret" is a form of intellectual property that can protect this form of information and offers the owner opportunities to benefit from their innovation. Trade secret law helps protect and encourage the development of new ideas. A wide range of commercially valuable information ranging from sales information, prototypes, manufacturing processes, and chemical formulas can constitute a trade secret.[39] Unlike patents, trade secrets do not have a finite time period, but endure as long as the information has value to the owner and is not known to competitors. As discussed in subsequent chapters, much of the U.S. economy is based on innovation and the development of new technologies and knowledge that makes trade secret protection especially critical. *Rockwell Graphic Sys., Inc. v. DEV Indus., Inc.*, 925 F.2d 174, 180 (7 Cor. 1991) stated, "Trade secret protection is an important part of intellectual property, a form of property that is of growing importance to the competitiveness of American industry" and that "the future of the nation depends in no small part on the efficiency of industry, and the efficiency of industry depends in no small part on the protection of intellectual property."

The theft of trade secrets, particularly by foreign governments, poses a direct threat to the competitiveness of the U.S. economy and thereby also affects national security. Many companies devote significant percentages of their budget to research and development. One recent estimate put the value of trade secrets for publicly traded U.S. companies at $5 trillion.[40] When the resulting trade secrets are misappropriated, competitors and other adversaries have a tremendous economic edge that can result in job losses and bankruptcies. As the U.S. economy transitions from an industrial to a more service- and information-based economy, greater amounts of innovation are tied up intangible assets. For instance, Standard and Poor's 500 index consists of the marketplace value of five hundred large, publicly held companies.[41] In 1975, it was reported that 16.8 percent of the value of S&P 500 consisted of intangible assets. That value increased to 79.7 percent of total value by 2005.[42]

The value of trade secrets in the global marketplace has been increasing as the world becomes ever more interconnected. Increased global competitiveness provides an incentive for foreign governments and foreign companies to employ a variety of means to target U.S. companies, people, academic institutions, and government agencies to obtain an economic advantage. Some tactics are considered accepted business practice, including mergers, acquisitions, licensing agreements, and the gathering of publicly available information. Although legal and accepted, these practices can pose significant risk to the innovation of U.S. organizations that may be more focused on short-term gain and neglect to adequately consider the risks of such activities. Furthermore, legal tactics may be precursors to illicit collection activities when the former fail to achieve desired results.[43]

Advances in computer technology and electronic communications have facilitated corporate spying by making it cheaper and easier. It is no longer necessary to physically trespass (although this low-technology approach still occurs) or steal paper documents. Now much industrial espionage occurs by cyber means from remote locations. Vast amounts of data can be exfiltrated from a company's server in an instant, just as similarly large quantities of information can be removed via thumb drives and other removable storage media. Using cyber techniques can afford the adversary a certain amount of anonymity and allow the perpetrator to remain outside of U.S. legal jurisdiction. These developments pose great challenges to U.S. law enforcement and intelligence agencies tasked with protecting U.S. innovation.

By the mid-1990s, the U.S. government recognized that the systematic theft of U.S. proprietary information was a grave problem for the economy and for national security. As Senator Herb Kohl stated in 1996, "It would not be unfair to say that America has become a full-service shopping mall for foreign governments and companies who want to jump start their businesses with stolen trade secrets. Sadly, we are under-equipped to fight this new war. Our laws have glaring gaps, allowing people to steal our economic information with virtual impunity."[44]

Until 1996, federal prosecutors lacked an effective tool to prosecute trade secret theft. There were no federal statutes that directly addressed economic espionage. Prosecutors typically relied on the Interstate Transportation of Stolen Property Act (18 U.S.C. 234), passed in the 1930s. It was intended to prevent the movement of stolen property across state lines by criminals attempting to evade local law enforcement. This act was not well suited to deal with intellectual property, which is inherently not transported physically from state to state. Similarly, other statutes such as the mail fraud statute or fraud by wire statute have limited applicability to intellectual property.

In 1996, senators Kohl and Arlen Specter introduced a bill to specifically prohibit economic espionage activity. The Economic Espionage Act of 1996 advances two primary objectives: the protection and promotion of national and economic security. The act makes the theft or misappropriation of a trade secret a federal crime. Unlike the Espionage Act of 1917 (18 U.S.C. §§792–799), the offense involves business information rather than classified or national defense information. This is of particular national security interest as some of the country's most cutting-edge technologies are now solely the domain of private industry.

The Economic Espionage Act provides two distinct but related offenses, 18 U.S.C. §§1831–1832. The first violation, §1831, outlaws theft of trade secrets for the benefit of a foreign entity (economic espionage). Economic espionage involves the intent to benefit a foreign entity or at least the knowledge the theft could have that result. It does not require intent to injure the owner of the trade secret. The second violation, §1832, criminalizes the misappropriation of trade secrets with the intent to convert the trade secret to the economic benefit of anyone other than the owner and to injure the owner of the trade secret. According to the U.S. Attorney's Manual, some of the factors assessed in determining whether to initiate an economic espionage or trade secret case under §1831 or §1832 include the following:[45] a) the scope of the criminal activity, including evidence of involvement by a foreign government, foreign agent, or foreign instrumentality, b) the degree of economic injury to the trade secret owner, c) the type of trade secret misappropriated, d) the effectiveness of available civil remedies, and e) the potential deterrent value of the prosecution.

Although economic and industrial espionage involve different intent elements, both require proof that the intellectual property is a trade secret. As such, a trade secret must have three elements as defined under 18 U.S.C §1839(3)(A),(B)(1996). First, the trade secret must involve information. Information may include "all forms and types of financial, business, scientific, technical, economic, or engineering formation . . . whether tangible or intangible, and whether or how stored, compiled, or memorialized physically, electronically, graphically, photographically, or in writing."[46] Second, it must have independent economic value from not being generally known to the public and not being readily ascertainable through proper means by the public (18 U.S.C. §1839[3][B][1996]). The value of the trade secret can include the competitive advantage of the owner by using the trade secret, the costs for an outsider to duplicate the trade secret, and the lost advantages to the trade secret owner resulting from the disclosure to a competitor. Third, the owner of the trade secret must have taken reasonable measures to keep the information a secret. These steps can involve physical security like locks, passwords, limiting access, use of nondisclosure agreements, labeling, and adequate training for employees. It is not necessary for the trade secret owner to have taken every conceivable step to protect the property but taken "reasonable measures."[47]

Recognizing the seriousness of the economic espionage threat, Congress passed the Economic Espionage Act in 1996. Congress took a traditional approach to the problem by criminalizing trade secret misappropriation. Although the Economic Espionage Act provides for significant prison terms and fines for violations, its effectiveness in deterring trade secret theft remains in question.[48] For a foreign company, the penalty for a violation may be considered merely a cost of doing business and well worth the risk. The number of prosecutions under the act is relatively few considering the magnitude of the

Table 1.1.   Penalties for economic and industrial espionage under §1831 and §1832

	Title 18 U.S.C., Section 1831	Title 18 U.S.C., Section 1832
Knowingly targets or acquires	Trade secrets	Trade secrets
For the benefit of	Foreign government, instrumentality, or agent	Anyone other than the owner
Maximum imprisonment (individual)	15 years	10 years
Maximum fine (individual)	$5,000,000	$250,000
Maximum fine (organization)	$10 million (3 times the value)[1]	$5 million

[1] Foreign and Economic Espionage Penalty Enhancement Act of 2012, Pub.L. 112-269.

problem. As of 2013, there had been approximately one hundred indictments under the Economic Espionage Act.[49] However, it has been more common for prosecutors to charge defendants under the theft of trade secrets rather than espionage because the former charge does not require the prosecution to prove that the defendant acted with the intent to benefit the foreign power.[50] There are a variety of factors that limit the number of cases and prosecutions under the Economic Espionage Act as discussed by Susan W. Brenner, a member of the law faculty of the University of Dayton, and Anthony C. Crescenzi, security expert. First, economic espionage cases are inherently complex, often involving much scientific jargon and novel technology. The technical aspects of these cases require that prosecutors spend much time to prepare the case. Second, these cases involve the culture of the Department of Justice, whose conservative approach often makes it reluctant to take on cases it is uncertain to win. Furthermore, economic espionage cases can involve serious diplomatic repercussions when a foreign government is accused of trade secret misappropriation. An additional factor concerns the possibility that the trade secret in question will be disclosed during the litigation process.[51] All of these factors diminish the effectiveness and frequency that the Economic Espionage Act is used.

In 2012, the Theft of Trade Secrets Clarification Act updated the Economic Espionage Act in a significant way. With the passage and enactment of the clarifying legislation, the definition of trade secret was expanded beyond goods to include services. It also broadened the scope of secrets protected by the law from those placed in interstate or foreign commerce to those that were used in or intended for the use of interstate or foreign commerce. The government recognized the need for this modification, following the trial of Goldman Sachs employee Sergey Aleynikov, who allegedly stole the code for high-speed computerized trading operations but was not convicted under the Economic Espionage Act because the code was in-house proprietary information that was never intended as an item for commercialization (unlike most trade secrets, which provide the foundation of an eventually lucrative product).[52]

CONCLUSION

Innovation does not occur in a vacuum, but rather within the context of international affairs. Indicating the shifting nature of what must be preserved, U.S. authorities for disruption of foreign threats to innovation have broadened from the government-centric Espionage Act to the amended Economic Espionage Act, which affords specific protection to U.S. companies' proprietary work. Measures of mitigation such as these are the only viable response, but they must keep current with an evolving international environment. Globalization cannot be stopped, nor should it be. Rather, the objective should be mitigation of the threats, which exploit open borders, by identifying nefarious actors and decreasing exposure of U.S. assets while taking full advantage of legitimate, worldwide talent.

NOTES

1. *A Strategy for American Innovation* (Washington, D.C.: National Economic Council and Office of Science Technology Policy, 2015).

2. Gregory F. Treverton and Seth G. Jones, *Measuring National Power* (Santa Monica, CA: Rand, 2005), 4.

3. Ibid., 1.

4. National Security Strategy, 2015, 8.

5. Ibid., 16.

6. James Bamford, "Frozen Assets: The Newest Front in Global Espionage Is One of the Least Habitable Locales on Earth—the Arctic," *Foreign Policy*, May 2015.

7. *National Intelligence Strategy* (Washington, D.C.: Office of the Director of National Intelligence, 2014).

8. Ibid.

9. *National Counterintelligence Strategy* (National Counterintelligence Executive, 2007), 7.

10. Ibid.

11. Muro, Rothwell, Andes, Fikri, and Kulkarni, *America's Advanced Industries*, 14.

12. David J. Berteau, Scott Miller, Bryan Crotty, and Paul Nadeau, *Leveraging Global Value Chains for a Federated Approach to Defense* (Washington, D.C.: Center for Strategic and International Studies, 2014), 4.

13. Muro, Rothwell, Andes, Fikri, and Kulkarni, *America's Advanced Industries*, 50.

14. American Energy Innovation Council, *Restoring American Energy Innovation Leadership: Report Card, Challenges, and Opportunities* (Washington, D.C.: Bipartisan Policy Center, 2015), 24.

15. John Fialka, *War by Other Means: Economic Espionage in America* (New York: W. W. Norton, 1999), 22.

16. David M. Kennedy, *Over Here: The First World War and American Society* (Oxford: Oxford University Press, 2004).

17. Cornell Law School: Title 18, Part 1, Chapter 37, accessed December 4, 2010.

18. Allen Weinstein and Alexander Vassiliev, *The Haunted Wood* (New York: Random House, 1999), 180–85.

19. Raymond Batvinis, *The Origins of FBI Counterintelligence* (Lawrence: University Press of Kansas, 2007), 252.

20. *The Federal Lobbying Disclosure Laws: Hearings before the Subcommittee on Oversight of Government Management of the Committee on Governmental Affairs,* 102nd Cong. 38 (1991).

21. http://www.justice.gov/usao/eousa/foia_reading_room/usam/title9/crm02062. htm (Foreign Agents Registration Act Enforcement).

22. *The Federal Lobbying Disclosure Laws.*

23. Ibid.

24. *Modification of the Foreign Agents Registration Act of 1938: Hearings before the Subcommittee on Administrative Law and Governmental Relations of the Committee on the Judiciary House of Representatives,* 102nd Cong. 33 (1991).

25. Gary Lee, "Rep. Glickman Introduces Lobbying Bill; Foreign Agents Would Have to File Reports," *Washington Post,* April 12, 1991.

26. *The Federal Lobbying Disclosure Laws,* 5.

27. Gary Lee, "Bill Targets Lobbyist Activities; Levin Wants to Cast Light on Dealmakers," *Washington Post,* February 28, 1992; Catherine Collins, "Senators Take a Fresh Look at Rules for Lobbyists and Foreign Agents," *Los Angeles Times,* July 14, 1991.

28. Barry Meier, "Lawmakers Seek to Close Foreign Lobbyist Loopholes," *New York Times,* June 12, 2008.

29. Jack Maskell, *Legal and Congressional Ethics Standards of Relevance to Those Who Lobby Congress* (Washington, D.C.: Congressional Research Service, 1996).

30. Jack Maskell, *Lobbying Congress: An Overview of Legal Provisions and Congressional Ethics Rules* (Washington, D.C.: Congressional Research Service, 2010).

31. Batvinis, *The Origins of FBI Counterintelligence,* 50.

32. Committee on Foreign Relations, U.S. Senate, Nondiplomatic Activities of Representatives of Foreign Governments: A Preliminary Study Prepared by the Staff of the Committee on Foreign Relations, at 8 (1962).

33. Eric Engleman and Jonathan D. Salant, "Chinese Firm Beefs up Its Lobbying Amid National Security Probe on Hill," *Washington Post,* August 27, 2012.

34. *United States of America v. Evgeny Buryakov (a/k/a "Zhenya"), Igor Sporyshev, and Victor Podobnyy.*

35. Ibid.

36. Ibid.

37. Ibid.

38. Terry Aguayo, "National Briefing: South Florida Couple Pleads Not Guilty to Spying," *New York Times,* January 20, 2006; John-Thor Dahlburg, "The Nation: Florida Couple Indicted as Cuban Agents," *Los Angeles Times,* January 10, 2006.

39. Uniform Trade Secret Act.

40. See Elizabeth A. Rowe, "Contributory Negligence, Technology, and Trade Secrets," *George Mason Law Review* 17 (2009): 1.

41. See http://www.standardandpoors.com.

42. James E. Malackowski, "The Intellectual Property Marketplace: Past, Present and Future," *The John Marshall Journal of Intellectual Property Law* 5 (2006): 605.

43. National Counterintelligence Center, *Annual Report to Congress on Foreign Economic Collection and Industrial Espionage: 1997* (National Counterintelligence Center, 1998).

44. 104th Cong. Rec. S737-S742 (1996).

45. Economic Espionage Act of 1996 18 U.S.C. 1831–1837 Prospective Policy, United States Department of Justice Criminal Division, February 27, 2013.

46. H.R. Rep. No 788, 104th Cong., 2d Sess. 7 (1996).

47. Ibid., 12.

48. Susan W. Brenner and Anthony C. Crescenze, "State-Sponsored Crime: The Futility of the Economic Espionage Act," *Houston Journal of International Law* 28 (2006): 389.

49. The Commission on the Theft of American Intellectual Property, *The IP Commission Report* (Washington, D.C.: National Bureau of Asian Research, 2013).

50. Ibid., 41.

51. Brenner and Crescenze, "State-Sponsored Crime," 389.

52. Michael J. De La Merced and Peter Lattiman, "Appeals Court Limits Federal Law Used in Goldman Programmer Case," *New York Times*, April 12, 2012.

Chapter Two

Entities Responsible for Securing U.S. Capacities for Innovation

The U.S. government has multiple agencies that contribute to the protection of innovation. The agencies both collect intelligence against adversaries and disrupt specific threat activities. The most significant entities include:

- Federal Bureau of Investigation (FBI): part of the Department of Justice
- Defense Security Service (DSS): part of the Department of Defense
- Homeland Security Investigations (HSI): part of the Department of Homeland Security
- Bureau of Industry and Security (BIS): part of the Department of Commerce
- Office of Intelligence of the Department of Energy

In addition to these operational agencies, several other entities also contribute to the protection of innovation by analyzing developments that may prove harmful to U.S. interests. The interagency Committee on Foreign Investment in the United States (CFIUS), chaired by the Department of the Treasury, is responsible for adjudicating foreign purchases in sensitive sectors such as technology and infrastructure. Finally, the National Counterintelligence and Security Center provides analysis to the director of national intelligence (DNI). DNI contributes to the policymaking process and may mitigate emerging threats.

FEDERAL BUREAU OF INVESTIGATION
(U.S. DEPARTMENT OF JUSTICE)

The Federal Bureau of Investigation, an element of the U.S. Department of Justice, is the agency with primary responsible for counterintelligence. Counterintelligence refers to the disruption of foreign state and nonstate actors' illicit acquisition of information. However, the FBI's effectiveness in this area is restricted by factors of organization and corporate culture. For instance, the organization's structure is reactive in nature (despite efforts to make it more proactive), which means that its first emphasis is investigating crimes and incidents that have already occurred rather than forward-leaning approaches to prevent crimes. Furthermore, the geographic territorialization of the Bureau's structure does not correspond with the realities of how threats operate. This limited optic both informs and compounds a corporate culture that does not encourage its special agents and intelligence analysts to become specialists in their respective fields of work.

Organization

The FBI is the oldest continually operating, domestically focused member of the U.S. intelligence community. It can trace its lineage to the Bureau of Investigation, which began operating as part of the U.S. Department of Justice in 1908. Its Counterintelligence Division and Cyber Division are the entities that have primary responsibility for collecting intelligence about state and nonstate actors that are exploiting U.S. entities for an informational advantage. The Criminal Investigative Division, by identifying white-collar crime, public corruption, and foreign corrupt practices, may identify the dynamics that threat actors exploit to obtain information. The Counterterrorism Division may also develop information of value for understanding the threat to innovation by identifying sabotage directed at degrading or destroying U.S. capabilities. The Bureau's WMD Directorate and Intelligence Branch play valuable roles analyzing the intelligence that FBI collectors provide.

Counterintelligence Division

The Counterintelligence Division is a key component in the FBI's efforts to prevent the illicit transfer of information pertaining to the United States' capacity for innovation. The Bureau's early foray into the field of counterintelligence was during World War I, as it attempted to identify the saboteur responsible for the explosion at Black Tom Island (an attack with a nexus to innovation, in its objective of destroying U.S. military technology). In 1939, the FBI created its General Intelligence Division to handle foreign counterintelligence as well as other intelligence work. However, it was not until 2001 that the Bureau officially designated a "Counterintelligence Division."[1] Prior to this, in 1994, the Bureau established an Economic Counterintelligence Program and, following the establishment of a Counterintelligence Division, it created an Economic Espionage Unit within the Division.[2]

The FBI's counterintelligence priorities are: keeping weapons of mass destruction, advanced conventional weapons, and related technology from adversaries; protecting the U.S. intelligence community against espionage and insider threats; safeguarding critical assets in the public and private sectors; and mitigating the threat from foreign operatives.[3] According to FBI director James B. Comey, spies continue to pose "as diplomats or ordinary citizens," but he added that the threat has "evolved." He cited their use of "students, researchers, or business people operating front companies" as new iterations of an old threat. Comey summarized the nature of the threat as consisting of "not only secrets, but trade secrets, research and development, intellectual property, and insider information from the federal government, U.S. corporations, and American universities."[4]

The Bureau has made efforts to adapt its strategies to deal with these evolving threats. In 2005, it dispatched hundreds of counterintelligence agents, many of whom had a specific focus on China, to the FBI's field offices. A principal FBI team, including undercover components focused on Chinese economic espionage, was established on an unmarked floor in a Silicon Valley office park.[5] More recently, in 2015, the FBI's assistant director for counterintelligence, Randall Coleman, stated that because the Chinese government was linked to wide-ranging targeting of trade secrets, U.S. authorities planned to make increased use of Foreign Intelligence Surveillance Act authorities in collecting against economic espionage.[6]

However, the FBI has not always recognized the continuing necessity for counterintelligence. In 1992, following the end of the Cold War, the Bureau reassigned several hundred agents from its foreign counterintelligence division to criminal investigative work.[7] (This despite publicly voiced concerns preceding this decision and exemplified by a June 1991 *Wall Street Journal* article headlined "Corporate Targets: As Cold War Fades, Some Nations' Spies Seek Industrial Secrets.") The Bureau identified that Moscow had no intention of ceasing its own espionage activities in the United States, a point driven home with the arrest of multiple Russian "illegals" in 2010. In this episode, ten individuals that were supported by the Russian intelligence service (SVR) posed as ordinary Americans. None had sensitive access or influence, but they all had the potential to infiltrate sensitive businesses and government areas in the future and thus compromise U.S. national security and innovation. The long-term nature of this infiltration operation and potential damage to U.S. security was largely lost on mainstream media reporting who could not get past the fact that no classified defense information was compromised.

FBI counterintelligence collection has not necessarily been postured to fully exploit intelligence to provide the U.S. government with information that would be of value for decision makers. For example, following the Soviet Union's detonation of an atomic bomb in 1949, the Joint Atomic Energy Intelligence Committee (JAEIC) advised the Scientific Intelligence Committee that "if the JAEIC had known of the implications of the [Klaus] Fuchs case in June 1949 at the time when the July estimate was being written, the estimate of the time by which the Soviets could have obtained their first bomb would have been appreciably advanced, as no allowance was made in making that estimate for successful espionage on details of bomb design and construction." This principle is no less valid today, as a state or nonstate actor's efforts to surreptitiously acquire information contributes to the U.S. government's strategic understanding of what capabilities that actor is attempting to develop.

Cyber Division

The FBI's Cyber Division is located under the Criminal, Cyber, Response, and Services branch. According to FBI director James B. Comey, speaking in 2014, "cyber security has topped the Director of National Intelligence list of global threats for the second consecutive year" and the FBI is "targeting high-level intrusions—the biggest and most dangerous botnets, state-sponsored hacks, and global cyber syndicates."[8] The Bureau founded this component in 2002 as part of a broader reorganization.[9] As of 2012, the division had twenty computer scientists and the Bureau was endeavoring to acquire fifty more in order to have at least one for each of the fifty-six field offices.[10] According to Comey:

> [The] FBI's mission in cybersecurity is not to study computer networks to patch vulnerabilities, nor is the FBI's jurisdiction confined to only those assets owned by the U.S. government or critical infrastructure providers. Rather, the FBI's mission focuses on countering the threat by investigating intrusions to determine criminal, terrorist, and nation-state actor identities, and engaging in activities which reduce or neutralize these threats. At the same time, the FBI also collects and disseminates information significant to those responsible for defending networks, including information regarding threat actor targets and techniques.[11]

However, cyber is not a threat; it is a vector that state and nonstate actors use to conduct a wide variety of malfeasance. Isolating cyber in a vacuum is problematic because assessing and mitigating the threat requires awareness of the actors manipulating the bits and bytes. Their intentions and objectives define how they will adapt their actions to take advantage of new technology.

Counterterrorism and Criminal Investigative Divisions

The Bureau's Counterterrorism and Criminal Investigative Divisions have the potential to contribute to the U.S. government's efforts to protect the capacity for U.S. innovation. Since the explosion at Black Tom Island during World War I, the Bureau has had to contend with state and nonstate actors employing violence against a variety of targets, including those engaged in innovation, such as the U.S. government research facilities attacked by antiwar radicals in the 1960s. However, the Bureau did not establish a dedicated Counterterrorism Division until 1999. Up until this point, the function of counterterrorism had been handled, at various times, by the Criminal Investigative Division and the National Security Division. (Part of the reason why the FBI created a distinct Counterterrorism Division was concern that the counterterrorism mission was playing second fiddle to the NSD's counterintelligence responsibilities.[12])

The FBI's disruption of criminal threats, overseen by its Criminal Investigative Division (CID), is its oldest mission. CID is its largest operational division, with nearly five thousand field special agents and three hundred intelligence analysts.[13] Criminal behaviors, such as white-collar crime, foreign corrupt practices, and more, can create conditions that nefarious actors can exploit to acquire proprietary information. Part of CID's mission includes investigating trade secret theft. In 2012, the intellectual property rights program was realigned from the Cyber Division to CID with the expectation that putting the Intellectual Property Rights (IPR) Unit with traditional criminal programs such as Organized Crime would lead to more effective and broader investigations.[14] The Criminal Division has in recent years enhanced its capabilities in the area of protecting intellectual property—a key to innovation—by training and placing fifty-one agents dedicated to intellectual property enforcement in twenty-one major U.S. cities, four of which are home to intellectual property investigative squads, and establishing an IPR Unit.[15]

International Operations

The FBI has an extensive presence abroad through its legal attachés—who are posted to U.S. diplomatic establishments—in seventy countries. However, it is worth noting that even before the creation of the CIA, the Bureau was operating abroad to protect U.S. interests in the area of innovation. For instance, during World War II, the Bureau expanded its Plant Survey Program abroad to strategically significant facilities in Latin America as part of its Special Intelligence Service. More recently, in 2011, the FBI deployed a special agent with an IPR background to the U.S. Embassy in Beijing, China, for a tour of one year. The agent contributed to the FBI's IPR mission by meeting with a large number of rights holders, law firms, U.S. government entities, nonprofit organizations, and foreign government agencies in Beijing, Shanghai, and Mongolia.[16]

Analytic Components

The FBI's Intelligence Branch is the repository of the FBI's analytical resources. Its creation in 2014 superseded the Directorate of Intelligence as the structure responsible for organizing these resources (and belatedly created an executive assistant director for intelligence position that the Intelligence Reform and Terrorism Prevention Act of 2004 had mandated).

In 2006, the FBI established its Weapons of Mass Destruction Directorate (WMDD). The Bureau, in its FY 2015 budget justification, identified four WMD threat areas that "constitute the greatest vulnerabilities": development and use of biological weapons; domestic acquisition of chemical agents; proliferation of WMD materials; and smuggling and proliferation of WMD technology.[17] Included in the WMD and of particular importance when assessing the illicit transfer of technology is the FBI's Counterproliferation Center (CPC), which the Bureau created in 2011 and "combines the operational activities of the Counterintelligence Division, the subject matter expertise of the WMDD, and the analytical capabilities of both components to identify and disrupt proliferation activities." According to Frank Figluzzi, the former assistant director for counterintelligence, the CPC is responsible for pursuing cases of illegal technology transfer, whether the technology is intended for WMDs or for other uses.[18] This positions the CPC to play a significant role in disrupting foreign efforts to acquire knowledge and facilitate innovation illicitly via the transfer of cutting-edge items.

Field Structure

In addition to its headquarters components, the Bureau has a far-flung presence, including fifty-six field offices in major U.S. cities and over 360 resident agencies (RAs)—satellite offices within the United States—as well as sixty legal attachés and twenty suboffices in seventy countries. The Bureau employs, as of 2014, more than thirty-four thousand people, with nearly fourteen thousand of those being Special Agents and more than three thousand of those being intelligence analysts.[19] Although this territorial approach does not align with the nature of all modern threats, the FBI's Domestic Investigations and Operations Guide, which the Bureau issued in 2011, provided direction for "systematically assessing particular geographic areas or sectors to identify potential threats, vulnerabilities, gaps, and collection opportunities." This obsolete approach may be changing, as Comey, in his efforts to address threat actors' use of cyber venues, has used field-based expertise to achieve national-level impacts. According to the *New York Times*, the FBI's top cyber security squad, which was responsible for the charging of Chinese intelligence officials with cyber theft of trade secrets and by disrupting a Russian-led hacking ring, is based in the Pittsburgh, Pennsylvania, field office.[20]

The Impact of Corporate Culture on the FBI's Efficacy in Mitigating the Threat to Innovation

An organizational structure that emphasizes *counter*terrorism, *counter*intelligence, and law *enforcement* intelligence has framed collection as something to respond to, rather than to anticipate. Critics have argued that evolution from a law enforcement agency stymied its ability to operate as a forward-looking intelligence organization capable putting U.S. decision makers at an informational advantage, rather than simply disrupting already known threats.[21] Attorney General Edward Levi developed the first set of guidelines for FBI investigations in 1976. These imposed a "criminal predicate" on domestic security investigations—distancing the Bureau from activities directed at intelligence gathering as opposed to collection for potential prosecution. A Senate Judiciary Committee report found that this set of AG Guidelines "tended to inhibit the gathering of information pertinent to internal security and law enforcement."[22] Compounding this problem, between the intelligence scandals of the 1970s and the issuance of the first set of AG guidelines, "higher officials tended to interpret the rules conservatively. If a decision fell anywhere in a grey area, they vetoed it to be on the safe side." The outcome of such timidity was that "investigators no longer did things they were in fact allowed to do."[23]

Since September 11, the FBI has struggled to transcend its legacy of a case-constrained organization. Former director Robert Mueller stressed that the Bureau was moving from thinking about intelligence as a case and instead finding intelligence within the case.[24] However, Mueller's formulation missed the point because identifying intelligence within a case tacitly accepts the idea that something must go wrong before opportunities for collection can be exploited, rather than identifying legitimate opportunities for collection in order to distance U.S. interests from emerging threats. Similarly, the Bureau in its 2011 Domestic Investigations and Operations Guide (DIOG) stated that "in order to protect against national security and criminal threats through intelligence-driven operations, the FBI should integrate intelligence activities into all investigative efforts." Like Mueller's paradigm, the DIOG portrayed intelligence as a byproduct of an investigation.

The Threat Review and Prioritization (TRP) process is a recent manifestation of the FBI's approach to intelligence as responsive to predications, rather than oriented toward answering U.S. government informational needs. Introduced in FY2013, TRP is informed by the work of FBIHQ "fusion cells" that "examine the national and international picture and provide intelligence on current and emerging threats across programs."[25] This provides the field with "guidance and a consistent process to identify priority threats."[26] TRP, although having the potential to move the Bureau away from its stove piped approach that focuses on cases, it is still anchored in an approach that highlights threats only after they have become demonstrated problems. The 9/11 Review Commission, which released its report in 2015, assessed that "emerging threats . . . receive little emphasis in the TRP" and that TRP "underemphasize[d] critical, over-the-horizon threats."[27] This posture puts the Bureau where it was prior to 9/11, when analytic pieces such as the "Phoenix memo" expressing concerns about foreign students attending U.S. aviation schools were disregarded by analysts.

Lack of Subject Matter Specialization

The FBI has struggled to develop a workforce that is characterized by subject matter specialization. This has not been helped by an organization structured to focus on methodology and tactics (for example, terrorism, cyber, WMD usage), rather than the actors who employ these tools to harm U.S. interests. For instance, according to a former unit chief of the FBI's Terrorist Research and Analytic Center, in the 1980s, "One of the things that the unit had been doing historically was writing these big long historical books on terrorist groups and events. . . . They were these big thick monographs that I was afraid nobody was reading." The unit chief's solution to this perceived problem was to "produce some operational things that were two, three pages." He assessed that these were "a big hit in the field because Agents would read two pages or three pages."[28] Contemporaneously, as the Center eviscerated institutional knowledge, the U.S. Senate was criticizing such thinking, stating in 1989 that the SSCI was "concerned that FBI Terrorism Section personnel . . . lack background knowledge of foreign political developments and personalities relevant to FBI international terrorism investigations."[29]

The Bureau's attitude toward subject matter specialization is apparent in its establishment of intelligence analyst positions. Prior to 9/11 there was no "intelligence analyst" role by name. Instead, two categories of employees—

intelligence research specialists (IRSs) and intelligence operations specialists (IOSs)—handled analytic functions. In theory, the IRSs were expected to have subject matter expertise about "a particular terrorism group, program, or target." All IRSs at the FBI had college degrees, and some had advanced degrees.[30] However, according to the 2004 Department of Justice, Inspector General report on handling of information prior to 9/11, IRSs, who were supposed to handle strategic analysis, were viewed as a support function that IOSs and special agents used to conduct research and analysis projects in support of ongoing investigations or prosecutions. Several IRSs interviewed by the OIG told the interviewers that IRSs were often used to perform the work that IOSs did not like to do, such as conducting name searches in the FBI's internal computer system or performing research on the Internet. A CIA manager detailed to the FBI told the OIG that IRSs were considered "second-class citizens" at the FBI."[31] IOSs, on the other hand, were not held to the stringent IRS requirements, and a number of these IOSs had no formal training in analytical work, but instead advanced to their positions from clerical positions within the FBI.[32]

The creation of an intelligence analyst position within the FBI post-9/11 has not demonstrably placed any greater value on developing a culture of expertise. According to a 2005 Department of Justice, Inspector General report, the Bureau purposely lumped all analysts under the same designation, rather than encouraging specialization, because it provided greater flexibility in assigning analysts when they could perform any function. Furthermore, analysts were not only interchangeable with other analysts, but also with other support staff. According to a 2005 DOJ OIG report, "If an intelligence analyst resigned, FBI management could decide to replace the intelligence analyst with a financial analyst or some other category of support staff."[33]

Unfortunately, when the Bureau created its intelligence analyst role, it built it on the above-described failures. In a 2002 internal review, the Bureau determined that 66 percent of its own analysts were unqualified for their jobs. An attempt to purge these holdovers by the Office of Intelligence, "improve the quality of the FBI's analytical corps by requiring a college degree for the intelligence analyst position," and "mandate[e] that analysts reapply for their current jobs" was "canceled before the process was completed."[34] According to a 2004 CRS report, even the new recruitment standards did not require a bachelor's degree (in place of the degree the FBI allowed a candidate for Intelligence Analyst to substitute a minimum of one year of related law enforcement or military experience).[35]

FBI agents also struggle to obtain adequate subject matter specialization. Agents are hired with diverse backgrounds and prior job expertise. Everyone has had some type of career prior to being hired as an agent. Many join the organization expecting to utilize the skill sets that landed them the extremely coveted and competitive position of FBI agent. However, organizational culture is such that pre-Bureau expertise is not often effectively utilized. The attitude "an agent is an agent is an agent" is quite prevalent. Little effort is made to direct new agents to squads or divisions where their prior expertise, experience, or interests can best be utilized. An agent's training emphasizes diverse experiences and broad skill sets that can be deployed in a variety of investigations. As an agent gains experience and expertise on the job, the agent is frequently transferred to new squads or divisions, often where different skills are needed. All too often, practical expertise acquired on the job is lost when internal transfers occur. Part of this is due to the Bureau's field office model, which discourages the use of resources geographically located in one area from working on issues in another—even if they are uniquely suited to the work. Additionally, "reinvention of the wheel"—through such dubious efforts as the 2008 Strategic Execution Team implementation and the 2013 institutionalization of the Threat Review and Prioritization process—waste precious time and resources that could be utilized protecting U.S. innovation and national security.

Subject matter expertise is not likely to take hold in the current conditions. As of 2003, the FBI planned to start from the bottom by hiring individuals at lower grade levels.[36] However, analysts who began their employment with the FBI prior to FY2002 were thirty times more likely to have less than a bachelor's degree than the analysts who entered on duty in FYs 2002–2004. Field visits by the 9/11 Commission staff discovered multiple situations in which poorly qualified administrative personnel were promoted to analyst positions in part as a reward for performance in other positions.[37] The result is that those in more senior positions were likely to lack an education and yet be supervising analysts who have been well educated. In a 2005 report, the Department of Justice determined that analysts with advanced degrees were more likely to leave within two years of being hired. This mismatch of managers and talent is likely to self-perpetuate, as the holdovers set the tone for successive generations, while more qualified analysts depart in frustration. Finally, the FBI's current structure does not create a need for expertise. The division of responsibilities across fifty-six field offices and the focus on "domain" requires special agents and intelligence analysts to treat threats as local entities, rather than to assess them in the context of a national or international problem.

Outlook

The FBI is not currently optimally organized to effectively disrupt foreign actors' illicit acquisition of innovation through tactical responses such as arrests or by driving strategic-level mitigation such as providing intelligence to inform the U.S. policymaking process. Its planning allocates resources based on present threats, rather than for collection against and disruption of threats before they can compromise areas of concern for national security, including U.S. public and private capabilities for innovation. Furthermore, this reactive approach, encouraged by TRP, does not orient the Bureau toward an approach that would take advantage of unique opportunities to develop intelligence regarding foreign actors' interests, as those interests become manifest through acquisitions or other activities in the domestic environment where the FBI has primary responsibility. This proactive collection on foreign intentions and capabilities is a particularly important function when examining innovation, as the capabilities of threat actors, such as China, may be readily indicated by what they are attempting to accomplish in the United States, whether through investment or through espionage. Although this information may not be predicable and consequently not of immediate value to the Bureau, it could provide value to other U.S. agencies seeking to understand foreign capabilities and identify resources that the United States needs in order to contend with those capabilities.

DEFENSE SECURITY SERVICE (U.S. DEPARTMENT OF DEFENSE)

The Department of Defense's Defense Security Service (DSS) contributes to the preservation of innovative capacities by protecting cleared industries, many of which have a nexus to cutting-edge technology. Consistent with the themes of this book, DSS is responsible for measures to guard against illicit, surreptitious acquisition of knowledge via espionage, as well as the transfer of knowledge via foreign investments that could result in a non-U.S. entity acquiring control of American capabilities.

DSS views its mission as playing out in a complex, global environment. Its world is defined by "rapid change" where "today's technology-oriented environment compels organizations to be open to new ideas, to swiftly adapt to shifting situations, to handle unexpected demands, and to be willing and able to change strategy in order to remain relevant"; greater global interdependence, where industry must be able to sort through complex supply chains; and new alliances, which may "expose unforeseen partnerships that involve potential adversaries or present other security concerns." The threat, according to DSS, emanates from "across the globe," "insiders," and "cyber." However, this seems to be a conceptual mistake, not unique to DSS, that does not differentiate between threats and vectors (for example, cyber is not a threat, it is an agnostic vector that can be used for both good and ill).[38]

Evolution of Mission

DSS was originally created to remedy a lack of coordination among military components on issues of personnel security (a function with significant ramifications for counterespionage activities). Its initial iteration was as the Defense Investigative Service (DIS), which became operational in 1972. Behind its creation was the recommendation of a blue ribbon defense panel. In accordance with the panel's findings, then Secretary of Defense Melvin Laird created a separate agency reporting directly to the Secretary of Defense.[39] By FY1984, DIS was an entirely civilian organization. In 1997, DIS became DSS, in a reflection of the service's broadened responsibilities.

Personnel security was the initial area of focus for DIS. Prior to its creation, each military service had conducted its own investigations. The agencies that had been responsible for these functions were the U.S. Army Intelligence Command, the Army Criminal Investigative Command, the Naval Investigative Service, and the Office of Special Investigation, Air Force.[40] Consistent with its emphasis on personnel security, DIS became the agency responsible for the Defense Central Index of Investigations.

Although DIS was originally established as an agency focused on vetting personnel, it evolved to assume responsibilities for safeguarding items and ideas. In 1980, DIS acquired responsibility for the Defense Industrial Security Program from the Defense Logistics Agency.[41] DISP covered industrial contractor facility clearances, industrial personnel security, safeguarding of classified information, and physical security for all Department of Defense (DoD) contractors involved with classified material.[42] As part of this, DIS inherited the Key Assets Protection Program and the Arms, Ammunition, and Explosives Program.[43] In 1993, Executive Order 12829 mandated the creation of the National Industrial Security Program, a successor to the Industrial Security Program, that expanded security measures beyond the DoD to safeguard classified information held by contractors, licensees, and grantees of the U.S. government.[44] This incorporated the industrial activities of entities such as the Central Intelligence Agency, the Department of Energy, and the Nuclear Regulatory Commission.[45] DSS administers the NISP for approximately thirty military and civilian agencies.

A distinct threat to U.S. innovation is the acquisition of domestic enterprises by foreign entities, which may take associated knowledge and technology out of American control. DSS addresses this phenomenon by promoting better awareness of foreign ownership control and influence (FOCI). A company is considered to be operating under FOCI whenever a foreign interest has power, direct or indirect, whether or not exercised, and whether or not exercisable, to direct or decide matters affecting the management or operations of that company in a manner that may result in unauthorized access to classified information or may adversely affect the performance of classified contracts. The following factors are reviewed to determine if a company is under FOCI: record of economic and government espionage against U.S. targets; record of enforcement and/or engagement in unauthorized technology transfer; the type and sensitivity of the information that shall be accessed; the source, nature, and extent of FOCI; record of compliance with pertinent U.S. laws, regulations, and contacts; the nature of any bilateral and multilateral security and information exchange agreements that may pertain; and ownership or control, in whole or in part, by a foreign government.[46] Specific DSS steps to mitigate these concerns are discussed in the subsequent chapter on USG partnerships with industry.

DIS/DSS established a component solely focused on counterintelligence (CI) that allowed DSS to use what it was learning through its interactions with industry to inform the larger picture of threats to the country's technological resources and incubators of innovation. In 1993, DIS created a CI office "in response to a recognized need for information of intelligence and counterintelligence value collected by DSS in the performance of its assigned functions. The information was analyzed and referred to agencies and contractors with an official interest in the information."[47] This office was originally staffed by detailees from each of the armed services.[48] Consistent with this perspective, DSS is now aligned under the Undersecretary of Defense for Intelligence.[49]

Organization

The DSS presence in the United States consists of forty-eight field locations spread across four geographic regions. The DSS mission is carried out by four operational elements. The first of these is the Industrial Security Field Operations Directorate. The Industrial Policy and Programs Directorate includes the International Division, which provides security and administrative oversight of exports resulting from sales by U.S. defense contractors to foreign governments and foreign contractors.[50] It also includes the Assessment and Evaluation Division and the International Division, which examines FOCI issues. The Counterintelligence Directorate, discussed above, and the Center for Development of Security Excellence Directorate are the other two divisions.

IMMIGRATION AND CUSTOMS ENFORCEMENT/ HOMELAND SECURITY INVESTIGATIONS (U.S. DEPARTMENT OF HOMELAND SECURITY)

The Department of Homeland Security's primary involvement with safeguarding U.S. capabilities for innovation is through Immigration and Customs

Enforcement (ICE) and its intelligence collection arm, Homeland Security Investigations (HSI). ICE has a dual-faceted mission in this area, with responsibilities for intellectual property (IP) and for counterproliferation. Foreign entities seeking new knowledge in the form of purloined IP increase their own capabilities and degrade U.S. advances. Similarly, the illicit acquisition of controlled dual-use technology not only provides opportunities for reverse engineering and acquiring new capabilities, but may also represent a direct military threat to the United States and its international interests.

ICE's roles are informed by an overarching set of DHS missions, which address various aspects of knowledge transfer via both IP and controlled technology. According to the DHS Strategic Plan for 2014–2018, Mission One is prevention of terrorism and enhancement of security. It includes prevention and protection against the unauthorized acquisition or use of chemical, biological, radiological, and nuclear materials and capabilities. Specifically, DHS's mission is to:

> Identify and interdict unlawful acquisition and movement of chemical, biological, radiological, and nuclear precursors and materials by leveraging investigative and enforcement assets towards domestic and international movement of these materials by engaging in information sharing with all stakeholders to monitor and control the technology.

Innovation is not simply an economic problem, but also includes state and nonstate actors gaining sensitive knowledge, such as that associated with WMDs, that could position them to harm U.S. interests. Securing and managing the borders is Mission Two, with goal 2.3 being to disrupt and dismantle transnational criminal organizations. Of particular concern is these organizations' reliance on counterfeit goods, which represent stolen intellectual property, some of which may be proprietary in nature (rather than simply the illegal use of copyrights and trademarks). Mission Four is safeguarding and securing cyberspace, including goal 4.4, which entails strengthening the cyber ecosystem. The increasing use of cyber as a vector to pilfer IP means that securing the cyber environment has clear implications for protecting U.S. capabilities for innovation. DHS has operational responsibilities for securing unclassified federal civilian government networks and working with owners and operators of critical infrastructure to secure their networks. To carry out these responsibilities, DHS conducts cyber threat analysis, risk assessment, mitigation, and incident response.[51]

ICE has multiple responsibilities within the DHS missions. It is "the only federal law enforcement agency with full statutory authority to investigate and enforce criminal violations of all U.S. export laws related to military items, controlled 'dual-use' commodities and sanctioned or embargoed countries."[52] This prominently positions it to address the threats that could accrue from foreign entities' acquisition of WMD technology, as well as prevent U.S. defense companies' loss of revenue share through the loss of proprietary IP. ICE is responsible for the National Intellectual Property Rights Coordination Center (NIPRCC), which is led by HSI. The NIPRCC is the government's clearing house for the exchange of information and intelligence related to export enforcement and is a conduit between federal law enforcement agencies and the intelligence community for export licensing and enforcement activities.[53] As part of its work, the NIPRCC addresses "the theft of innovation that threatens U.S. economic stability and national security."[54] However, the NIPRCC goes beyond the problems of innovation and also addresses issues, such as product counterfeiting, that are beyond the scope of this book. In 2010, ICE created local IP Theft Enforcement Teams, which were federal partnerships with state, local, and tribal law enforcement. These teams were structured around an informal task force approach. They were based on best practices that the NIPRCC had identified.[55] ICE also created the Interagency Federal Export Coordination Center, which replaced HSI's National Export Enforcement Coordination Network, in 2010, and which, unlike its predecessor, was mandated by Executive Order to include intelligence community participation.

HSI plays a significant role in several ICE missions. As of 2014, HSI was the principal intelligence collection component of DHS and the second largest federal criminal investigative agency, with authority to enforce more than four hundred federal statutes.[56] It had 6,400 investigators, including 250 special agents and 170 support staff to sixty-three offices in forty-six countries.[57] Aside from its own personnel, HSI works with specially trained U.S. CBP officers stationed at ports of entry to inspect suspect export shipments. In 2014, it opened 1,656 intellectual property rights investigations.[58] Of its eight divisions, those most relevant to evaluating and conducting activities to disrupt foreign innovation are National Security Investigations, Domestic Operations, the IPR Coordination Center (discussed above), International Operations, Investigative Programs, and the Office of Intelligence. HSI has twenty-six field offices throughout the United States.

The National Security Investigations Division (NSID) includes the Counter-Proliferation Investigations (CPI) Program, which focuses on export law violations. The primary goal of HSI CPI investigations is to detect and disrupt illegal exports before they or the actors behind them cause damage to the national security interests of the United States.[59] This highlights the unique nature of halting illicit activities aimed at innovation, as there is a window of opportunity between the theft of the item or information and the point at which it can be absorbed by a foreign actor. HIS's three-pronged approach to attacking the problem of illicit innovation involves detecting illegal exports, investigating potential violations, and obtaining international cooperation. CPI targets the trafficking and illegal export of conventional military equipment, firearms, and controlled technology. It also addresses attempts to acquire and transmit materials used to manufacture weapons of mass destruction, including chemical, biological, radiological, and nuclear materials. Additionally, CPI has specific responsibilities through its enforcement of the Arms Export Control Act, the Export Administration Act, the International Economic Emerging Powers Act, and the Smuggling Goods from the United States Act for enforcing export laws including statutes pertaining to goods destined for sanctioned or embargoed countries.[60] CPI Centers were established to serve as regional HSI resources for manpower, expertise, deconfliction, undercover operational support, and other CPI assistance that HSI required.[61] This concept allows for dedicated and experienced HSI agents to be strategically placed in high-risk domestic areas to improve HSI's ability to combat illegal exports and illicit procurement networks that pose a threat to the United States.

NSID also houses the Student and Exchange Visitor Program (SEVIP), which "acts as a bridge for government organizations that have an interest in information on non-immigrants whose primary reason is coming to the United States to be students." SEVIP manages F and M visa classifications, while the U.S. Department of State handles J visa classifications. Both agencies facilitate this through the Student and Exchange Visitor Information System (SEVIS), which is maintained by DHS. These are valuable systems when identifying risks to innovation, as foreign students and visitors engaged in commercial activities are significant conduits for both the legitimate and illicit transfer of knowledge.

The HSI Investigative Programs Division (IPD) is notable for several entities that it contains. One of these is the Cyber Crimes Center's Cyber Crimes Unit, which oversees cyber-related investigations by focusing on criminal organizations that use cyber capabilities to perpetrate crimes. The Unit is particularly interested in cyber economic crimes involving financial fraud, the theft of digital intellectual property and technical data controlled under export law, and the targeting of cross-border illicit Internet marketplaces.[62] The IPD's National Targeting Center focuses on a number of issues, including intellectual property rights and counterproliferation. (However, it also deals with wide-ranging topics including human trafficking, gang enforcement, and financial crime, which raises questions about the adequacy of its resources.)

The Office of Intelligence, in addition to coordinating information throughout HSI to maintain global awareness, features several entities with bailiwicks that include topics relevant to the transfer of knowledge that would spur innovation. Its analysis component includes an Illicit Trade Unit, which provides intelligence on the flow of illegal goods in and out of the United States. Areas of emphasis include technology transfers and the spread of technology and products that endanger public safety. The Illicit Travel Unit addresses issues of vulnerabilities that criminal organizations exploit, as well as criminal activities and structures.

An interesting problem is HSI's diplomatic engagement with foreign actors that are targeting the very information that HIS is attempting to protect. Notably, the NIPRCC regularly liaises with Chinese Ministry of Public Security representatives from the Chinese embassy in Washington, D.C.[63] HIS's International Operations Division is the primary point of interaction with foreign governments. Within this Division are the Transnational Criminal Investigative Units, which have allowed HSI to formalize relations with foreign law enforcement entities.[64] Of course, this is a problem by which DHS writ large is characterized. In 2015, DHS Secretary Jeh Johnson explained to Congress that:

> [DHS] participated in frank discussions with officials of the People's Republic of China on cyber issues of concern to both our nations. This culminated in our Presidents announcing several key cybersecurity commitments. As part of these commitments, we agreed to investigate cyber crimes, collect electronic evidence, and mitigated malicious cyber activity emanating from its territory, and to provide timely responses to requests for information and assistance concerning those activities.[65]

Expecting China to give up on its massive cyber campaign against the United States based on a friendly chat seems a bit naïve.

HSI's publicity has not been consistent with its public image. It has claimed (likely to the annoyance of FBI, DEA, and several other entities) to "set the standard for federal law enforcement/intelligence agencies." However, the FBI has provided it with platforms from which to operate, such as the JTTF. HSI's self-proclaimed standard setting may be an overreach. Recent media reports portray the organization's role as something less than earth shattering. For instance, in 2013, the *New York Times* reported "Federal Officials Return Looted Afghan Artifacts"; in 2014 the *New York Times* reported "Two Men, Long on N.F.L.'s Radar Are Charged with Making Counterfeit Tickets"; also in 2014, the *New York Times* reported that "Authorities to Seize a Roman Statue in Queens That They Say Was Stolen."

TEXTBOX 2.1

In another instance of passing off foreign forgeries as U.S. products, a former CEO of Powerline Inc., a battery distributor, was found guilty of selling more than USD $2.6 million of counterfeit batteries to the U.S. Department of Defense. A joint investigation by ICE and Defense Criminal Investigative Service identified that the battery assemblies and batteries that the U.S. Navy used for emergency backup power on aircraft carriers, minesweepers, and ballistic submarines were affixed with counterfeit labels falsely identifying the batteries as originating from approved manufacturers. The former CEO used chemicals to remove "Made in China" markings from the batteries. He was arrested when two undercover HSI agents hired him to sail his yacht to the U.S. Virgin Islands after he had spent more than two years near St. Martin. Once the CEO entered U.S. territory, he was arrested and the yacht was seized.[1]

These episodes could not have occurred had Chinese companies not acquired the capabilities to undercut U.S. prices. While it is not clear from the information available whether knowledge that facilitated the counterfeiting was obtained in an unethical or illegal manner, these examples certainly demonstrate how counterfeit or cheaply produced goods can put U.S. entities at risk.

NOTE

1. "Written testimony of ICE Homeland Security Investigations International Operations Assistant Director Lev Kubiak for a House Committee on Homeland Security, Subcommittee on Border and Maritime Security Haring titled 'The Outer Ring of Border Security: DHS's International Security Programs,'" June 2, 2015; "Statement for the Record, U.S. Immigration and Customs Enforcement, before the U.S. House of Representatives Committee on Homeland Security, Subcommittee on Oversight, Investigation and Management on 'Homeland Security Investigations: Examining DHS's Efforts to Protect American Jobs and Secure the Homeland,'" July 28, 2011.

OFFICE OF INTELLIGENCE AND COUNTERINTELLIGENCE (U.S. DEPARTMENT OF ENERGY)

With its purview over seventeen laboratories, the Department of Energy (DOE) is an integral part of the U.S. government's own efforts to facilitate innovation. DOE's intelligence component is responsible for exploiting the department's expertise to assist other federal (including the intelligence community, of which DOE is a part) and nonfederal entities. It also has responsibilities for counterintelligence, protecting DOE components from adversarial and competitive state and nonstate actors. The sensitivity of the data with which DOE works is indicated by the need for a cadre of employees who maintain "Q" or Top Secret clearances with SCI accesses.

DOE intelligence can trace its beginnings to the Atomic Energy Commission, which was established approximately three decades before the inauguration of the department. However, it was not until 1990 that DOE consolidated its intelligence functions in an Office of Intelligence that brought together the Office of Foreign Intelligence, Threat Assessments, and Counterintelligence.[66] In 1998, the Office of Energy Intelligence (which was located in the Office of Nonproliferation and National Security) split into an independent Office of Intelligence and an Office of Counterintelligence.[67] It was not until 2006 that intelligence components were reconsolidated into the current Office of Intelligence and Counterintelligence under which intelligence and counterintelligence exist as separate directorates.[68] In addition to its headquarters intelligence component, DOE has several Field Intelligence Elements (FIEs) at locations including Los Alamos National Laboratory (LANL) and Sandia National Laboratories, both of which are located in New Mexico.[69] The Field Intelligence Element at LANL has been described as "providing critical information to the Nation's most senior national security policymakers" and as possessing "unique science and technology expertise."[70] Further insight about FIEs is given by the description by Argonne National Laboratory, which describes its FIE as a facility that "provides tools and resources to enable and strengthen connections between government sponsors and the broad set of scientific and engineering capabilities at the Laboratory, with the overall goal of improving the national security of the United States."[71]

The 1998 CI Implementation Plan made an important change to how DOE looked at hostile state and nonstate actors' attempts to compromise its work. Until the 1998 plan, counterintelligence had been subordinate to security at the laboratories. Subsequently, it gained its own programmatic and operational identity, with assured access to the laboratory director.[72] This indicated a change in perspective that broadened the understanding of counterintelligence beyond local, limited considerations to greater strategic awareness of threat actors' intentions. The linking of DOE counterintelligence to U.S. strategic concerns was also evident in the decision that, beginning in FY1998, DOE CI programs would be programmed in the National Foreign Intelligence Program (NFIP).[73] The changes have clearly informed the perspective of the Department's counterintelligence component. A 2007 inspection report described the CI directorate's responsibility as including operations against espionage or other intelligence activities by foreign entities.[74] This outlook stresses the role of entities that threaten the United States at the most strategic level, rather than specific activities that may compromise an individual facility.

Part of the Department's intelligence mission is provision of subject matter expertise to internal and external customers. DOE serves as the premier technical intelligence resource in the areas of nuclear weapons, nonproliferation, energy, science, and technology, as well as emerging nuclear threats.[75] The Office of Energy Intelligence established the practice of using the nuclear expertise scattered throughout the various Department laboratories.[76] With the 1998 Counterintelligence Implementation Plan, the DOE analysis program would complete products to assist CI field personnel to better target their scarce operational and analytical resources.[77] Additionally, the analytic program would participate in and contribute to assessments of the threat to DOE weapons and facilities.[78] In addition to internal customers, DOE analysis—including foreign intelligence analysis that could support nonproliferation activities and policymaking—serves external entities throughout the federal government, including the intelligence community, the counterintelligence community, and law enforcement.[79] Products are developed based on the input not only of DOE officials but also of other U.S. government agencies' officials.[80]

DOE also engages in limited collection and other counterintelligence and counterterrorism activities. According to the Department's Inspector General, "pursuant to Executive Order 12333, the Intelligence Directorate can engage in limited overt collection activities" but it "does not engage in primary covert collection."[81] There are historical indicators that DOE planned to engage in signals intelligence (SIGINT) collection. In 1991, the Department discovered and ordered confiscated wiretapping and surveillance equipment, which security personnel at nuclear weapons plants and laboratories had purchased.[82] Additionally, DOE indicated that it cooperated with the United States' key SIGINT entity, the National Security Agency.[83] However, more recently, as of May 2009, the Office of Intelligence and Counterintelligence reported that it had not engaged in any electronic surveillance.[84]

Interagency involvement by DOE Office of Intelligence and Counterintelligence includes operational and information-sharing functions. Operational cooperation notably occurs between DOE and the FBI. As of 1999, the then Office of Counterintelligence requested the FBI to recruit and station foreign counterintelligence (FCI)-experienced special agents in the five nuclear laboratory jurisdictions.[85] This by 2011 had evolved into the "Agents in the Lab" initiative that placed FBI agents in DOE facilities to raise CI awareness and to broaden the FBI's access to intelligence within the facilities.[86] DOE also offers specialized technology and "operation support" to intelligence and law enforcement agencies.[87] Integration with the broader intelligence community is apparent in the conduits for information between DOE and other government agencies (OGAs). The Office of Intelligence and Counterintelligence is responsible for nominating individuals to the Consolidated Terrorism Watchlist if DOE acquires applicable information.[88] As of 1999, OCI planned to work with the CIA to develop an expanded DOE distribution for CIA CI analytical products.[89] Working groups have provided another opportunity for the sharing of DOE information. For instance, one laboratory established a "Counterintelligence Coordination Committee" that included representatives from the Energy laboratory, the Energy Operations Office, the FBI, the CIA, and the U.S. Customs Service.[90] The Office of Intelligence and Counterintelligence also serves as the liaison to the FBI-run National Joint Terrorism Task Force.[91]

In addition to operational cooperation and information sharing, DOE provides interagency analytical assistance. Analyses that could assist other government agencies' efforts to counter the illicit transfer of U.S. technology to foreign governments have been made available to appropriate entities.[92] Analytic products have included nuclear-related technology assessments at the request of other agencies.[93] Furthermore, DOE has provided analytical assistance for exploitation of other agencies' information. For instance, DOE has provided help to the FBI with respect to its Foreign Intelligence Surveillance Act (FISA) collection activities.[94]

BUREAU OF INDUSTRY AND SECURITY
(U.S. DEPARTMENT OF COMMERCE)

The Bureau of Industry and Security (BIS) is an element of the Department of Commerce that plays an integral role in ensuring that sensitive technology, including items that could enhance a hostile actor's ability to engage U.S. innovation, is not furnished to state or nonstate entities of concern. BIS's decision-making process takes into account U.S. strategic interests (for example, how the proliferation of a specific technology will impact policy options, etc.) and leverages interagency expertise to determine the implications of a specific technology's proliferation. Once it has received these external inputs, BIS interprets regulations in order to make a decision, and then takes steps to ensure that the technology has not been diverted from the declared end-user to an undesirable party. Ultimately, BIS provides feedback, notably through its annual report to Congress, that illustrates the evolving threat environment (that is, the state and nonstate actors engaged in illicit acquisition of technology) that can then be used by policymakers to make decisions about those actors.

BIS's focus is on those items that are primarily commercial in nature but are potentially dual-use because of their applicability to conventional arms, weapons of mass destruction, terrorist activities, or human rights abuse. It has both offensive and defensive responsibilities directly pertinent to preserving the United States' capability for innovation. According to its 2014 report to Congress, BIS has a responsibility for "promoting continued U.S. leadership in strategic technologies." In 2009, export control reforms stipulated a defensive role for BIS "to create more effective safeguards, or 'higher fences,' to keep the most sensitive items and technology away from foreign entities that seek to harm our national interests."[95]

The above-articulated mission is conducted within the context of strategic U.S. interests. In making its determinations about export license applications, BIS must weigh "divergent or even competing" U.S. interests, ensuring that U.S. companies can operate competitively and globally, while mitigating the risks of dual-use technology ending up in the wrong hands.[96] This task is further complicated by the emergence of new threats that result in the shifting of BIS priorities. According to a Government Accountability Office (GAO) report, senior BIS officials have had to make regulatory changes that reflected the dynamic geopolitical environment, such as changing licensing requirements for exports to India, Iraq, Libya, and Syria.[97] BIS also has a responsibility for supporting U.S. policy decisions related to U.S. participation in multiple international agreements and treaties. These include the Australia Group, which focuses on stemming the proliferation of chemical and biological weapons; the Missile Technology Control Regime; the Nuclear Suppliers Group; the Wassenaar Arrangement, which addresses export controls on conventional arms and sensitive dual-use goods and technologies; the Chemical Weapons Conventions; the Additional Protocol to the U.S. International Atomic Energy Agency Safeguards Agreement; and the Biological Weapons Convention.[98] These multilateral arrangements ultimately inhibit the transfer of technology and the capabilities for innovation—that are inherent in activities, such as reverse engineering—to malignant actors.

BIS operates in conjunction with multiple U.S. government agency partners. It contributes a deputy director (with the other coming from the U.S. Department of Justice) to the Export Enforcement Coordination Center and is a participant in the CFIUS process.[99] Additionally, multiple agencies may review any license application submitted to BIS for decision. Per Executive Order 12981, these are the Departments of Defense, Energy, and State.[100] BIS's referrals to the Department of Energy came about as a result of the events of September 11, 2001, and focused on missile technologies and chemical or biological agents as well as nuclear-related applications.[101] BIS may also refer applications to the Central Intelligence Agency to determine whether foreign parties of concern may be involved in the proposed export.[102]

Decisions by the BIS center on the Export Administration Regulations (EAR), which require that potential exporters obtain a license from BIS or reach a determination that a government licenses are not necessary for the item in question. (BIS also has export control authorities under the Energy Policy and Conservation Act, the Mineral Leasing Act, the Naval Petroleum Reserves Production Act, the Outer Continental Shelf Lands Act, and the Forest Resources Conservation and Shortage Relief Act.[103]) Whether an export license is required depends on multiple factors, including the item being exported, country of ultimate destination, individual parties involved in the export, parties' involvement in proliferation activities, and planned end use of the item. Perhaps because of the shifting dynamics described above, BIS, according to a GAO report, did not have an official definition or explanation as to what constituted an export control concern. This according to GAO meant that "the decision as to whether a party should be added to the watchlist is left to the judgment of BIS personnel responsible for maintaining the watchlist." Instead, BIS mandates only that entities under investigation must be placed on the watchlist of export concerns. Historically, in addition to the murky definitions of the entities to be watchlisted, BIS did not routinely review and update the list. According to a GAO assessment, "BIS officials do not regularly review the watchlist to ensure its completeness. BIS officials said they do not conduct periodic checks as to whether particular parties have been added to the list. They also do not compare BIS watchlist to other federal agencies' lists or databases use for similar purposes to determine whether BIS watchlist is missing pertinent parties." The watchlist is concerned with recipients. However, BIS also historically experienced difficulty with identifying the suitability of items for export as it had failed to implement GAO recommendations to ensure that items are properly classified to guard against the improper export of defense-related items.[104]

In addition to adjudicating export license applications, BIS has also deployed assets internationally to ensure that items are reaching the declared end-users for the declared purposes (rather than being diverted to an undeclared third party of concern). To facilitate this process of end-user checks, BIS maintains Export Control Offices in U.S. embassies and consulates in Moscow, Beijing, Hong Kong, New Delhi, Abu Dhabi, and Singapore. Export Control officers, Office of Export Enforcement special agents deployed from the United States, and Foreign Commercial Service officers conduct the checks.[105] In FY2014, BIS conducted 1,044 end-user checks in fifty-one countries.[106] BIS used the results of checks that identified illicit activities, such as unauthorized reexport, to prevent future exports to unsuitable end-users and to take enforcement action.[107]

The Office of Export Enforcement, in addition to end-user checks, is BIS's law enforcement component and is thus key to the disruption of threat activities.[108] It employs both criminal investigators and enforcement analysts who are singularly focused on export controls and who work closely with BIS licensing officers. Additionally, Export Enforcement has developed force-multiplying relationships with law enforcement and intelligence agencies as well as with partners in industry.[109] Export Enforcement officials participate in the export licensing process by making recommendations on license applications, detaining shipments that may have been undertaken in violation of the EAR, and in some significant cases seeking the issuance of Temporary Denial Orders to prevent imminent export violations.[110]

BIS also has analytical duties that are directly pertinent to ensuring the United States' capability for innovation. Central to these is its responsibility for monitoring the strength of the U.S. defense industrial and technological base, which involves reviewing the potential for domestic impact of U.S. technology transfers on a continuing basis.[111] It also regularly initiates studies of specific sectors significant to innovation. These have included the NASA industrial base, telecommunications, the U.S. space industrial supply chain, and the U.S. integrated circuit fabrication and design capabilities.[112]

As a U.S. government component integral to preventing illicit foreign acquisition of capacity for innovation, it is not surprising that BIS was the target of a cyber attack by Chinese entities. This is consistent with China's relentless, aggressive pursuit of U.S. technology, with little regard for the legality of methods employed to obtain it. In 2006, BIS discovered that entities operating through the Chinese Internet had made a targeted effort to access BIS user accounts.[113] The objective of the attacks was unknown, but the end result was tantamount to sabotage. The hackers used a "rootkit" that so thoroughly compromised BIS's system that workstations were deemed unsalvageable and a new network had to be built.[114] Making things worse, it took technicians eight days from identifying the penetration to install a filter, which turned out to be the wrong type.[115]

China's attack on BIS illustrates how the war over innovation is never strictly a private sector problem. BIS's role as the entity responsible for governing the transfer of technology by the private sector, as opposed to anything that BIS developed in its own right, made it a target for actors hostile to U.S. interests. Its information technology inefficiency, indicated by the excessive amount of time it took to identify and mitigate the threat activity, speaks to another element of the relationship, preservation of innovation, between government and industry. Specifically, government is ill-equipped to secure innovation when its knowledge and capabilities lag behind the innovators.

COMMITTEE ON FOREIGN INVESTMENTS IN THE UNITED STATES (U.S. DEPARTMENT OF THE TREASURY)

The Committee on Foreign Investment in the United States (CFIUS) is a relatively obscure interagency body that has a significant role in governing the acquisition of assets—including those essential to innovation—by entities abroad. CFIUS's mandate is to assess the implication of foreign powers' buying into the United States through foreign direct investment acquisitions of existing American entities. It currently operates under the auspices of the Department of the Treasury and draws its authorities from section 721 of the Defense Production Act of 1950, as amended by the Foreign Investment and National Security Act (FINSA) of 2007, section 721 and as implemented by Executive Order 11858 as amended and regulations at 31 Code of Federal Regulations, Part 800.[116] What CFIUS does not assess are new "greenfield" outposts of foreign enterprises or the implications of U.S. companies' expansion abroad (which are significant, from a counterintelligence perspective, as they may create new vulnerabilities).

President Gerald Ford created CFIUS by Executive Order in 1975. As with subsequent evolutions of the body, CFIUS's creation was the result of political pressure: an attempt to placate Congress, which had grown increasingly concerned about the rapid increase in investments by the Organization of the Petroleum Exporting Countries (OPEC) countries in American portfolio assets and a belief that some of the OPEC members' investments were being driven by political rather than by economic motives. The International Investment Survey Act of 1976 strengthened the Executive Branch's hand in reviewing foreign transactions by providing the president clear and unambiguous authority to collect information on international investment.[117]

The next significant development in the evolution of CFIUS occurred in 1988, with the passage of the Exon-Florio Amendment to the Omnibus Trade and Competitiveness Act. Again, congressional concerns provided the impetus for legislation, with the issue in question being the proposed sale of Fairchild Semiconductor by its owner, the French firm Schlumberger Limited, to the Japanese firm Fujitsu, in 1987.[118] This contributed to a broader concern that foreign takeovers of U.S. firms could not be stopped by anything less than the president's declaration of national emergency or regulators' invocation of federal anti-trust, environmental, or securities laws.[119] Exon-Florio gave the president the authority to block proposed or pending foreign mergers, acquisitions, or takeovers of persons engaged in interstate commerce in the United States that threatened to impact national security.[120] (Before the president can invoke this authority, he/she must determine that other U.S. laws are inadequate or inappropriate for protection of the national security.

Additionally, the president must have credible evidence that the foreign investment will impact national security, which represented an effort to distinguish legitimate concerns from political considerations.) President Ronald Reagan implemented provisions of the Omnibus Trade Act, via Executive Order 12661, and, as part of this, delegated to CFIUS the president's authority to conduct reviews, undertake investigations, and make recommendations. This was despite the fact that the legislation did not specifically mention CFIUS. As a Congressional Research Service report noted, "This transformed CFIUS from a purely administrative body to one with a broad mandate and significant authority."[121] With this authority, companies were increasingly inclined to negotiate with or shy away from CFIUS in advance of a potential denial of a transaction.

Under Exon-Florio, the president must consider twelve factors when deciding to block a foreign acquisition. (CFIUS, as the body to which these considerations have been delegated, must also take these into consideration.) Most relevant to the preservation of an American innovative edge are whether the potential effects of the transaction on U.S. technological leadership are in areas affecting U.S. national security; the potential effects on U.S. critical technologies; the capability and capacity of domestic industries to meet national defense requirements, including the availability of human resources, products, technology, materials, and other supplies and services; the control of domestic industries and commercial activity by foreign citizens as it affects the capability and capacity of the United States to meet the requirements of national security; and the long-term projection of the U.S. requirements for sources of energy and other critical resources and materials.

In addition to the ability to engage in innovation, factors also reflect concerns that existing technologies may be used against the United States. Specific issues include the potential effects of the transactions on the sales of military goods, equipment, or technology to a country that supports terrorism or proliferates missile technology or chemical and biological weapons. It also includes transactions identified by the Secretary of Defense as "posing a regional military threat" to the interests of the United States.[122]

The Byrd Amendment to the National Defense Authorization Act for FY1993 gave additional responsibilities to CFIUS. Until this point, reviews happened either at the voluntary submission of a proposal to CFIUS process or a CFIUS member agency's request for the review of a specific transaction. However, the Byrd Amendment made it mandatory for CFIUS to investigate proposed mergers, acquisitions, or takeovers in cases where two criteria are met: (1) the acquirer is controlled by or acting on behalf of a foreign government, and (2) the acquisition results in control of a person engaged in interstate commerce in the United States that could affect the national security.[123] The mandatory review of "covered" transactions has evolved to identify whether a transaction threatens to impair the national security, the foreign entity is controlled by a foreign government, or would result in control of any critical infrastructure that could impair national security.[124]

In 2007, Congress passed the National Security Foreign Investment Reform and Strengthened Transparency Act of 2007 (FINSA), PL 110-49. As with previous legislation, the political climate provided context for the legislation. In the years leading up to FINSA, the Chinese had attempted to acquire the oil company Unocal, and more recently, Dubai Ports World pursued purchase of a British firm that had operated several key U.S. ports. (In both cases, the potential buyers abdicated the playing field after encountering hostile public opinion.) FINSA addressed six problems identified by Congress: (1) the principal members of CFIUS at times seemed not to be well informed concerning the outcomes of reviews and investigations regarding proposed or pending investment transactions; (2) CFIUS had incorrectly interpreted the requirements under the statutes for investigation of transaction that involve firms that are owned or controlled by a foreign government; (3) reporting requirements had not provided Congress with enough information about the operations and actions of CFIUS for members to fulfill their oversight responsibilities; (4) CFIUS had exercised too much discretion in choosing which transaction it investigated; (5) the definition of national security used by CFIUS was no longer adequate post–September 11; and (6) deadlines placed on CFIUS to complete reviews and investigations of investment transactions did not always provide adequate time for the committee to complete its reviews and investigations.[125]

FINSA introduced several significant changes to the CFIUS process. Significantly, it gave statutory recognition to CFIUS and established the Secretary of the Treasury as its chair. It also added the Department of Energy as a member and granted the president permission to add any other members deemed necessary.[126] Executive Order 13456, which implemented FINSA, added five members of CFIUS to observe and, as appropriate, participate in and report to the president: director of the Office of Management and Budget, chairman of the Council of Economic Advisors, the National Security Advisor, Assistant to the President for Economic Policy, and the Assistant to the President for Homeland Security and Counterterrorism.[127] Reflecting the recent foreign efforts to acquire U.S. infrastructure, the PL 110-49 built upon the Exon-Florio's consideration of critical infrastructure by specifically modifying the definition of entities relevant to national security to include critical infrastructure, including energy deposits and power plants. It also included "homeland security" and "critical industries" as broad categories of economic activity that could be subject to a CFIUS review.[128] Consistent with the physical concerns of critical infrastructure, CFIUS also considers the location of an acquired business and the proximity to certain government facilities such as military outposts.[129] It also introduced the director of national intelligence (DNI) as a participant in the process. Although legislation did not make the DNI a member of the committee, it did require the DNI to carry out an analysis of any threat to U.S. national security resulting from any merger, acquisition, or takeover.[130] This analysis includes incorporation of the views from all affected or appropriate intelligence agencies with respect to the transaction.[131] Furthermore, the DNI must ensure that the intelligence community remains engaged in the collection, analysis, and dissemination to CFIUS of any additional relevant information that may become available during the course of any investigation conducted.[132] Presumably, this requires ongoing awareness of the foreign presence because a 2006 change to CFIUS process by the administration allowed CFIUS to reopen a review of a deal and to overturn its approval at any time if CFIUS believed that the companies materially failed to comply with the terms of the arrangement.[133]

A recent judicial decision has curbed the president's freedom of action in blocking transactions. In 2014, a federal appeals court ruled that a Chinese-owned company was entitled to review the unclassified information that President Barack Obama used in his decision to block the transaction and that the company should be provided an opportunity to respond to the information.[134] Up until this point, foreign firms had been given little insight into the process.

CFIUS Today

CFIUS, as of 2015, reflects a forty-year evolution of legal authorities. It is composed of heads of the Department of Treasury (chair), Department of Justice, Department of Homeland Security, Department of Commerce, Department of Defense, Department of State, Department of Energy, Office of the U.S. Trade Representative, and the Office of Science and Technology Policy. Additionally, the Office of Management and Budget, Council of Economic Advisors, National Security Council, National Economic Council, and the Homeland Security Council observe and participate when appropriate.[135] As noted above, the DNI advises but does not participate in policy discussions. Similar to the DNI, the Secretary of Labor provides input on conformity with U.S. employment law.[136]

Scrutiny of a transaction can be initiated in several ways. The president or any member of CFIUS can trigger a review of an investment transaction. These steps are in addition to a formal notification by parties, which would prompt a formal investigation. Prior to filing a voluntary notice, parties may consult with CFIUS or submit a draft notice. Once a formal inquiry is initiated, CFIUS members examine the transaction to identify and address any concerns for national security inherent to it. If CFIUS finds that the covered transaction does not present any national security risks or that other provisions of law provide adequate and appropriate authority to address the risks, then CFIUS will advise the parties in writing that CFIUS has concluded all action in respect to such transaction. If CFIUS finds that a covered transaction presents national security risks and that other provisions of law do not provide adequate authority to address the risks, then CFIUS may enter into an agreement with or impose conditions on parties to mitigate such risks or may refer the case to the president.

CFIUS is, at present, more thoroughly integrated into the national security enterprise than it was when initiated. As a result of PL 110-49, CFIUS must now provide confidential briefings to Congress as requested and produce an annual report. These measures make investment regulation a subject of national policy debate, as opposed to a technocratic decision. The divergence of the two is demonstrated by the proposed acquisition of P&O (which operated several major U.S. ports) by Dubai Ports World in 2006, which CFIUS approved but which Congress opposed, as well as concerns about the Chinese-owned CNOOC's attempt to purchase Unocal, an oil company. Political decision making also introduces a broader rubric than the formal CFIUS process. For instance, according to the *Economist* in 2007, the United States has made it clear that it will consider the openness of other countries' markets when their governments are trying to buy American companies.[137]

Shortcomings of CFIUS

CFIUS is an incomplete mechanism for regulating the cross-border investments that could result in foreign acquisition of capabilities for innovation. There is a basic conceptual problem of "national security" being ill defined. According to the Congressional Research Service, neither Congress nor the administration had attempted to define the term *national security* as it appears in the Exon-Florio statute. Rather, Treasury Department officials have suggested that during a review or investigation each member of CFIUS is expected to apply the definition of national security consistent with the constituent agency's legislative mandate.[138] Additionally, as noted above, it does not regulate U.S. companies' investments abroad, which could expose those entities to greater vulnerability from foreign actors. Furthermore, CFIUS does not cover the full scope of foreign investments on U.S. soil because it does not address "greenfield" developments by foreign companies. This became a concern in 2013, when the Russian space agency Roscomos proposed building approximately half a dozen global positioning system monitor stations in the United States.[139] CFIUS does not regulate the purchase of specific intellectual property or the hiring of employees.[140] As discussed in a subsequent chapter, the Chinese telecommunication company Huawei attempted to invoke this to avoid a review.

TEXTBOX 2.2

CFIUS has formally recommended against only two transactions. However, others, including the attempted CNOOC purchase of Unocal and the investment by Dubai Ports World, which brought CFIUS into the spotlight, were actually withdrawn when the political climate grew increasingly skeptical of these deals. Similarly indicating the role that politics can play in allowing or prohibiting a company from buying into the United States was an incident in 2000 when the White House requested that the FBI tone down its congressional testimony warning of the risks posed by foreign government ownership of communications companies.[1] The FBI's concern was that such a shift in control increased the risks to U.S. national security and reduced the ability of U.S. security forces to do their job.[2]

NOTES

1. Kathy Chen, "White House Asks FBI to Curb Warnings on Foreign Ownership of Telecom Firms," *Wall Street Journal*, September 8, 2000.
2. Ibid.

NATIONAL COUNTERINTELLIGENCE AND SECURITY CENTER (OFFICE OF THE DIRECTOR OF NATIONAL INTELLIGENCE)

The National Counterintelligence and Security Center (NCSC) is a component of the Office of the Director of National Intelligence. It is headed by the National Counterintelligence Executive (NCIX). NCSC develops, coordinates, and produces the National Threat Identification and Prioritization Assessment, the National Counterintelligence Strategy of the United States of America, and espionage damage assessments, among other products. It identifies priorities for counterintelligence collection, investigations, and operations and is responsible for counterintelligence program budgets and evaluations.

Created by the Office of the Director of National Intelligence in December 2014, the NCSC is the latest iteration of interagency counterintelligence bodies. It was preceded by the Office of the National Counterintelligence Executive, which was created in 2002 as a result of the Counterintelligence Enhancement Act. The NCIX succeeded the National Counterintelligence

Center (NACIC), which was established in 1994. This was initially led by a senior FBI official, with a military counterintelligence component executive as deputy. The chair would then rotate between the FBI, CIA, and the Department of Defense, with the FBI serving as deputy when it was not acting as chair.[141] Also in 1994, the U.S. government established the National Counterintelligence Policy Board, which is now chaired by the NCIX.[142]

Journalist Mark Riebling cites 1988 as the beginning of an interagency Counterintelligence Center (CIC).[143] However, this was the CIA's in-house CI component rather than the NACIC. But starting in 1994, the head of the CIC's Counterespionage Group was to be an FBI executive.[144]

CONCLUSION

The current collection and analytical process that informs U.S. government decisions to prevent compromise of innovation by foreign entities seeking to acquire existing entities is currently incomplete. The Department of Energy and the Department of Commerce have collection components that are oriented toward ensuring that their own operations are not degraded by threat actors. The two intelligence agencies that have wider responsibilities for identifying and disrupting threat activities beyond the confines of their departments—the Federal Bureau of Investigation and Homeland Security Investigations—are reactive in nature. Their collection activities focus on already identified acts of malfeasance rather than the production of intelligence of strategic value that can help decision makers anticipate new challenges. This backward-looking posture likely shortchanges entities such as NCSC and CFIUS, which must analyze and interpret information not to understand what actors have already committed an offense, but to anticipate which actors might pose challenges in the future.

Effective protection of innovation is one of several topics that suggest a need to rethink how intelligence collection and analysis is done in the domestic environment. The current agencies are not structured to collect strategic intelligence. Instead, they are set up to obtain a subset of intelligence—the information that comes to light as a result of efforts to disrupt identified malfeasance—which leaves opportunities to collect information of foreign intelligence value, which happens to be present in the United States, unexploited (and unused by decision makers). While the FBI has put significant effort into remaking itself as an intelligence agency since 9/11 (and does have some valuable legacies in this area that reach back to the 1930s), its corporate culture is still weighted toward the reactive approach of law enforcement. Consequently, reform efforts have been skewed (for example, TRP, which focuses on identified issues, rather than identifying opportunities to develop an informational advantage for decision makers such as CFIUS). While beyond the scope of this book, the systemic flaws of the current collection and analytical functions that protect innovation suggest that responsibilities should be reallocated across agencies. (It is neither likely that the American public will accept a dedicated domestic intelligence service nor is such a drastic step advisable, given the effort that is still being spent on getting existing agencies to function properly.) One approach would be to divest the FBI of as many of its criminal investigative missions as possible, keeping only those that are transnational in nature, and parceling these (along with the workforce most heavily invested in them) to agencies with a strong law enforcement culture such as DEA and ATF. Following the division of labor, the Bureau could be reoriented toward intelligence, with each component aligning its responsibilities toward intelligence requirements that lead to identifying threats for disruption. This stands in contrast to the current paradigm that treats intelligence collection as a byproduct of the investigations of known threats.

Table 2.1. Executive branch agencies and their functions

Executive Branch Agency	Component	Function
U.S. Department of Justice	Federal Bureau of Investigation (FBI)	The FBI is the primary intelligence agency within the domestic setting. Its role in securing U.S. innovation falls under its counterintelligence and criminal investigative divisions. Its cyber division has a significant role in identifying activities of concern. However, cyber, despite the Bureau's organizational structure, is not a threat in and of itself, but rather a vector used by malign and benign actors alike.
U.S. Department of Defense	Defense Security Service (DSS)	DSS has significant responsibilities for personnel and physical security at U.S. defense contractor facilities. Prominent among its duties is administering the National Industrial Security Program. Additionally, DSS addresses the complications created by foreign ownership control and influence (FOCI) of companies that develop proprietary information that adds value to U.S. capabilities.
U.S. Department of Homeland Security (DHS)	Homeland Security Investigations (HSI) (Part of Immigration and Customs Enforcement [ICE])	ICE is the only federal law enforcement agency with full statutory authority to investigate and enforce criminal violations of all U.S. export laws related to military items, controlled "dual-use" commodities, and sanctioned or embargoed countries. HSI is the principal intelligence collection component of DHS and the second largest federal criminal investigative agency, with authority to enforce more than four hundred federal statutes.

(continued)

Executive Branch Agency	Component	Function
U.S. Department of Energy (DOE)	Office of Intelligence and Counterintelligence	DOE's intelligence component is responsible for exploiting the department's expertise to assist other federal (including the intelligence community, of which DOE is a part) and nonfederal entities. It also has responsibilities for counterintelligence, protecting DOE components from adversarial and competitive state and nonstate actors.
U.S. Department of Commerce	Bureau of Industry and Security (BIS)	BIS's focus is primarily on those items that are primarily commercial in nature but are potentially dual-use because of their applicability to conventional arms, weapons of mass destruction, terrorist activities, or human rights abuse. It has both offensive and defensive responsibilities. It adjudicates export license requests and also deploys assets to ensure that sensitive exports are not diverted and instead reach the declared end user.
U.S. Department of the Treasury	Committee on Foreign Investment in the United States (CFIUS)	CFIUS is an interagency body that vets proposed purchases of U.S. entities by foreign parties. Following a CFIUS review, the president may opt to block a proposed acquisition. CFIUS shortcomings include a limited purview (only certain categories of acquisitions are subject to CFIUS scrutiny), and it does not address "greenfield" investments (the establishment of entirely new commercial entities, as opposed to the acquisition of existing assets).
Office of the Director of National Intelligence	National Counterintelligence and Security Center (NCSC)	NCSC is the point of interagency coordination on counterintelligence (CI) matters. CI is the prominent discipline under which state-sponsored exfiltration of sensitive technology is disrupted.

TEXTBOX 2.3

With recent high-profile cyber attacks like those on Target, Home Depot, and Sony Pictures, there is an increase in awareness among U.S. businesses for cyber security. Cyber security was once handled almost exclusively by the U.S. government. However, private cyber security companies are increasingly stepping in and conducting cyber security investigative work and developing innovative tools to not only help prevent cyber attacks, but also to actively respond to them. Companies like Mandiant, FireEye, and Crowd Strike represent a changing dynamic in this arena. Executives at many large U.S. corporations targeted by hackers such as banks, credit card companies, and utilities find it difficult to learn about foreign hackers from government investigators because much of the information is classified.[1] Private security companies can be much more public about their activities. In fact, Mandiant was one of the first such companies to actively publicize what they are doing and make a business out of it.

Cyber investigations have traditionally been handled very discreetly. Many cyber security companies are staffed by former military and investigators from law enforcement agencies. Consequently, the tendency to not talk about what they are doing is strong. FireEye, on the other hand, will routinely discuss security breaches when its customers allow it. FireEye CEO David DeWalt explained, "We want to become an extension of the government, we can be a little more neutral globally as a public company, we can be a little more able to disclose."[2] Indeed, Mandiant (now owned by FireEye) attracted much attention in 2013 when it released a very detailed report on an elite Chinese cyber hacking team carrying out attacks on U.S. companies. Mandiant directly linked the cyber attacks of 141 U.S. and foreign entities to China's military. They traced the attacks back to a single group designated as "Advanced Persistent Threat One" (APT1). APT1 was identified as a Chinese military unit within the People's Liberation Army unit 61398.[3] The directness and specificity of the Mandiant report helped focus public attention on the cyber espionage activities.

Company Profiles of High-Profile Cybersecurity Firms:

Mandiant:
Founded in 2004
CEO: Kevin Mandia (former U.S. Air Force Officer)
Acquired by FireEye in December 2013
Revenue: $100 million (2012)

(continued)

Employees: 300 (2013)
Headquarters: Alexandria, Virginia

FireEye
Founded in 2004 by Ashar Aziz, formerly of SunMicrosystems
CEO: Dave DeWalt
Acquired Mandiant in 2013
Headquarters: Milptas, California
Revenue: $635 million
Employees: 1,000+ (2013)

CrowdStrike
Founded in 2011 by Dmitri Alperovitch and George Kurtz
CEO: George Kurtz
Senior former FBI executives on board: Shawn Henry, former executive director, and Steve Chabinsky, former deputy assistant director of cyber division
Revenue: $13.8 million
Employees: 160
Headquarters: Irvine, California

The emergence of cyber expertise for the private sector is not an entirely new phenomenon and follows in the tradition of competitive intelligence firms. However, it is a new variant on this theme, as it is filling a role that the government is not only unwilling but increasingly unable to fill for several reasons. Increasingly, government reliance on the expertise, rather than simply the labor (which is usually provided by government contractors), has been apparent for a number of years. For instance, in 2011, the Office of the Director of National Intelligence's Office of the National Counterintelligence Executive released a report that explicitly cited Mandiant's 2010 findings that information was pilfered from the corporate network of a U.S. Fortune 500 manufacturing company during business negotiations in which the company was looking to acquire a Chinese firm. The purloined information, according to Mandiant, may have helped the Chinese firm attain a better negotiating and pricing position.[4] Such a citation could plausibly be attributed to the use of publicly available information as a means to protect sources and methods. However, prior to this reference, Joel F. Brenner, head of ONCIX, noted that there was a "seismic shift" toward increasing reliance on the private sector in the intelligence world.[5]

The private sector has increasingly identified threats to the U.S. government, at times in areas where the government might never have recognized that it had a problem. Particularly notable is the report that in 2015 the information technology firm CyTech accidentally discovered the breach of twenty-one million federal employees' personal data during a product demonstration for the Office of Personnel Management (a claim that OPM has denied).[6] That same year, FireEye Inc. determined through forensic analysis that Chinese hackers may have accessed U.S. military technology when they hacked into systems of the engineering department at Pennsylvania State University.[7] Although the Federal Bureau of Investigation brought the university's attention to the fact that a hack had occurred, the university had to resort to assistance from the private sector to identify the fact that U.S. government information may have been compromised. CrowdStrike, similarly, through its research, was able to release a white paper about state-sponsored penetrations of more than seventy entities, including government agencies.[8]

Nimbleness by private sector cyber security has resulted in increased reliance by the government on these entities. As of 2015, the FBI had paid Mandiant more than USD $17 million in the preceding decade for services that including teaching employees about hacking cases.[9] Furthermore, Secretary of Defense Ashton Carter noted in 2015 that firms such as FireEye and Crowdstrike were leaders in the field of attribution—linking cyber attacks to perpetrators—and that when they outed a malicious group, the U.S. government took notice.[10] A high-profile example of such an attribution was Mandiant's identification of the Chinese PLA's Unit 61398 as a perpetrator of widespread cyber attacks.[11]

The government is unlikely to keep pace with the private sector's acumen for several reasons. There is an ongoing failure within the U.S. government to identify the talent it needs, much less acquire it. According to a former Bush administration official, in 2009, federal information technology managers did not know what skills they actually needed to combat cyber threats; this sentiment had not changed by 2015, when the United States' Chief Information Officer Tony Scott admitted that recruiting of digital specialists and putting them in the right positions was going to be a challenge.[12] The Partnership for Public Service, a think tank focused on assisting the development of the federal workforce, stated similarly in a 2015 report that "currently the Government still does not know exactly how many cyber workers it employs, what skills they have, where they work and what skills they need."[13]

(continued)

These unique problems are compounded by more general trends that characterize the current workforce. According to the Partnership for Public Service, millennials do not view government as a permanent career path, unlike previous generations.[14] Their willingness to remain in positions once they have been hired is likely negatively influenced by perceptions that their career development was shifted to a slow track with minimal recognition from supervisors, shrinking opportunities for training, and few assignments to which they apply unique talents.[15] This is exacerbated, especially in the area of cyber talents, where there is such a disparity in pay, by the lure of the private sector. Once trained by the federal government, cyber-capable employees become very attractive to the private sector, and even the National Security Agency has lost more technical people at much higher rates, early on in their careers, than employees with other skill sets.[16] The result is a shift in expertise to private cyber security, as illustrated by Shawn Henry's decampment from the FBI.

Finally, private cyber security offers unique capabilities that make it an attractive alternative to reliance on federal government entities (even if those entities were operating at full competency). CrowdStrike, for instance, employs a concept known as "active defense" that entails identifying the source of attack to networks and using this identification to inform limited offensive measures such as misinformation and malware against the attacker.[17] This may be done through tactics such as using decoys to lure hackers into a controlled environment where their behaviors can be observed.[18] As Henry explained to the *Los Angeles Times*, "We will not break the law, but there's a lot organizations can do behind their own firewall on their own networks to make life difficult for the adversary."[19]

This phenomenon is uniquely relevant to this book. The U.S. government is losing the capacity for understanding innovation in the cyber milieu to private industry (just as the U.S. government writ large has ceded much of its ability for innovation to private industry). It is through the vector of cyber, an area requiring an innovative approach, that threat actors are targeting innovation in other sectors, through penetration of government, industry, and academic networks.

NOTES

1. Danny Yadron, "Latest Cyber Deal Shows Security Is Hot Sector," *Wall Street Journal*, January 3, 2014.

2. Elizabeth Weise, "FireEye Has Become Go-To Company for Breaches," *USA Today*, May 21, 2015.

3. Mandiant Intelligence Center Report, *APT1: Exposing One of China's Cyber Espionage Units*, http://intelreport.mandiant.com/ (accessed March 9, 2016).

4. Office of the National Counterintelligence Executive, *Foreign Spies Stealing US Economic Secrets in Cyberspace, Report to Congress on Foreign Economic Collection and Industrial Espionage, 2009–2011* (Office of the National Counterintelligence Executive, 2011), 5.

5. Ariana Eunjung Cha, "Even Spies Embrace China's Free Market," *Washington Post*, February 15, 2008.

6. Damian Paletta, "Cybersecurity Firm Says It Found Spyware on Government Network in April," *Wall Street Journal*, June 15, 2015.

7. Andrew Grossman, "U.S. Charges Six Chinese with Economic Espionage," *Wall Street Journal*, May 20, 2015.

8. Ken Dilanian, "Cyber Security Gets Confrontational," *Los Angeles Times*, December 4, 2012.

9. Danny Yadron, "Cybersecurity Firm's Strategy Raises Eyebrows," *Wall Street Journal*, September 9, 2015.

10. Anna Mulrine, "Pentagon Cybersecurity Strategy Comes with Olive Branch to Silicon Valley," *Christian Science Monitor*, April 23, 2015.

11. Chris Lew, *Chinese Motivations for Corporate Espionage—a Historical Perspective* (FireEye, 2013).

12. Joe Davidson, "Lack of Digital Talent Adds to Cybersecurity Problems," *Washington Post*, July 19, 2015.

13. Partnership for Public Service, *Cyber In-Security II: Closing the Federal Talent Gap* (Washington, D.C.: Partnership for Public Service, 2015), 6.

14. Lisa Rein, "Millennials Working in Government Are at Their Lowest Levels in Five Years, New Report Finds," *Washington Post*, August 24, 2015.

15. Ibid.

16. Partnerships for Public Service, *Cyber In-Security II*, 24; Patrick Semansky, "In Fierce Battle for Cyber Talent, Even NSA Struggles to Keep Elites on Staff," Nextgov.com, April 14, 2015.

17. "The Surveillance State and Its Discontents," *Foreign Policy*, December 2013.

18. Ibid.

19. Ken Dilanian, "Cyber Security Gets Confrontational," *Los Angeles Times*, December 4, 2012.

NOTES

1. "Counterintelligence. History and Evolution," *Federal Bureau of Investigation*, http://www.fbi.gov/about-us/investigate/counterintelligence/history-and-evolution (accessed June 23, 2014).

2. National Counterintelligence Center, *Annual Report to Congress on Foreign Economic Collection and Industrial Espionage: 1996* (National Counterintelligence Center, 1997), 5; Office of the National Counterintelligence Executive, *Annual Report to Congress on Foreign Economic Collection and Industrial Espionage: 2004* (Office of the National Counterintelligence Executive, 2005), 13.

3. "FBI Counterintelligence National Strategy: A Blueprint for Protecting U.S. Secrets," *Federal Bureau of Investigation*, last updated November 4, 2011, http://www.fbi.gov/news/stories/2011/november/counterintelligence_110411 (accessed June 23, 2014).

4. Statement of James B. Comey, Director of the Federal Bureau of Investigation, before the United States Senate Committee on the Judiciary, May 21, 2014.

5. Jay Solomon, "Phantom Menace, FBI Sees Big Threat from Chinese Spies," *Wall Street Journal*, August 10, 2005.

6. Barrett Devlin, "U.S. News: FBI to Use Spy Law to Battle Trade Theft," *Wall Street Journal*, July 24, 2015.

7. Sharon LaFraniere, "FBI Reassigns 300 Counterspies to Crime-Fighting," *Washington Post*, January 9, 1992.

8. Statement of James B. Comey, Director of the Federal Bureau of Investigation, before the United States Senate Committee on the Judiciary.

9. "Panel Chairman Seeks Study of FBI Reorganization; Rep Wolf Cites Concerns on Impact of Shifting Agents to Counterterrorism Effort," *Washington Post*, June 5, 2002.

10. Ellen Nakashima, "Fierce Fight for Expert Workers," *Washington Post*, November 13, 2012.

11. FBI FY 2014 Budget Justification, 9.

12. David A. Vise and Lorraine Adams, "FBI to Restructure, Adding Emphasis on Crime Prevention," *Washington Post*, November 11, 1999.

13. "Ten Years After: The Bureau Since 9/11," *Federal Bureau of Investigation*, http://www.fbi.gov/about-us/ten-years-after-the-fbi-since-9-11 (accessed July 20, 2014).

14. 2013 Joint Strategic Plan on Intellectual Property Enforcement, U.S. Intellectual Property Enforcement Coordinator, June 2013, 72.

15. Ibid., 21.

16. Ibid., 72.

17. FBI FY 2015 Budget Justification, 8.

18. *Hearing Entitled Economic Espionage: A Foreign Intelligence Threat to American Jobs and Homeland Security before the Subcommittee on Counterterrorism and Intelligence, Committee on Homeland Security*, 112th Cong. (2012). (Statement of C. Frank Figluzzi, Assistant Director, Counterintelligence Division, Federal Bureau of Investigation).

19. U.S. Department of Justice, Federal Bureau of Investigation, FY2015 Budget at a Glance (Washington, D.C., 2014)

20. "Premier FBI Cybersquad in Pittsburgh to Add Agents," *New York Times*, August 17, 2014.

21. Todd Masse and William Krouse, *The FBI: Past, Present, and Future* (Washington, D.C.: Congressional Research Service, 2003), 14.

22. Committee on the Judiciary, Subcommittee on Security and Terrorism, Impact of Attorney General's Guidelines for Domestic Security Investigations (The Levi Guidelines), S. Rep 98-134 (1984) (November 1983), 7, 9.

23. Brian Michael Jenkins, Sorrel Wildhorn, and Marvin M. Lavin, *Intelligence Constraints of the 1970s and Domestic Terrorism: Executive Summary* (Santa Monica, CA: Rand, 1982), 11.

24. Masse and Krouse, *The FBI: Past, Present, and Future*, 16.

25. Bruce Hoffman, Edwin Meese III, and Timothy J. Roemer, *The FBI: Protecting the Homeland in the 21st Century* (Washington, D.C.: 9/11 Review Commission, 2015), 56.

26. U.S. Department of Justice, Statement of James B. Comey, Director of the Federal Bureau of Investigation, before the United States Senate Committee on the Judiciary (Washington, D.C., May 21, 2014).

27. Hoffman, Meese, and Roemer, *The FBI: Protecting the Homeland in the 21st Century*, 57.

28. Stanley A. Pimentel, Society of Former Special Agents, "Interview of Former Special Agent Richard A. Marquise" (unpublished interview, April 11, 2008).

29. Select Committee on Intelligence, The FBI and CISPES, S. Prt. 101-46, at 8 (1989).

30. U.S. Department of Justice, Office of the Inspector General, *The Federal Bureau of Investigation's Efforts to Hire, Train, and Retain Intelligence Analysts* (Washington, D.C.: U.S. Department of Justice, Office of the Inspector General, 2005), 18.

31. U.S. Department of Justice, Office of the Inspector General, *Review of the FBI's Handling of Intelligence Information Related to the September 11 Attacks* (Washington, D.C.: U.S. Department of Justice, Office of the Inspector General, 2006), 86.

32. Ibid., 15.

33. U.S. Department of Justice, *The Federal Bureau of Investigation's Efforts to Hire, Train, and Retain Intelligence Analysts*, viii, 5.

34. Ibid., 104.

35. Alfred Cumming and Todd Masse, *FBI Intelligence Reform Since September 11, 2001: Issues and Options for Congress* (Washington, D.C.: Congressional Research Service, 2004).

36. U.S. Department of Justice, Office of the Inspector General, *The Federal Bureau of Investigation's Efforts to Improve the Sharing of Intelligence and Other Information* (Washington, D.C.: U.S. Department of Justice, Office of the Inspector General, Audit Division, 2003), 30.

37. U.S. Department of Justice, *The Federal Bureau of Investigation's Efforts to Hire, Train, and Retain Intelligence Analysts*, 2.

38. Defense Security Service, Strategic Plan 2020, 13.

39. "DSS Marks 40th Anniversary," *DSS Access* 1, no. 3 (Fall 2012), 8–11.

40. www.dss.mil.

41. Defense Security Service, Strategic Plan 2020, 5.

42. Ibid., 5.

43. www.dss.mil.

44. Defense Security Service, Strategic Plan 2020, 5.

45. "DSS Marks 40th Anniversary."

46. www.dss.mil.

47. "DSS Marks 40th Anniversary."

48. "DSS Counterintelligence Celebrates 20th Anniversary," *DSS Access* 2, no. 2 (Summer 2013), 14.

49. "DSS Marks 40th Anniversary."

50. "International Division Oversees Industry Involvement with Foreign Governments," *DSS Access* 1, no. 2 (Summer 2012), 17–21.

51. Statement for the Record, "DHS Cybersecurity: Roles and Responsibilities to Protect the Nation's Critical Infrastructure," Deputy Secretary Jane Hall Lute, U.S. Department of Homeland Security, before the House Committee on Homeland Security, March 13, 2013.

52. *Homeland Security Investigations: Examining DHS's Efforts to Protect American Jobs and Secure the Homeland before the U.S. House of Representatives Committee on Homeland Security, Subcommittee on Oversight, Investigation and Management*, Statement for the Record, U.S. Immigration and Customs Enforcement, July 28, 2011.

53. "Written Testimony of ICE Homeland Security Investigations International Operations Assistant Director Lev Kubiak for a House Committee on Homeland Security, Subcommittee on Border and Maritime Security Hearing Titled 'The Outer Ring of Border Security: DHS's International Security Programs,'" June 2, 2015.

54. "Written Testimony of U.S. Immigration and Customs Enforcement Homeland Security Investigation Assistant Director John Wood for a House Committee on Homeland Security Subcommittee on Counterterrorism and Intelligence Hearing Titled 'Economic Espionage: A Foreign Intelligence Threat to American Jobs and Homeland Security,'" June 27, 2012.

55. "Testimony of John Morton, Director, U.S. Immigration and Customs Enforcement, Before the U.S. House of Representatives Committee on the Judiciary, Subcommittee on Intellectual Property, Competition and the Internet on 'Promoting Investment and Protecting Commerce Online: Legitimate Sites v Parasites, Part II,'" April 5, 2011.

56. "Written Testimony of ICE Homeland Security Investigations Executive Associate Director Peter Edge for a Senate Committee on Appropriations Subcommittee on Homeland Security Hearing Titled 'Investing in Cybersecurity: Understanding Risks and Building Capabilities for the Future,'" May 7, 2014.

57. "Written Testimony of ICE Homeland Security Investigations International Operations Assistant Director Lev Kubiak for a House Committee on Homeland Security, Subcommittee on Border and Maritime Security Haring Titled 'The Outer

Ring of Border Security: DHS's International Security Programs,'" June 2, 2015; "Written Testimony of ICE Deputy Director Daniel Ragsdale for a House Committee on Appropriations Subcommittee on Homeland Security Hearing on ICE's FY 2015 Budget Request," March 13, 2014.

58. Budget-in-Brief Fiscal Year 2016, Homeland Security.

59. "Written Testimony of U.S. Immigration and Customs Enforcement Homeland Security Investigation Assistant Director John Wood for a House Committee on Homeland Security Subcommittee on Counterterrorism and Intelligence Hearing Titled 'Economic Espionage: A Foreign Intelligence Threat to American Jobs and Homeland Security,'" June 27, 2012.

60. "Written Testimony of ICE Homeland Security Investigations International Operations Assistant Director Lev Kubiak for a House Committee on Homeland Security, Subcommittee on Border and Maritime Security Hearing Titled 'The Outer Ring of Border Security: DHS's International Security Programs,'" June 2, 2015.

61. "Written Testimony of U.S. Immigration and Customs Enforcement Homeland Security Investigation Assistant Director John Wood for a House Committee on Homeland Security Subcommittee on Counterterrorism and Intelligence Hearing Titled 'Economic Espionage: A Foreign Intelligence Threat to American Jobs and Homeland Security,'" June 27, 2012.

62. "Written Testimony of ICE Homeland Security Investigations Executive Associate Director Peter Edge for a Senate Committee on Appropriations Subcommittee on Homeland Security Hearing Titled 'Investing in Cybersecurity: Understanding Risks and Building Capabilities for the Future,'" May 7, 2014.

63. "Testimony of John Morton, Director, U.S. Immigration and Customs Enforcement, Before the U.S. House of Representatives Committee on the Judiciary, Subcommittee on Intellectual Property, Competition and the Internet on 'Promoting Investment and Protecting Commerce Online: Legitimate Sites v Parasites, Part II,'" April 5, 2011.

64. "Written Testimony of ICE Homeland Security Investigations International Operations Assistant Director Lev Kubiak for a House Committee on Homeland Security, Subcommittee on Border and Maritime Security Haring Titled 'The Outer Ring of Border Security: DHS's International Security Programs,'" June 2, 2015.

65. "Prepared Testimony on 'Worldwide Threats and Homeland Security Challenges' Secretary of Homeland Security Jeh Charles Johnson, House Committee on Homeland Security," October 21, 2015.

66. Jeffrey T. Richelson, *The US Intelligence Community*, 6th ed. (Boulder, CO: Westview Press, 2011), 141.

67. Ibid.

68. Ibid., 142.

69. U.S. Department of Energy, Office of Inspector General, *Office of Inspection and Special Inquiries Inspection Report: Internal Controls Over Sensitive Compartmented Information Access for Selected Field Intelligence Elements* (Washington, D.C.: U.S. Department of Energy, 2008).

70. "Intelligence Team Given National Honor," *Los Alamos National Laboratory*, www.lanl.gov, February 28, 2011.

71. "National Security Facility," *Argonne National Laboratory*, www.anl.gov (accessed January 24, 2016).

72. U.S. Department of Energy, Office of Inspector General, Office of Audit Service, *Audit Report: Review of the Status of the U.S. Department of Defense's Counterintelligence Implementation Plan* (Washington, D.C.: U.S. Department of Energy, 1999).

73. Ibid.

74. U.S. Department of Energy, Office of Inspector General, Office of Inspections and Special Inquiries, *Inspection Report: Internal Controls Over Computer Property at the Department's Counterintelligence Directorate* (Washington, D.C.: U.S. Department of Energy, 2007).

75. *Inspection Report: Internal Controls Over Sensitive Compartmented Information Access for Selected Field Intelligence Elements.*

76. U.S. Department of Energy, Office of Inspector General, *Inspection Report: Follow-On Review of the Status of the U.S. Department of Energy's Counterintelligence Implementation Plan* (Washington, D.C.: U.S. Department of Energy, 2000).

77. *Audit Report: Review of the Status of the U.S. Department of Defense's Counterintelligence Implementation Plan, U.S. Department of Energy.*

78. Ibid.

79. *Inspection Report: Follow-On Review of the Status of the U.S. Department of Energy's Counterintelligence Implementation Plan.*

80. Ibid.

81. U.S. Department of Energy, Office of Inspector General, Office of Inspections and Special Inquiries, *Inspection Report: The Consolidated Terrorism Watchlist Nomination Process at the Department of Energy* (Washington, D.C.: U.S. Department of Energy, 2007).

82. Keith Schneider, "U.S. Confiscating A-Plant Wiretaps," *New York Times*, August 2, 1991.

83. *Audit Report: Review of the Status of the U.S. Department of Defense's Counterintelligence Implementation Plan.*

84. U.S. Department of Energy, *Letter Report on Selected Aspects of the Department of Energy's Activities Involving the Foreign Intelligence Surveillance Act* (Washington, D.C.: U.S. Department of Energy, 2009).

85. *Audit Report: Review of the Status of the U.S. Department of Defense's Counterintelligence Implementation Plan.*

86. "Ten Years After: The FBI Since 9/11: Counterintelligence," www.fbi.gov (accessed August 19, 2015).

87. *Inspection Report: Internal Controls Over Sensitive Compartmented Information Access for Selected Field Intelligence Elements.*

88. *Inspection Report: The Consolidated Terrorism Watchlist Nomination Process at the Department of Energy.*

89. *Audit Report: Review of the Status of the U.S. Department of Defense's Counterintelligence Implementation Plan.*

90. *Inspection Report: Follow-On Review of the Status of the U.S. Department of Energy's Counterintelligence Implementation Plan.*

91. U.S. Department of Energy, Office of Inspector General, Office of Audits and Inspections, *Inspection Report: Continuity of Operations Planning and Intelligence Readiness* (Washington, D.C.: U.S. Department of Energy, 2012).

92. *Inspection Report: Follow-On Review of the Status of the U.S. Department of Energy's Counterintelligence Implementation Plan.*

93. Ibid.

94. *Letter Report on Selected Aspects of the Department of Energy's Activities Involving the Foreign Intelligence Surveillance Act.*

95. U.S. Department of Commerce, Bureau of Industry and Security, *Annual Report to the Congress for Fiscal Year 2014* (Washington, D.C.: U.S. Department of Commerce, 2015), 3, 5.

96. U.S. Government Accountability Office, *Export Controls: Improvements to Commerce's Dual Use System Needed to Ensure Protection of U.S. Interest in the Post-9/11 Environment* (Washington, D.C.: Government Accountability Office, 2006).

97. Ibid.

98. U.S. Department of Commerce, *Annual Report to the Congress for Fiscal Year 2014*, 18–19.

99. Ibid., 6; U.S. Department of Commerce, Bureau of Industry and Security, *Annual Report to the Congress for Fiscal Year 2011* (Washington, D.C.: U.S. Department of Commerce, 2012), 18.

100. *Export Controls: Improvements to Commerce's Dual Use System Needed to Ensure Protection of U.S. Interest in the Post-9/11 Environment.*

101. Ibid.

102. Ibid.

103. U.S. Department of Commerce, Bureau of Industry and Security, *Annual Report to the Congress for Fiscal Year 2009*, 28.

104. *Export Controls: Improvements to Commerce's Dual Use System Needed to Ensure Protection of U.S. Interest in the Post-9/11 Environment* (Government Accountability Office, 2006).

105. U.S. Department of Commerce, *Annual Report to the Congress for Fiscal Year 2011.*

106. U.S. Department of Commerce, *Annual Report to the Congress for Fiscal Year 2014*, 11.

107. U.S. Department of Commerce, *Annual Report to the Congress for Fiscal Year 2011*, 10.

108. U.S. Department of Commerce, *Annual Report to the Congress for Fiscal Year 2014*, 11.

109. Ibid.

110. U.S. Department of Commerce, *Annual Report to the Congress for Fiscal Year 2011.*

111. Ibid., 19; U.S. Department of Commerce, *Annual Report to the Congress for Fiscal Year 2014*, 66.

112. U.S. Department of Commerce, *Annual Report to the Congress for Fiscal Year 2011*, 19; U.S. Department of Commerce, *Annual Report to the Congress for Fiscal Year 2009*, 16.

113. Alan Sipress, "Computer System Under Attack: Commerce Department Targeted; Hackers Traced to China," *Washington Post*, October 6, 2006.

114. Ibid.

115. Ellen Nakashima and Brian Krebs, "As Cyberattacks Increase, U.S. Faces Shortage of Security Talent," *Washington Post*, December 23, 2009.

116. www.treasury.gov.

117. James K. Jackson, *The Committee on Foreign Investment in the United States* (Washington, D.C.: Congressional Research Service, 2014).

118. Ibid.

119. James K. Jackson, *The Exon-Florio National Security Test for Foreign Investment* (Washington, D.C.: Congressional Research Service, 2013), 3.

120. Jackson, *The Committee on Foreign Investment in the United States.*

121. Jackson, *The Exon-Florio National Security Test for Foreign Investment*, 4.

122. Jackson, *The Committee on Foreign Investment in the United States*, 18.

123. Ibid., 6.

124. Ibid., 13.

125. Jackson, *The Exon-Florio National Security Test for Foreign Investment*, 3.

126. "CFIUS Reform: The Foreign Investment and National Security Act of 2007," www.treasury.gov.

127. Jackson, *The Committee on Foreign Investment in the United States*, 8.

128. Ibid., 13.

129. Spencer Ante and William Mauldin, "IBM, Lenovo Deal Likely to Spark Security Review," *Wall Street Journal*, January 24, 2014.

130. Jackson, *The Committee on Foreign Investment in the United States*, 16.

131. www.treasury.gov.

132. Ibid.

133. Jackson, *The Exon-Florio National Security Test for Foreign Investment*, 8.

134. William Mauldin and Brent Kendall, "Court Backs Chinese Firm over White House—Ruling Says Company's Rights Were Violated in National Security Review of Purchase of Wind Projects Near Naval Facility," *Wall Street Journal*, July 16, 2014.

135. www.treasury.gov.

136. "CFIUS Reform: The Foreign Investment and National Security Act of 2007," www.treasury.gov.

137. "Keep Your T-Bonds, We'll Take the Bank, Sovereign Wealth Funds," *Economist*, July 28, 2007.

138. Jackson, *The Exon-Florio National Security Test for Foreign Investment*, 7.

139. Jackson, *The Committee on Foreign Investment in the United States*, 13.

140. Shayndi Raice, "China's Huawei Draws Scrutiny for Deal to Buy Small U.S. Tech Firm," *Wall Street Journal*, November 19, 2010.

141. Richard Gid Powers, *Broken: The Troubled Past and Uncertain Future of the FBI* (New York: Free Press, 2004), 389.

142. Counterintelligence and Security Enhancement Act of 1994.

143. Mark Riebling, *Wedge: The Secret War between the FBI and the CIA* (New York: Knopf, 1994), 393.

144. Powers, *Broken*, 389.

Chapter Three

Institutions of Innovation Intelligence Collection

From Strategic Intention to Tactical Implementation

The fluid movement of knowledge has been and will likely continue to be exploited by threat actors seeking to develop an even greater informational advantage than what they can achieve through licit measures. Two factors indicate that this targeting will continue to be an ongoing and potentially increasing challenge to the integrity of U.S. innovation. The first of these considerations is the growing number of states that in the decades following the end of the Cold War have targeted the United States. In the early 1990s, Robert Gates, who was the nominee for the position of the director of Central Intelligence, claimed that nearly twenty governments were engaged in economic intelligence collection against the United States.[1] As of the late 1990s, at least twenty-three countries were targeting U.S. private industry.[2] These accumulating actors included "some U.S. allies and partners" who "use their broad access to U.S. institutions to acquire sensitive U.S. economic and technology information" according to the National Counterintelligence Executive (NCIX). This is not surprising, as global dynamics shifted from a unified Western bloc focused on the shared objective of countering the Soviet Union to competing economic interests. Second, established adversaries of the Cold War have not disappeared and their expertise in targeting U.S. information has gained momentum over the decades.

Multiple foreign governments have developed systems to facilitate the coordinated overt and covert collection of information that contributes to innovation by their state and private sector entities. Implementation of collection requires operational awareness—the identification of the environments where information can be targeted—and tactical-level tradecraft by which specific individuals with access to proprietary information can be exploited by foreign operatives either in person or virtually and whether wittingly or unwittingly.

CHINA

According to the NCIX's 2011 report to Congress (the most recent of these reports publicly available), regarding foreign economic collection and industrial espionage between 2009 and 2011, "Chinese actors are the world's most active and persistent perpetrators of economic espionage." China's institutionalized entrenched targeting of foreign knowledge dates to at least 1986 when Deng Xiaoping created the 863 Program, which was directed at narrowing the gap in astronautics, information technology, laser technology, automation technology, energy technology, and materials between China and the West by 2000.[3] The 863 Program was succeeded by the Super 863 Program in 1996, which extended the acquisitions horizon to 2010.[4] Consistent with China's focus on applied research (which can be viewed as a reliance on innovation co-opted from foreign entities), the 863 Program has increasingly directed funding toward Chinese enterprises rather than research institutes.[5]

China's State Commission of Science, Technology, and Industry for National Defense (COSTIND), created in 1982, managed the 863 Program. COSTIND had oversight responsibilities for a network of institutions—including the Chinese Aerospace Corporation, the China National Nuclear Corporation, China Northwest Industries Group, Aviation Industries Corporation of China, and the Cha State Shipbuilding Corporation—which is dedicated to the specification, appraisal, and application of advanced technologies to the PRC's military.[6] Super 863 was managed jointly by COSTIND and the Chinese Ministry of Science and Technology (MOST) and focused on biotechnology, information technology, automation, nuclear research, and exotic materials. Under this initiative, COSTIND was specifically responsible for the fields of laser and space technology.[7]

China's National Key Basic Research Program, also known as the 973 Program, was established to develop a body of scientific knowledge that could provide a foundation for innovation. It funded small and medium Chinese enterprises in furtherance of establishing a technologically advanced indigenous scientific and manufacturing base.[8] However, as of 2012, portions of the 973 Program had evolved to focus on applied research.[9] The U.S.–China Economic and Security Review Commission assessed that this shift demonstrated that basic science remained secondary to applied research.[10] Furthermore, the 973 Program, like the 863 Program, drew on international outreach to develop expertise.[11] The focus on specific technology coupled with pursuit of external knowledge is consistent with the longstanding reality that Chinese innovation is reliant on foreign knowledge and—with the relegation of a scientific foundation to a secondary status—will likely remain so.

Without an indigenous engine for innovation, China will likely continue to exploit licit and illicit access to foreign government and company resources to fill its gaps.

Emphasis on practical applications, rather than the development of a foundation of scientific knowledge, was further codified in the National Medium-to Long-Term Plan for Science and Technology Development (2006–2020). This plan emphasizes the enterprise sector as the core of China's innovation system.[12] It also set the aggressive goal of making China a global leader in science and technology by 2050. The plan set the tone for China's interaction with foreign entities by introducing the concept of "indigenous innovation," the impetus for China's subsequent efforts to effect the transfer of foreign technologies and intellectual property.

This process of acquiring and assimilating knowledge and resultant technology through initiatives such as the 863 and 973 Programs is a de facto intelligence-gathering enterprise directed at a strategic level and leveraging multiple entities for collection. COSTIND has attempted to monitor all U.S. and foreign technologies brought into China through joint ventures.[13] The Peoples' Liberation Army (PLA), under the leadership of the Chinese Communist Party's eight-member Central Military Commission, which is a beneficiary of the COSTIND-driven collection, has its own intelligence component that has engaged in clandestine collection activities against U.S. targets. This entity is known as the Second Department of the PLA.[14] Facilitation of this collection can occur on U.S. soil. Science and technology representatives in PRC embassies are used to assist in the targeting of technology and to encourage collaboration between Chinese entities and U.S. firms.[15] Although certain Chinese practices have been subject to WTO scrutiny, Beijing has continued to coerce foreign companies into transferring knowledge. According to the U.S. Trade Representative, in 2015 standards for development bodies in China often deny membership or participation rights to foreign entities.[16] This makes it more difficult for foreign companies to develop products consistent with the Chinese government's requirements upon which purchase is contingent.

Collection in the context of foreign innovation is a precursor to exploitation of information. China has enshrined acquisition (that is, collection) in its strategic policy. In late 2009, three Chinese agencies—the Ministry of Science and Technology, the Ministry of Finance, and the National Development and Reform Commission (NDRC)—announced a National Indigenous Innovation Product Accreditation System.[17] Under this system, the Chinese government based its procurement on multiple factors that included that the product must have originally been trademarked in China and independent of overseas brands.[18] The objective of these requirements was to force companies doing business with the Chinese government to transfer R&D activities to China, where they could be observed and absorbed. China has also exploited the setting of standards by demanding that, in exchange for participation in the process, a firm enter into a joint venture with a Chinese company and maintain only a minority ownership stake, license intellectual property at terms favorable to China, or transfer technology.[19] Such absorption, of course, could take place not only via legitimate (if ill-considered) transfer of knowledge, but also via surreptitious acquisition through intelligence activities. According to the Office of the U.S. Trade Representative, in 2014 theft of trade secrets to benefit Chinese companies has occurred in China.[20] Additionally, the requirement that intellectual property be trademarked in China has made it susceptible to misappropriation once it has been submitted to the government for approval.[21] Chinese provincial- and local-level government bodies have also pressured foreign firms to transfer intellectual property rights.[22]

China, in addition to collecting specific knowledge externally, also engages in acquisition of companies, informed by Beijing's interests. The NDRC and China's Export-Import Bank issued a guidance in 2004 that encouraged investment abroad in specific areas including research and development centers to utilize international advanced technologies, managerial skills, and professions.[23] This represented the implementation of Jiang Zemin's "going out" policy, which encouraged investment abroad that was first articulated in the early 2000s. The concept is codified in the Overseas Investment Industrial Guidance Policy, which periodically establishes the parameters for the Overseas Investment Industrial Guidance Catalogue, which provides details about the sectors in which investment is encouraged.[24]

Once China has acquired information, it is blatantly employed to enhance the country's elements of national power, particularly the military element. Since at least the 1990s, China has emphasized civil-military integration to facilitate the military use of civilian technologies.[25] Civilian enterprises have been encouraged to participate in military research and development and participate in the formal Central Special Committee, which coordinates R&D projects for military modernization.[26] This has significant implications for any foreign entity doing business or conducting research in conjunction with China, as China's engagement of external industry or academia is likely to be driven by this dual-use calculation. As Kathleen Walsh, an associate professor at the Naval War College, has theorized, China's defense innovation ecosystem is layered on top of the country's existing measures to spur innovation.[27] This suggests that there is not an effective way to control the use of knowledge or technology once it reaches China.

RUSSIAN FEDERATION (THAT IS, RUSSIA)

Like China, Russia's collection activities against U.S. innovation build on long-established institutions' deeply entrenched practices. A 2011 NCIX report states that "Russia's intelligence services are conducting a range of activities to collect economic information and technology from US targets." Under the Soviet Union, these activities were conducted in a strategically coordinated fashion. The Military Industrial Commission (VPK), under the Presidium of the Council of Ministers, was a body meant to help the Soviet Union improve the technological sophistication of its weapons and military systems, as well as to advance the technology of the manufacturing process.[28] VPK membership included the heads of key Soviet defense manufacturing ministries. Full VPK membership was given to the Ministers of Aviation, Machine Building (projectiles and explosives), Defense Industry (armor and electro-optics), General Machine Building (strategic missiles and space), Communications Equipment, Radio (radars and large-scale computers), Medium Machine Building (nuclear weapons and high-energy lasers), Shipbuilding, and Electronics.[29]

The VPK integrated the capabilities of state-controlled intelligence and nonintelligence entities to effect a coordinated collection of information. Based on the requirements for Western technologies that it developed based on inputs from its government clients, the VPK tasked five agencies: Soviet military intelligence (GRU); the KGB's First Chief Directorate, Directorate T (represented by Line X officers in diplomatic establishments); the State Committee for Science and Technology (GKNT); a secret unit in the Academy of Sciences; and the State Committee for External Economic Relations.[30] Additionally, the VPK used intelligence agencies of Soviet satellite states including Bulgaria, Romania, Czechoslovakia, and East Germany.[31] The extent of VPK-driven collection is indicated by its provision of instructions for 3,617 S&T acquisition tasks in 1980.[32]

Simple acquisition was not the end goal. Rather, as with most collection against innovation, the objective was to integrate the acquired knowledge into the state's capabilities. This was done largely by exploiting the concepts identified in both equipment and documents.[33] As a U.S. government description of the program stated, copying and reverse engineering were major characteristics of the VPK program.[34]

The Soviet intelligence services (GRU and KGB) were significant participants in the VPK-orchestrated collection campaign. KGB Line X officers were usually assigned under diplomatic cover positions as science attachés or equivalent positions in the commercial or economic sections of Soviet missions or at international organizations. Most of these intelligence officers were scientific specialists by both academic and professional training. This undoubtedly made them more effective at targeting information of interest. Unlike the KGB, the GRU did not have a separate cadre of career scientific specialists in the field; its officers tended to have technical and military specializations. The GRU deployment broadened the Soviet footprint and its opportunities for collection, as GRU officers, in addition to assignments at diplomatic establishments (where all military attaches were GRU officers), held positions within Aeroflot and Morflot (the Soviet merchant marine).[35]

Other nondiplomatic or military institutions also provided cover for intelligence activities. The Soviet Ministry of Foreign Trade, with its global presence, provided a platform for Soviet targeting of technology. At one level, the Ministry pursued its VPK requirements overtly. Additionally, the Soviet Ministry of Trade, like the Soviet diplomatic establishments, provided a cover for GRU and KGB officers who could take advantage of the Ministry's overt missions related to technology acquisition. Soviet trade activity had long served as a platform for intelligence officers, as demonstrated by reporting about the use of Amtorg, the Soviet state-run trading company, as a cover. Soviet intelligence also used scientific and academic exchanges and positions as "acceptance engineers" at companies with Soviet contracts as positions for its officers.[36]

The outcome of this vast intelligence enterprise was apparent in Soviet technological advances. Gains included a clone of the U.S. airborne radar system, AWACS; the Russian Blackjack bomber, which was copied from the American B1-B; the RYAD series of computers, which were plagiarized from their IBM originals; and integrated circuits purloined from Texas Instruments.[37] Additionally, the Russian space shuttle was created from documents stolen from NASA.[38] (In this context, the United States' recent partnership with Russia for launches is appalling.) In at least one instance, theft led to the Soviets fielding an American-designed weapon, the Kirov class destroyer, even before the United States had introduced it.[39] Furthermore, in some areas, such as cold-rolled steel armor for ships, the Soviets did not even bother to conduct research because they had the U.S. formulas.[40] The extent of success was indicated by the claim by Leonid Sergeyevich Zaitsev, head of Directorate T, that the S&T acquisitions covered the entire KGB's operating costs.[41]

It is unlikely that the Russian Federation has deviated from its established practices. The KGB never truly disappeared—its foreign collection arm became the SVR—and the GRU continued to operate uninterrupted. The institutionalized nature of Russian intelligence activities in the United States was indicated by the fact that there continued to be Russian embassy and United Nations slots that were traditionally held by intelligence personnel.[42] The GRU that, as indicated by its role in the VPK, was already focused on innovation continued to pursue economic espionage, particularly against civilian research and development activities.[43] Beyond bureaucratic momentum, Russian leadership consistently demonstrated a blatant willingness to improve the country's position through theft. Then Russian intelligence chief Yevgeny Primakov suggested in 1991 that Russian intelligence would shift to the commercial sphere.[44] Putin's willingness to appropriate property with impunity is no different in motivation. Such a climate hardly bodes well for Western participants in projects such as Skolkovo. His pressure on Russia's "near abroad" makes it plausible that in the future Moscow may be able to coerce assistance with collection activities from those countries.

Finally, the VPK program provides a widely applicable lesson about the nature of ostensibly open-source information in advancing a hostile state's capabilities. During the 1980s, when the program was operational, the U.S. government estimated that 90 percent of the approximately 100,000 documents that the Soviets obtained worldwide each year were unclassified.[45] Collection of unclassified documents included exploitation of commercial and government databases where abstracts were unclassified but that, if analyzed, in aggregate could reveal sensitive information concerning U.S. strategic capabilities and vulnerabilities.[46]

ALLIES(?)

However, it is not only the United States' clear adversaries that have consistently attempted to exploit U.S. efforts at innovation for their own gain. France tasked the SDECE chief of station in Washington, D.C., to begin spying on U.S. scientific research in 1962.[47] Subsequently, the French intelligence services (SDECE and DGSE) established an economic information section with an emphasis on industrial technology and developed its collection requirements based on meetings with French companies to develop a sense of the foreign technology that was needed.[48] This is consistent with the claim by Pierre Marion, former head of French intelligence, who described creating a unit to gather information about secret technology and marketing plans of private companies globally.[49] Then, in the early 1990s, the Central Intelligence Agency authenticated, allegedly formulated by French intelligence, a list containing forty-nine companies (including at least twenty U.S. firms), twenty-four financial institutions, and six USG agencies that the French planned to target.[50] In 1995, the United States expelled two French diplomats after they attempted to develop information about Osprey aircraft technology.[51] The DGSE reportedly subsidized its operations by selling what it had collected to French companies.[52]

Israel, supposedly a close ally of the United States, has been alarmingly duplicitous by running a persistent campaign of espionage against U.S. innovation. In 1996, Israel was one of approximately half a dozen countries (including France) that the Central Intelligence Agency identified as engaged in economic espionage, and was identified again in 2011 as a perpetrator of these activities.[53] As early as the late 1960s, following the 1967 Six Day War, U.S. industry executives began reporting approaches by Israeli Mossad agents who were affiliated with the Mossad's Science Liaison Bureau.[54] More recently, a large U.S. Department of Defense contractor who had hosted an Israeli delegation discovered that equipment had disappeared during field testing related to the manufacture of a radar system.[55] The contractor learned the destination of the stolen property when, two years later, it received a request from Israel to repair a piece of the missing equipment.[56] Israel has mitigated the consequences of such behavior through several measures. The first was a very aggressive, long-running public relations campaign that dates back to the formation of Israel and that led to the formation of the American Israeli Political Affairs Committee (AIPAC). Additionally, historical reporting indicates that it has been effective at playing U.S. government entities against each other. After the FBI discovered an Israeli who appeared to be working on behalf of Mossad to conduct science and technology collection, Israel complained through its liaison at the CIA.[57]

METHODOLOGIES OF THEFT AND INNOVATION

The loss of innovation by U.S. organizations, business and academic alike, is enormous. It terms of monetary damage, it is difficult to ascribe an accurate figure. A 2013 report by the Blair-Huntsman IP commission examining the theft of U.S. intellectual property estimated the loss to be in the hundreds of billions of dollars.[58] According to National Security Director General Keith Alexander (who was double-hatted as the head of Cyber Command), economic espionage now represents the greatest transfer of wealth in human history.[59] So just how are foreign adversaries, be it foreign governments or foreign companies, stealing so much U.S. intellectual property? Although cyber intrusions are an all too common method for a threat actor to pilfer large amounts of data, many less sophisticated and pedestrian methods are also routinely utilized, often in combination. Many of these methods pose threats that are underappreciated by U.S businesses and academic institutions.

Foreign government apparatuses for identifying, collecting, and exploiting information in furtherance of innovation succeed or fail based on implementation at the human level. The previously discussed programs represent the strategic aspect of innovation via collection. They formulate the requirements for acquisition based on the states' needs and marshal the gamut of resources that will engage in collection. The operational level is a step down from the strategic perspective and is closely associated with methodology—the determination of environments and patterns of activity that will likely yield targets vulnerable to foreign intelligence collection activity. It is analogous to a specific military theater. Finally, the tactical level of intelligence is concerned with the interactions between a foreign operative, whether physically or remotely, with his or her target of information, regardless of whether the target is witting or unwitting.

Insider Threat

The biggest threat to an organization's intellectual property is from a trusted insider who may be witting or unwitting (such as in the case of an employee who opens a spear-phishing email that compromises information on a company's or government agency's system). The employee on the inside of an organization that has legitimate access to the proverbial crown jewels is in the best position to recognize and access the most valuable information with the organization and also best avoid detection. Indeed, law enforcement agencies like the FBI are most concerned about the insider threat. Often the insider can operate for long periods of time, even decades, without being identified, a reality highlighted by the Chi Mak case. The insider's activities severely damage national security as well as destroy an organization's competiveness. The problem has become so severe that in 2011 President Barack Obama issued Executive Order 13587 establishing a national insider threat taskforce and required all federal agencies handling classified information to develop an insider threat program. These programs teach employees to look for odd behavior or "indicators." Technology has been employed to scan internal email communication and track employee computer key strokes. The difficulty of detecting an insider, amassing direct evidence, mounting an investigation, and finally prosecuting an insider is so daunting that law enforcement agencies focus on prevention.

A foreign government or business wishing to illegally acquire proprietary information and trade secrets can benefit greatly from placing or obtaining a spy on the inside of the target. Such an insider affords the best opportunity for the threat actor to obtain the desired information. Even when other methodologies are used, such as cyber network intrusions, the trusted insider can be of tremendous value in implementing the technical attack. A cyber attack like the one that occurred in November 2014 is thought to be the responsibility of the North Korean government, yet many suggest an insider in the company would have been necessary to implement the attack. Such an insider could have provided a nation-state like North Korea valuable information regarding passwords, network architecture, and personal details of executives (useful for crafting spear-phishing attacks).

The insider threat comes about through three broad mechanisms: recruitment of existing employees, infiltration or placement of a witting insider (that is, a mole) in the target, and capitalizing on volunteers already within the target organization.

Variation 1 of the Insider Threat: Recruitment

Recruitment refers to the often gradual process intelligence services and other threat actors use to acquire the services of an insider who is in a position to supply, wittingly or unwittingly, the desired sensitive information. Recruitment involves identifying vulnerabilities of the intended target and utilizing those to manipulate attitude and behavior. The recruiter is then able to step in and address the vulnerability, usually in exchange for the recruit's services.

Foreign entities can most effectively exploit divided loyalties in areas of culture or ideology to create commonalities with and ultimately recruit individuals who have access to proprietary information of value. The National Counterintelligence Center advised Congress that foreign collectors specifically target foreign employees working for U.S. companies.[60] Several countries have demonstrated a willingness to exploit the ties of émigrés and foreign ethnic scientists to facilitate technology transfer.[61] According to the Department of Defense's Personnel Security Research Center, spying prompted by divided loyalties has become the most common motive for espionage by U.S. persons.[62]

China is particularly notorious for its exploitation of cultural ties. It does not recognize the concept of Chinese Americans and instead views all individuals of Chinese descent, regardless of location, as "overseas Chinese."[63] Such targeting is made easier by groups such as the Silicon Valley Chinese Overseas Business Association, which includes individuals who hold positions as advisors to Chinese industries and universities.[64] Israel holds a similar view of the international Jewish community. This is apparent in the Israeli government–sponsored "Taglit-Birthright Israel" program, which provides Jews under twenty-six years of age with a free ten-day trip to Israel.[65] The stated purpose of these trips is to encourage an interest in Judaism. However, by tying this increased interest to a nation-state, the trips may also inculcate a divided loyalty problem similar to that which China actively encourages. This is problematic, given that Israeli companies have aggressively attempted to engage in technology transfer, and according to Oliver "Buck" Revell, the FBI has had a number of economic espionage cases that involved Israeli companies.[66] According to the National Counterintelligence Executive, the Russian intelligence services may increasingly target the many Russian immigrants with advanced technical skills who work for prominent U.S. companies.[67]

According to what is now the National Counterintelligence and Security Center, foreign governments may create entities such as friendship societies and international exchange organizations to collect intelligence and provide cover for personnel engaged in collection.[68] The U.S. National Counterintelligence Executive assessed that foreign governments can establish and exploit such quasi-official organizations to identify the accesses that their nationals have to sensitive information. These nationals can be debriefed upon returning home.[69] This circumvents the need for clandestine tradecraft within the United States, making it more difficult for the intelligence community to identify activities that facilitate the transfer of innovation. China brazenly connects the concepts of cultural exchange and collection. The China Association for International Exchange of Personnel established "liaison organization" offices in the United States and is a conduit through which Beijing has attempted to illegally acquire technology from Western scientists and engineers.[70]

Related to the vulnerability inherent in shared culture is the vulnerability of shared ideology. If Russia is using culture as a way to reach well-connected members of its diaspora, it is following in the footsteps of its Soviet predecessor's exploitation of the shared ideology of communism. The Soviet Union exploited a shared ideology with greatest effectiveness in the United States during the 1930s and 1940s to facilitate the transfer of sensitive information, with the most infamous example being research on the atomic bomb. (The Soviet Union continued to supply the Communist Party of the United States of America—CPUSA—with funding until at least 1980.[71] Its contribution that year was USD $2,775,000.) More recently, Cuba recruited multiple spies in the State Department and in the Defense Intelligence Agency based on ideological affinity.

Foreign governments have also exploited non-country-specific ideologies. For instance, during the Cold War, the Soviet bloc used the "peace" and anti-nuclear movements to counter U.S. objectives. Altruism and idealism are similarly susceptible to manipulation by foreign governments, which may play on an individual's belief that they are doing the "right" thing. In the late 1980s, a group called "Corporate Professionals for Social Responsibility" attempted to raise USD $35,000 to equip a Moscow-based group with computers.[72] While there is no indication that this was nefarious, it demonstrates how a hostile foreign country may benefit from well-intentioned individuals.

Foreign governments, as discussed previously, aggressively and brazenly exploit shared cultural heritages as a means to tap into the expertise of globally distributed diaspora populations. Unfortunately, possibly due to political correctness, naiveté, or perhaps simply an overabundance of optimism, this dark side of globalization is often overlooked. For instance, the Center for Strategic and International Studies (CSIS), a prominent Washington think tank, opined that "America's immigrant communities provide a rich source of international understanding within our borders. Many Americans have a connection to other parts of the world, are fluent in their ancestral language, and could serve as citizen diplomats abroad. Too few of these people take part in exchange programs or are accepted into civilian service within the U.S. government."[73] While these thoughts are doubtlessly well intended, foreign governments and nonstate actors will certainly exploit individuals who are encouraged to maintain deep roots in globally distributed culturally connected populations and who also attain positions of access to information that those state and nonstate actors have an interest in acquiring.

While foreign entities can take steps to create sympathetic responses that might, in turn, lead arrogant individuals who believe they can take foreign policy into their own hands by passing information, there are other motivations that a foreign entity can exploit. A foreign entity can provide an opportunity for an employee with access to sensitive information to seek revenge by damaging an employer's interests through compromise of information. Related to revenge-seeking behavior is the vulnerability of ego and self-image, which may lead an individual to become involved with and seek approval from an individual who, in turn, may be working for a foreign government and make requests for information accordingly. Similarly, greed or a need for money due to financial problems has been a motivating factor in some of the most notorious espionage cases of the past half century, with Aldrich Ames at the CIA and Robert Hanssen at the FBI both selling U.S. secrets to the Russians. Finally, the trauma of personal crises may skew an individual's thinking and create a sense of loss that a foreign entity may seek to exploit (for example, an individual who has gone through an ugly divorce may be targeted by an all-too-perfect companion who, in actuality, is controlled by a foreign entity).

Several of these conditions are uniquely applicable when assessing the threat to innovation. Divided loyalty is ripe for manipulation in an environment that encourages transnational collaboration and multinational presences of corporations. In this fluid setting, an individual is arguably more susceptible to the emotional tug of culture and affinity than one whose bottom line is anchored in and reliant upon the United States. This amorphous environment is also a breeding ground for individuals dominated by ego, as they seek ways to distinguish themselves and bolster their identity. The transactional nature of international commerce is, of course, an invitation for foreign entities to play upon greed, especially when the information they want is subject to export restrictions.

Organizational deficiencies can make it easier for a recruited agent to misappropriate valuable information. Factors include the availability and ease of acquiring proprietary information, poor education among employees about the sensitivity of information, the ease with which an employee may exit the facility or network system with proprietary information (that is, a lack of appropriate monitoring at physical and virtual chokepoints), and an insufficient emphasis on security that results in other demands to take precedence over it. Finally, access is often as important as expertise. Support and administrative employees can be useful recruitments for several reasons. First, secretaries, computer operators, technicians, maintenance personnel, and other support employees all often have access to sensitive information.[74] Their lower pay may give those employees predisposed to unscrupulousness a motivation to provide information to a competitor, including a foreign government and its intelligence service. Beyond these factors, the administrative and support staffs are the human equivalent of wallpaper—arguably giving them greater opportunity to gather proprietary information unnoticed.

TEXTBOX 3.1. THE STEPS OF RECRUITMENT

An insider is an individual with legitimate access to information that wittingly or unwittingly provides that information to a foreign intelligence service. The insider threat is one of the most damaging types of threats to the United States and its institutions. A foreign actor's recruitment of an insider is often a gradual process that can take place over an extended period of time. The recruitment process typically consists of the following six steps:

Spotting

The intelligence operative is continually looking for people that may have influence or access to desired information. Spotting may occur in any number of settings, ranging from official business to social functions. According to the Senate Select Committee on Intelligence, "social occasions and situations [were] a favorite hunting ground for Soviet bloc intelligence officers" as were restaurants, bars, and clubs in the vicinity of defense contractors.[1]

(continued)

Assessing

Once a potential recruit is identified, the intelligence officer assesses that person for "vulnerabilities" that can be used to manipulate the person. Such vulnerabilities include greed, financial difficulties, sex, ideology, revenge, ego, and others. Intelligence services understand the concepts of Maslow's hierarchy of needs and they use it to their advantage.

Developing

The intelligence officer gradually develops rapport with the potential recruit. Often trivial favors are exchanged for one another. There is often a change in the nature of the relationship—that is, a professional relation becomes personal. The foreign intelligence operative may begin requesting that a contact provide assistance with seemingly innocuous information in a clandestine manner. This is a means of a) identifying whether the individual is willing to take tasking and b) conditioning the individual to intelligence tradecraft.

Recruiting

At the recruitment phase, some threshold with legal or ethical consequences is crossed. The intelligence officer may attempt to initiate a pattern of paying the potential recruitment for seemingly benign tasks. The purpose is to avoid scaring off the potential recruit with an immediate request for proprietary information.[2] Information that should not be shared is passed on. The recruited individual is now under the control, wittingly or unwittingly, of the intelligence service.

Handling

Handling refers to the day-to-day operation of the source by the intelligence officer. Frequently, secretive methods of communication and other tradecraft are used. The recruit and the handler often cease to meet in person, with information being passed via means such as "dead-drops." The recruit is typically asked not to acknowledge or tell others about the relationship.

Termination

At termination, the relationship between the intelligence officer and the recruit ends or goes dormant. Termination can occur when the recruit loses access to the information or when there is a compromise of security. The relationship can go dormant for long periods of time before being rekindled, sometimes by a new handler.

NOTES

1. *Meeting the Espionage Challenge: A Review of United States Counterintelligence and Security Programs. Report of the Select Committee on Intelligence. United States Senate*. Report No. 99-522, at 26 (1986).
2. Ibid.

Variation 2 of the Insider Threat: Volunteer

Many individuals that commit economic espionage by acquiring trade secrets and transferring them illicitly to a competitor or foreign government do so under their own accord. Employees that recognize the value of the information they have access to look for ways to benefit personally, satisfying the desire that foreign actors exploit for recruitment from that information. This is a particular problem with employees leaving an organization. For instance, the head of the Cleveland Clinic's Alzheimer's laboratory left the United States with stolen biological material after the Japanese Institute of Physical and Chemical Research offered to relocate his research program.[75] Exiting employees often take valuable information with them when they leave. This information can be valuable to competitors that may have wooed the employee with a job offer. Nondisclosure agreements can be helpful in delineating the information that can be legally disclosed upon departure for an employee, but it is not a perfect solution. Disgruntled employees are of particular concern because they have the added motivation of revenge to motivate the illicit transfer of information.

Variation 3 of the Insider Threat: Infiltration (that is, a Mole)

Infiltration of a witting participant is another mechanism that may produce an insider threat. Infiltration attempts to place a person into a position of access or influence rather than manipulate a person already in such a position (recruitment) or capitalize on a volunteer. Infiltration is frequently gradual and subtle, as it can take years for an individual to get the right education and work their way through low-level positions in order to eventually land in the desired sensitive location. The gradual and natural career progression of the individual makes detection of the insider very difficult. Russia, China, and Cuba all have intelligence services that have demonstrated a willingness to wait years, even decades, for a recruit to gain a position of access to sensitive information. Sponsoring intelligence services or other organizations may cultivate large numbers of individuals to infiltrate a given target because the chances of any one obtaining the position with desired access is low. This type of long-term methodical approach to insider threat development is utilized most by intelligence services and governments that can be patient and formulate a long-term strategic plan. This approach may seem hard to comprehend for Western organizations that tend to focus on short-term profits and sales and are often unable to support a strategy in which immediate payoff is not likely.

An example of an infiltration attempt was the Russian spy ring identified in 2010. In December 2010, ten individuals of Russian descent were arrested for acting as agents for Russia's SVR, the foreign intelligence agency. On the surface, these Russian spies seemed to be living ordinary American lives. None of them held clearances or had access to classified national defense information. Many had children and concerned themselves with typical family life. The American public had a hard time understanding the significance of the arrest. These spies were in the process of infiltrating American society. By getting the right jobs and the right education, one or more of them could eventually work themselves into a sensitive position. Indeed, even the spies' children were likely being groomed to enter the spy business.[76] They were deep undercover, sleepers, known in intelligence terms as *illegals*—individuals who had created entirely new lives to effect long-term penetration of a country—who had been dispatched to blend in with U.S. society before engaging in espionage. This approach is not new. The Russian SVR's predecessor, the Soviet KGB, made extensive use of such illegals internationally, including in the United States, as in the case of Rudolf Abel. They aimed to become so Americanized that no one could connect them with the Russian government.[77] Clearly, the Russian government took the long-term approach with this operation. Although there was no immediate payoff in terms of sensitive information, each spy had the potential to infiltrate a sensitive area and do tremendous damage to the U.S. national security and economic interests.

Elicitation

Elicitation is a technique commonly used to gather sensitive information not otherwise available without raising suspicion that particular information is being sought. Elicitation is simply conversation steered toward topics of interest in which the true purpose is obscured. It is nonthreatening, deniable, and easy to disguise. Such conversations can occur in person or via telephone, email, online chat programs—anything that affords a human-to-human give and take. When conducted by a skilled business collector or foreign intelligence collector, sensitive nonpublic proprietary information can easily be gathered. Such collectors may even collect personal information about an individual that can be used for future targeting or recruitment attempts. An elicitor recognizes and manipulates psychological and cultural predispositions and exploits those to gather intelligence.[78] It is critical that employees that interact with competitors and customers understand what is appropriate to discuss and what is not. A skilled elicitor can blur those lines and lead the target into saying too much. This is especially true when the target's guard is down, such as in social situations and when being entertained by foreign hosts.

Academics are particularly susceptible to exploitation via elicitation because of a professional culture that emphasizes openness and collaboration. The compromise of science, due to a lack of security awareness, has been a problem since at least the compromise of the Manhattan Project by a Soviet spy ring. More recently, NASA expressed concern that one of its facilities was "strongly biased toward maintaining an academic reputation, rather than meeting U.S. industry and national needs" in relation to FBI concerns about espionage at the facility.[79] The willingness of U.S. scientists and scholars can be manipulated by foreign entities who, in their approaches, know the right questions to ask.[80] China is notorious for its efforts to elicit information from visiting academics and scientists. It employs a number of techniques against visitors. These include inviting scientists to make a presentation in an academic setting in which audience questions are directed at increasingly sensitive topics and wearing down visitors with grueling itineraries, compounded with copious quantities of alcohol.[81] Furthermore, as scientists get together and exchange ideas about ways to address problems, they may not be aware of elicitation because there is often no exchange of documents that might otherwise serve as a red line of what can be shared.[82]

TEXTBOX 3.2. ELICITATION

Elicitation is the strategic use of conversation to extract information from people without revealing the true purpose of the conversation. Skilled elicitors can extract proprietary information from victims without creating suspicions. Elicitation represents one of the most common ways in which U.S. innovation can be lost to foreign adversaries. Ploys play on some of the same vulnerabilities that foreign intelligence operatives use in recruitment of insiders. Ego may be played on by posturing to demonstrate knowledge, which can lead a target to prove his or her greater knowledge of a topic and, in the process, confirm or divulge additional information. Also appealing to ego is the use of feigned ignorance, providing an invitation to an individual with proprietary knowledge to feel superior by lecturing by an all-too-attentive foreign intelligence operative. Another tack directed at prompting an ego-driven response is the use of a provocative statement, meant to draw a response that confirms or provides additional sensitive information. In the same way that an intelligence service may cater to an individual's self-doubt by providing a "honey trap," elicitation techniques can similarly focus on insecurity. A foreign operative's use of confidential bait—feigning the release of sensitive information to a recipient to establish rapport—is directed at an individual who may be seeking intellectual or other companionship. Similarly, foreign intelligence operatives may prove to be exceptionally good listeners—which not only appeals to insecure individuals but, of course, ensures that foreign governments get a full accounting of the information provided. Finally, several methods of positive feedback may appeal equally to egotistical and insecure individuals. Flattery is the blunt force form of positive feedback, and foreign intelligence operatives will use this. A more complex method is an interview request. Foreign government–run news services function at times as appendages of the country's intelligence apparatus, and an interview may be crafted to raise specific questions about which a government wants information. Another variation of the interview may be job related, such as a call from a foreign intelligence operative posing as a "headhunter" who is interested in specific, recent projects on which a target has worked.

Open-Source Collection

Foreign competitors and adversaries can accumulate a treasure trove of information simply by combing through the information U.S. organizations post to their websites, print in company brochures, or advertise at trade show exhibition tables. In an effort to attract sales and attention, companies may reveal much about their products and corporate strategies. Foreign actors may also attempt to exploit commercial entities in a more targeted manner by making requests for information (RFI) that are directed at filling the actors' understanding of specific technologies. RFIs are especially useful to countries such as China that are trying to catch up with Western innovation and may find information deemed commonplace by U.S. industry to be of significant value. As a congressional report noted, collection of open-source intelligence (OSINT) by China's PLA accelerated the country's military technology development by emulating proven development options.[83] The problem is not a new one. A visiting Soviet scientist once explained to an employee of a U.S. research organization in 1962 that Soviets needed only to come to the United States and buy all of the technical information that they needed.[84] Extensive research may ultimately lead one into a gray area where classified insights become available or where leads to identifying such information can be obtained.[85] All an adversary has to do is a little legwork and a bit of shopping to gain valuable insights.

Aspects of source development have highlighted the importance that foreign governments place on obtaining OSINT. Soviet intelligence, for instance, attempted to spot, assess, and develop selected librarians who would work wittingly or unwittingly to help Moscow meet its intelligence collection requirements.[86] Soviet exchange students participated in this process by identifying scientific-technical libraries and how those libraries functioned.[87] Soviet efforts to establish sources capable of open-source collection are not unique. According to a 2008 DoD report, foreign agents are often recruited and sustained in countries of interest to collect publicly available information.[88]

Collection of open-source information is a way for foreign actors to get closer to their ultimate objective of sensitive information. Gathering OSINT can produce leads that can help a foreign adversary identify entities possessing desired information and to focus its clandestine collection.[89] According to a National Counterintelligence Center report, some traditional intelligence services have resorted to clandestine methods even in gathering OSINT.[90] This suggests that foreign intelligence services perceive OSINT to be of value to U.S. intelligence in identifying a foreign intelligence service's ultimate objectives. Not only can OSINT provide the trail of technical breadcrumbs toward sensitive information, but it can also yield personality profile data, which can be used to target an individual either for recruitment or as an unwitting assistant.[91] For instance, membership lists of international business and technical societies can be used to identify individuals who have access to areas of interest.[92]

Foreign governments have demonstrated a willingness to use open-source collection of seemingly mundane information to assemble a better understanding of the United States. Some governments debrief their citizens after foreign travel and ask for any information acquired abroad.[93] (For the record, the U.S. intelligence community engages in similar activities through the Central Intelligence Agency's National Resources Division, according to its former chief Henry Crumpton.) Such mundane details may not equate to sensitive information but rather may be used to help refine the targeting of such information by providing insights about facilities and individuals who might have access to it. China is notorious for seeking information from the hundreds of thousands of Chinese who visit the United States annually.[94]

An indicator of how OSINT fits into a foreign government's broader collection is indicated by its use of clandestine methods in obtaining information to which it has open access. According to what is now the National Counterintelligence and Security Center, practitioners of economic and industrial espionage may use legal but misleading steps to hide an actor's true interest, affiliation, or location.[95] This is prompted by foreign intelligence services' belief that they are closely monitored by U.S. counterintelligence.[96] Historically, Soviet intelligence recruited sources who could steal microfiches containing specific reports from technical libraries and might request that similar seemingly innocuous relationships be kept confidential.[97] (In some instances, cloak-and-dagger tactics employed in the collection of mundane material may be a way to condition an agent to eventually apply tradecraft to collection of sensitive information.) The use of the Internet has increased foreign intelligence collectors' ability to maintain relative anonymity in their collection of open-source information. As early as the 1980s, the Soviet Union had discovered that electronic databases provided an efficient means to identify and procure unclassified technical information.[98] The ability to operate with a minimum of contact or exposure, even when collecting open-source information, stymies counterintelligence services' ability to identify indicators of foreign governments' collection interests. Not only does this put CI services at a disadvantage when assessing what sectors/entities a foreign intelligence service may attempt to penetrate for proprietary information, but it also deprives the broader intelligence community (and ultimately its policymaking customers) of information that indicates foreign governments' longer-term intentions.

"Dumpster Diving"—Physical Surveillance by Foreign Entities in the United States

Another low-tech approach to gathering sensitive information involves recovering discarded information in refuse. Many discarded documents, personal items, and even prototype products are discarded by the unsuspecting companies only to be recovered by an interested competitor. Much information that may appear innocuous by itself can be quite valuable to an adversary when pieced together with other bits of information. Another overlooked method employed by adversaries is to recover discarded office equipment like copy machines, fax machines, and computers. These items frequently contain hard drives that may contain proprietary business information. Extreme care must be taken to destroy documents and wipe discarded equipment memories.

Surveillance—Physical and Communications—of U.S. Entities Abroad

With the advent of miniaturized electronics, the ease with which a threat actor can deploy audio or video surveillance equipment greatly increases. Multiple countries have recruited hotel personnel to provide intelligence officers with access to visitors' luggage and rooms.[99] Hotel rooms, particularly in foreign hotels, are frequently bugged. The U.S. business traveler can no longer expect privacy while traveling. Cameras and listening devices can be planted in the walls and appliances. Information placed in hotel safes is not secure. U.S. business travelers have reported indicators that their briefcases and laptop computers had been accessed when left unattended in hotel rooms.[100] Even Air France was alleged to have bugged its first-class cabins to collect economic intelligence.[101] (France, not surprisingly, denied the allegation.[102]) Email, Internet traffic, telephone calls, and faxes can also be intercepted, particularly in foreign countries. It is quite easy for an adversary to intercept electronic communication and obtain valuable trade secrets from unsuspecting travelers. There are also indicators that travelers have been photographed, likely to facilitate future targeting, during business meetings abroad.[103]

Exploitation of Site Visits

A common practice in academia and industry is to host foreign visitors who are in the United States for industry site visits, conferences, and trade shows. Frequently, the hosts proudly display their latest and greatest products, prototypes, and facilities—all with the hopes of increasing market share, coaxing foreign graduate students to pay high tuition to attend U.S. universities, and fostering business partnerships with foreign entities. Foreign actors can take advantage of these visits to acquire items of proprietary information. Hosts are frequently unaware of how a competitor can brazenly ignore the security measures put in place by the host. Furthermore, some countries will add intelligence officers to such delegations.[104] Multiple Near East firms allow their government to include intelligence officers within company delegations to cleared facilities; these companies may even receive direction to target specific cleared contractors.[105] Europe and Eurasia region delegations to cleared defense facilities at times included known or suspected intelligence officers who were affiliated with the countries' U.S. embassies.[106] Furthermore, as observed by what is now the U.S. National Counterintelligence and Security Center, foreign visitors to sensitive U.S. facilities tend to be among their nations' leading experts and are far more effective than traditional intelligence officers at recognizing and acquiring esoteric information that fills specific gaps.[107] The following are some common techniques used during onsite visits:

1. Recording devices: With the miniaturization of electronics in recent years, it is becoming increasingly easy for a visitor to conceal an audio or recording device. Cameras can be hidden in sunglasses, pens, cigarette packs, and buttons. Even a cell phone can be used to record pictures while the user appears to innocently be checking a text message. Microelectronics have also made it possible to introduce malware contained on portable storage devices into the host's network. Simply inserting a thumb drive into a USB port of an unattended computer may be sufficient to introduce malware capable of exfiltrating the company's data. Portable memory storage devices are often given away as small gifts by a potential threat actor to unsuspecting hosts.

2. Elicitation: Onsite visits afford the visitors opportunities to interface with the host's employees. Much valuable information can be extracted unwittingly from employees not adequately trained in security procedures. As the Defense Security Service has noted, delegations, even when they do not include intelligence officers, often try to steer discussions beyond the agreed-upon topics.[108] The FBI also determined that the deputy chief of a Soviet high-technology concern who had met with Silicon Valley executives and acquired company information was actually an intelligence officer.[109]

3. Sample collection: Visitors can collect samples and equipment during site visits. One example involved members of a scientific delegation who discreetly dipped their ties into a photo processing solution manufactured by Agfa during a trade show in order to obtain a sample.[110] In another example, a Soviet visitor to a Boeing plant applied an adhesive to his shoes

in order to surreptitiously obtain samples of alloys that Boeing was using to build its 747s, which the Soviets who were visiting ostensibly had an interest in purchasing.[111] Subsequent analysis could determine the metal alloys used in the host's aircraft.

4. Facility information: Observing and photographing a facility and equipment can be advantageous for a threat actor. According to the Defense Security Service, Near East entities have attempted to make unauthorized use of cameras, cell phones, and laptops during visits to cleared defense contractors and conferences.[112] The observation of a factory layout or the model number of equipment in a research lab, for instance, may seem innocuous, but can provide the foreign entity clues about how a product is made or how to set up and run their own competing facility. In additional to the physical makeup of a facility, DSS assessed in its 2014 report that some intelligence officers from services of European and Eurasian governments likely leveraged facility visits to assess employees who might be targeted for future recruitment.[113]

Exploitation of Joint Ventures

Joint ventures represent another method for U.S. organizations to lose innovation and intellectual property to adversaries. Partnering with foreign entities often proves enticing for companies trying to reach foreign markets or cut labor and manufacturing costs of their products. Joining forces with a foreign partner can make good business sense. Even academic institutions pride themselves on their worldliness and readily engage with foreign universities. In the case of academia, the National Counterintelligence Center noted that the assumed credibility of a foreign academic institution adds a measure of legitimacy.[114] This legitimacy can be exploited by foreign intelligence services. For instance, according to a report from the Senate Select Committee on Intelligence, an East German scientist attempted to recruit U.S. counterparts.[115]

However, many of these partnerships come with strings attached. Frequently, the intellectual property must be divulged to the foreign partner as a condition of the deal. Once the proprietary information is provided to the foreign partner, it is no longer under the control of the owner. There is little recourse should the foreign partner decide to absorb the proprietary information and then sever the business arrangement. Many U.S. companies have found themselves in positions in which they have given away their secrets and now have a new competitor with which to contend.

Joint ventures may also provide foreign governments and their intelligence services avenues to establish relationships with U.S. entities that can be leveraged for future collection activities. An employee of a Near East entity who had worked with a cleared contractor on a U.S. Army aviation program began emailing colleagues employed by the contractor with whom he had worked on the project after it concluded. The emails initially contained follow-up questions germane to the project, but subsequent communications segued into probing questions about the contractor's other platforms.[116] This was likely an instance of an attempt to exploit a relationship to obtain access to sensitive information. Additionally, the involvement of foreign employees with intelligence or security ties may help a foreign company target a U.S. partner. For instance, IBM partnered with Beijing Teamsun Technology Co.—the primary point of contact for managing the relationship is a cyber warfare specialist who was formerly employed by the PLA.[117]

Front Companies

Countries engaging in economic espionage frequently establish front companies internationally and in the United States to facilitate their operations. For instance, according to the FBI, as of 2005 there were more than three thousand Chinese front companies in the United States.[118] Front companies appear to function as domestic enterprises without revealing their foreign ties. In the Chinese case, they are even more difficult to identify because Beijing expects them to be self-sustaining.[119] This means they are not merely a front but instead a functioning business that exists to hide illicit activities. Front companies are often used to proliferate restricted technology. Some sensitive dual-use products that have both commercial and military applications are restricted from sale to certain countries or from foreign sales altogether. Front companies can acquire the items domestically and be instrumental in the eventual transfer of the goods to prohibited end users. Sometimes this involves the use of a front company in a third country, where an item can be legitimately shipped as regulated by the Bureau of Industry and Security, prior to being forwarded on to a country that is not permitted to acquire it from the United States. Front companies may, in some instances, form joint ventures with domestic companies that have developed sensitive technology. The foreign joint venture partner may transfer the technology to a third party in violation of the joint venture agreement. Front companies may also be used to facilitate other intelligence activities. Chinese individuals who had stolen technology from U.S. companies Avago and Skyworks established a front company that served as an explanation of where technology that they presented to Tianjin University originated.[120] Finally, front companies can serve as a beachhead for targeting of other U.S. entities. According to a congressional report, PRC front companies may be used to sponsor the visit of delegations, which may include intelligence officers, to the United States.[121]

THE CYBER COROLLARY TO
TRADITIONAL METHODS OF INFILTRATION

It is important to note that while the cyber milieu presents unique challenges, it is simply the newest environment in which foreign actors apply the fundamental methodologies of intelligence and counterintelligence. It provides an opportunity for remote collection of open-source information from the websites of relevant entities (for example, government, defense contractors, academic institutions, etc.) without requiring HUMINT tradecraft. Furthermore, governments, just as in the HUMINT realm, use both official intelligence services as well as unaffiliated actors to collect information. The National Counterintelligence Executive has identified that sometimes independent hackers augment government capabilities for computer intrusions.[122] As an example, Chinese freelance hackers appear to at times take orders from the military or state-owned companies.[123] (Foreign governments may also recruit operatives from among this milieu. For instance, a Russian hacker was arrested, released on a technicality, and was subsequently identified as working for Moscow.)[124]

However, the use of the cyber vector does create unique opportunities that hostile actors can exploit. In the late 1990s, the FBI's MOONLIGHT MAZE operation developed information about Russian hacker attacks against Department of Energy laboratories, NASA, the Department of Defense, and defense contractors. Part of the concern was that an attack might be used to identify a scientist and use that information as a starting point to determine how that individual might be recruited as a human source.[125] According to a report by the National Counterintelligence Executive, foreign intelligence services may engage in "cyber spotting" to identify resumés of interest and responses to surveys in furtherance of identifying individuals who have access to information of value.[126]

An individual need not be a witting agent of a cyber-enabled foreign intelligence service. Rather, the accumulated assessment data may be used to craft a spear-phishing attack. This is a fake email that exploits familiarity using known name, known email address, and information about the recipient.[127] For instance, a Chinese intelligence operative emailed approximately twenty U.S. Steel employees with a communication that purported to be from the company's CEO.[128] Unit 61398, otherwise known as the Second Bureau of the Chinese PLA General Staff Department's Third Department, recruited operatives who were proficient in English and who initiated attacks by researching specific individuals who could then be targeted with an email containing malware.[129] Additionally, Europe- and Eurasia-region collectors have used social networking sites to target cleared contractor employees.[130] This takes the classic pattern of spotting and assessing into the cyber realm and could obviously be used to help target individuals of interest with tailored, compromised communications. Kevin Mandia, founder of cyber-security firm Mandiant, explained that the effectiveness of spear phishing was due to attackers' evolution to "target human inadequacies and weaknesses" rather than exploiting vulnerabilities in the software.[131] The 2010 cyber attack from China on Google was accomplished by assessing and targeting specific Google employees based on data from their social networking accounts.[132] The Chinese hacker then established a chat session, masquerading as an acquaintance, and within this session provided a link to a photo-sharing website administered by the attack's perpetrators. The malware embedded in the site allowed the Chinese hackers to gain access to the victim's username and password information.[133] When an agent is witting, he or she can provide information without ever meeting the foreign intelligence operative who is the recipient of the information.[134] This takes tradecraft a step beyond the typical, physical dead-drop.

Cyber attacks may obtain information not for its own sake but as a way to reach more sensitive targets, similarly to other types of collection. For instance, a single attack against RSA compromised at least three defense contractors and an estimated 20 percent of the Fortune 100 companies.[135] Similarly, Chinese hacking related to unmanned aerial vehicle technologies initially, according to cyber-security firm FireEye, targeted large defense companies before narrowing in on specific UAV-specific entities.[136]

The results of cyber attacks can be massive, which differentiates them in scope from HUMINT collection. Chinese hackers targeted all three of the primary contractors for the F-35 Joint Strike Fighter, while six to eight of the contractors working on the project were completely compromised.[137] Also, in 2012 NASA disclosed that Chinese hacks against its Jet Propulsion Laboratory had allowed intruders to gain full functional control over the laboratory's network.[138] This meant that the intruders had the ability to copy, delete, or modify sensitive files, manipulate user accounts for mission-critical systems, and steal user credentials to access other NASA systems.[139]

Compromises conducted in furtherance of future actions have also impacted the commercial viability of the private sector. According to a 2011 report by the National Counterintelligence Executive, a range of U.S. companies advised the NCIX that their networks were being targeted for client lists, mergers and acquisitions data, company information on pricing, and financial data. This was especially true of those companies that were doing business with China.[140]

Another problem that bridges the HUMINT-cyber intelligence disciplines is the collection of technology that can then be used to penetrate information technology systems. As of 1986, the Soviet Union had obtained more than three hundred different types of Western computer hardware and software that provide the baseline for a technical capability to penetrate various U.S. automated systems.[141]

The cyber aspect has implications for the tradecraft of traditional HUMINT operations. An insider threat no longer needs to meet with the entity for which he or she is clandestinely collecting information. The obsolescence of physical meetings makes it more difficult to identify acts of theft and espionage.[142] Huge quantities of data can be transferred instantaneously, either via email to a threat actor or onto removable media with which an insider threat or visitor can depart the premises.

CONCLUSION

Foreign governments do not simply collect through their designated intelligence services. Rather, they may use a variety of vectors, often in coordination with intelligence operatives, to acquire information that contributes to the governments' requirements for innovation. Furthermore, information need not be proprietary to be valuable, and open-source collection is of demonstrated interest, particularly to states seeking to close an innovation gap that may exist between them and the United States (or possibly between them or other regional competitors).

By applying multiple methodologies and forms of tradecraft toward a specific target, foreign actors may increase their chances of successful acquisition. The Defense Security Service in its 2013 report discussed how collectors from the East Asia and the Pacific region used government, industry, and academic platforms to address a national strategy articulated through collection requirements.[143] Countries may also employ multiple methodologies in succession. When one approach is unsuccessful, they may turn to another concept. For instance, the Defense Security Service assessed that the use of transshipment—the use of a middleman to prevent a country from identifying the ultimate destination of an item—by East Asia and Pacific research institutes' reflected a lack of previous successes in obtaining desired components from U.S. companies.[144] The wide-ranging collection attributable to China is one example of how a foreign government may deploy multiple operatives under a variety of guises. According to a congressional report, it was likely that PRC citizens, whether on scientific visits, delegations, or exchanges, who were allowed to travel to the United States received collection requirements to address.[145]

The U.S. intelligence community, in conjunction with private industry and academia, should be identifying ways in which it can use observation of foreign government objectives for intelligence value as well as develop strategies to exploit foreign governments' demonstrated interests for purposes of disruption when appropriate. As an open society, the United States is limited in what it can do to halt foreign acquisition of nonproprietary or otherwise controlled information. However, awareness of what foreign governments' operatives are attempting to collect can provide indicators that will help the U.S. government assess countries' capabilities (based on the gaps they are trying to fill). Furthermore, such awareness of collection can be parlayed into opportunities for disruption. As noted by the 2007 National Counterintelligence Strategy, "Intelligence activities of foreign powers afford us opportunities to exploit their operations and gain access to their intelligence in order to corrupt its integrity."[146] However, for these activities to succeed, industry and academia that engage with foreign actors (not all of whom even pretend to be friendly to the United States) must avoid trading the long-term well-being of the United States for short-term institutional gains.

NOTES

1. John Burgess and John Mintz, "CIA FBI Chiefs Warn Panel Over Economic Espionage; U.S. Advanced Technology Is a Target," *Washington Post*, April 30, 1992.

2. Jack Nelson, "Spies Took $300 Billion Toll on U.S. Firms in '97," *Los Angeles Times*, January 12, 1998.

3. *PRC Acquisition of U.S. Technology, Select Committee of the United States House of Representatives*, 11.

4. Ibid., 12.

5. Micah Springut, Stephen Schlaikjeer, and David Chen, *China's Program for Science and Technology Modernization: Implications for American Competitiveness* (Arlington, VA: Centra Technology, 2011), 27.

6. *PRC Acquisition of U.S. Technology*, 8.

7. Ibid., 13.

8. *Report to Congress of the U.S. China Economic and Security Review Commission*, 110th Cong. 127 (2007).

9. *Report to Congress of the U.S. China Economic and Security Review Commission*, 112th Cong. 407 (2012).

10. Ibid.

11. *Report to Congress of the U.S. China Economic and Security Review Commission*, 110th Cong. 127 (2007).

12. *Report to Congress of the U.S. China Economic and Security Review Commission*, 112th Cong. 387 (2012).

13. *Report of the Select Committee on U.S. National Security and Military/Commercial Concerns with the People's Republic of China*, 105th Cong. 13 (1999).

14. Ibid., 7.

15. Ibid., 28.

16. U.S. Trade Representative, *2015 Special 301 Report* (Washington, D.C.: U.S. Trade Representative, 2015), 41–42.

17. U.S. Trade Representative, *2011 Special 301 Report* (Washington, D.C.: Office of the U.S. Trade Representative, 2011).

18. Ibid.

19. U.S. Trade Representative, *2015 Special 301 Report*, 41–42.

20. U.S. Trade Representative, *2014 Report to Congress on China's WTO Compliance* (Washington, D.C.: U.S. Trade Representative, 2014).

21. U.S. Trade Representative, *2015 Special 301 Report*, 36.

22. U.S. Trade Representative, *2013 Special 301 Report* (Washington, D.C.: U.S. Trade Representative, 2013), 32.

23. Nargiza Salidjanova, *Going Out: An Overview of China's Outward Foreign Direct Investment* (Washington, D.C.: U.S. China Economic and Security Review Commission, 2011), 5.

24. Andrew Szamossegi, *An Analysis of Chinese Investments in the U.S. Economy* (Washington, D.C.: U.S. China Economic and Security Review Commission, 2012), 73.

25. *2014 Report to Congress of the U.S. China Economic and Security Review Commission*, 113th Cong. 293 (2014).

26. Ibid.

27. *Assessing China's Efforts to Become an "Innovation Society": A Progress Report. Hearing before the U.S. China Economic and Security Review Commission*, 112th Cong. 156 (2012).

28. U.S. Department of Defense, *Soviet Acquisition of Military Significant Western Technology: An Update* (Washington, D.C.: Office of the Secretary of Defense, 1985), 2.

29. Ibid., 4.

30. Christopher Andrew and Oleg Gordievsky, *KGB: The Inside Story* (New York: HarperCollins, 1990), 621–22.

31. Fialka, *War by Other Means*, 68.

32. Andrew and Gordievsky, *KGB: The Inside Story*, 621–22.

33. U.S. Department of Defense, *Soviet Acquisition of Military Significant Western Technology: An Update*, 2.

34. Ibid., 101.

35. Ibid., 6.

36. Ibid., 16, 20.

37. Andrew and Gordievsky, *KGB: The Inside Story*, 621–22.

38. Fialka, *War by Other Means*, 9.

39. Ibid., 75.

40. Ibid., 70.

41. Andrew and Gordievsky, *KGB: The Inside Story*, 621–22.

42. Walter Pincus, "Russian Spies on Rise Here; Administration Worried about 'Aggressive' Economic Espionage," *Washington Post*, September 21, 1999.

43. Ibid.

44. Fred Hiatt, "Soviets Shift to Commercial Spying; Primakov Says Traditional Espionage Against U.S. Has Declined," *Washington Post*, December 13, 1991.

45. U.S. Department of Defense, *Soviet Acquisition of Military Significant Western Technology: An Update*, 17.

46. Ibid.

47. Fialka, *War by Other Means*, 88.

48. Ibid., 91–92.

49. Ronald J. Ostrow and Paul Richter, "Economic Espionage Poses Major Peril to U.S. Interests Spying," *Los Angeles Times*, September 28, 1991.

50. Fialka, *War by Other Means*, 95–96; Walter Pincus, "CIA Targets Overseas Firms but Draws a Line," *Washington Post*, March 5, 1995.

51. Robin Wright, "France Accuses U.S. Diplomats of Espionage," *Los Angeles Times*, February 23, 1995.

52. Fialka, *War by Other Means*, 93.

53. Paul Blustein, "France and Israel Alleged to Spy on U.S. Firms," *Washington Post*, August 16, 1996; Siobhan Gorman, "China Singled Out for Cyberspying," *Wall Street Journal*, November 4, 2011.

54. Riebling, *Wedge*, 245–46.

55. Paul Blustein, "France and Israel Alleged to Spy on U.S. Firms," *Washington Post*, August 16, 1996.

56. Ibid.

57. Riebling, *Wedge*, 247.

58. "The IP Commission Report."

59. The Fourth Annual Cybersecuity Summit on September 25, 2013, at the National Press Club in Washington, D.C. (see *The Staggering Cost of Economic Espionage Against the US*, October 23, 2013).

60. National Counterintelligence Center, *Annual Report to Congress on Foreign Economic Collection and Industrial Espionage: 1997* (National Counterintelligence Center, 1998), 14.

61. National Counterintelligence Center, *Annual Report to Congress on Foreign Economic Collection and Industrial Espionage: 1995* (National Counterintelligence Center, 1996), 19.

62. Katherine L. Herbig, *Changes in Espionage in Americans: 1947–2007* (U.S. Department of Defense, Defense Personnel Security Research Center, 2008), 69.

63. Jay Solomon, "Phantom Menace: FBI Sees Big Threat from Chinese Spies," *Wall Street Journal*, August 10, 2005.

64. Edward Wong and Didi Kirsten Tatlow, "China Seen in Push to Gain Technology Insights," *New York Times*, June 5, 2013.

65. Naomi Schaefer Riley, "Young, Jewish and Going to Israel; Taglit-Birthright Has Given Away 300,000 10-Day Trips, Hoping to Stir an Appreciation of Jewish Heritage," *Wall Street Journal*, November 1, 2012.

66. Eli Lake, "FBI Took Long Look at AIPAC Activities: Probe Targeted Suspected Spies," *Washington Times*, January 18, 2011.

67. Office of the National Counterintelligence Executive, *Foreign Spies Stealing US Economic Secrets in Cyberspace*, 8.

68. National Counterintelligence Center, *Annual Report to Congress on Foreign Economic Collection and Industrial Espionage: 1995* (National Counterintelligence Center, 1996), 20.

69. National Counterintelligence Executive, *Annual Report to Congress on Foreign Economic Collection and Industrial Espionage: 2005* (National Counterintelligence Executive, 2006), iv.

70. *PRC Acquisition of U.S. Technology*, 38.

71. John Barron, *Operation SOLO: The FBI's Man in the Kremlin* (Washington, D.C.: Regnery Publishing, 1994), 341.

72. Evelyn Richards, "Americans Conducting 'Computer Diplomacy'; Goal Is to Liberate Soviets, Promote Peace," *Washington Post*, August 28, 1989.

73. Center for Strategic and International Studies, *CSIS Commission on Smart Power* (Washington, D.C.: Center for Strategic and International Studies, 2007), 52.

74. National Counterintelligence Center, *Annual Report to Congress on Foreign Economic Collection and Industrial Espionage: 1995*, 17.

75. Justin Gillis, "Scientists Accused of Theft; Espionage Alleged against Japanese," *Washington Post*, May 10, 2001.

76. Barrett Devlin, "Russian Spy Ring Aim to Make Children Agents," *Wall Street Journal*, July 26, 2012.

77. Jerry Markon and Philip Rucker, "The Suspects in a Russian Spy Ring Lived All-American Lives," *Washington Post*, June 30, 2010.

78. U.S. Department of Justice, FBI brochure "Elicitation," www.fbi.gov.

79. Judy Pasternak and Robert C. Paddock, "Possible Espionage Probed at NASA Research Center," *Los Angeles Times*, November 19, 1992.

80. Office of the National Counterintelligence Executive, *Annual Report to Congress on Foreign Economic Collection and Industrial Espionage: 2003* (Office of the National Counterintelligence Executive, 2004), 6.

81. *PRC Acquisition of U.S. Technology*, 40.

82. David Wise, *Tiger Trap: America's Secret Spy War with China* (New York: Houghton Mifflin Hartcourt, 2011), 13.

83. *PRC Acquisition of U.S. Technology*, 30.

84. Amos K. Wylie, "Unfair Exchange," *Studies in Intelligence* (Fall 1962).

85. Ibid.

86. *FBI Counterintelligence Visits to Libraries: Hearings before the Subcommittee on Civil and Constitutional Rights of the Committee on the Judiciary, House of Representatives*, 100th Cong. 115 (1988) (Testimony of James H. Geer, Assistant Director, Intelligence Division, Federal Bureau of Investigation).

87. Ibid.

88. Herbig, *Changes in Espionage in Americans: 1947–2007*.

89. National Counterintelligence Center, *Annual Report to Congress on Foreign Economic Collection and Industrial Espionage: 1995*, 20.

90. Ibid.

91. Ibid.

92. Office of the National Counterintelligence Executive, *Annual Report to Congress on Foreign Economic Collection and Industrial Espionage, 2001* (Office of the National Counterintelligence Executive, 2002), 2.

93. National Counterintelligence Center, *Annual Report to Congress on Foreign Economic Collection and Industrial Espionage: 1995*, 19.

94. Jay Solomon, "Phantom Menace: FBI Sees Big Threat from Chinese Spies," *Wall Street Journal*, August 10, 2005.

95. National Counterintelligence Center, *Annual Report to Congress on Foreign Economic Collection and Industrial Espionage* (National Counterintelligence Center, 2000).

96. National Counterintelligence Center, *Annual Report to Congress on Foreign Economic Collection and Industrial Espionage: 1995*, 20.

97. *FBI Counterintelligence Visits to Libraries: Hearings before the Subcommittee on Civil and Constitutional Rights of the Committee on the Judiciary, House of Representatives*, 100th Cong. 107 (1988) (Testimony of James H. Geer, Assistant Director, Intelligence Division, Federal Bureau of Investigation); National Counterintelligence Center, *Annual Report to Congress on Foreign Economic Collection and Industrial Espionage: 1995*, 20.

98. U.S. Department of Defense, *Soviet Acquisition of Military Significant Western Technology: An Update*, 17.

99. National Counterintelligence Center, *Annual Report to Congress on Foreign Economic Collection and Industrial Espionage: 1995*, 17.

100. Office of the National Counterintelligence Executive, *Annual Report to Congress on Foreign Economic Collection and Industrial Espionage: 2001*, 3.

101. Thomas Omestad, "Cloak and Dagger as R&D. The French Do It. The Brits Do It. But Corporate Spying May Not Be for Us," *Washington Post*, June 27, 1993.

102. "World Wire: Airline Denies Business Spying," *Wall Street Journal*, September 16, 1991.

103. Office of the National Counterintelligence Executive, *Annual Report to Congress on Foreign Economic Collection and Industrial Espionage: 2001*, 3.

104. Defense Security Service, *Targeting U.S. Technology: A Trend Analysis of Cleared Industry Reporting* (Defense Security Service, 2014), 30.

105. Ibid., 40.

106. Ibid., 63.

107. Office of the National Counterintelligence Executive, *Annual Report to Congress on Foreign Economic Collection and Industrial Espionage: 2004* (Office of the National Counterintelligence Executive, 2005).

108. Defense Security Service, *Targeting U.S. Technology: A Trend Analysis of Cleared Industry Reporting* (2014), 30.

109. Dan Morain, "Spies Never Came in from the Cold," *Los Angeles Times*, September 24, 1990.

110. Statement by Nicholas Eftimiades, "'Chinese Intelligence Operations' before the Joint Economic Committee, United States Congress," Wednesday, May 20, 1998.

111. Gus W. Weiss. "The Farewell Dossier: Duping the Soviets" *Studies in Intelligence* 39, no. 5 (1996), 121–26; Jim Drinkhall, "Security Loophole: East Bloc Businessmen Freely Come and Go In U.S. Defense Areas," *Wall Street Journal*, January 23, 1984.

112. Defense Security Service, *Targeting U.S. Technology: A Trend Analysis of Cleared Industry Reporting* (2014), 42.

113. Ibid., 63.

114. National Counterintelligence Center, *Annual Report to Congress on Foreign Economic Collection and Industrial Espionage.*

115. *Meeting the Espionage Challenge: A Review of United States Counterintelligence and Security Programs. Report of the Select Committee on Intelligence. United States Senate.* Rep. No. 99-522 (1986).

116. Defense Security Service, *Targeting U.S. Technology: A Trend Analysis of Cleared Industry Reporting* (Defense Security Service, 2013), 34.

117. Defense Group Inc., *Open Power, Hidden Dangers: IBM Partnerships in China* (Vienna, VA: Defense Group Inc., 2015), 3.

118. Jay Solomon, "Phantom Menace: FBI Sees Big Threat from Chinese Spies," *Wall Street Journal*, August 10, 2005.

119. *China's Propaganda and Influence Operations, Its Intelligence Activities That Target the United States, and the Resulting Impacts on U.S. National Security. Hearing before the U.S.-China Economic and Security Review Commission*, 111th Cong. 133 (2009).

120. Ellen Nakashima, "Grand Jury Indicts Six Chinese Citizens in Alleged Plot to Steal Trade Secrets," *Washington Post*, May 20, 2015.

121. *PRC Acquisition of U.S. Technology*, 35.

122. Office of the National Counterintelligence Executive, *Foreign Spies Stealing US Economic Secrets in Cyberspace*, 1.

123. Danny Yadron, James T. Areddy, and Paul Mozur, "China Hacking Deep, Diverse—Internet Spies Stretch Beyond Government Offering Beijing Cover, Experts Say," *Wall Street Journal*, May 30, 2014.

124. Lillian Ablon, Martin C. Libicki, and Andrea A. Golay, *Hacker's Bazaar Markets for Cybercrime Tools and Stolen Data* (Santa Monica, CA: Rand, 2014), 19.

125. Bob Drogin, "Yearlong Hacker Attack Nets Sensitive U.S. Data Technology," *Los Angeles Times*, October 7, 1999.

126. Office of the National Counterintelligence Executive, *Annual Report to Congress on Foreign Economic Collection and Industrial Espionage: 2002* (Office of the National Counterintelligence Executive, 2003), 10.

127. Robert Faturechi, "Chinese Accused of Email Hacking Scam," *Los Angeles Times*, May 21, 2014.

128. Ibid.

129. Kevin Mandia, Written Testimony before the Subcommittee on Crime and Terrorism, Judiciary Committee, United States Senate, May 8, 2013.

130. Defense Security Service, *Targeting U.S. Technologies: A Trend Analysis of Cleared Industry Reporting* (2013), 53.

131. Mandia, Written Testimony before the Subcommittee on Crime and Terrorism.

132. *2010 Report to Congress of the U.S. China Economic and Security Review Commission*, 111th Cong. 237-239 (2010).

133. Ibid.

134. Office of the National Counterintelligence Executive, *Foreign Spies Stealing US Economic Secrets in Cyberspace*, 2.

135. "The IP Commission Report," 43.

136. Edward Wong, "Hacking U.S. Secrets, China Pushes for Drones," *New York Times*, September 20, 2013.

137. *Report to Congress of the U.S. China Economic and Security Review Commission*, 112th Cong. 155 (2012).

138. Ibid.

139. Testimony of Larry M. Wortzel. Cyber Espionage and the Theft of U.S. Intellectual Property and Technology before the House of Representatives. Committee on Energy and Commerce Subcommittee on Oversight and Investigations, July 9, 2013.

140. Office of the National Counterintelligence Executive, *Foreign Spies Stealing US Economic Secrets in Cyberspace*, 5.

141. *Meeting the Espionage Challenge: A Review of United States Counterintelligence and Security Programs. Report of the Select Committee on Intelligence. United States Senate*, Rep. No. 99-522, at 36 (1986).

142. Office of the National Counterintelligence Executive, *Foreign Spies Stealing US Economic Secrets in Cyberspace*, 2.

143. Defense Security Service, *Targeting U.S. Technology: A Trend Analysis of Cleared Industry Reporting* (2013), 23–24.

144. Defense Security Service, *Targeting U.S. Technology: A Trend Analysis of Cleared Industry Reporting* (2014).

145. *PRC Acquisition of U.S. Technology*, 39.

146. The National Counterintelligence Strategy of the United States of America, 2007, 1.

Chapter Four

Selling Out

The Risks for Companies
Seeking Markets Abroad

Multiple foreign governments have offered incentives to attract foreign direct investment (FDI) by U.S. companies, notably those companies that possess technologies of interest. While FDI gives commercial enterprises access to new markets, it also gives foreign state and nonstate actors greater access to proprietary information and experienced human capital. The National Counterintelligence Center warned as early as 1995 that foreign companies could use technology-sharing agreements, which required U.S. companies to divulge large amounts of information about their processes and products as a means to exploit U.S. companies' interest in expanding into markets abroad. Even in the best-case scenario these would result in a transfer of knowledge.

However, less scrupulous foreign entities have been known to go further to achieve a one-sided benefit. Their tactics may include requiring divulgence of more information than the project being negotiated warrants, terminating negotiations once the information changes hands, or demanding the provision of additional information as a prerequisite to continuing the negotiating process.[1] As the National Counterintelligence Executive observed, "Even the process of negotiating a joint venture—where no agreement is actually reached—can be a goldmine for foreign firms seeking to collect sensitive information."[2] This is not a new problem. The intelligence service of Nicalai Ceaucescu's Romania would lure Western companies into negotiations for contracts to build large industrial projects and use these negotiations as an opportunity to obtain sufficient details for Romanian engineers to complete the project.[3]

The threats to U.S. innovation-fueling knowledge and technology do not dissipate even when a contract is successfully negotiated and implemented. The NCIX articulated several indicators of trouble once an arrangement had been established, including foreign partners making repeated requests for

99

unrestricted access to facilities or to computer networks, overstaffing by a foreign partner, and targeted requests for information, particularly if sensitive in nature, that go beyond the scope of the relationship or that are purposely directed at working-level personnel who may not be fully cognizant about the rules regarding the release of information.[4]

This is a particularly problematic paradigm in the case of U.S. competitors bordering on adversaries, specifically the Russian Federation and the Peoples' Republic of China, which have both attempted to draw U.S. companies into establishing a local presence that brings intellectual property with it. Even when production is not in the midst of a hostile country, U.S. industry in third countries is susceptible to targeting by foreign intelligence services. According to a U.S. government report on the Soviet targeting of military technologies, "as a result of various coproduction arrangements and contract bidding among foreign firms, the availability of much US defense contractor technology overseas in US subsidiaries and in other firms has increased. This enables Soviet Bloc intelligence to seek priority US technologies in many countries around the world."[5] With ever-increasing globalization, combined with the increasingly internationalized identity of U.S. firms, this lesson is even more applicable today.

RUSSIA

The Russian Federation's Skolkovo project was an ambitious effort directed at establishing the Russian version of Silicon Valley by attracting foreign companies to establish platforms for developing and deploying intellectual property on Russian soil. Two elements that characterized Skolkovo were ingrained in previous Russian efforts to modernize. The first of these was the top-down and sometimes ruthless approach to development exemplified by Peter the Great, Alexander II, Stalin, and Khruschev. A close predecessor to Skolkovo and associated entities was Moscow's creation of several dozen science cities throughout the Soviet Union.[6] The second was the importation of foreign innovation. In 1929, the Soviet Union, in an effort to establish an automotive industry, asked Henry Ford to establish a massive manufacturing facility, which became the Gorky Automobile Plant.[7] Almost half a century later, in 1973, the Soviet Union proposed that Lockheed build and equip an "aircraft city" in the USSR in exchange for Moscow's purchase of fifty Lockheed transports; the Soviets offered a similar arrangement to Boeing.[8]

Skolkovo is a clear successor to Soviet attempts to benefit from the direct investment of foreign companies. Initiated by then president Dimitri Medvedev, this project was an attempt to create a technology cluster in a special economic zone outside of Moscow.[9] The Russian government planned to offer tax breaks and relaxed visa and customs regulations to companies that established a presence in Skolkovo.[10] Indicating the persistence of the Russian government's continuing authoritarian approach to development, Skolkovo represented an attempt to create a Silicon Valley–like development out of whole cloth, with four hundred hectares demarcated for up to one thousand start-ups, a research university with 1,800 students, and forty corporate research and development centers.[11] Further indicating the development by diktat approach, Skolkovo was intended to serve as the linchpin for a national innovation ecosystem that would bring together researchers, entrepreneurs, and investors in five "clusters" focused on information technology, biomedical, energy efficiency, space, and nuclear technologies.[12] These new techno-parks were located at Tomsk, Duna, Zelenograd, and St. Petersburg.[13] Additionally, Russia's attempt to catch up with the West was apparent in the Ministry of Education and Science's attempt to develop Western-style research centers at Russian universities.[14]

The reliance on foreign expertise showed Skolkovo to be a hollow project that would be a one-way transfer of international knowledge to Russia. A leaked Russian government report made clear Moscow's intentions, stating that the country needed to seek opportunities to use "American technological potential" as well as forming "alliances of modernization" to attract technology from Europe.[15] In 2010, Medvedev visited Silicon Valley and met with representatives of companies such as Apple and Google.[16] Furthermore, Medvedev suggested establishing videoconferencing links to have "virtual hallway discussions" between the tech-savvy employees of companies in Russia and Silicon Valley.[17] This would allow Skolkovo not only to attract U.S. innovation to Russia but also give Russia an excuse to reach into a hotbed of U.S. innovation. Indicating that business with Russia was appealing to innovation-oriented companies, Microsoft, Google, Motorola, Boeing, and Intel had research centers in Russia.[18] In addition to industry, the Massachusetts of Technology (MIT), for USD $300 million, agreed to set up the Skolkovo Institute of Science and Technology.[19] (Russia had also approached Stanford and California Institute of Technology.[20]) In October 2011, at a ceremony at the RUSNANO International Nanotechnology Forum, the Skolkovo Foundation Sk Tech (the twenty-first-century-sounding truncation of a name for the Skolkovo Institute of Science and Technology) and MIT signed an agreement to "collaborate in building capacity in education, research and entrepreneurship programs."[21] Sk Tech's foci, across approximately fifteen centers, would be energy science and technology, biomedical science and technology, information science and technology, space science and technology, and nuclear science and technology.[22] As of 2012, approximately twenty companies, including Cisco, IBM, and SAP, planned to open a sizeable R&D laboratory and cooperate with the Skolkovo Institute.[23] While in the United States, such corporate partnerships would foster gains for the United States' bottom line; they instead generate new knowledge to which Russia would have ready access.

The balance between government control of Skolkovo and the participation of foreign investors is troubling. The government-financed Skolkovo Foundation was responsible for building and running the city.[24] (Similarly, the five techno-parks discussed previously would be government owned and leased to high-tech entities.[25]) Moscow established a tight grip on the management of Skolkovo from the outset. Medvedev directly appointed Victor Vekselberg to lead the project.[26] Medvedev's chief of staff, Vadislav Surkov, who was responsible for the Skolkovo Innovation Center, was a proponent of a stronger government and compared the project (apparently favorably) to the state-planned science cities of the Soviet era.[27] The board would also include the directors of Russian state-financed tech companies, including RUSNANO, headed by Anatoliy Chubais.[28] RUSNANO was a creation of the Kremlin that invested approximately USD $1 billion annually in nanotechnology and other high-tech sectors.[29] The acquisitive aims of RUSNANO, a key sponsor of Skolkovo, indicate the project's objective of bolstering the Russian government's capabilities for innovation. Meanwhile, the U.S. representation on the Skolkovo Foundation Council consists of private sector figures including executives from Intel and Google.[30]

This is a dangerously unbalanced partnership. The Russian government has demonstrated that it is more than willing to appropriate private assets. A notable example is the case of the energy company Yukos, owned by Mikahil Khordokovsky, a political rival to Vladimir Putin. The private sector can realistically do little to seek redress from an authoritarian government such as Russia's. Investments, especially those that bring new technology desired by Moscow, are ill advised.

A troubling tangent of Russian attempts to create Skolkovo and a broader innovation network is the involvement of a U.S. subfederal politician in a similar mismatched relationship with Russian leadership. In 2010, California governor Arnold Schwarzenegger visited Russia, along with twenty-three potential investors, to help attract high-tech business and investment.[31] Schwarzenegger showed enthusiasm for opportunities present in Russia, referring to the country as a "gold mine."[32] This kind of boosterism is inexplicable and dangerous. Schwarzenegger was shilling for a foreign government (given Moscow's clear control of the Skolkovo project) and encouraging U.S. companies to submit themselves to the whims of an increasingly unreliable and hostile regime.

CHINA

For several decades, the Peoples' Republic of China has made a concerted endeavor to attract foreign investment that would bring technology to China. This behavior started with Deng Xiaoping, who initiated an open door policy. Beijing created its first special economic zone in 1980 in Shenzhen.[33] These special economic zones were meant to attract foreign investment, skills, and imports. In addition to five special economic zones, China designated fourteen coastal open cities with various freedoms and tax breaks as incentives for foreign investments and trade.[34] For instance, in Hainan foreign investors did not need visas and were able to lease land for seventy years. They were promised the ability to manage businesses without interference from the Communist Party and the right to keep a significant portion of their profits.[35] To further prod investment, China and other Far East countries have deliberately established consulting firms to facilitate U.S. companies' creation of business abroad.[36] Its 1,000 Talent Program, sponsored by the Organization Department of the Chinese Communist Party, is aimed at convincing talented Chinese to return to China.[37] The Chinese Academy of Sciences launched a similar initiative—the 100 Talent Program—in 1994, which offered an attractive salary, research support, and housing incentives for young scientists who had been working abroad.[38] Additionally, China's provincial cities have targeted tax breaks toward and created business parks for returning entrepreneurs.[39] This leveraging the skills and resources of the diaspora is a theme in both China's licit and illicit pursuits of capability for innovation. U.S. companies responded to these blandishments, particularly after 2000, when China became a member of the World Trade Organization.[40] According to the U.S.–China Economic and Security Review Commission, China has also directed efforts at immigration of non-Chinese with expertise to China.[41]

China is also paying greater attention to and learning from Western innovation practices and, like Russia, has attempted to establish R&D incubators. The government has encouraged multinational corporations to establish R&D centers within larger, high-technology zones, such as Beijing's Zhongguancun. Multinational companies feel compelled to develop their relationships with Chinese universities and research institutes, not only to obtain access to talent but also to establish and maintain connections to Chinese government officials. The China Economic and Security Review Commission has highlighted the possibility that "Chinese researchers in [multinational corporation] R&D centers form technological communities that, in principle, could then be harnessed by Chinese firms to re-innovate and develop products under their own brands."[42] However, it is not simply specific knowledge that China is attempting to acquire. Rather, as indicated by the 973 Program,

China has attempted to understand the fundamental components of innovation—so as not simply to replicate technology but to replicate the process that produces breakthroughs. Assuming that an authoritarian country such as China or Russia can produce a viable culture of innovation (which is unlikely), the investment of U.S. firms in those locations brings these countries one step closer to closing the gap with U.S. innovation and its implications for elements of national power.

Almost from the point of deciding to open the country to foreign direct investment, China has used U.S. companies' presence as an opportunity to siphon off the results of innovation. In 1979, the McDonnell aircraft company reached a deal to build parts in China. In return, China demanded the technology and the right to produce increasingly large pieces of the planes that it purchased from McDonnell in Chinese factories. As Chinese factories absorbed the manufacturing know-how, from production of nose cones and fuselages for airliners, emerging versions of Chinese fighter aircraft began featuring better-produced fuselages and smoother aluminum skins.[43] This represented not simply an opportunity for reverse engineering, but rather an opportunity to master technological processes upon which the Chinese could innovate to enhance their military capabilities. This pilfering of intellectual property to enhance China's baseline knowledge has continued to be a concern. As Robert Atkinson of the Information Technology and Innovation Foundation wrote in 2012, China, in exchange for allowing foreign companies to invest, often required the transfer of technology that sometimes occurred "in the form of a requirement to establish [research and development] facilities where the technology often [went] out the back door, in the form of Chinese researchers who [left] or [took] the technology to Chinese firms."[44] China further coopts U.S. capabilities because the required joint venture agreements often keep profits in China and allow Chinese firms to learn from foreign firms, against which the Chinese firms will independently compete. With no organization monitoring outgoing U.S. technology, U.S. companies that operate in pure pursuit of short-term profits may degrade the United States' long-term national interest by entering an environment rife with commercial coercion.

China has used foreign investment to target specific expertise and technology for acquisition. In 2002, China scrapped its substandard high-speed rail system. The government then structured foreign procurement as a way to force foreign technology transfer in exchange for providing market access.[45] (In 2015, China amazingly became a frontrunner to produce the trains for California's proposed high-speed rail line.)[46] A similar situation occurred when Japan's Kawasaki Heavy Industries saw its partnership dissolve and then saw China produce remarkably similar technology that it planned to sell internationally.[47] Kawasaki Heavy Industries had originally entered into a joint venture with China South Locomotive and Rolling Stock Corporation Ltd. (CSR), which concluded with Kawasaki accusing CSR of copying and selling its bullet train technology on the domestic and global markets.[48] Siemens had a similar experience, entering into a joint venture with China National Railway (CNR) to build the Beijing-Tianjin high-speed railway.[49] Of sixty trains, CNR built fifty-seven at its facility in China. CNR then won the contract to build the Beijing-Shanghai rail line. One wonders how much of this newfound expertise was "found" from foreign investors.

Innovation by arm-twisting has not simply been pervasive throughout Chinese industry; it has also been enshrined in government policy. In the mid-2000s, Beijing unveiled its National Medium- and Long-Term Program for Science and Technology Development (2006–2010), which sought to establish an environment that would encourage indigenous innovation and urged that China "master core technologies" in 402 areas. By implementing this program in all sectors, industries, and regions, China hoped to drastically enhance the country's competitiveness.[50] The program gave impetus to absorbing Western technologies. Because WTO regulations prohibited overt demands for technology, China instead used a variety of implicit insistences on transfers by barring U.S. companies' goods from purchase by the Chinese government unless they agreed to transfer technology.[51] The transfer of capacities for innovation to China is not simply a benefit to its economy but instead is a contribution to its military and intelligence services. As of 2014, Chinese companies that acquire advanced technology are legally required by state security laws to share these acquisitions with the PLA and Chinese intelligence if they are requested to do so.[52]

Even as China is using the transfer of technology in furtherance of innovation that benefits its military and other elements of national power, the U.S. government is encouraging American companies to hand over technology. For instance, the U.S. Department of Energy and China's NDRC signed a memorandum of understanding (MOU) that encouraged cooperation on nuclear energy and reiterated U.S. approval for transfer of third-generation nuclear technology to China.[53] With this agreement as context, Westinghouse signed a contract to build four AP1000 reactors in China—the first time such a reactor had been built in that country. A technology transfer arrangement was part of this deal, requiring seventy-five thousand documents related to the construction of the reactors to be handed over.[54] China has since set a goal of indigenizing this technology with the objective of building a reactor based on the AP1000.[55]

The next extension of this commercial coercion is outright theft, including espionage. The National Bureau of Asian Research has stated the reality that trade secret theft is a risk inherent in expansion to overseas markets, as each piece of information sent abroad exposes intellectual property to increased risk.[56] This has been the case with foreign direct investment into China. As Robert Atkinson put it, "Many foreign companies in China just assume that their electronic communications will be monitored by the Chinese government, even if they are encrypted. This is not about a poor country that doesn't want to pay for software. This is about government-supported attacks to steal intellectual property from foreign companies."[57] Chinese theft from foreign companies ranges from the interception of electronic communications to basic, thuggish snatch and grab of technology. After Monsanto opened production and research facilities in China for advanced corn technology, the advanced corn was systemically stolen—likely by the Chinese government—to obtain the advanced intellectual property.[58]

In addition to identifying ways to steal specific U.S. technology, China has encouraged foreign companies to create ground-level R&D research facilities. IBM established a wholly owned research facility in Beijing in 1995. Intel, Microsoft, Hewlett-Packard, General Electric, 3M, and Panasonic followed suit.[59] As of 2011, China's Ministry of Commerce claimed that there were more than 1,200 foreign multinational corporation R&D centers in China. U.S. companies have discovered that they must increasingly allocate money to bench science, product development, and clinical trials all conducted within China.[60] Indicators that U.S. companies are pursuing China-based R&D—rather than simply adapting existing products to Chinese standards—include: Microsoft's establishment of Microsoft Research China, which subsequently became Microsoft Research Asia; its opening of a Shanghai Science and Technology Park in 2010, which was its only comprehensive research center outside of the United States; and the Hewlett Packard laboratories in China, which work with Chinese universities and research institutes.[61] The indigenization of research processes, rather than specific technologies, is consistent with China's 973 Program—an effort to develop its capacity for basic science. However, it is also encouraged by U.S. policy and has included a series of bilateral relationships in the sciences.

U.S. ACADEMIA ABROAD

The expansion of U.S. universities abroad creates vulnerabilities that foreign governments can exploit to target institutions and human capital essential to innovation. Three distinct phenomena—traditional exchange programs, the establishment of U.S. programs abroad, and the temporary or permanent migration of academics to foreign institutions—present a variety of channels through which the capacity for innovation can transfer adversaries. Exploiting these conduits of information exchange can facilitate espionage and poses a serious national security risk.

U.S. universities' footprints abroad are widening. According to the Institute of International Education, 283,332 U.S. students studied abroad during the 2011/2012 academic year. (Out of these, 14,887 studied in China, making that country, a pervasive threat to American innovation, the fifth highest-ranking destination.) Additionally, multiple U.S. institutions have developed a presence in a range of countries, some of which are associated with efforts to target U.S. innovation. The Harvard School of Engineering and Applied Sciences and the Harvard University Center for the Environment are engaged with Chinese universities in the field of environmental studies.[62] Yale and Peking University established the Peking-Yale Joint Research Center for Plant Molecular Genetics and Agro Biotechnology.[63] Many other U.S. universities have links to Chinese universities on topics ranging from technology and innovation to stem cell research to pharmaceuticals. These U.S. universities include George Mason University, the Levin Institute, State University of New York, University of Houston Medical Center, Indiana University, Purdue University, and the University of California at Santa Barbara.[64] In 2005, the Zhejiang Provincial Government worked with Zhejiang University and the California Nanosystems Institute at UCLA to found the Zhejiang-California International Nanosystems Institute.[65] In addition to a physical presence, at least one U.S. institution, the Massachusetts Institute of Technology, assisted the Russian Federation with establishing an institute at its Skolkovo project. The failure of one such partnership, between Johns Hopkins University and the Singaporean government in 2006 due in part to the failure to transfer technology to local industry, demonstrates that foreign governments expect such partnerships to bolster their own private sector capabilities, as opposed to a good faith effort to partner for academic progress.[66]

Beyond the establishment of foreign campuses, U.S. institutions have engaged foreign academic entities on specific joint projects. Microsoft as of 2015 had worked with China's Tsinghua University for approximately twenty years.[67] The Scripps Institute of Oceanography at the University of California at San Diego (UCSD) reached an agreement with China's Ningbo University, which included USD $50 to $100 million of Chinese funding for a Scripps UCSD research center at Ningbo University for development of renewable marine resources and technologies and the formation of a USD $25 million marine innovation and technology fund for commercialization in China of Scripps UCSD discoveries.[68] The Scripps example is consistent with China's pattern vis-à-vis commercial entities—the attraction of R&D activities to China, which can then be appropriated by the Chinese government. Oceanographic technology will likely be of unique interest to Beijing as it continues to expand its presence via such novel approaches as building islands in the South China Sea. Chinese regional governments have also encouraged cooperation with U.S. institutions.

The inherent vulnerabilities of engaging foreign academic institutions are due in part to foreign governments' use of those entities to pursue innovation, either of a cutting-edge variety or in an attempt to close a gap in knowledge. China, through its 863 Program, funds military and civilian research at Chinese civilian universities.[69] This indicates that partnering with Chinese universities may directly contribute to Beijing's ability to wield elements of national power. One example of particular concern is the Chinese government's funding a variety of academic programs to develop expertise in information warfare and computer network operations.[70] Aside from the value that China places on information operations in wartime, the cultivation of cyber capabilities may be contributing to malicious computer activities conducted against U.S. entities by Chinese actors including the Peoples' Liberation Army. Additionally, China's universities have contributed technology to the Chinese bottom line. For instance, the Northwestern Polytechnical University was associated with the ASN Technology Group, which claimed to produce 90 percent of China's unmanned aerial vehicles.[71]

The United States' willingness to engage with universities that the government clearly employs as a means to acquire specific technology may be attributable to the logical fallacy of mirror imaging—the belief that the other side is thinking in the same way about a given situation. However, American and foreign academic partnerships can be alarmingly mismatched. U.S. universities usually pursue research in furtherance of scientific advancement—seeking funding from the U.S. government when the interests of the researcher and the interest of a funder such as the National Science Foundation coincide. Universities in places such as China pursue research as appendages of the state—addressing requirements levied by their governments. The concept that the Chinese government uses academia to serve the interest of the state, including the military, is not new. During the 1990s, China relied on foreign scientists and engineers for information to advance its weapons development projects. It exploited academic exchanges as one venue through which to exploit this expertise for necessary data.[72]

Historically, the Soviet Academy of Sciences, despite its academic veneer, functioned as a collector at Moscow's behest. Along with several other Soviet entities, the Academy of Sciences was principally involved with the acquisition of information for nondefense industries and at times worked jointly with the KGB.[73] This is consistent with reporting about other Soviet institutes, including the Institute of the USA and Canada, as well as the Institute of World Economics and International relations, where one-third of the members were

KGB personnel.[74] Considering the similarities between Soviet and Russian intelligence operations (for example, the use of "illegals"), it is possible that the current Russian Academy of Sciences has continued the cooperation with the KGB's successor, the SVR, as a means to gather information on behalf of an authoritarian state.

Foreign governments are also actively recruiting academic human capital to fill the ranks of universities abroad, including those in countries that have been associated with instances of targeting U.S. technology. For instance, South Korea, under the auspices of its Science and Engineering Foundation, launched its USD $800 million World Class Universities Program in 2008, which was an endeavor to import foreign professors on a part-time basis to teach and conduct research.[75] Both activities contribute to foreign countries' bottom line. Teaching creates a cadre of indigenous talent, and research develops new knowledge on foreign soil. The program received one thousand applicants in its first ten months, 40 percent of whom were from the United States, including eleven Nobel laureates and eighteen members of the U.S. National Academy of Engineering.[76]

China, as in other efforts to facilitate the transfer of knowledge, has targeted overseas Chinese to staff its institutions (which are often closely tied to government interests) and other Chinese entities. China expert James Mulvenon has observed that China is trying to woo back thousands of ethnic Chinese scientists who have trained or worked in the United States.[77] Education scholar Ben Wildavsky characterized Beijing's approach as "aggressively recruiting" individuals and attracting professors from American universities to fill positions at a number of Chinese science-oriented institutions. Starting in 2005, China's National Natural Science Foundation (NSFC) launched a program to provide incentives intended to attract Chinese of foreign nationality to work full time for Chinese institutions.[78] What China is doing fits within a broader trend, as noted by the U.S. National Counterintelligence Executive, which stated that "several countries have found repatriation of emigres and foreign ethnic scientists to be the most beneficial technology transfer methodology. One country, in particular, claims to have repatriated thousands of ethnic scientists back to their home country from the United States." The recruitment of U.S.-trained academics to fill positions abroad also provides opportunities for the illicit transfer of technology.

China's attraction of U.S.-trained academics has benefited Beijing at several levels. The most visible result has been that many of these individuals have assumed leadership positions in Chinese research institutes and universities, and the results are apparent. According to the U.S.–China Economic and Security Review Commission, the top ten universities in China, which the Chinese government has selected to become world-class institutions, have an increasingly large number of Western-trained faculty members.[79] As of 2012, the dean of the school of engineering at Peking University had worked at the U.S. Department of Energy's Los Alamos National Laboratory.[80] A former Johns Hopkins University professor took a position as head of Peking's Engineering Institute, a Northwestern University professor became dean of the School of Life Sciences at Peking, a Georgia Tech professor became dean at the College of Environmental Science, and a Princeton University professor became the vice president of Tsinghua's Institute of Biomedicine.[81] These individuals have also returned to China with knowledge of the policy and institutional environments necessary for successful innovation.[82] The internationalization of academia has produced instances in which academics have a position with a university in the United States and an association with a university or lab in China.[83] As the next chapter illustrates, this dynamic has led to the illicit exfiltration of knowledge and technology from the United States and added to China's capability for innovation at a cost to the United States.

Established academics are not the only ones who the Chinese government has targeted to return to China with knowledge obtained in the West. Chinese regional government delegations visiting the United States have routinely paid visits to multiple cities in which there are large Chinese student populations. Delegations make a pitch to these students to return to China.[84]

China's ability to benefit from Western-educated academics extends to the informal exchanges of information between scholars. There is a general tendency for researchers to develop contacts with colleagues for collaboration. Because of the trends of Chinese study and research in the United States followed by a return to China, there is a pronounced transnational academic community. A number of Chinese in the United States with scientific backgrounds have organized ethnic Chinese professional societies, which often include support for China's S&T development as part of their mission.[85] This fluid dynamic provides an environment that Beijing can exploit to develop knowledge.

Despite China's clear use of academia to exploit U.S. entities, the U.S. government and U.S. industry has encouraged academia to engage with Chinese institutions on research. For instance, the U.S.–China Clean Energy Research Center (CERC) was initiated as the result of a meeting between President Barack Obama and Chinese president Hu Jintao.[86] Under the auspices of CERC, the U.S. Department of Energy awarded grants to teams of researchers from U.S. and Chinese universities. The CERC Clean Vehicle Consortium brought together representative of the University of Michigan, Ohio State University, the Massachusetts Institute of Technology, Tsinghua University, Beihang University, Beijing Institute of Technology, Hunan University, North China Electric Power University,

Shanghai Jiao Tong University, Tianjin University, Tongji University, and Wuhan University of Technology.[87] Collaboration on the topic of clean vehicles is interesting because this is also an area in which China has invested in the United States and attempted to openly compete against at least one U.S. company. Under the auspices of the Clean Vehicle Consortium, Ohio State University and Tsinghua University collaborated on the degradation of lithium ion batteries, which is significant given China's acquisition of A123 Systems, which entered bankruptcy after drawing down funding from the DOE.

OTHER COUNTRIES

While China and Russia present the two most persistent threats based on their investments in attracting U.S. companies capable of driving innovation and their long histories of state-directed and resourced acquisition of technology, other countries have employed related tactics against U.S. companies. Japan, for instance, used a Byzantine patenting process that resulted in U.S. companies licensing their intellectual property to Japanese firms (effectively handing over the products of innovation) rather than run the bureaucratic gauntlet. Between 1950 and 1978, U.S. firms licensed 32,000 patents to Japanese companies. While Japanese firms paid USD $9 billion for the licenses, journalist John Fialka argues that the actual worth was approximately USD $1 trillion.[88] More recently, India has positioned itself to absorb the capability and products from U.S. innovation. In September 2015, Indian prime minister Narendra Modi met with executives of various Silicon Valley technology companies to attract investment in India.[89] However, India has not been a safe environment for foreign innovation. The National Counterintelligence Executive highlighted that in 2004 a U.S. software manufacturer was the victim of a theft that resulted in the loss of portions of its source code and confidential design documents from a recently opened research and development center in Mumbai, India.[90] The process of innovation in India is hindered by challenges in securing and enforcing patents. Specific sectors that the USTR identified as particularly vulnerable to patent enforcement included biopharmaceuticals, agricultural chemicals, and green technology.[91] Should U.S. companies eventually pursue R&D operations in India, they will encounter a climate in which they are unable to realistically claim ownership for their results. Finally, the U.S. Defense Security Service believed that unspecified countries in Europe and Eurasia would take advantage of U.S.-cleared defense contractors' financial difficulties in a less than robust economy and encourage them to develop facilities abroad.[92]

TEXTBOX 4.1.   ARGUMENTS FOR ENGAGEMENT

While the perception of profit opportunities explains industry's willingness to transfer innovation to China, the U.S. government and academia are driven by different factors. The U.S. government first engaged China on scientific matters in 1979, and the development of a scientific relationship was viewed, first and foremost, as a diplomatic initiative to formalize relations with Beijing.[1] However, the ongoing relationships between the Chinese government and multiple U.S. government agencies have created vulnerabilities that China has attempted to exploit. From the outset the U.S. government gave China access to information that could help the country catch up in areas of innovation. For instance, starting in 1979, the U.S. Department of Energy began working with China on high-energy physics.[2] While the United States saw science as a diplomatic initiative, China has used its access to international science and technology to catch up with the international scientific and technological advancements.[3] This intent to acquire accrued knowledge is further indicated by Chinese who, while abroad, will acquire mastery of a technology common in the United States but distinctly in short supply in China.[4] The U.S. government's numerous agreements on scientific cooperation with China—thirty agency-to-agency agreements with forty subagreements as of 2014—even if evaluated from a purely diplomatic perspective, may ultimately be self-defeating. As China advances technologically, its willingness to accede to U.S. desires will change—especially because its pursuit of objectives such as control of the South China Sea are in direct opposition to American interests.

There are certainly opportunities for the United States to use engagement as an avenue for acquiring insights about Chinese innovation. One indication that U.S. institutions are becoming savvier is evident in a 2007 report that indicated that the U.S. Navy's Office of Naval Research (ONR) recognized that its awareness of Chinese S&T activities was limited and believed that it needed to develop a closer relationship with Chinese institutions to better understand Chinese capabilities.[5] However, this seems to be the exception rather than the rule. Commercial entities have developed footprints in China based on short-term concerns about market share, rather than long-term considerations of what dissemination of current technology will mean for China's capability to innovate in the future. Similarly, the U.S. government's encouragement of partnerships with Beijing is based on a 1979 agreement that was inspired by U.S. diplomatic considerations.

Subfederal governments in the United States have also pursued relations with Chinese entities. Subfederal governments are less concerned with national strategy than the local creation of jobs and the attraction of foreign capital.[6] Despite not being concerned about national strategy, subfederal government officials nonetheless deal with Chinese leaders. During a 2011 visit to the United States by Hu Jintao, a U.S.–China Memorandum of Understanding (MOU) was signed to strengthen cooperation between U.S. governors and Chinese provincial leaders.[7] Such relationships can border on state usurpation of foreign policy responsibilities. In 2013, California governor Jerry Brown signed an MOU with Xie Zhenhua, the vice minister of the National Development and Reform Commission of China, regarding lowering carbon dioxide emissions, which included sharing of information and experiences regarding policies and programs as well as cooperative research on clean and efficient energy technologies.[8] This appearance of usurpation is furthered by states' establishment of offices in China. As of 2015, twenty-five states had offices there.[9] China is not the only country with which U.S. subfederal governments have worked directly—as indicated by Schwarzzenger's boosterism vis-à-vis Russia—but it is the most prominent.

Academia partners with China for practical and ideological reasons. At the practical level, U.S. institutions see R&D cooperation with Chinese entities as a source of revenue for U.S. schools.[10] Scholars also cite the public diplomacy value of educational exchanges. The Center for Strategic and International Studies, a Washington think tank, actually called for an expansion of students in fields including medicine, engineering, and computer sciences.[11] There is also a perception that Chinese students provide a bridge between the United States and China.[12] However, this results in a phenomenon similar to the transnational community of scholars discussed previously, which facilitates the transfer of technology and knowledge and which the government of China, and presumably other governments, can exploit.

NOTES

1. Suttmeier, *Trends in U.S. China Science and Cooperation*, 29.
2. Ibid.

3. Ibid.

4. Springut, Schlaikjeer, and Chen, *China's Program for Science and Technology Modernization*, 97.

5. *2007 Report to Congress of the U.S. China Economic and Security Review Commission*, 110th Cong. 61 (2007).

6. Szamossegi, *An Analysis of Chinese Investments in the U.S. Economy*, 110.

7. Ibid., 112.

8. *2014 Report to Congress of the U.S. China Economic and Security Review Commission*, 113th Cong. 219 (2014).

9. Koch-Weser and Ditz, *Chinese Investment in the United States*, 4.

10. Ibid., 24.

11. Center for Strategic and International Studies, *CSIS Commission on Smart Power*, 57.

12. *China's Propaganda and Influence Operations, Its Intelligence Activities That Target the United States, and the Resulting Impact on U.S. National Security: Hearing before the U.S. China Economic and Security Review Commission*, 111th Cong. 67 (2009) (Statement of Ross Terrill).

CONCLUSION

The U.S. government has unwisely prompted U.S. industry and academia to establish presences in a number of countries. Particularly alarming are ventures in China and Russia, countries that have both demonstrated a consistently hostile relationship with the U.S. government. Adding to those countries' innovational bottom line empowers their adversarial actions. As with foreign investment into the United States, the most troubling implication of outward investment from the United States is the transfer of tools for innovation—human capital that returns to its home country, teaching the fundamentals of the R&D process, and more—as opposed to the transfer of a specific technology. The patterns of collaboration also set U.S. entities up for exploitation by foreign intelligence services.

NOTES

1. National Counterintelligence Center, *Annual Report to Congress on Foreign Economic Collection and Industrial Espionage: 1995*, 21.

2. Office of the National Counterintelligence Executive, *Annual Report to Congress on Foreign Economic Collection and Industrial Espionage: 2002*, 8.

3. Fialka, *War by Other Means*, 90.

4. Office of the National Counterintelligence Executive, *Annual Report to Congress on Foreign Economic Collection and Industrial Espionage: 2002*, 8.

5. *Soviet Acquisition of Military Significant Western Technology: An Update*, 17.

6. Will Englund, "Russia's Fading Scientific Prospects," *Washington Post*, December 22, 2011.

7. "Lurching into the Fast Lane: Industry in Russia," *Economist*, July 14, 2012.

8. Gus W. Weiss, "The Farewell Dossier: Duping the Soviets," *Studies in Intelligence* (Fall 1962).

9. "Lurching into the Fast Lane: Industry in Russia," *Economist*, July 14, 2012; "Can Russia Create a New Silicon Valley? Innovation in Russia," *Economist*, July 14, 2012.

10. Oliver Staley, "For MIT the Launch of a Russian Satellite," *Washington Post*, May 12, 2013.

11. "Can Russia Create a New Silicon Valley? Innovation in Russia," *Economist*, July 14, 2012.

12. Ibid.

13. Andrew E. Kramer, "Innovation, By Order of the Kremlin," *New York Times*, April 11, 2010.

14. Will Englund, "Russia's Fading Scientific Prospects," *Washington Post*, December 22, 2011.

15. Will Bland, "Innovation on Demand; Russia Is Trying to Build Its Very Own Version of Silicon Valley," *Wall Street Journal*, June 16, 2010.

16. Yuliya Chemova, "Russia's Tech Startup Scene Retreats Amid Ukraine Conflict," *Wall Street Journal*, September 8, 2014.

17. Don Clark, "Medvedev's Silicon Valley Visit Yields Deal with Cisco," *Wall Street Journal*, June 24, 2010.

18. Will Bland, "Innovation on Demand; Russia Is Trying to Build Its Very Own Version of Silicon Valley," *Wall Street Journal*, June 16, 2010.

19. "Can Russia Create a New Silicon Valley? Innovation in Russia," *Economist*, July 14, 2012; Oliver Staley, "For MIT the Launch of a Russian Satellite," *Washington Post*, May 12, 2013.

20. "Can Russia Create a New Silicon Valley? Innovation in Russia," *Economist*, July 14, 2012; Oliver Staley, "For MIT the Launch of a Russian Satellite," *Washington Post*, May 12, 2013.

21. "Skolkovo Foundation and MIT to Collaborate on Developing the Skolkovo Institute of Science and Technology," October 26, 2011, ww.mit.edu.

22. Oliver Staley, "For MIT the Launch of a Russian Satellite," *Washington Post*, May 12, 2013.

23. "Can Russia Create a New Silicon Valley? Innovation in Russia," *Economist*, July 14, 2012.

24. Andrew E. Kramer, "Innovation, By Order of the Kremlin," *New York Times*, April 11, 2010.

25. Ibid.

26. Chrystina Freeland, "The Next Russian Revolution," *Atlantic*, October 2011.

27. Will Bland, "Innovation on Demand; Russia Is Trying to Build Its Very Own Version of Silicon Valley," *Wall Street Journal*, June 16, 2010.

28. Andrew E. Kramer, "Innovation, By Order of the Kremlin," *New York Times*, April 11, 2010.

29. Chrystina Freeland, "The Next Russian Revolution," *Atlantic*, October 2011; "Medvedev Ups the Tempo of Change; the Russian President Wants His Country to Attain Greater Heights," *Wall Street Journal*, June 16, 2010.

30. Chrystina Freeland, "The Next Russian Revolution," *Atlantic*, October 2011; "Medvedev Ups the Tempo of Change; the Russian President Wants His Country to Attain Greater Heights," *Wall Street Journal*, June 16, 2010.

31. Kathy Lally, "Medvedev, iPad in Hand, Tries to Stress High-Tech at News Conference," *Washington Post*," May 19, 2011; Sergei Loiko, "Russian Leader Fetes Schwarzenegger; Medvedev, Seeking Economic and Tech Ties, Take Him to a Silicon Valley-Type Hub He's Planning," *Los Angeles Times*, October 12, 2010.

32. Michael Schwirtz, "Russia Asks Schwarzenegger to Help in a Tough Task," *New York Times*, October 12, 2010.

33. "Political Priority, Economic Gamble: Special Economic Zones," *Economist*, April 4, 2015.

34. "The South China Miracle: A Great Leap Forward," *Economist*, 1991.

35. "China Throws Open Its Seaboard," *Economist*, March 12, 1988.

36. Fialka, *War by Other Means*, 22.

37. *A Progress Report: Hearing before the U.S. China Economic and Security Review Commission*, 112th Cong. 90 (2012).

38. Springut, Schlaikjeer, and Chen, *China's Program for Science and Technology Modernization*, 38.

39. "Gone but Not Forgotten: Diasporas," *Economist*, June 27, 2015.

40. Robert D. Atkinson, *Enough Is Enough: Confronting Chinese Innovation Mercantilism* (Washington, D.C.: Information Technology and Innovation Foundation, 2012), 8.

41. *Assessing China's Efforts to become an "Innovation Society": A Progress Report. Hearing before the U.S. China Economic and Security Review Commission*, 112th Cong. 90 (2012).

42. Springut, Schlaikjeer, and Chen, *China's Program for Science and Technology Modernization*, 89–90.

43. Fialka, *War by Other Means*, 32.

44. Atkinson, *Enough Is Enough*, 33.

45. Ibid., 34.

46. Robin Respault and Rory Carroll, "China May Have Edge in Race to Build California's Bullet Train," *Reuters*, May 21, 2015.

47. Michael Fitzpatrick, "Did China Steal Japan's High-Speed Train?" www.wsjonline.com (accessed July 12, 2015).

48. *2014 Report to Congress of the U.S. China Economic and Security Review Commission*, 113th Cong. 299 (2014).

49. Dennis C. Shea. "The Impact of International Technology Transfer on American Research and Development before the Committee on Science, Space, and

Technology Subcommittee on Investigations and Oversight, United States House of Representatives," December 5, 2012.

50. Atkinson, *Enough Is Enough*, 8.

51. Ibid., 34.

52. *2014 Report to Congress of the U.S. China Economic and Security Review Commission*, 113th Cong. 298 (2014).

53. *2007 Report to Congress of the U.S. China Economic and Security Review Commission*, 110th Cong. 165 (2007).

54. *2014 Report to Congress of the U.S. China Economic and Security Review Commission*, 113th Cong. 201 (2014).

55. Ibid., 202.

56. "The IP Commission Report," 41.

57. Atkinson, *Enough Is Enough*, 40.

58. Ibid., 39.

59. Springut, Schlaikjeer, and Chen, *China's Program for Science and Technology Modernization*, 88.

60. *Report to Congress of the U.S. China Economic and Security Review Commission*, 113th Cong. 165 (2014).

61. Springut, Schlaikjeer, and Chen, *China's Program for Science and Technology Modernization*, 89.

62. Ibid., 100.

63. Ibid., 99.

64. Ibid., 100.

65. Ibid., 52.

66. Ben Wildavsky, *The Great Brain Race: How Global Universities Are Reshaping the World* (Princeton, NJ: Princeton University Press, 2010), 83.

67. Melissa Korn, "Microsoft Brings U.S. and China Universities Together," *Wall Street Journal*, June 19, 2015.

68. Iacob Koch-Weser and Garland Ditz, *Chinese Investment in the United States: Recent Trends in Real Estate, Industry, and Investment Promotion* (Washington, D.C.: U.S. China Economic and Security Review Commission, 2015), 24.

69. Bryan Krekel, Patton Adams, and George Bakos, *Occupying the Information High Ground: Chinese Capabilities for Computer Network Operations and Cyber Espionage* (Washington, D.C.: U.S. China Economic and Security Review Commission, 2012), 60.

70. Ibid., 59.

71. Edward Wong, "Hacking U.S. Secrets, China Pushes for Drones," *New York Times*, September 20, 2013.

72. *2007 Report to Congress of the U.S. China Economic and Security Review Commission*, 110th Cong. 132 (2007).

73. *Soviet Acquisition of Military Significant Western Technology: An Update*, 21.

74. Brian D. Dailey and Patrick J. Parker, eds., *Soviet Strategic Deception* (Lexington, MA: Lexington Books, 1987), 30.

75. Wildavsky, *The Great Brain Race*, 81.

76. Ibid., 81.

77. Christopher Drew, "New Spy Game," *New York Times*, October 18, 2010.

78. Springut, Schlaikjeer, and Chen, *China's Program for Science and Technology Modernization*, 38.

79. *Assessing China's Efforts to Become an "Innovation Society": A Progress Report. Hearing before the U.S. China Economic and Security Review Commission*, 112th Cong. 78 (2012).

80. Ibid., 132.

81. Wildavsky, *The Great Brain Race*, 72–73.

82. Richard P. Suttmeier, *Trends in U.S. China Science and Cooperation: Collaborative Knowledge Production for the Twenty-First Century?* (Washington, D.C.: U.S. China Economic and Security Review Commission, 2014), 39.

83. *Assessing China's Efforts to Become an "Innovation Society": A Progress Report. Hearing before the U.S. China Economic and Security Review Commission*, 112th Cong. 87 (2012).

84. Ibid., 90.

85. Suttmeier, *Trends in U.S. China Science and Cooperation*, 39.

86. *2014 Report to Congress of the U.S. China Economic and Security Review Commission*, 113th Cong. 10 (2014).

87. Ibid., 197.

88. Fialka, *War by Other Means*, 58.

89. Vindu Goel, "Narendra Modi, Indian Premier, Courts Silicon Valley to Try to Ease Nation's Poverty," *New York Times*, September 27, 2015.

90. Office of the National Counterintelligence Executive, *Annual Report to Congress on Foreign Economic Collection and Industrial Espionage: 2005* (Office of the National Counterintelligence Executive, 2006).

91. U.S. Trade Representative, *2015 Special 301 Report*, 48.

92. Defense Security Service, *Targeting U.S. Technology: A Trend Analysis of Cleared Industry Reporting* (2014), 65.

Chapter Five

Selling Out

Part II

When foreign actors invest (or follow the investment paradigm), they commit capital—whether money or intelligence resources—to accessing entities on U.S. soil. They control the process from the outset—when they opt to target an entity—to the exploitation of knowledge gained from that entity. However, foreign entities have also benefited from the desire of U.S. entities, whether individuals, companies, and even elements of government to engage, either for profit or politics. Illicit exploitation of this dynamic may occur in two ways. The first is the case of corporations or other entities that establish a presence abroad that foreign entities can target on their own turf to acquire information. Individuals who choose to engage in the illegal sale of technology or information based on the motives previously discussed provide another conduit for innovation to travel from its originators and rightful possessors to unauthorized actors. Foreign governments can encourage (that is, recruit) volunteers by offering incentives, such as specific business opportunities or less quantifiable measures such as appeals to an individual's misplaced sense of loyalty and duty. Although foreign actors' use of perception management is the topic for another book, it is worth noting that incentives must be advertised in some way (for example, the attempt to portray outward direct investment by U.S. companies as an opportunity for profit, the creation of cultural or ideological solidarity that can be played upon, etc.) before a volunteer will respond.

There are several categories of illicit activities that fit within the context of U.S. entities reaching outward, physically or virtually, to do business with foreign entities. Individuals may establish new platforms abroad, contributing to a state or nonstate actor's physical resources. Individuals may travel abroad temporarily to provide assistance. U.S. industry, in doing business with foreign entities, may be susceptible to exploitation through providing services as well as through visiting contractors, as both scenarios give foreign actors a point of access. A particularly susceptible venue for businesses seeking to connect with foreign clients who may, in turn, be interested in obtaining proprietary information are trade shows and other industry events. These provide a buffet of options for individuals who are collecting information on behalf of foreign governments, an environment that is characterized by an interest in engagement (sellers meet buyers) and opportunities for anonymity.

Front companies and related concepts fit within this paradigm because they rely on being perceived as U.S. companies, rather than as foreign-sponsored investments. These serve two purposes. The first and most widely recognized use is as a façade to facilitate the transfer and hide the ultimate destination of restricted technology. Additionally, foreign entities may employ sham companies in the United States to siphon human capital from U.S. industry. These sham companies hire individuals who possess proprietary knowledge and seek to employ it to compete with the U.S. firm and to contribute to foreign countries' overall capacity for innovation.

EXAMPLES OF FOREIGN-DIRECTED
INNOVATION EXFILTRATION

A subset of targeting against foreign companies doing business abroad is the use of joint ventures to obtain sensitive information. U.S. industry reporting from FY2013 indicated that East Asia and Pacific region state-owned enterprises exploited partnerships with cleared companies in furtherance of obtaining unauthorized access to U.S. information and technology.[1] Specifically, according to U.S. intelligence, community reporting joint ventures were pursued as a vector through which to obtain sensitive aerospace information.[2] (This is an especially problematic issue because East Asia and the Pacific region producers of commercial aircraft, which work with the U.S. commercial aerospace industry, regularly share personnel and research with government entities.[3]) As former FBI agent I. C. Smith explained to Congress in 2009, "If you're going to have Chinese nationals in [a factory built by a foreign company in China] you're going to lose something."[4] The problem is not limited to East Asia and the Pacific region. DSS has assessed that governments in the Europe and Eurasia region would encourage joint commercial ventures that would provide opportunities for foreign collectors to exploit cleared contractors.[5]

Furthermore, companies doing business with entities abroad may be at risk from manipulation and exploitation by foreign government interests masquerading as commercial concerns. For instance, IBM's Chinese partners include Beijing-based Teamsun Technology Company. Shen Changxiang, the individual primarily responsibility for managing the relationship between the two companies, is a cyber warfare specialist who was previously employed by the PLA.[6] An individual with this background would be well positioned to exploit a relationship built around information technology transfer to fill gaps and to help China assess U.S. capabilities. Other IBM customers in China have business interests in the PLA, the MSS, and multiple Chinese government ministries.[7]

Individuals employed by U.S. entities have engaged in activities to benefit foreign governments by misappropriating technology (and the knowledge that it represents). Xiaodong Sheldon Meng was sentenced in June 2008 for providing a trade secret from his former employer, Quantum3D Inc., to the PRC Navy Research Center.[8] The technology that Meng provided included the source code for a visual simulation software program intended for training both commercial and military fighter pilots.[9] Not only did he sell the software, but he also installed it on the Chinese computers and attempted to alter it so that it would appear as though the Chinese had developed the software.[10] China's gain via Meng's economic espionage is consistent with the previously discussed trend of acquiring graphics and simulation capabilities and is a demonstration of how foreign governments use multiple channels—licit and illicit—to acquire capabilities.

China has also been the intended recipient of agricultural research. In December 2011, Kexue Huang, a Chinese national, was sentenced for economic espionage after stealing trade secrets from DowAgroSciences and providing them to researchers.[11] Huang's intention was to use the stolen materials to engage in unauthorized research that would benefit universities that were instrumentalities of the Chinese government.[12] His ability to share information with China was facilitated by his acceptance of a job as a visiting professor at a Chinese university.[13] Backed by Chinese government grants from China's National Natural Science Foundation, Huang ultimately intended to start a business in China based on the purloined information and attempted to identify manufacturing facilities in China for this endeavor.[14] Additionally, after leaving Dow, Huang took a position with Cargill as a biotechnologist. While employed by that company, he stole a trade secret pertaining to the manufacture of a new food product, which he provided to a student at Hunan Normal University.[15]

Agricultural innovation was also the target of another incident of Chinese collection. In May 2011, Mo Hailong and Wang Lei were caught digging up a DuPont research farm in Iowa. Mo and his associates had visited numerous seed-testing fields that large agriculture companies used. Additionally, Zhang Weiqiang and Yan Wengui (who was affiliated with the U.S. Department of

Agriculture) allegedly traveled to China where they discussed—with Chinese scientists—research they had performed in the United States. Zhang and Yan also arranged for a delegation from the Chinese Academy of Agricultural Science and the Crop Research Institute in China to travel to the United States. Members of this delegation were discovered attempting to smuggle proprietary rice seeds out of the United States.[16]

Consistent with China's demonstrated desires in the field of transportation technology, multiple examples of theft against U.S. companies have demonstrated that Beijing is willing to complement any overt activities with clandestine collection. According to a 2011 Department of Justice report, Xiang Dong Yu, a product engineer with Ford, copied thousands of Ford documents, including sensitive design information, onto an external hard drive with the intent of supplying them to the Beijing Automotive Company.[17] In 2013, the DOJ reported that Shanshan Du and her husband, Yu Qin, copied more than fifteen thousand General Motors files to an external hard drive and used it to provide hybrid vehicle technology to a China-based automotive company.[18]

RETURNEES TO CHINA
POSSESSING PROPRIETARY INFORMATION

China poses a particular problem in the area of innovation transfer. It has endeavored to coopt the worldwide Chinese diaspora as a means of collection and influence. Furthermore, it has attempted to develop affinities for Chinese culture that could be leveraged to promote divided loyalties through initiatives such as its Confucius Centers. China has also made a significant effort not simply to collect information, but rather to encourage the emigration of talent from the United States to China. The following examples illustrate how these factors can inspire the theft of proprietary information as a means to enhance an individual's opportunities in China.

Multiple individuals in the U.S. private sector have stolen information of value to innovation with the intent of returning to China with it. David Yen Lee, a chemist with the Valspar Corporation, began stealing paint formulas in 2008; at the time of his arrest in 2009, the approximately 160 proprietary formulas for paints and coatings that he had downloaded from the company's computer system were valued at USD $20 million.[19] Lee planned to take this information with him to a new job that he had accepted as vice president of technology and administrator of research and development with Nippon Paint in Shanghai.[20] Hanjian Jin was another example of an individual who traded on her access in the United States to obtain sensitive corporate information that she could then use in furtherance of a career in China. In 2006, Jin took a leave of absence from her job at Motorola and returned to China, where she went to work for Sun Kaisens on projects for the Chinese military.[21] She returned to Motorola in early 2007, only to turn around and attempt to leave the United States on a one-way ticket with more than one thousand documents.[22] This incident was just one of Motorola's unfortunate encounters with China, which also included the previously discussed theft of information by Huawei.

Chinese academic institutions, in addition to industry (although both contribute to the government's capabilities), are beneficiaries of defections. In mid-2009, Hong Meng, who was employed by the DuPont Corporation, downloaded sensitive information about organic light-emitting diodes, which he intended to transfer to Peking University, College of Engineering, Department of Nanotechnology, where he had obtained a faculty position. Meng also sought Chinese government funding to commercialize the research that he had stolen from DuPont.[23] Meng conducted his theft from DuPont through multiple conduits, including emailing his Peking University account with the protected chemical process from his DuPont computer, downloading the chemical process from his DuPont computer to a thumb drive, and obtaining 109 samples of DuPont intermediate chemical compounds that he enlisted a colleague at Northwestern University to send to him in China.[24]

TEMPORARY DEFECTION: CLANDESTINE PROVISION OF ASSISTANCE TO FOREIGN GOVERNMENTS AND OTHER ENTITIES DURING VISITS ABROAD

Foreign governments have used invitations to experts in specific fields to provide presentations on technologies of interest—which provide opportunities for collection. As noted previously, China obtained information about the U.S. space shuttle in this manner. Another example of this tradecraft was the case of Sixing Liu, an employee of L-3 Communications. Liu, in addition to stealing thousands of electronic files, including information about the performance and design of guidance systems for missiles, rockets, target locators, and UAVs, delivered presentations at multiple Chinese universities, the Chinese Academy of Sciences, and Chinese government-organized conferences.[25] His intention, at least in part, was to position himself for employment in China.[26] This corresponds with China's efforts to effect the relocation of human capital with desired skills and knowledge. Gwo Bao Min, an aerospace engineer who was employed by the U.S. Department of Energy's Lawrence Livermore Laboratory and who possessed a Q clearance, delivered a number of lectures in China and consented to answer question from Chinese government scientists.[27] Peter Lee, a contractor for Lawrence Livermore who had previously worked at Los Alamos National Laboratory, traveled to China in 1997 at the expense of the Chinese Institute of Applied Physics and Computational Mathematics.[28] According to DSS, Lee shared classified information during lectures he delivered while in China, both in 1997 and earlier in 1985.[29] Dongfan Chung, discussed in a previous chapter, traveled to China on multiple occasions between 1985 and 2003 to give lectures on topics including the U.S. space shuttle.[30]

Like Meng and Liu, Noshir Gowadia assisted China at least in part through physical travel to that country. Gowadia, who was an engineer for the Northrop Grumman Corporation between 1968 and 1986, provided classified knowledge of military design technologies and between 2003 and 2005 took six trips to China during which he provided defense services that involved design, test support, and test data analysis of technologies to assist China's cruise missile system.[31] Gowadia was charged with providing the PRC with designs for a low-signature cruise missile exhaust system capable of rendering a PRC cruise missile resistant to detection by infrared missiles.[32] Gowadia also communicated classified information regarding lock-on range for infrared missiles against the U.S. B-2 bomber and exporting classified information about the B-2.[33]

Another example of individuals providing illegal assistance to China on technology issues came to light in 2010 with the arrest of David Zhang and his wife, Leping Hunag, the owners of California-based company General Technology Systems Integration (GTSI), based on charges that GTSI had entered into contracts with the Twenty-Fourth Research Institute of the China Electronic Technology Corporation Group to design two types of high-performance analog-to-digital converters for the PRC. In furtherance of this, GTSI hired two engineers to design the technology and provide training in China.[34]

FRONT COMPANIES

A more complex effort to acquire technology, often of a restricted nature, is the use of a front company (or a legitimate company that also engages in front company–like activities). During the Cold War, the Soviet Union directed the establishment of a network of Bulgarian front companies that were set up to acquire Western technology.[35] Countries may also position themselves to be approached by unscrupulous brokers. For instance, the Soviet Ministry of Foreign Trade and its industrial ministries operated foreign trade organizations, commercial offices, joint companies, and foreign procurement offices staffed with individuals that knew the hardware markets and were poised to engage with technology traders and diverters, as well as spotting opportunities for diversions of controlled technologies.[36] Emphasizing the theme of this book—that licit and illicit collection are not distinct but fluid—the Soviet organizations responsible for diversion were staffed by legitimate soviet trade officials, intelligence officers under trade official cover, and trade officials who were cooperating with intelligence officers.[37] As of 2005, according to the FBI, China had approximately three thousand front companies operating in the United States.[38]

Two Chinese front company cases, Bin Wu and Chai-Wai Tsu, illustrate that multiple Chinese intelligence and military entities benefit from the use of front companies. Wu established multiple front companies in Norfolk, Virginia, which he and at least two other PRC nationals solicited technology, including third-generation night vision equipment, from U.S. companies.[39] Wu then forwarded the item to China's MSS through intermediaries in Hong Kong.[40] In another instance, a Chinese front company operating in the United States functioned to provide the Chinese government with aerospace technology. Chai-Wai Tsu, an employee of a Beijing military contracting company called Dimigit, also served as the vice president of the California-based front company Cheerway Inc.[41] Tsu exported in excess of four hundred restricted integrated circuits with applications in military radar systems, many of which he purchased from U.S. distributors with the false assurances that he was not exporting them.[42] In reality, Tsu supplied restricted technology to entities including the "704 Research Institute" (a.k.a. the Aerospace Long March Rocket Technology Company), which is affiliated with the China Aerospace and Technology Corporation.[43]

China has also benefited from questionable to illicit practices of companies operating in the United States. In 2008, Virginia-based WaveLab was sentenced for exporting controlled power amplifiers to China after purchasing these items from U.S. companies with the assurance that they would not be sent abroad. In 2008, Qing Li was sentenced for conspiring with an individual in China to locate and procure thirty accelerometers that have military applications for "smart" bombs and missile development as well as calibrating the g-forces of nuclear and chemical explosions for a scientific agency in China. In 2009, Michael Ming Zhang, the president of J. J. Electronics, a California-based firm, was charged with exporting dual-use electronic items to China. Zhang's China-centric business also allegedly imported and sold approximately 4,300 Cisco electronics components bearing counterfeit marks from China.[44] In 2009, Shu Quan-Sheng, a Chinese-born naturalized U.S. citizen who was the president, secretary, and treasurer of AMAC International, a company with offices in both Virginia Beach, Virginia, and Beijing, was sentenced for illegally exporting space launch technical data and defense services to the PRC. Shu provided the PRC with assistance on the design and development of a cryogenic fueling system for space launch vehicles. Sam Ching Sheng Lee, part owner and chief operations manager of Multimillion Business Associate Corporation (MBA), an import-export company, pled guilty to illegally exporting national security–controlled thermal imaging cameras to China. Lee, using MBA, exported the cameras to entities in China, including a company in Shanghai that was engaged in the development of infrared technology. Jason Jian Liang, the owner and operator of Sanware International, a California-based company, pled guilty to the illegal export of thermal imaging cameras to China. Fu-Tain Lu, the owner and founder of California-based Fushine Technology Inc., was sentenced in 2012 for selling sensitive microwave amplifiers to Everjet Science and Technology Corporation in the PRC. In 2013, Philip Chaohui He, a Chinese citizen, was sentenced for exporting radiation-hardened circuits to China while attempting to bring the circuits aboard a Chinese ship in Long Beach, California. He was the only employee of Sierra Electronic Instruments, an Oakland, California, company through which He arranged for the purchase of more than three hundred radiation-hardened circuits from a Colorado-based company (and assured that the items would not be exported).[45] Proliferation of sensitive technology is a demonstrably consistent threat activity that hides behind the trappings and practices of international commerce, rather than traditional intelligence tradecraft.

China is not the only country that has benefited from U.S.-based companies willing to engage in illegal commerce. Russia and its Soviet predecessor have both used front companies to obtain sensitive technology. In 1983, the Belgium government expelled six Russians and Romanians after discovering that an electronics company was in actuality a front for collection of technology.[46] Almost three decades later, the FBI broke up a Russian procurement network that used the Houston, Texas–based Arc Electronics to obtain cutting-edge microelectronics from U.S. manufacturers and illegally export them to Russian entities.[47] The items—including analog-to-digital converters, static random access memory chips, microcontrollers, and microprocessors—have a wide variety of military applications.[48] Alexander Fishenko, the president and chief executive officer of Apex, is also a part owner of the Russian Apex Systems LLC, which is a certified supplier of military equipment for the Russian government.[49] The FBI was able to identify that Russia's internal security service, the FSB, obtained microchips from Arc.[50]

Iran has collaborated directly with individuals in the United States to obtain proprietary information. In 2009, Ali Amirnazmi, a dual U.S./Iranian citizen who resided in Pennsylvania, was convicted for conspiracy to violate the International Emergency Economic Powers Act. Amirnazmi and his company, Trantech Consultants, engaged in illegal business transactions with companies controlled by the government of Iran, and Amirnazmi worked at the express direction of the highest level of the Iranian government, including Mahmoud Ahmadinejad, to advance the Iranian petrochemical industry.[51] Among multiple actions, he licensed software to Iranian companies that was designed to help buyers locate the best prices for chemicals internationally.[52]

THE THIRD-COUNTRY CONUNDRUM

The vulnerabilities to businesses doing business abroad are made more complex by foreign entities' use of third countries to hide their involvement in efforts to acquire knowledge. Such exploitation occurs in two ways. The first is a foreign entity from a third country attempting to collect against a U.S. corporation's international presence in a second country (for example, a U.S. company establishes a factory in country X, which country Y attempts to infiltrate because it is easier than infiltrating the U.S. company's presence in the United States). The Soviet Union, according to a 1985 U.S. government report, took advantage of co-production agreements and contract bidding by foreign firms that resulted in significant technology being present abroad to seek U.S. technologies that were a priority target for collection in multiple countries, rather than needing to operate in the United States.[53] Foreign actors may also attempt to purchase restricted items through a third country–based straw purchaser that is not subject to restrictions. (A variation of the straw company in a third-country approach is a foreign entity's cooperation with a U.S.-based freight forwarder that provides the foreign recipients with a U.S. address.[54] In this scenario, a U.S. company with a sensitive item will believe it is sending it to a U.S. address when, ultimately, the item will be sent onward to a country that is subject to restrictions.)

Use of straw purchases is usually associated with foreign governments against which the United States has enacted restrictions for various reasons. For instance, in 2009, DHS's Immigration and Customs Enforcement determined that a Canadian/Iranian citizen who was being tasked by an Iranian handler had requested pressure transducers from a U.S. company.[55] Iran also attempted to obtain GPS engines and a peak power meter via transshipment through Singapore, according to a 2013 DSS report.[56] The trail grows even more complicated when multiple countries are involved. In a 2011 report to Congress, the Department of Commerce identified an attempt to export aircraft parts to Iran via Singapore and Malaysia.[57] Another individual attempted to export aircraft parts to Iran but this time via the United Arab Emirates (a common transshipment point for such activities) and France.[58] There are indications that foreign entities may strategically select third countries from which to target U.S. interests. According a 2014 DSS report, collectors from other regions often use front companies that operate in the western hemisphere.[59] Therefore, according to DSS, many of the incidents of western hemisphere entities requesting sensitive information are actually driven by third-country actors.[60]

Iran has repeatedly orchestrated and used front companies in third countries to obtain restricted technology. In 2006, Jamshid Ghassemi, an officer in the Iranian Air Force, was indicted as part of an effort to obtain twelve Honeywell military accelerometers and gyroscopes from an individual in the United States that would be shipped to Romania and transshipped to Iran.[61] In 2013, the Iranian company Business Machinery World Wide (BMWW) as well as various subsidiaries and business partners was indicted for the illegal export of computer equipment from the United States to Iran.[62] BMWW began soliciting computer parts from the United States in 2008. To hide the destination of the components, BMWW directed that the U.S. goods be shipped to its UAE subsidiaries, which, according to the U.S. DOJ, "were created solely to illicitly transship the U.S. goods to Iran and evade the export embargo."[63] While these examples demonstrate that Iranian entities are actively engaged in circuitous routing in furtherance of subterfuge, Iran benefits from other instances of individuals routing contraband through third countries. For instance, between 2002 and 2005 Mohammad Reza Vaghari operated the Pennsylvania-based Saamen Company through which he purchased items from U.S. companies and then routed to Iran via the UAE. Among the items that Vaghari transmitted or attempted to transmit in this manner were a centrifuge, fuel cell systems, ultrasonic liquid processors, and laboratory equipment.[64] Jirair Avanessian, owner of the California-based XVAC, was sentenced in 2011 for arranging to provide Iran with vacuum pumps that have applications for uranium enrichment via the UAE.[65]

The Soviet Union made repeated use of acquisitions via third-country companies. For instance, in 1983 a West German citizen attempted to divert several Digital Equipment Corporation VAZ super minicomputers to the Soviet Union. These would have helped the Soviets to engage in computer-aided design and applications for microelectronics fabrication.[66] According to a congressional report, the Soviets' overall program of trade diversion had as of the mid-1980s reduced the Western technological lead from approximately ten to twelve years, where it had been a decade previously, to approximately five to six years.[67]

There are also instances of countries that have acquired technology re-exporting those capabilities. China, which had gained expertise through the project that it contracted with Westinghouse, provided assistance to

Pakistan's nuclear program as of 2012. The China Nuclear Industry Huaxing Construction Co., Ltd. conspired to export high-performance epoxy paint, certified as meeting "Level 1" nuclear industry standards, for use in the reactor and core of a PAEC-owned and -controlled nuclear power plant. The PAEC is a BIS-listed entity.[68] Furthermore, China's drone program appears to owe at least some of its development to U.S. innovation. In 2013, it displayed its Wing Loong drone at the Paris Air Show—the first display of a Chinese armed UAV at an international defense exhibition—and, as of that year, China was entertaining interest in purchasing the technology from six African and Asian countries.[69]

Countries to which the United States sells technology may prove careless about preventing its acquisition by third countries that are of concern to Washington. According to a 2014 U.S. government report, Near East governments with access to U.S. technology have a history of transferring sensitive U.S. technology to countries of concern, without obtaining U.S. permission.[70] Even when not actively transferring technology, those Near East governments have shown a low willingness to protect the technology against exploitation and diversion.[71] Those governments' relationship and likeliness to continue cooperating with third-country governments in proliferating U.S. technology is indicated by Near East commercial efforts to acquire U.S. technology specifically on behalf of third parties.[72] The United States had experienced similar problems with European and Eurasian governments that have a "low willingness to safeguard U.S. technology and information acquired."[73] Similar thinking is apparent in Soviet targeting of Israel, following the 1973 Yom Kippur War, to gain information about U.S. weapons used by the Israeli army.[74]

A spin on the problem of third-country acquisition is when illicit collectors of country A collect illicitly from collectors of country B, who in turn acquired items clandestinely from country C. This convoluted progression of technology occurred during the Cold War, when Russians cultivated Japanese collectors of U.S. technology. The Russians, according to John Fialka, discovered their job to be relatively simple because the Japanese collectors tended to care little about the items once they had reached Tokyo.[75] Countries known to collect against the United States either licitly or illicitly could also do business with third countries that the United States has sanctioned. Israel, for instance, was identified by the CIA as one of the countries engaged in economic collection against the United States. Israel, as indicated by its sale of one hundred Harpy drones to China in the 1990s, is less discriminating about which countries it does business with and will do so despite U.S. protestations, as indicated by the Pentagon's request that the China-bound Harpy drones not be upgraded.[76]

PRETENSE PURCHASES: FOREIGN ENTITIES'
USE OF BUSINESS TRANSACTIONS AS OPPORTUNITIES
TO ACCESS AND EXPLOIT U.S. INDUSTRY

Foreign actors attracted by services premised on advanced technology may exploit relationships with U.S. companies through which they can illicitly acquire proprietary knowledge and technology. Shan Yan Ming, a Chinese national employee of PetroChina who was receiving training on software by its California-based developer, 3DGeo Development Inc., illegally down-loaded the source code for the software, a powerful tool for locating oil and gas deposits, transferred it to his laptop, and was attempting to leave the country with it when he was arrested at San Francisco International Airport.[77] This case illustrates U.S. companies' willingness to accept the risks in dealing with China despite their awareness that Beijing employs less-than-legal tactics. 3DGeo had instructed its employees to maintain awareness about Shan's activities, as two years prior another PetroChina employee had entered the company's offices on a weekend and accessed the company's computer net-work without permission.[78] However, the private sector's willingness to court risk not only imperils its own interests but it may also have the potential to shift the balance of national power between countries.

The U.S. government's provision of opportunities to Chinese researchers and its encouragement of U.S. entities in the academic and commercial sectors to do similarly has resulted in losses. The U.S. Department of State acknowledged that the 1979 U.S.–China Agreement on Cooperation in Science and Technology, the cornerstone of cooperation in the field of innovation, may have produced an unintended side effect of bleedover of U.S. knowledge into China's military sector.[79] Consistent with this, multiple U.S. agencies have expressed concerns that China has targeted specific laboratories and fields of study for cooperation.[80] It is unclear how the U.S. government could avoid thinking that this would happen, given China's longstanding application of civilian technology to military capabilities.

A related problem to cooperation is the concept of deemed export—the provision of information that would normally be restricted from export to a specific country to nationals of that country while they are in the United States. The provision of services can be a route to this, as demonstrated by the case of Lattice Semiconductor Corporation, which between 2000 and 2002 released controlled technology to Chinese nationals who were in the United States for technical training.[81] Employment of foreign nationals provides another opportunity for deemed export violations. Intevac provided national security–controlled technology made by a U.S. company to a Russian national employee in the United States.[82] This can also occur in the academic realm. University of Tennessee professor Reece Roth employed Chinese and Iranian students on plasma research that he was conducting on a classified U.S. Air Force project that specifically stipulated that foreign nationals could not participate.[83] Such issues could continue to be a problem for academia, as institutions have demonstrated opposition to restrictions on deemed exports. When the U.S. government attempted to amend requirements surrounding deemed exports, the Department of Commerce was deluged by letters from professors who feared that such changes would cripple their research due to their dependence on foreign students.[84]

COUNTERINTELLIGENCE CONCERNS
FOR TRADE SHOWS AND INDUSTRY EVENTS

Trade shows and industry events provide foreign intelligence services and other threat actors with unique opportunities to collect against sensitive information. Trade shows, particularly in areas of cutting-edge civilian and military technology, provide a perfect storm of technology, company representatives who are eager to sell the technology, and attendees who are present specifically to become familiar with that information. This provides an environment in which foreign intelligence operatives can assess the technology, as well as the personnel with access to it. In fact, they are encouraged to do so. Similarly, industry and professional events are often characterized by participants' desire to demonstrate their proficiency in an area of expertise and who will readily share information. Foreign state and nonstate intelligence collectors—whether through formal intelligence services or competing industries—can exploit this collegial environment to elicit data of specific interest.

Targeting Trade and Industry Events: An Established Intelligence Methodology

Foreign governments' and their respective intelligence services' practice of targeting trade and industry conferences is well established. According to a 1985 U.S. government report, the Soviet Union in the late 1970s identified at least thirty-five conferences internationally that could provide information of value to military research problems.[85] Furthermore, the Soviets judged some of this information to be among the most significant contributions to the various military projects.[86] For instance, targeting an international radar conference by Soviet military intelligence (the GRU) led to improved circuit design for synthetic aperture satellite radars and aircraft over-the-horizon radar.[87] On the civilian side, the Soviet KGB's attention to a conference on integrated optics assisted with identifying ways to produce a new category of Soviet-integrated optical devices for fiber optics communications.[88] Events that Soviet military and civilian intelligence agencies targeted included the Conference on Integrated Optics, the International Conference on Radar, the Conference of the Aerospace and Electronic Systems Society of IEEE, the International Conference on Nontraditional Energy Transformation Systems, the Conference on Millimetric and Submillimetric Equipment, and the Symposium on Solar Energy Convention.[89] Individuals from the Soviet Academy of Sciences, who were usually not allowed to travel abroad unless they agreed to assist the KGB, traveled to the United States to attend conferences at which they could determine the nature of research being conducted for military applications as well as the individuals and companies doing the research.[90] Such collection not only identified technology but also potentially channels through which it could be procured in the future through the recruitment of individuals with access.

Present-Day Indicators of Intent to Target Trade Shows and Conferences

Conferences have consistently been venues in which foreign governments and their proxies have targeted U.S. information and technology. The appeal for foreign collectors is obvious because these events bring together a concentrated group of specialists in a given field.[91] In 2013, Near East collection entities (for example, intelligence services) tasked Near East companies to collect specific information and technologies associated with U.S. companies at defense conferences.[92] During an annual armed service–related convention, two East Asia and the Pacific individuals—one of whom was known to have represented a foreign government–affiliated institution—queried an employee of a cleared contractor about micro-air vehicles.[93] According to the National Counterintelligence Executive, the audiences at international technically oriented events are often experts whose level of technical understanding and ability to exploit the intelligence they collect potentially make them more of a threat than the traditional intelligence officers.[94]

Tradecraft Employed by Foreign Entities to Exploit Opportunities for Collection at Trade and Industry Events

There have been multiple specific instances of foreign collection activities in the midst of these events. During a 2013 unmanned aerial vehicle (UAV) conference, an individual from a company in the Near East region dropped three pages that contained instructions for collectors on which companies to target, what information to obtain and report, and how to do so.[95] Collectors were to attend relevant events, take photographs, obtain copies of presentations, clarify terms, and collect product lists, brochures, and advertising materials.[96] On another occasion, foreign collectors dipped their ties into a photo processing solution that was on display, presumably to obtain a sample that could be analyzed and reverse engineered later.[97] According to the National Counterintelligence Executive, another standard collection tactic involves stealing exhibitors' technical reference manuals.[98] In addition to direct approaches to vendors, foreign entities may benefit from sidebar conversations.[99] For instance, Chi Mak, who was convicted of providing U.S. defense information to China, had received instructions from his handler to engage in networking through professional associations and conferences.[100] Additionally, Evgeny Buryakov, an officer of the Russian SVR's Directorate ER (which collects economic intelligence) who was working under nonofficial cover as part of a Russian bank office, attended a trade association conference. He used the event as an opportunity to gather information during confidential meetings.[101] Informal conversations among experts can become detailed to the point of inadvertently communicating information that might not be releasable due to export controls.

Photography and visual media provide an opportunity for passive collection that foreign intelligence services and other entities can subsequently analyze. Clandestine filming of equipment is a standard collection technique.[102] Chinese nationals were observed videotaping every static display and taking accompanying notes during an international arms exhibit. The group also stole a videocassette that showed the U.S. Theater High Altitude Air Defense System when the DoD contractor left it unattended.[103]

An additional HUMINT problem is the level of expertise present at such events. Rather than intelligence officers, international gatherings can attract the leading scientific and technical experts from their respective countries. These scientists and technical experts often work directly on their home countries' sensitive projects and were consequently familiar with the knowledge that was still needed to successfully complete a given endeavor.[104] This makes them more effective than intelligence officers because they are not only capable of collecting information but also of analyzing its applicability and value.[105]

The Role of Trade and Industry Events in Complex Targeting Operations

Foreign operatives may use trade shows as opportunities to spot information on which they will follow up later. According to the National

Counterintelligence Center, international technical and academic conferences provide an opportunity to assess experts in a specific field of interest.[106] Foreign personnel using these events as a starting point for future exploitation may collect membership lists of international business and technical executives, as these compilations are increasingly used to identify potential U.S. targets.[107] Additionally, registration forms usually require biographic details about individuals—including data about corporate experience and areas of expertise, which can be useful in assessing an individual as a potential recruit.[108] Foreign operatives may also use contacts established through conferences, as well as through membership in professional organizations, to broker visits by foreign collectors.[109]

An example of a foreign actor's follow-up involved a representative of a Europe- and Eurasia-region company who approached a representative of a U.S. company and indicated interest in purchasing certain computer chips that were export controlled. The representative of the Europe- and Eurasia-region company subsequently called the U.S. representative's mobile phone and left messages, after which he attempted to contact the U.S. company representative at home.[110]

The other side of this is that foreign entities may view events as a means to follow up on targeting that has already been pursued through other channels. For instance, in 2012 a professor at an engineering university in the East Asia and Pacific region provided a request for information to a cleared contractor for an item of dual-use technology.[111] The professor subsequently approached the cleared contractor's booth at a navigation conference in the United States and made inquiries about the dual-use technology, even though the booth did not display any information about the item.[112]

In a similar instance, a national of a Europe- and Eurasia-region country who was assigned as an intelligence officer to a Washington, D.C., embassy, made an unannounced visit to a cleared contractor and claimed to be soliciting vendors who could address concerns about hacking of the embassy's network.[113] The same intelligence officer subsequently approached a cleared contractor's display booth at a cyber security conference.[114]

Foreign Actors' Engineering of Trade and Industry Events Abroad as Opportunities for Targeting and Collection

Foreign entities may exploit the hosting of conferences as a means to draw industries of interest into an operational environment where they can be more easily exploited. For instance, Chinese cities have been chosen more frequently as locations for international science and technology conferences and exhibitions.[115] Reporting from U.S. industry to the Defense Security Service has included conference organizers' solicitations to U.S. companies for participation in conferences hosted outside of the United States.[116] Foreign intelligence collectors, according to a report by what is now the National Security and Counterintelligence Center, sometimes attempt to recruit scientists by inviting them on all-expenses-paid trips abroad for conferences and other events. The individuals are treated very well, and their advice is solicited.[117] For instance, representatives of Chinese organizations have debriefed drone experts who attended conferences in China.[118] Collectors viewing them as an avenue through which to access sensitive information may contact the expert once he or she returns to the United States.[119]

SIPHONING OF HUMAN CAPITAL

Multiple foreign entities have built upon the concept of acquiring human capital through purchases of U.S. firms and instead sponsored, to varying degrees, the formation of ventures that lure human capital in possession of proprietary information away from their former employers, with sensitive data in tow. Journalist John Fialka referred to this as "tunneling." In this scenario, company A can avoid research and development expenses by establishing an arm near company B and hiring company B's disgruntled employees.[120] For instance, a Japanese firm hired V-22 test pilot engineers who helped to design the aircraft's software, its fuselage, and its landing gear.[121]

South Korea, a U.S. ally that relies on Washington for military support, nonetheless has engaged in collection against proprietary information that is the result of and basis for innovation. The South Korean company Kolon Industries allegedly recruited current and former DuPont employees over the course of several years in an attempt to obtain proprietary information about the manufacture of a substance considered to be a competitor to Kevlar.[122] In another instance of commercial competition, an employee of the Cleveland, Ohio–based Lubrizol Corp. provided proprietary information, including product specifications, to the South Korean company and Lubrizol competitor SK Chemicals.[123] Between 2001 and 2008, the employee downloaded materials and met on seventeen occasions with SK Chemical representatives.[124] Furthermore, as of 2009 the Department of Commerce identified an attempt to illicitly export night vision goggles to South Korea.[125] Furthermore, as of 2012 the Department of Commerce identified that South Korea was the intended recipient of illicitly exported infrared focal plane array detectors and camera engines.[126] The incidents are part of an established trend that dates to at least the late 1990s, when South Korea was identified as one of several U.S. allies that nonetheless engaged in economic espionage against U.S. interests.[127]

China has also employed this strategy after setting its sights on a proprietary DuPont formula for chloride route titanium dioxide. Titanium dioxide is in itself a valuable white pigment and the chloride route process also produces titanium tetrachloride, which has military and aerospace applications.[128] The Chinese government–owned company Pangang endeavored to arrange a joint venture in which DuPont would open a plant in China.[129] When this arrangement did not come to fruition, China turned to theft, engaging in an act of corporate date rape. In 1991, a Chinese Communist Party leader (who later became a member of the CCP Politburo) asked Liew to obtain the process for manufacturing titanium dioxide.[130] The Chinese state–owned enterprise awarded Walter Liew, a California resident, a USD $17 million contract to build a factory in China capable of producing 100,000 metric tons of titanium dioxide.[131] Liew in turn was to develop a team of former DuPont employees who were knowledgeable about the DuPont process, and over the course of fifteen years hired multiple former employees of the company.[132] His company, USA Performance Technology Inc., was eventually found guilty of conspiracy to commit economic espionage, conspiracy to commit theft of trade secrets, attempted economic espionage, attempted theft of trade secrets, possession of trade secrets, conveying trade secrets, and conspiracy to obstruct justice.[133]

Starting in 2003, Tze Chao, a former DuPont employee, began providing consulting services to Pangang.[134] He had worked for DuPont from 1966 to 2002.[135] In 2008, Chao bid to design a 100,000-ton-per-year titanium dioxide plant for the Pangang Group, and while he did not win the contract, the Pangang Group asked him to review the designs that Liew's company USA Performance Technology Inc. provided to Pangang.[136] Chao, consistent with the vulnerability of divided loyalty, claimed that China appealed to his Chinese ethnicity and presented cooperation as a way for the good of China.[137] Thanks to the perfidy of Liew, Chao, and others who participated in this scheme, Pangang as of 2013 was running the largest titanium dioxide complex in China and was one of the country's leading producers of titanium dioxide—which had hitherto been a product unique to DuPont.[138]

Another case, again with a China connection and using a similar ploy of siphoning off expertise, involved targeting the Dow Chemical company. Wen Chyu Liu, who worked for Dow from 1965 until 1992, is in the same category of the Chinese engineers discussed previously who used academia as a way into the United States, as Liu originally arrived in the country for graduate work. Liu, a research scientist, worked on elastomers that have applications for automotive industrial hoses, electrical cable jackets, and vinyl siding. In collaboration with at least four individuals who were former or current employees of Dow, Liu misappropriated information in order to market elastomer process packages to multiple Chinese companies. Although unlike Liew Liu did not establish a formal company, he paid his collaborators for information, including a cash bribe of USD $50,000 in exchange for Dow's process manual and other information related to its work on elastomers.[139]

Yet another example of Chinese theft of U.S. innovation involved network technology. In 2001, two former Lucent Technologies scientists—Hai Lin and Kai Xu—participated in a joint venture with Datang Telecom Technology Company to sell a copy of Lucent's Pathstar data and voice transmission system product in China.[140] The third conspirator in this plot was Yong Qing Cheng—an employee of an optical networking vendor.[141] Lin, Xu, and Cheng founded ComTriad, which requested that Datang provide venture capital, which resulted in an investment from Datang of USD $500,000.[142] This theft, according to the U.S. Department of Justice, injured not only Lucent but also those companies that had licensed portions of their software to Lucent for use in Pathstar and sold Lucent custom-designed circuit boards for the product.[143] The lesson is that in an era of collaborative ventures, one instance of trade secret theft/economic espionage can damage multiple companies' capabilities for innovation.

The tech sector of Silicon Valley, California, has also been the victim of innovation via the establishment of companies to implement the stolen technology. In 2007 Lan Lee and Yuefei Ge were indicted on charges of stealing data sheets and confidential documents from their employer, NetLogic Microsystems, and forming a company, SICO Microsystems, to develop components based on the purloined designs.[144] They then approached multiple Chinese government agencies, including the General Armaments Department and the 863 Program.[145]

SIMPLE THEFT

In 2002, the U.S. Department of Justice indicted two individuals for the theft of proprietary information from multiple Silicon Valley companies, which they intended to use to advance China's capability for develop superintegrated circuit design. The defendants, Fei Ye and Ming Zhong, were born in China—Ye was a U.S. citizen and Zhong was a U.S. permanent resident—and employed by the Transmeta Corporation and Trident Microsystems Inc. Ye had also worked for Sun Microsystems and NEC Electronics Corporation. They claimed to be collecting information for the "Supervision" project, which they represented as being funded by the city of Hangzhou and in the process of applying for funding from China's 863 Program. When arrested in November 2001 at San Francisco International Airport as Ye and Zhong were about to board a flight to China, authorities discovered trade secrets from Transmeta and Sun in their luggage. Ye also possessed trade secrets belonging to NEC, Sun, and Trident at his residence, while Zhong possessed trade secrets belonging to Trident. That the two defendants were inspired not simply by personal gain but rather by ideological and cultural affinity—the powerful motives described in a previous chapter—was indicated by their interest in providing China with the capability to compete with worldwide leaders' core development technology and products in the field of integrated circuit design.[146]

A 2014 incident provides another example of how China's luring of foreign talent to establish businesses in that country can result in the theft of proprietary information. Yu Long, who had been employed by a Connecticut defense contractor, was charged with attempting to travel to China with sensitive proprietary documents that contained information about the development of technologically advanced titanium that would be used for U.S. military aircraft.[147] Long's intentions were clear, based on registration documents for a new corporation being established in China, as well as a nearly completed application for work with a state-sponsored aviation and aerospace research center.[148]

CONCLUSION

The paths of commerce and scientific collaboration established by Americans seeking opportunities beyond the United States have been steadily exploited for the illicit transfer of knowledge via superficially similar transactions. Theft/espionage does not occur in a vacuum, and it cannot be disrupted with a cookie-cutter approach. The dynamic of "selling out" illustrates how new norms in global interaction provide new methodologies—opportunities for operation—that unscrupulous actors can exploit. Half a century ago, many of the activities discussed above would have stood out because they were anomalies. However, in the first decades of the twenty-first century, the idea of sustained linkages between U.S. entities and institutions in countries—including those that pose a geopolitical challenge to U.S. interests—are commonplace. This results in new opportunities for state and nonstate entities seeking to surreptitiously obtain proprietary information, particularly because it means that information is increasingly on their home turf. Focusing only on the tactical, granular aspects of tradecraft (toward which the law enforcement–informed counterintelligence community is biased) without first assessing how threat actors can exploit changing dynamics—which provides the context for what tradecraft might look like—is too little, too late.

NOTES

1. Defense Security Service, *Targeting U.S. Technology: A Trend Analysis of Cleared Industry Reporting* (2014), 33.

2. Ibid.

3. Ibid.

4. *China's Propaganda and Influence Operations, Its Intelligence Activities That Target the United States, and the Resulting Impacts on U.S. National Security: Hearing before the U.S.-China Economic and Security Review Commission*, 111th Cong. 138 (2009).

5. Defense Security Service, *Targeting U.S. Technology: A Trend Analysis of Cleared Industry Reporting* (2014), 65.

6. Defense Group Inc., *Open Power, Hidden Dangers*, 3.

7. Ibid., 3.

8. U.S. Department of Justice, *PRO IP Act, First Annual Report 2008–2009* (Washington, D.C.: U.S. Department of Justice, 2009), 14.

9. Ibid.

10. *2007 Report to Congress of the U.S. China Economic and Security Review Commission*, 105.

11. U.S. Department of Justice, *Pro IP Act, Annual Report FY 2012* (Washington, D.C.: U.S. Department of Justice, 2012), 17; Christopher Drew, "New Spy Game," *New York Times*, October 18, 2010.

12. U.S. Department of Justice, *Pro IP Act, Annual Report FY 2011* (Washington, D.C.: U.S. Department of Justice, 2011).

13. Christopher Drew, "New Spy Game," *New York Times*, October 18, 2010.

14. Ibid.; U.S. Department of Justice, *Chinese National Charged with Economic Espionage Involving Theft of Trade Secrets from Leading Agricultural Company Based in Indianapolis* (Washington, D.C.: U.S. Department of Justice, 2010).

15. U.S. Department of Justice, *Summary of Major U.S. Export Enforcement, Economic Espionage, Trade Secret and Embargo-Related Criminal Cases (January 2008 to the Present: Updated March 26, 2014)* (Washington, D.C.: U.S. Department of Justice, 2014), 48.

16. John Eligon and Patrick Zuo, "Designer Seed Thought to Be Latest Target by Chinese," *New York Times*, February 5, 2014.

17. U.S. Department of Justice, *Pro IP Act FY 2011*, 18; National Counterintelligence Executive, *Foreign Spies Stealing US Economic Secrets in Cyberspace*, 4.

18. U.S. Department of Justice, *PRO IP Act, Annual Report FY 2013* (Washington, D.C.: U.S. Department of Justice, 2013), 17.

19. Office of the National Counterintelligence Executive, *Foreign Spies Stealing US Economic Secrets in Cyberspace*, 4.

20. Ibid.; U.S. Department of Justice, *Summary of Major U.S. Export Enforcement, Economic Espionage, Trade Secret and Embargo-Related Criminal Cases* (January 2008 to the Present: Updated March 26, 2014), 66.

21. Nathalie Tadena, "Engineer Gets 4 Years In Motorola Secrets Case," *Wall Street Journal*, August 30, 2012.

22. Ibid.

23. Office of the National Counterintelligence Executive, *Foreign Spies Stealing US Economic Secrets in Cyberspace*, 4.

24. U.S. Department of Justice, *Summary of Major U.S. Export Enforcement, Economic Espionage, Trade Secret and Embargo-Related Criminal Cases* (January 2008 to the Present: Updated March 26, 2014), 66.

25. U.S. Department of Justice, *PRO IP Act, Annual Report FY 2013*, 17.

26. Ibid.

27. Wise, *Tiger Trap*, 46.

28. Ibid., 154, 156.

29. Central Intelligence Agency, *Report to Congress on Chinese Espionage Activities Against the United States*, www.cia.gov (accessed October 14, 2015).

30. U.S. Department of Justice, *Former Boeing Engineer Convicted of Economic Espionage in Theft of Space Shuttle Secrets for China* (Washington, D.C.: U.S. Department of Justice, 2009).

31. "Statement of Robert S. Mueller, Director, Federal Bureau of Investigation, before the Committee on Judiciary, United States Senate, Regarding Oversight of the Federal Bureau of Investigation," December 14, 2011; U.S. Department of Justice, *Summary of Major U.S. Export Enforcement, Economic Espionage, Trade Secret and Embargo-Related Criminal Cases* (January 2008 to the Present: Updated March 26, 2014), 63.

32. U.S. Department of Justice, *Summary of Major U.S. Export Enforcement, Economic Espionage, Trade Secret and Embargo-Related Criminal Cases (January 2008 to the Present: Updated March 26, 2014)*, 62.

33. Ibid., 66.

34. U.S. Department of Justice, *PRO IP Act, Annual Report FY 2013*, 17; U.S. Department of Justice, *Summary of Major U.S. Export Enforcement, Economic Espionage, Trade Secret and Embargo-Related Criminal Cases* (January 2008 to the Present: Updated March 26, 2014), 68.

35. Fialka, *War by Other Means*, 86.

36. *Soviet Acquisition of Military Significant Western Technology: An Update*, 26.

37. Ibid.

38. Jay Solomon, "Phantom Menace: FBI Sees Big Threat from Chinese Spies," *Wall Street Journal*, August 10, 2005.

39. *PRC Acquisition of U.S. Technology*, 35.

40. Ibid.

41. U.S. Department of Justice, *Summary of Major U.S. Export Enforcement, Economic Espionage, Trade Secret and Embargo-Related Criminal Cases* (January 2008 to the Present: Updated March 26, 2014), 77.

42. Ibid.

43. Ibid.

44. Ibid.

45. U.S. Department of Justice, *PRO IP Act, Annual Report FY 2013*, 17; U.S. Department of Justice, *Summary of Major U.S. Export Enforcement, Economic Es-*

pionage, Trade Secret and Embargo-Related Criminal Cases (January 2008 to the Present: Updated March 26, 2014), 31, 42, 45, 70, 81, 84, 87, and 92.

46. "Six Now Expelled in Belgian Espionage," *New York Times*, August 23, 1983.

47. "Russian Agent and Other Members of Procurement Network of Russian Military and Intelligence Operating in the U.S. and Russia," U.S. Attorney's Office, October 3, 2012, www.fbi.gov (accessed November 8, 2015).

48. Ibid.

49. Ibid.

50. Ibid.

51. U.S. Department of Justice, *Summary of Major U.S. Export Enforcement, Economic Espionage, Trade Secret and Embargo-Related Criminal Cases* (January 2008 to the Present: Updated March 26, 2014), 74.

52. Ibid.

53. *Soviet Acquisition of Military Significant Western Technology: An Update*, 20.

54. Office of the National Counterintelligence Executive, *Annual Report to Congress on Foreign Economic Collection and Industrial Espionage: 2001*, 2.

55. "Statement for the Record, U.S. Immigration and Customs Enforcement, before the U.S. House of Representatives Committee on Homeland Security, Subcommittee on Oversight, Investigation and Management on 'Homeland Security Investigations: Examining DHS's Efforts to Protect American Jobs and Secure the Homeland,'" July 28, 2011.

56. Defense Security Service, *Targeting U.S. Technology: A Trend Analysis of Cleared Industry Reporting* (2013), 23.

57. U.S. Department of Commerce, Bureau of Industry and Security, *Annual Report to the Congress for Fiscal Year 2011* (Washington, D.C.: U.S. Department of Commerce, 2012), 29.

58. Ibid., 30.

59. Defense Security Service, *Targeting U.S. Technology: A Trend Analysis of Cleared Industry Reporting* (2014), 68.

60. Ibid.

61. U.S. Department of Justice, *Summary of Major U.S. Export Enforcement, Economic Espionage, Trade Secret and Embargo-Related Criminal Cases* (January 2008 to the Present: Updated March 26, 2014), 13–14.

62. Ibid., 15–16.

63. Ibid.

64. U.S. Department of Justice, *PRO IP Act, Annual Report FY 2013*, 17; U.S. Department of Justice, *Summary of Major U.S. Export Enforcement, Economic Espionage, Trade Secret and Embargo-Related Criminal Cases* (January 2008 to the Present: Updated March 26, 2014), 57.

65. U.S. Department of Justice, *Summary of Major U.S. Export Enforcement, Economic Espionage, Trade Secret and Embargo-Related Criminal Cases* (January 2008 to the Present: Updated March 26, 2014), 55.

66. *Meeting the Espionage Challenge: A Review of United State Counterintelligence and Security Programs. Report of the Select Committee on Intelligence. United States Senate* Rep. No. 99-522 at 30 (1986).

67. Ibid.

68. U.S. Department of Commerce, Bureau of Industry and Security, *Annual Report to the Congress for Fiscal Year 2013* (Washington, D.C.: U.S. Department of Commerce, 2014), 36.

69. *2013 Report to Congress of the U.S. China Economic and Security Review Commission*, 223.

70. Defense Security Service, *Targeting U.S. Technology: A Trend Analysis of Cleared Industry Reporting* (2014).

71. Ibid.

72. Ibid.

73. Ibid.

74. Shlomo Shpiro, "Soviet Espionage in Israel, 1973–1991," *Intelligence and National Security* 30, no. 4 (2014): 486–507.

75. Fialka, *War by Other Means*, 70.

76. Edward Wong, "Hacking U.S. Secrets, China Pushes for Drones," *New York Times*, September 20, 2013.

77. John R. Wilke, "Two Silicon Valley Cases Raise Fears of Chinese Espionage," *Wall Street Journal*, January 15, 2003; Jay Solomon, "Phantom Menace: FBI Sees Big Threat from Chinese Spies," *Wall Street Journal*, August 10, 2005.

78. John R. Wilke, "Two Silicon Valley Cases Raise Fears of Chinese Espionage," *Wall Street Journal*, January 15, 2003.

79. *2004 Report to Congress of the U.S. China Economic and Security Review Commission*, 108th Cong. 185 (2004).

80. Suttmeier, *Trends in U.S. China Science and Cooperation*, 36.

81. U.S. Department of Commerce, Bureau of Industry and Security, *Don't Let This Happen to You: An Introduction to U.S. Export Control Law. Export Enforcement* (Washington, D.C.: U.S. Department of Commerce, 2008), 23.

82. U.S. Department of Commerce, Bureau of Industry and Security, *Annual Report to the Congress for Fiscal Year 2014* (Washington, D.C.: U.S. Department of Commerce, 2015), 38.

83. *2014 Report to Congress of the U.S. China Economic and Security Review Commission*, 297.

84. *China's Propaganda and Influence Operations, Its Intelligence Activities That Target the United States, and the Resulting Impact on U.S. National Security: Hearing before the U.S. China Economic and Security Review Commission*, 111th Cong. (2009) (Statement of James Mulvenon).

85. *Soviet Acquisition of Military Significant Western Technology: An Update*, 19.

86. Ibid.

87. Ibid., 19–20.

88. Ibid.

89. Ibid.

90. *FBI Counterintelligence Visits to Libraries: Hearings before the Subcommittee on Civil and Constitutional Rights of the Committee on the Judiciary, House of Representatives*, 100th Cong. 107 (1988) (Testimony of James H. Geer, Assistant Director, Intelligence Division, Federal Bureau of Investigation); Fialka, *War by Other Means*, 68.

91. National Counterintelligence Center, *Annual Report to Congress on Foreign Economic Collection and Industrial Espionage: 1995*, 19–20.

92. Defense Security Service, *Targeting U.S. Technology: A Trend Analysis of Cleared Industry Reporting* (2014), 44.

93. Defense Security Service, *Targeting U.S. Technology: A Trend Analysis of Cleared Industry Reporting* (2013), 28.

94. Office of the National Counterintelligence Executive, *Annual Report to Congress on Foreign Economic Collection and Industrial Espionage, 2001*, 2.

95. Defense Security Service, *Targeting U.S. Technology: A Trend Analysis of Cleared Industry Reporting* (2014), 46.

96. Ibid.

97. Statement by Nicholas Eftimiades, "Chinese Intelligence Operations before the Joint Economic Committee, United States Congress," Wednesday, May 20, 1998.

98. Office of the National Counterintelligence Executive, *Annual Report to Congress on Foreign Economic Collection and Industrial Espionage: 2004*, 7.

99. Office of the National Counterintelligence Executive, *Annual Report to Congress on Foreign Economic Collection and Industrial Espionage: 2002*, 10.

100. *2009 Report to Congress of the U.S.-China Economy and Security Review Commission*, 155.

101. *United States of America v. Evgeny Buryakov (a/k/a "Zhenya"), Igor Sporyshev, and Victor Podobnyy.*

102. Office of the National Counterintelligence Executive, *Annual Report to Congress on Foreign Economic Collection and Industrial Espionage: 2004*, 7.

103. *PRC Acquisition of U.S. Technology*, 41.

104. Office of the National Counterintelligence Executive, *Annual Report to Congress on Foreign Economic Collection and Industrial Espionage: 2002*, 10.

105. Office of the National Counterintelligence Executive, *Annual Report to Congress on Foreign Economic Collection and Industrial Espionage: 2001*, 2.

106. National Counterintelligence Center, *Annual Report to Congress on Foreign Economic Collection and Industrial Espionage: 2000*.

107. Office of the National Counterintelligence Executive, *Annual Report to Congress on Foreign Economic Collection and Industrial Espionage: 2001*, 2.

108. Office of the National Counterintelligence Executive, *Annual Report to Congress on Foreign Economic Collection and Industrial Espionage: 2002*, 10.

109. National Counterintelligence Center, *Annual Report to Congress on Foreign Economic Collection and Industrial Espionage: 2000*.

110. Defense Security Service, *Targeting U.S. Technology: A Trend Analysis of Cleared Industry Reporting* (2014), 64.

111. Ibid.

112. Ibid.

113. Defense Security Service, *Targeting U.S. Technologies: A Trend Analysis of Cleared Industry Reporting* (2013), 55.

114. Ibid.

115. *2007 Report to Congress of the U.S. China Economic and Security Review Commission*, 132.

116. Defense Security Service, *Targeting U.S. Technology: A Trend Analysis of Cleared Industry Reporting* (2014).

117. National Counterintelligence Center, *Annual Report to Congress on Foreign Economic Collection and Industrial Espionage: 1995*, 19–20.

118. Edward Wong, "Hacking U.S. Secrets, China Pushes for Drones," *New York Times*, September 20, 2013.

119. National Counterintelligence Center, *Annual Report to Congress on Foreign Economic Collection and Industrial Espionage: 1995*, 19–20.

120. Fialka, *War by Other Means*, 45.

121. Ibid., 44.

122. United States Department of Justice, *PRO IP Act, Annual Report FY 2013*, 17; U.S. Department of Justice, *Summary of Major U.S. Export Enforcement, Economic Espionage, Trade Secret and Embargo-Related Criminal Cases* (January 2008 to the Present: Updated March 26, 2014), 33.

123. Evan Perez, "FBI's New Campaign Targets Corporate Espionage," *Wall Street Journal*, May 11, 2012.

124. Ibid.

125. U.S. Department of Commerce, Bureau of Industry and Security, *Annual Report to the Congress for Fiscal Year 2009* (Washington, D.C.: U.S. Department of Commerce, 2009), 30.

126. U.S. Department of Commerce, Bureau of Industry and Security, *Annual Report to the Congress for Fiscal Year 2013*, 36.

127. Jack Nelson, "Spies Took $300 Billion Toll on U.S. Firms in '97," *Los Angeles Times*, January 12, 1998.

128. "Walter Liew Sentenced to 15 Years in Prison for Economic Espionage: Court Orders Lengthy Prison Term, $27.8 Million Forfeiture, and $511,000 in Restitution After First Ever Jury Trial for Economic Espionage," U.S. Attorney's Office. July 11, 2014. www.fbi.gov (accessed October 24, 2015).

129. Justin Scheck and Evan Perez, "FBI Traces Trail of Spy Ring to China," *Wall Street Journal*, March 9, 2012; "IP Commission Report," 39-40.

130. Ibid.

131. "The IP Commission Report," 39-40.

132. Justin Scheck and Evan Perez, "FBI Traces Trail of Spy Ring to China," *Wall Street Journal*, March 9, 2012

133. "Walter Liew Sentenced to 15 Years in Prison for Economic Espionage: Court Orders Lengthy Prison Term, $27.8 Million Forfeiture, and $511,000 in Restitution After First Ever Jury Trial for Economic Espionage," U.S. Attorney's Office, July 11, 2014, www.fbi.gov.

134. Justin Scheck and Evan Perez, "FBI Traces Trail of Spy Ring to China," *Wall Street Journal*, March 9, 2012; "Statement of Robert S. Mueller III, Director, Federal Bureau of Investigation, before the Committee on the Judiciary, United States Senate, at a Hearing Entitled 'Oversight of the Federal Bureau of Investigation'"; "Former DuPont Scientist Pleads Guilty to Economic Espionage: Admits He Provided Trade Secrets to Companies Controlled by Chinese Government," U.S. Attorney's Office, Northern District of California, March 2, 2012, www.fbi.gov.

135. "Former DuPont Scientist Pleads Guilty to Economic Espionage: Admits He Provided Trade Secrets to Companies Controlled by Chinese Government," U.S. Attorney's Office, Northern District of California, March 2, 2012, www.fbi.gov.

136. Ibid.

137. Justin Scheck and Evan Perez, "FBI Traces Trail of Spy Ring to China," *Wall Street Journal*, March 9, 2012.

138. IP Commission Report, 39–40.

139. "Former Dow Research Scientist Convicted of Stealing Trade Secrets and Perjury," February 7, 2011, www.fbi.gov.

140. "Three Indicted in Lucent Trade-Secret Case," *New York Times*, June 1, 2001.

141. Ibid.; John R. Wilke, "Two Silicon Valley Cases Raise Fears of Chinese Espionage," *Wall Street Journal*, January 15, 2003.

142. "New Indictment Expands Charges against Former Lucent Scientists Accused of Passing Trade Secrets to Chinese Company," April 11, 2002, www.justice.gov.

143. Ibid.

144. "Two Engineers Indicted in Economic Espionage," *Los Angeles Times*, September 27, 2007.

145. Ibid.; "Two Bay Area Men Indicted on Charges of Economic Espionage," September 26, 2007, www.justice.gov.

146. "Pair from Cupertino and San Jose, California, Indicted for Economic Espionage and Theft of Trade Secrets from Silicon Valley Companies," December 4, 2002, www.justice.gov.

147. U.S. Department of Justice, *Summary of Major U.S. Export Enforcement, Economic Espionage, Trade Secret and Embargo-Related Criminal Cases* (January 2009 to the Present: Updated August 12, 2015).

148. Ibid.

Chapter Six

Buying In

The Inherent Risks of Foreign Direct Investment

The counterpoint to U.S. investments and other transfers of technology and knowledge outward is the admission of foreign investment into the United States. Of specific concern is foreign direct investment (FDI), which allows foreign entities to influence and control entities on U.S. soil. FDI, whether the acquisition of existing entities or "greenfield" investments, allows foreign governments to increase their capacity for innovation using U.S. assets in sectors that have a direct impact on elements of national power. Not only does access to U.S. innovation provide foreign actors—including adversarial countries such as China—with the opportunity to catch up with the United States, but it also furnishes the knowledge and access that an adversary needs in order to compromise U.S. capabilities, especially in the field of information technology.

THE CHINA CASE

China is one of multiple countries that have sought to improve their capabilities for innovation by purchasing U.S. entities. What sets China apart is a set of factors that should make the United States wonder about the advisability of allowing such purchases to continue. As of 2014, China was the fastest growing source of U.S.-bound foreign direct investment.[1] Yet it has also been identified by the U.S. Department of Defense as the world's most active and persistent perpetrator of cyber-facilitated economic espionage.[2] Previously, in 2007, Joel Brenner, the national counterintelligence executive, identified that out of 140 countries' intelligence entities, Chinese intelligence was consistently the most aggressive.[3]

Chinese investment in the United States provides a way for Beijing to acquire existing U.S. capabilities and leverage the knowledge of its human capital. Chinese firms are encouraged to pursue joint ventures with foreign firms or acquire them outright in order to absorb cutting-edge technologies that will allow them to leapfrog several phases of development.[4] While this can occur through the attraction of R&D to China as previously discussed, it has also led Chinese entities to pursue investments in the United States. This is at times due to the miniscule nature of firms engaged in the most interesting work. China has attempted to acquire U.S. companies engaged in cutting-edge work that were too small to invest in China in order to acquire unique capabilities.[5]

Beyond existing technology, the most important asset that a foreign government can acquire from an acquisition in the United States is the associated human capital—the knowledge that individuals possess and can utilize that ultimately leads to innovation. As the consultancy the Rhodium Group discussed in a 2015 report on Chinese foreign direct investment in the United States, acquisitions in the United States provide access to a diverse and well-educated workforce. The intent to exploit these new accesses is summed up by the Rhodium Group's observation that "in many cases, new Chinese owners have doubled down on local expertise by expanding R&D-related activities at their new subsidiaries." A related phenomenon is China's strategic investment in entities that give it access to hotbeds of innovation. This is apparent in "greenfield" developments within broader innovation clusters, such as Baidu's establishment of an artificial intelligence laboratory in Sunnyvale, California.[6] Of course, as discussed previously, "greenfield" developments also have the advantage of not being subjected to CFIUS review.

China's acquisition of U.S. firms that have developed advanced technology and that possess the human capital for innovation is made even more problematic because of the possibility for bleedover from the civilian to the military sector. This does not occur by chance but by design, as in 2003 China promulgated a doctrine of civil-military integration, which included promoting coordination and cooperation between commercial and military entities and locating military potential in civilian capabilities.[7] Therefore, in addition to contributing to China's economic and informational elements of national power, Chinese acquisition in the United States is primed to be picked over by Beijing to enhance its military capabilities. Furthermore, the very process of closing the innovation gap contributes to China's emphasis on degrading an opponent's technological advantages.[8] This arguably contributes to the PIA's ability to assume a more assured and aggressive posture.

Information Technology

China's investments in the U.S. information technology sector represent acquisitions that bolster Beijing's "information" element of national power. In Chinese strategic thinking, this is a particularly important capability. The Peoples' Liberation Army (PLA) has traditionally viewed acquisition of information dominance as a prerequisite to winning high-technology conflicts.[9] To accomplish this, the PLA must be able to protect its own systems while disrupting those of its opponent. China's investment in the United States not only gives it access to the technologies that it needs to bolster its offensive and defensive resources, but also positions it to compromise U.S. systems. As testimony to the U.S.–China Economic and Security Review Commission indicated, PLA strategic and doctrinal writings on information confrontation stress the importance of attacking or shaping the adversary's perceptions, sometimes via the network or systems themselves with false or corrupted data during a conflict or crisis.[10] This means not only being able to disable systems, but also to manipulate them because the delivery of corrupted information requires that the networks not be destroyed or disabled. Another aspect of network exploitation that may be furthered through Chinese investment in the U.S. IT sector is the collection of information. Chinese entities, through repeated cyber attacks against seemingly all facets of U.S. society, have established their willingness to engage in such activities. Again, China must have access to but not damage U.S. networks in order to ensure that information of interest continues to move across them (and be intercepted).

The most prominent progression of acquisitions—both technology and of access to human capital—has been the Chinese telecommunications company Huawei. The Huawei Shenzhen Technology Company (Huawei) was founded in 1988 by Ren Zhengfei, a former director of the Information Engineering Academy, which is believed to be the 3PLA's primary center for telecommunications research.[11] The 3PLA is the signals intelligence division, and Zhenfei is believed to maintain connections with this intelligence entity.[12] Furthermore, Sun Yafang, the chairwoman of Huawei as of 2012, had been previously affiliated with the Chinese Ministry of State Security (MSS).[13] The MSS is China's primary civilian intelligence agency. The company also received technical assistance in order to catch up with the telecommunications sector from Chinese government-sponsored research institutes including the Posts and Telecommunications Universities of Beijing, Nenjing, and Shanxi.[14] (The Beijing Institute of Posts and Technology maintains links to the PLA.)[15] This further illustrates the previously discussed substantial differences between U.S. and Chinese academic institutions and the possibility that contributions by U.S. institutions may eventually be used to assist Chinese companies seeking to compete with American firms and possibly serve as proxies for Chinese intelligence activities.

The association of Huawei with Chinese intelligence services that target U.S. interests is more troubling because of the control exerted by China that could turn Huawei's capabilities against the West (even more than Huawei has already done through instances of theft). The Chinese State Owned Assets Supervision and Administration Commission, which identifies state-owned enterprises with strategic value to China's national security, formally designated Huawei as a "national champion."[16] State support is not an insignificant nationalist gesture, given that Huawei is the world's second largest manufacturer of telecommunications equipment.[17] Furthermore, the Chinese Communist Party maintains a party cell within Huawei.[18] Company officials have claimed that the Chinese government requires such cells within all companies.[19] However, this does not lessen the possibility that such a party cell may be used to exert control and actually suggests that this is more likely because it was imposed by the government, rather than done at the company's own volition. Experts on Chinese industry have advised U.S. policymakers that the Chinese government uses these groups to exert influence and monitor corporate developments.[20]

Despite the extent of the Chinese government's control over Huawei, the company during the past decade and a half has been allowed to develop a presence in the United States—a presence that is closely controlled by its China-based parent. According to a 2012 congressional investigation, Huawei's board of directors sets terms for operations in the United States and is empowered to mobilize resources and establish strategy.[21] There are indications that Huawei closely controls its U.S. subsidiary's decisions. In one instance, a senior-level executive in the United States could not sign a contract to provide cyber security services without approval from China.[22] On another occasion, the parent company repudiated a contract that a senior-level U.S. executive had previously approved.[23]

Huawei's U.S. presence is a challenge to U.S. innovation in multiple ways. It has partnered with U.S. telecommunications providers, which provides it access to U.S. technology, as well as an opportunity to compromise U.S.-developed capabilities should the Chinese government attempt to leverage Huawei as an element of information warfare. Furthermore, Huawei has demonstrated a desire to acquire U.S. technology—both through purchases and via illicit acquisitions. Finally, by establishing an R&D footprint in the United States and hiring local talent, Huawei has coopted U.S. knowledge, which effectively contributes to the advances of a company that may be turned against the United States at the direction of the Chinese government.

By partnering with or leveraging existing U.S. entities, Huawei has been able to access technology and human capital within the United States. As of 2013, Huawei customers included Cricket Communications, Clearwire, Cox TMI Wireless, Hibernia Atlantic, Level 3/BTW Equipment, Suddenlink, Comcast, and Bend Broadband.[24] As of 2015, Huawei (as well as China's ZTE) has been associated with reports by U.S. companies of odd or alerting behavior.[25] Huawei had operations in fourteen U.S. states.[26] Its California R&D center employed over two hundred people as of 2015, and its location in Plano, Texas, employed approximately three hundred people as of that year.[27] At the same time as it has leveraged U.S. human capital for R&D, Huawei has maintained an ongoing relationship with the PLA and developed technology including transport network products, data products, videoconferencing products, and Voice over IP (VoIP) capabilities on the military's behalf.[28] Given the close control that Huawei has over its U.S. subsidiary, it should be considered possible that work done in the United States will ultimately benefit Chinese military capabilities and that requirements of the Chinese military may actually provide direction for the work being done by U.S. employees.

Huawei has pursued acquisitions—both licit and illicit—of U.S. technology. In 2008, Huawei, in conjunction with Bain Capital, attempted to acquire the U.S. communications technology company 3Com, but withdrew the bid after CFIUS signaled that it would object to the acquisition due to the national security risks posed by the sale of network gear.[29] In 2010, Huawei attempted a different approach vis-à-vis the bankrupt 3Leaf when it endeavored to purchase cloud computing assets (rather than the company).[30] It also hired fifteen of 3Leaf's employees, which could be viewed as an attempt to acquire the company's institutional knowledge, again without inviting CFIUS scrutiny.[31] However, Huawei divested itself of the assets in 2011 after CFIUS requested, at Department of Defense prompting, that the purchase be submitted for CFIUS review.[32] (Huawei claimed that the purchase should not be subject to such scrutiny because it was not purchasing the company, only its assets.[33]) However, because intellectual property is not a tangible asset that can be tracked, it is unknown whether Huawei was able to absorb the knowledge prior to divesting it. In the context of acquisitions, it should be noted that Huawei has allegedly engaged in the theft of intellectual property. In 2010, Motorola (which incidentally was eventually purchased by Lenovo, another Chinese IT company, discussed later) claimed that former employees, while still working for Motorola, established an outside firm, Lemko, in 2002 and proceeded to sell Motorola trade secrets to customers, including Huawei.[34] Ren Zhengfei, Huawe's PLA-connected founder, is alleged to have begun working with the Motorola employees in 2001.[35] Only four years prior to the beginning of this episode, in 1997 Motorola had established a joint laboratory with Huawei to develop a high-speed switching and routing equipment idea for an air defense network.[36] This succession of events is an additional indicator that Huawei may exploit its footprint in the United States to engage in future nefarious activity.

The Zhongxing Telecom Technology Corporation (ZTE), China's second largest telecommunications company—and the world's fifth largest mobile phone manufacturer as of 2012—has also pursued efforts to leverage U.S. innovation to enhance its own (and by extension China's) capabilities. Like Huawei, ZTE's roots are in Chinese government–sponsored R&D, specifically China Aerospace Industry Corporation, from which it was spun off in 1985.[37] Also, like Huawei, it has maintained a relationship with the PLA including collaborative research with military and civilian universities on technologies together with satellite navigation and data link jamming techniques as well as training active-duty PLA personnel.[38] ZTE, like Huawei, includes a Chinese Communist Party cell, which raises concerns about Chinese government control similar to those previously discussed. Manufacturers of Chinese mobile equipment such as ZTE may facilitate Chinese intelligence collection, as, according to the U.S.–China Economic and Security Review Commission, "sophisticated malware has propagated within China specifically targeting smart phones."[39] Furthermore, researchers in May 2012 identified a backdoor that could allow unauthorized users to gain full control over select model ZTE mobile phones.[40]

ZTE has pursued knowledge to support its innovation via several avenues. Notably, as of 2012 it had five R&D centers in the United States, which employed three hundred people.[41] Among these facilities was a laboratory in Richardson, Texas, focused on 4G, or Long-Term Evolution (LTE), which was attempting to develop a dual mode CDMA/LTE platform as the product basis for expanding their presence in the U.S. market.[42] In addition to its establishment of platforms for drawing on U.S. human capital, ZTE has involved itself in U.S. telecommunications infrastructure. A ZTE official advised that the company was willing to lose money on projects in the United States if it meant being able to better understand U.S. technology and standards.[43] This provides it access to networks that may be exploited for information warfare, consistent with the PLA-favored approach to conflict.

The third largest Chinese telecommunications company, Datang, is similar to other Chinese entities within the industry. It is one of multiple companies funded by the Chinese military or military-associated research institutes.[44] Datang was founded in 1998 by a group that included the Chinese Academy of Telecommunications Technologies (CATT) and the Tenth Research Institute, which was overseen by the Ministry of Information Industry.[45] Datang Telecom Technology and Industry Group—the parent company of Datang—

is closely linked to Chinese government interests, as indicated by its operation of multiple research institutes that it inherited from CATT.[46] Although it lacks the U.S. presence of Huawei and ZTE, Datang has nonetheless been a party to the targeting of U.S. technology. Two former employees of the technical staff at Lucent, Hai Lin and Kai Xu, attempted to develop a joint venture with Datang with the objective selling a clone of Lucent's PathStar data and voice transmission system to Internet providers in China.[47]

China has also become a notable presence in the field of U.S. computing. In 2005, it completed a high-profile purchase of IBM's personal computer business.[48] The acquisition was the first billion-dollar purchase in the United States by a mainland Chinese company.[49] Then in 2014, it acquired IBM's x86 server component, what was, at the time, the largest overseas technology acquisition by a Chinese company.[50] These acquisitions have provided Lenovo with access to U.S. knowledge as well as technology. As of 2012, Lenovo's workforce of nineteen thousand included nearly ten thousand former IBM employees.[51] That Lenovo was purchasing expertise and an ability to innovate, as well as market share, is indicated by multiple developments. By 2012, it had relocated its R&D facilities to North Carolina (site of its 2005 acquisition).[52] Following its 2014 acquisition of the IBM server business, Lenovo planned to relocate some of its server production to the United States.[53] In 2014, Lenovo purchased the Motorola Mobility from Google, and with that purchase planned to retain all 3,500 employees.[54] However, even as it is employing American aptitude in furtherance of its information technology development, Lenovo may be simultaneously using its products to facilitate cyber exploitation of U.S. networks. During a test of Lenovo computers, the U.S. Air Force discovered that the machines were attempting to make an unauthorized connection to China.[55]

TEXTBOX 6.1. HARDLY AMUSING: IMPLICATIONS OF CHINESE INVESTMENT IN THE ENTERTAINMENT INDUSTRY

China has given notable emphasis to leveraging culture as a means to develop support internationally, as indicated by the proliferation of its Confucius Centers and Confucius Classrooms. In this context, the acquisition of AMC Theaters by China's Dalian Wanda Group in 2012 could be a strategically significant purchase, which made the Chinese firm the largest theater owner in the world.[1] As Carolyn Bartholomew, a member of the U.S. China Economic and Security Review Commission, noted in 2013, "This investment in the entertainment industry, par-

(continued)

ticularly if you look at movies and other sort of cultural production, it's perhaps not quite as benign as we think that it might be. I'm waiting to see if there any forthcoming movies about Tibet and whether the AMC theatres will be allowed to show them."[2] In addition to censorship, Chinese control of theaters may facilitate its efforts to promote specific themes through cinema. In 2009, the China Film Group Corporation produced *Confucius* starring Chow Yun-Fat and pulled the American film from many theaters to make room for the movie.[3] With an international chain of theaters, China could conceivably arrange to similarly promote specific features over others, based not on profitability but on ideology.

Another nexus between entertainment and information that is a concern is Chinese acquisition of U.S. video game companies. China's Tencent owns Riot Games and Epic Games, and Cryptic Studios, a subsidiary of Perfect World, was also acquired by a Chinese firm. All three of these companies have U.S.-based R&D operations.[4] The underlying technologies associated with gaming have long been identified by the military as potential assets. In 1999, the U.S. Army formed, in conjunction with the University of Southern California, the Institute for Creative Technologies to create realistic training simulations that used new technologies such as virtual reality and artificial intelligence.[5] Even if China is not acquiring U.S. gaming companies for knowledge of artificial intelligence, virtual reality, graphics, and more, these entities could still be of value from a soft power perspective. Just as films can be used to propagate desired messages, the treatment of China in virtual combat settings (for example, casting it as an enemy, an ally, etc.) or incorporating Chinese mythology into a game could make effective use of high-end technology for purposes of perception management.

Finally, China has controlled the transmission of information via the Internet, a phenomenon often referred to as "the Great Firewall." However, even though the United States chastises Chinese censorship, Chinese companies are allowed to develop their capabilities—which will likely be deployed to disrupt free speech—in the United States. For instance, the Chinese search engine Baidu, which the U.S.–China Economic and Security Review Commission called "an important arbiter of the information accessible to Internet users in China" and which has "aggressively censored results from its web searches," has an R&D facility working on artificial intelligence in California.[6] Furthermore, the Chinese e-commerce company Alibaba indicated that it was interested, as of 2011, in purchasing the U.S. internet company Yahoo!.[7]

NOTES

1. James K. Jackson, *The Committee on Foreign Investment in the United States* (Washington, D.C.: Congressional Research Service, 2014), 8.
2. *Trends and Implications of Chinese Investment in the United States: Hearing before the U.S. China Economic and Security Review Commission,* 113th Cong. (2013).
3. John Dotson, *The Confucian Revival in Propaganda Narratives of the Chinese Government: U.S. China Economic and Security Review Commission Staff Research Paper,* July 20, 2011, 10.
4. *New Neighbors,* 60.
5. Karen Kaplan, Army, "USC Join Forces for Virtual Research Technology: Effort Could Provide More Realistic Military Training Simulations—and Better Hollywood Special Effects," *Los Angeles Times,* August 18, 1999.
6. Thilo Hanemann and Daniel H. Rosen, *High Tech: The Next Wave of Chinese Investment in America* (The Asia Society, 2014), 31; *2010 Report to Congress of the U.S.–China Economic and Security Review Commission,* 111th Cong., Second Session, November 2010, 221, 231.
7. Owen Fletcher, "Alibaba's Interest Poses Tests," *Wall Street Journal,* October 4, 2011.

China, through multiple entities, is likely collecting on developments within the IT environment to facilitate future targeting of technology and expertise. Catapult Systems, a Chinese IT consulting firm, maintains an office in San Antonio, Texas.[56] ChinaSoft acquired Deem, a business service operation, in 2014.[57] Just as they tap U.S. innovation expertise, Chinese firms may also rely on U.S. experts to help navigate into positions from which they can acquire technology. For instance, according to a 2012 congressional report, Huawei attributed its success to the services of Western consulting firms including IBM, Accenture, and PriceWaterhouseCoopers.[58]

Energy

Energy has been an area of notable concern for China. It has pursued resources through extensive bilateral engagement of multiple states, including some considered to be international pariahs. More recently, it has turned its focus to the innovative field of green technology. Successful deployment of these innovative approaches to fuel would enhance multiple elements of Chinese national power. The economic benefits are obvious, as are the military benefits, as China extends its footprint in the South China Sea. However, green technology would also provide China with important diplomatic and informational benefits. It has consistently been perceived as a laggard in reducing pollution, and the ability to portray itself as adopting environmentally friendly measures on a meaningful scale would help it to change the current narrative.

China's approach to energy technology acquisition can be divided into two key areas. The first is the development of energy generation (for example, wind power). The second is the ability to store generated energy via battery technology. Ultimately, China's objective is to deploy these capabilities to the power industry, notably the automotive sector. Beijing has pursued access to this technology through acquisition of U.S. assets through purchases as well as manipulation of commercial interactions to the detriment of U.S. companies such as American Semiconductor.

Green and Other Energy Generation

China has pursued far-reaching international investments to acquire energy resources. Its push into the U.S. energy sector can be viewed as a part of this broader trend. However, the U.S. experience has been characterized by an effort to obtain not natural resources (other than investment in shale plays), but rather the acquisition of technology to exploit natural resources, primarily in the "green" sectors, but also in the traditional petroleum field. Yet even while China is broadening its footprint in the U.S. green energy industry, multiple bilateral agreements between the U.S. and Chinese governments provide vehicles for information sharing that is arguably of far greater benefit to Beijing than to Washington.

Solar

Solar technology has been of consistent interest to China, and it has pursued capabilities for innovation using U.S. resources, as well as pilfering resources from the United States to compete with U.S.-based innovators. Zhenfa New Energy, a major producer of photovoltaic solar cells, controls a subsidiary, STR Holdings, in Connecticut.[59] Chinese firm Hanergy acquired the thin-film photovoltaic solar cell manufacturer MiaSole in 2013 and also purchased Alta, a solar power developer.[60] Zongyi Solar, the U.S. subsidiary of Chinese firm Jiangsu Zongyi, developed Tinton Falls, one of the largest solar farms in New Jersey.[61] China owns multiple solar companies in North Carolina.[62] As China has pursued a state-subsidized effort to acquire innovation assets in the solar and other energy fields, it has created financial difficulties for U.S. firms, which it has exploited to further expand its holdings. For instance, Evergreen Solar, which had been the third largest U.S. producer of solar panels and a beneficiary of subsidies from Massachusetts, found itself in financial difficulty due to excess Chinese production and exports.[63] Ultimately, the financial ramifications led to Evergreen entering a joint venture with China and, ultimately, moving its manufacturing facilities to China in 2011.[64] Such a move could only contribute to China's ability to exert control over the industry and benefit from future innovation in the field.

Wind

In recent years, China has become the primary producer of wind turbines. This is due in large part to Chinese government support, through a USD $6 billion low-interest loan from the China Development Bank. State-owned Xianjing Goldwind Science and Technology is one of the most dominant players in this sector. In 2009 the company entered the U.S. market with a USD $10.2 million pilot wind farm project in Minnesota and sales to projects in Illinois and Montana.[65]

TEXTBOX 6.2. INSIDER THREAT THREATENS U.S. BUSINESSES AND THEIR INTELLECTUAL PROPERTY: THE CASE OF AMERICAN SUPERCONDUCTOR (AMSC)

American Superconductor Inc. (AMSC) is a Massachusetts-based engineering company that provides software and designs for the wind power and power grid industry. AMSC was the victim of trade secret theft by their biggest customer, Sinovel Corporation, a Chinese manufacturer and exporter of wind turbines. One employee of AMSC was charged with stealing trades secrets, causing an alleged loss of more than $800 million to the company.[1]

NOTE

1. "Sinovel Corporation and Three Individuals Charged in Wisconsin with Theft of AMSC Trade Secrets," *Justice News; Department of Justice Office of Public Affairs*, June 27, 2013.

NOTES

1. *2014 Report to Congress of the U.S. China Economic and Security Review Commission*, 113th Cong. 11 (2014).

2. *Report to Congress of the U.S. China Economic and Security Review Commission*, 112th Cong. 156 (2012).

3. *2007 Report to Congress of the U.S. China Economic and Security Review Commission*, 106.

4. Nargiza Salidjanova, *Going Out: An Overview of China's Outward Foreign Direct Investment* (Washington, D.C.: U.S. China Economic and Security Review Commission, 2011), 8.

5. Szamossegi, *An Analysis of Chinese Investments in the U.S. Economy*, 73.

6. *New Neighbors: Chinese Investment in the United States by Congressional District. A Report by the National Committee on U.S.-China Relations and the Rhodium Group*, 2015, 60.

7. *2010 Report to Congress of the U.S. China Economic and Security Review Commission*, 100.

8. *2011 Report to Congress of the U.S. China Economic and Security Review Commission*, 184.

9. Bryan Krekel, Patton Adams, and George Bakos, *Occupying the Information High Ground: Chinese Capabilities for Computer Network Operations and Cyber Espionage* (Washington, D.C.: U.S. China Economic and Security Review Commission, 2012), 14.

10. Ibid., 41.

11. Ibid., 74; *Investigative Report on the U.S. National Security Issues Posed by Chinese Telecommunications Companies Huawei and ZTE: A Report by Chairman Mike Rogers and Ranking Member C.A. Dutch Ruppersberger of the Permanent Select Committee on Intelligence. U.S. House of Representatives.* 112th Cong 13–14 (2012).

12. *Investigative Report on the U.S. National Security Issues Posed by Chinese Telecommunications Companies Huawei and ZTE*, 13–14.

13. Ibid., 24.

14. Springut, Schlaikjeer, and Chen, *China's Program for Science and Technology Modernization: Implications for American Competitiveness*, 61.

15. Ibid., 125.

16. Krekel, Adams, and Bakos, *Occupying the Information High Ground*, 74.

17. Ibid.

18. *Investigative Report on the U.S. National Security Issues Posed by Chinese Telecommunications Companies Huawei and ZTE*, 23.

19. Ibid.

20. Ibid.

21. Ibid., 31.

22. Ibid.

23. Ibid.

24. *Investigative Report on the U.S. National Security Issues Posed by Chinese Telecommunications Companies Huawei and ZTE*, 30

25. Ibid., 10.

26. *New Neighbors*, 59.

27. Ibid., 44 and 49.

28. *Investigative Report on the U.S. National Security Issues Posed by Chinese Telecommunications Companies Huawei and ZTE*, 34.

29. *2013 Report to Congress of the U.S. China Economic and Security Review Commission*, 113th Cong. 108 (2013), 108.

30. Ibid.

31. Shayndi Raice, "U.S. Panel Poised to Recommend Against Huawei Deal," *Wall Street Journal*, February 11, 2011.

32. *2013 Report to Congress of the U.S. China Economic and Security Review Commission*, 108.

33. Shayndi Raice, "U.S. Panel Poised to Recommend Against Huawei Deal," *Wall Street Journal*, February 11, 2011; Yajun Zhang and Eliot Gao, "China Criticizes U.S. Review of Sensitive Deals," *Wall Street Journal*, February 18, 2011.

34. Springut, Schlaikjeer, and Chen, *China's Program for Science and Technology Modernization*, 107.

35. Ibid.

36. Ibid., 125.

37. Krekel, Adams, and Bakos, *Occupying the Information High Ground*, 70.

38. Ibid., 71; *Investigative Report on the U.S. National Security Issues Posed by Chinese Telecommunications Companies Huawei and ZTE*, 40.

39. *Report to Congress of the U.S. China Economic and Security Review Commission*, 112th Cong. 160 (2012).

40. Ibid., 163.

41. *Investigative Report on the U.S. National Security Issues Posed by Chinese Telecommunications Companies Huawei and ZTE*, 42.

42. Krekel, Adams, and Bakos, *Occupying the Information High Ground*, 73.

43. *Investigative Report on the U.S. National Security Issues Posed by Chinese Telecommunications Companies Huawei and ZTE*, 42.

44. Krekel, Adams, and Bakos, *Occupying the Information High Ground*, 68.

45. Ibid., 77.

46. Ibid., 79.

47. "Three Indicted in Lucent Trade-Secret Case," *New York Times*, June 1, 2001; John R. Wilke, "Two Silicon Valley Cases Raise Fears of Chinese Espionage," *Wall Street Journal*, January 15, 2003.

48. *New Neighbors*, 40.

49. Forelle and Hitt, "U.S. Panel Clears IBM Sale of Unit to Chinese Firm," *Wall Street Journal*, March 10, 2005.

50. "Start-Ups Join Microsoft Accelerator," *Washington Post*, August 18, 2014; Spencer Ante and William Mauldin, "IBM, Lenovo Deal Likely to Spark Security Review," *Wall Street Journal*, January 24, 2014.

51. Szamossegi, *An Analysis of Chinese Investments in the U.S. Economy*, 47.

52. Ibid.

53. *New Neighbors*, 40.

54. Rolfe Winkler, "Google Sells Handset Business to Lenovo; the Nearly $3 Billion Deal Comes Two Years after Google Bought Motorola for $12.5 Billion," *Wall Street Journal*, January 29, 2014.

55. Spencer E. Ante, "IBM, Lenovo Wrestle Security Worries," *Wall Street Journal*, June 26, 2014.

56. *New Neighbors*, 44.

57. Ibid., 48.

58. *Investigative Report on the U.S. National Security Issues Posed by Chinese Telecommunications Companies Huawei and ZTE*, 26.

59. *New Neighbors*, 13.

60. Ibid., 49.

61. Ibid., 17.

62. Ibid., 40.

63. Szamossegi, *An Analysis of Chinese Investments in the U.S. Economy*, 105.

64. Ibid., 105.

65. Ibid., 47–48.

Chapter Seven

Buying In

Part II

Foreign governments work within the paradigm of "buying" to conduct illicit intelligence activities. These encompass students and researchers who come to the United States with the purpose of acquiring knowledge and resultant technology on behalf of their home countries. They may take a longer route—embedding themselves into high-tech industries to gain access to propriety information—prior to leaving the United States with the results of their malfeasance. To target U.S. institutions, foreign entities must be able to effectively identify entities of interest and to move the information, once acquired, out of the country. On the front end is information gathering about placement and access identifying knowledge of value. On the back end of an intelligence collection, a foreign entity must have the ability to successfully exfiltrate the results of an operation from the United States or from a U.S. commercial or academic institution abroad.

Physical and cyber methodologies may be used for intelligence collection by foreign entities attempting to "buy in" or penetrate the United States. Physically present individuals include intelligence officers assigned under diplomatic cover and foreign operatives dispatched to infiltrate academia and industry. These individuals are responsible either for recruiting individuals who have access to information of interest or for directly purloining information to foreign customers. However, the cyber milieu provides opportunities for foreign governments to decrease their exposure. Open Source Intelligence assessment data, historically collected manually, is now often available online. Email or some other means of electronic communication provides a means to social engineer the divulgence of sensitive information.

PENETRATION OF ACADEMIA

The United States is a world leader in the area of academic institutions and associated research. However, this prominence also makes it a target for foreign entities seeking to find shortcuts to research breakthroughs or simply to catch up with U.S. capabilities. Threats to academic institutions are well-established and diverse. Foreign governments may use researchers from their respective countries to gain access to the results of ongoing work. Furthermore, students who come to the United States may use their admittance, via academia, as a point of entry to high-tech industries from which they can exfiltrate proprietary information in furtherance of foreign governments. Finally, the academic milieu provides opportunities for collection of open-source information, both for the inherent value of that information and the leads that it may yield that a foreign intelligence service can use to spot and assess individuals with additional information.

Historical Precedent

The Soviet Union historically used students to conduct intelligence collection in the United States. The Soviets, according to the congressional testimony of James Geer, assistant director of the FBI's Intelligence Division, placed KGB officers in cover positions as students.[1] Actual Soviet students were also involved with intelligence collection activities and met with Soviet intelligence officers who were working from various Soviet diplomatic establishments in the United States.[2] Soviet students at U.S. institutions were at times tasked to obtain, sometimes by covert means, any documents and material accessible to them either through an identified individual or through the school's library.[3]

The Soviet Union, in furtherance of its VPK program—the multifaceted technology acquisition effort discussed in chapter 3—identified Carnegie-Mellon, Cincinnati, Kentucky, Massachusetts Institute of Technology, Michigan, and Wisconsin as sources for information about high-strength, high-temperature alloys, lightweight structural alloys, and powder metal processing. The Soviets saw the California Institute of Technology and MIT as sources for transonic, supersonic, and hypersonic aerodynamic research. Additionally, the Soviet Union viewed Princeton, Stanford, Kansas, MIT, Ohio State, and Penn State as likely venues for obtaining information regarding electrohydraulic control systems. Furthermore, research applicable to future high-energy laser and particle beam weapons was the target of the Soviets at MIT, Denver, and Princeton.[4]

Foreign governments continue to exploit U.S. openness to academics and students as an avenue by which to collect against innovation. The Defense Security Service (DSS) assessed that regimes in the Near East region use professors, students, and researchers on U.S. student visas to collect against technology.[5] In a number of instances, these students appear to have targeted their applications to U.S. universities involved in sensitive or classified research projects for the Department of Defense.[6] This was consistent with the DSS report of the previous year indicating links between Near East governments and students' academic interests and solicitation to specific U.S. programs.[7]

Risks Inherent in Foreign Researchers

The case of foreign researchers is an example of the old adage that one gets what one pays for. In a report to Congress, the U.S. National Counterintelligence Center (now the National Counterintelligence and Security Center) discussed how foreign students served as research assistants at no cost to professors.[8] This arrangement provided students access to the professor's research and opportunities to learn the applications of the technology.[9] In at least one publicly identified incident, a student was specifically tasked by a foreign intelligence service to seek out a laboratory assistant position to acquire access to the unique research.[10] If such scenarios transpire in the way a foreign intelligence service intends, the technology has been misappropriated before it can even be commercialized or applied in the service of the U.S. government. Misappropriated research may also be used to speed a country's own work. According to the DSS's 2013 report, East Asia- and Pacific-region students and academics exploited access to sensitive and restricted technologies as a way to drive parallel research and development to benefit their home countries.[11] As of 2015, Bo Cai, who was employed by a technology company in China, attempted to work through his cousin, Wentong Cai, a Chinese national who was in the United States on a student visa, to obtain sensors manufactured primarily for sale to the U.S. Department of Defense.[12] These sensors had applications for line-of-sight stabilization and precision motion-control systems. Wentong invoked his status as a graduate microbiology student at Iowa State University to justify acquiring the sensors.[13] Authorities arrested Bo Cai in December 2014 while he was trying to smuggle the sensor onto a China-bound flight.[14]

Foreign academics, possibly working on behalf of their home governments, have also reached virtually into the United States to elicit information. DSS noted in its 2014 report that Near East students requested thesis assistance and review of draft scientific publications that in both instances could facilitate a transfer of knowledge in the form of corrections or comments.[15] Additionally, Near East–region students have requested access to U.S. research papers. Furthermore, studies in the United States provide opportunities to develop contacts that foreign students and researchers can subsequently leverage for intelligence collection. According to a U.S. congressional report, "many PRC scientists were educated in the United States and retain valuable contacts in the U.S. research and business community who can be exploited for technology transfer."[16]

Academic Institutions as a Venue for Collection of Open-Source (OSINT) Information

Foreign intelligence services, in addition to penetrating academia as students and researchers, have also pursued access to open-source information available through academic libraries. From a substantive perspective, these institutions are valuable targets for innovation-oriented intelligence collection. According to FBI testimony in the late 1980s, information about new technologies was often first available in the public sector and only later classified once military applications became apparent.[17] This appeared to be no less a problem as of 2008, when the National Counterintelligence Executive wrote that "often [sensitive] technologies are difficult to identify in their early phases."[18]

Soviet intelligence historically attempted to develop contacts with librarians responsible for technical collections as well as students who used these resources. Because collections of technical materials attracted scientists and engineers, Soviet intelligence used libraries as venues to spot and assess individuals of interest. The Soviets were able to get technical information and identify future human sources. In addition to direct contacts, the Soviets also tasked sources to steal microfiches containing specific technical reports from libraries. According to the FBI, Soviet intelligence also targeted librarians and library patrons because of their potential to gain future employment with the U.S. Department of Defense's Defense Technology Information Center.[19]

Academia as an Entry Point to Industry

Foreign governments may benefit from students who initially arrive in the United States for academic reasons but eventually segue into positions in the private sector. In May 2015, the U.S. Department of Justice charged six Chinese citizens with stealing wireless technologies from U.S. companies and establishing a joint venture with Chinese state-run Tianjin University to produce and sell the technology. Three of the defendants studied at the University of Southern California (USC), where they received graduate degrees in electrical engineering.[20] (In the course of earning their degrees, two of the defendants—Hao Zhang and Wei Pang—were permitted to work on a U.S. Department of Defense–funded project.)[21] Pang then went to work for Avago Technologies and Zhang for Skyworks Solutions.[22]

Pang and Zhang expropriated proprietary information regarding thin film bulk acoustic resonator technology from Avago and Skyworks. This technology allows wireless devices to filter out unwanted signals and that, in more advanced variations, is used in smaller wireless devices with military applications.[23] (Their DoD-sponsored work at USC also pertained to this technology.) In conjunction with the Chinese government–run Tianjin University (specifically its investment arm), the defendants established ROFS Microsystems, located within a district identified as Tianjin University's micro- and nanotechnology industry base.[24] The Chinese government had a particular interest in seeing Tianjin excel, as the university was part of the country's 985 Program, which identified ten Chinese universities that were intended to be "world class" by the early twenty-first century.[25] Tianjin's complicity was further notable in its authorization for Wei and Hao to incorporate Novana, a front company hiding the true source of the technology in the Cayman Islands.[26] Demonstrating the defendants' audacity, Peng stated the venture would beat competitors because they would save money by not having to invest in research and development.[27] The U.S. victims learned of their loss when Pang's former boss traveled to Tianjin to visit Pang and recognized the stolen Avago technology in Pang's laboratory.[28] Not only did the theft deprive U.S. companies and the U.S. government of the technology, but it also allowed ROFS to sell the technology to military entities.[29]

A similar case involved the theft of U.S. aerospace information. Steve Liu, a PRC national, came to the United States to work as a researcher at a U.S. university. Following this stint, Liu worked for several U.S. technology companies, including L-3 Communications, that developed precision navigation devices and innovative components for the U.S. Department of Defense.[30] Liu's objective in working for L-3 Communications was to steal thousands of electronic files detailing the performance and design of guidance systems for missiles, rockets, target locators, and unmanned aerial vehicles. The theft of these documents positioned him for employment in the PRC.[31] According to the FBI, Liu delivered presentations about the stolen technology at multiple Chinese universities, the Chinese Academy of Sciences, and conferences organized by PRC government entities.[32] This suggests that China's concerted effort to attract expatriates with technical knowledge back to China is having an impact on economic decision making. Liu also demonstrated divided loyalty in his role as co-chair of the Chinese government–sponsored International Workshop on Innovation and Commercialization of Micro and Nanotechnology, which brought together researchers, administrators, and engineers and provided an opportunity for the Chinese government to identify expatriates of interest.[33]

Yet another example of how China's universities play a role in the illicit exfiltration of U.S. technology and expertise involves Rongxing Li, an Ohio State University professor. Li had served as the endowed chair for OSU's Department of Civil, Environmental, and Geodetic Engineering. In 2014, Li attempted to obtain nearly USD $37 million from NASA for imaging work on the 2020 Mars mission. Li blatantly lied in his proposal, claiming that he had no relationships with Chinese scientists, even though he had spent most of 2012 on a sabbatical at Tongji University in Shanghai and maintained an ongoing association with Tongji. He even was listed as the director of a center for spatial information and as a professor. Not only would Li have obtained NASA monetary support, but under the terms of the proposal he also would have been able to access Department of Defense technical information. While in China in 2014, Li provided notice of his resignation from OSU. When his wife attempted to leave the United States, DHS agents found multiple thumb drives in her possession containing restricted defense information.[34]

Foreign researchers at U.S. institutions have also attempted to sell their technology to entities in their home country. Yudong Zhu, an associate professor in the radiology department of New York University's School of Medicine, obtained funding from the U.S. National Institutes of Health (NIH) to conduct research on magnetic resonance imaging.[35] Zhu arranged for two individuals to come to New York from China. All were charged with conspiring to take a bribe from a Chinese-sponsored research institute and a Chinese medical imaging company to share nonpublic information about the NIH-funded work.[36] All three individuals were associated with the Shenzhen Institute of Advanced Technology, which is known to recruit overseas Chinese with technical knowledge and to pursue ventures that may result in technology transfer.[37]

These examples suggest the need for caution when permitting foreign students to segue into high-tech industry. Yet U.S. institutions often ignore the danger. Indeed, it has been referred to as a positive trend. According to the China Economic and Security Review Commission, attracting Chinese investment into the United States can be accomplished by building on the U.S. competitive advantage in the academic sector to "integrate Chinese nationals into the fabric of U.S society."[38] Unfortunately, it appears that foreign governments, notably China, have exploited this openness. Greater integration of individuals into innovative industries provides them increasing access that they can exploit to benefit their home country at the expense of the United States.

Soviet exploitation of students also used academia as a point of entry to collect against technology. A Soviet official assigned at the United Nations in New York City attempted to enlist the services of students at Columbia

University and Queens College. This was likely a first step in the recruitment cycle that would eventually entail clandestine collection. The official in one instance promised that the Soviet Union would pay for a student's education in exchange for the student's pursuit of a position in the defense industry where the individual would have access to classified information. Targeting of students was an example of how open-source information, such as theses and term papers, in higher education could be exploited not only for the information contained within but also as a means to identify U.S. students who could be targeted for recruitment.[39]

Several foreign governments have applied the approach of leveraging cultural ties to exploit subject matter expertise in academia. According to the U.S. National Counterintelligence Executive (now the National Counterintelligence and Security Center), multiple countries have demonstrated effectiveness at tapping foreign-born recipients of doctorates from U.S. universities in science and engineering for access to U.S. technology.[40] Cultural initiatives involving specific academic institutions may provide a means to develop ties that can later be exploited for intelligence activities. As of 2014, China had established its Confucius Institutes at ninety colleges and universities in the United States and Canada.[41] Russia has also pursued efforts to establish cultural rapport with young Americans, including a Georgetown graduate student, by sponsoring paid trips to Russia. This was done through Yury Zaytsev, the head of the Russian Cultural Center in Washington, D.C.[42] The FBI is investigating whether Zaytsev and an organization he led, Roosotrudnichetsvo, used these trips as opportunities to recruit participants.[43]

The convergence of culture and academia provided the milieu for the activities of another suspected Chinese operative. As of 1978, the FBI was investigating Chien Ning, who it suspected of having been dispatched to the United States by the MSS. He established, with Chinese government backing, the Chinese-language magazine *Science and Technology Review*. This magazine played upon the concept of "overseas Chinese" and the exploitation of diaspora populations who had access to information and technology of interest. Ning also engaged in the exploitation of open-source information by reviewing the holdings of the libraries at the University of California at Berkeley and Stanford University for PhD theses and books, which he arranged to have photocopied and sent back to China.[44]

JOINT VENTURES

Foreign governments have attempted to gain access to U.S. innovation via joint ventures. According to a congressional report on the PRC's acquisition of U.S. technology, Beijing increased the resources it put toward identifying high-technology U.S. firms to which it could make overtures and used its science and technology representatives at its embassies to help with targeting and encourage collaboration.[45] However, negotiations may provide an opportunity for a foreign entity to milk a U.S. company for proprietary information before walking away from the table. Chinese delegations have made overtures to U.S. companies, ostensibly in pursuit of a joint venture. Throughout the course of negotiations, they elicited as much of the company's information as possible before pulling out of the deal at the last minute.[46] In 2013, the U.S. Trade Representative suggested the Chinese used failed joint ventures as a way to obtain trade secrets.[47]

Joint ventures have preceded targeting of companies' proprietary information, particularly in the case of China. According to a U.S. Congressional report, "U.S. businesses may be unaware that joint venture operations are also vulnerable to penetration by official PRC intelligence agencies."[48] Companies wishing to do business in China have little choice but to subject themselves to penetration by foreign intelligence collection because the Chinese government usually demands that establishing a corporate presence be done as a joint venture.[49]

Close quarters between U.S. and foreign participants in joint ventures also provide avenues for the illicit transfer of knowledge or resultant technology. Such transfers are often unintentional—the result of carelessness bred by familiarity. According to a 2001 report by the National Counterintelligence Executive, foreign employees who are in place for a long period of time will be accepted as full partners, which may result in the waning of security vigilance on the part of U.S. participants.[50]

MULTINATIONAL CORPORATIONS

The international reach of U.S. corporations not only puts them at risk of being targeted abroad but also offers a conduit through which foreign operatives might enter the United States. According to journalist John Fialka, during the 1970s and 1980s, French intelligence recruited and inserted moles into the French operations of IBM, Corning, and Texas Instruments.[51] Furthermore, as of 1990, U.S. intelligence authenticated a document that outlined French plans to target forty-nine U.S. companies as well as multiple financial institutions and government agencies.[52] More recently, starting in 2006, the Chinese PLA began to infiltrate 141 companies, in more than twenty major industries. They wished to acquire technical information, blueprints, proprietary manufacturing processes, test results, business plans, pricing documents, partnership agreements, and contact lists from victim organizations.[53] All of these companies were in what China considered to be strategic emerging industries.[54] Poland, while still a Soviet satellite, used the Polish American Machinery Company, a U.S.-incorporated firm, as the marketing arm of the Polish trade agency Metal Export. The West Coast branch manager, Marian Zacharski, was assigned by the Polish intelligence service to spot and recruit individuals in the California aerospace industry.[55]

Even when engaged in joint ventures, China may still target U.S. companies. For instance, Westinghouse, even as it was working in China to develop nuclear reactor technology, discovered that hackers had targeted it.[56] A similarly duplicitous approach marked the dealings of the Chinese telecom sector with U.S. counterparts. In 1997, Motorola established a joint lab with Huawei to develop high-speed switching and routing equipment.[57] In 2002, twelve former Motorola employees established a rival company, Lemko, while still employed by Motorola.[58] Huawei's founder, Ren Zhengfei, had reportedly been worked with the defendants since 2001 and Huawei was a beneficiary of the trade secrets obtained in the five years following its establishment.[59] As if Huawei had not done enough damage to Motorola, the company was also the victim of theft by a naturalized U.S. citizen, Hanjuan Jin, on behalf of a Chinese company that developed telecommunications technology for China's military.[60]

As discussed in a previous chapter, Chinese companies have established a footprint in the United States. On at least one occasion this has facilitated the theft of trade secrets. In 2012, Yuan Li, a former research chemist for the pharmaceutical company Sanofi-Aventis, pled guilty to stealing Sanofi trade secrets and making them available for sale through Abby Pharmatech Inc., the U.S. subsidiary of a Chinese pharmaceutical company.[61] These secrets were viewed by Sanofi as potential building blocks for future drugs and were a foundation for future innovation.

Foreign-owned corporations that establish presences in the United States may also provide platforms for foreign intelligence services to collect information. For instance, in 2015, the U.S. government identified Evgeny Buryakov as a Russian SVR operative who was operating under nonofficial cover, masquerading as an employee of a Russian bank's Manhattan office.[62] Buryakov, as well as two other SVR personnel, Victor Podobnyy and Igor Sporyshev, were tasked with collecting a variety of information, including material about U.S. efforts to develop alternative energy resources.[63] All three of these SVR personnel were members of the SVR's Directorate ER, which is dedicated to developing information on economic issues.[64] Foreign media, especially if state controlled, is another field that may be used by foreign intelligence collectors as it provides a plausible reason for pursuing information. For example, Sporyshev requested Buryakov to formulate questions for a Russian state-owned news organization national security journalist Shane Harris identified as Tass.[65]

INDIVIDUAL INFILTRATION OF U.S. COMPANIES

China, again, was the state sponsor of a clear-cut infiltration of the U.S. technology industry in furtherance of military know-how. In 1978, Chi Mak, who eventually gained a position working on sensitive U.S. defense technology, was dispatched to the United States explicitly to gather information on behalf of the Chinese government.[66] He began relaying information to China in 1983.[67] Mak became a naturalized U.S. citizen in 1985 and was able to obtain a Secret-level security clearance in 1996 through his work at Power Paragon, a subsidiary of L-3/SPD Technologies/Power Systems Group. He accessed and copied information about the Quiet Electric Propulsion Project for U.S. Navy warships, which he passed to China via his brother Tai Mak, who acted as a courier.[68] It was apparent that Chi Mak was tasked to collect specific information at the behest of China when FBI agents discovered his collection documents identifying seventeen categories of naval- and space-based military technology that Mak was supposed to obtain.[69]

The damage that Mak caused to U.S. defense innovation was severe in part because he was able to operate for a long time before being detected. He began providing information to China in 1983 but was not arrested until 2005. When authorities searched his residence they discovered thousands of pages of documents on military research and development that he had stolen from his employer.[70] China's use of individuals such as Mak to bolster its naval technology has serious implications for U.S. national security interests now more than ever, as China takes an increasingly aggressive posture in the South China Sea.

Although a volunteer rather than a dispatched agent, Dongfan Chung, a former Boeing engineer, is discussed here because of his role in the Chi Mak episode. Chung's participation in providing sensitive information to China emphasizes two previously discussed concerns—cultural identity and the close relationship of Chinese universities with the Chinese government. Chung, a naturalized U.S. citizen, volunteered his services because he wanted to contribute to China's modernization.[71] (The implicit tradeoff, of course, was that such action was at the expense of the United States.) In the letter by which he volunteered his service to help China modernize, Chung referred to himself as having been a "Chinese compatriot for over thirty years" and to China as "the motherland."[72] The other noteworthy aspect of Chung's work for the Chinese is that he initially indicated his willingness to spy to a professor at the Harbin Institute of Technology.[73] As previously discussed, Chinese institutions of higher education function as an appendage of the government and interaction with them provides an opportunity for exploitation of U.S. interests.

Chung had already worked his way into the U.S. defense industry by the time he volunteered to China. Having started work in 1973, he did not offer his services until 1979.[74] Chung held positions with Rockwell and Boeing and maintained a Secret-level clearance, which he obtained in 1973, six years before he volunteered his services to China.[75] After his initial contact with the Harbin Institute of Technology, Chung's Chinese government customers included the China National Aero Technology Import and Export Corporation, the Nan Chang Aircraft Company, and the China Aviation Industry Corporation.[76] Like Mak, Chung was not a simple "vacuum cleaner" collector, but instead received specific taskings from China for technical information as well as questions regarding aircraft development.[77] Topics included the U.S. space shuttle program, military and civilian aircraft, and helicopters.[78]

Once he compromised information, Chung communicated it in three different ways that illustrate how foreign governments may channel information to parties of interest. The Chinese diplomatic presence provided Chung an opportunity to hand information over, which he did, via the Education Consul at the Chinese consulate in San Francisco, California.[79] The items sent through the consul included twenty-four manuals from Rockwell's B-1 Bomber division, all of which carried the cover notice that "Possession of this publication is restricted to the engineering personnel of Rockwell International Aerospace Division. Its disclosure to organizations other than Rockwell International or selected federal agencies is prohibited."[80] Chung also traveled to China clandestinely—failing to report his travel to his cleared employer, a condition of his clearance—and delivered lectures on the U.S. space shuttle program and other sensitive topics.[81] Foreign governments use such personal interactions as opportunities to exploit unwitting participants and therefore it is plausible that a witting participant will divulge even greater information. In Chung's case, he was asked to prepare specific topics by his Chinese handlers. In 1985, the Deputy Director, Technical Import Department, China National Aero Technology Import and Export Corporation (CATIC) suggested that Chung provide lectures in China on "the entire process of the aircraft's fatigue life and its major links," "the static strength and principles of fatigue design when designing new aircraft," "the formulation of a fatigue test plant," and "the determination of a helicopter's rotor wings, blades, and propeller hub's load."[82] Chung also made presentations to Chinese aerospace workers—an activity that played on the ties of cultural affinity.[83] In 1987,

Gu Weihao of China's Ministry of Aviation and the China Aviation Industry Corporation advised Chung that it would be faster and safer to transmit information via Chi Mak.[84] This may have been Chung's undoing, as the FBI questioned him following the arrest of Mak.[85]

Like Mak, Chung had a long run as a foreign agent and exploited his access to acquire massive quantities of information that he was all too eager to provide to his "motherland." He began spying in 1979 and was not arrested until 2008. His career in defense ran from 1973 until 2006. When federal authorities searched his home, they discovered approximately three hundred thousand documents that included plans for the fueling system of a Delta-4 rocket and an antennae system for the space shuttle.[86]

ROLE OF DIPLOMATIC ESTABLISHMENTS

Foreign governments routinely use their diplomatic presence in the United States as a cover for intelligence officers who seek out opportunities to collect information of interest to their respective regimes. The Soviet Union's KGB Line X, which was responsible for science- and technology-related collection, tended to occupy science attaché positions at Soviet diplomatic establishments and at international organizations.[87] As noted in the Chung case, the Chinese have used diplomatic posts for intelligence activities. Chinese PLA military intelligence officers use the cover of military attachés at the Chinese embassy in Washington, D.C., and at the United Nations in New York.[88] Even less prominent countries have been persistent in their efforts to obtain technology. For instance, in 1972, the FBI informed Congress that Cuba, through its mission at the United Nations, pursued electronic equipment for shipment back to Cuba.[89] This is consistent with reporting that Cuban officials were obtaining plans for computer chips from Bill Gaede, an engineer at Advanced Micro, who started providing information to them in 1982 out of ideological affinity for the Cuban regime.[90]

CYBER CAMPAIGNS

Foreign-originated cyber attacks are an unfortunate reality of life. As discussed previously, the cyber vector is an effective technique for intelligence collection. It can be used to exfiltrate a massive quantity of information, meaning that espionage need not only target one lab or office but rather entire industries. Between July and September 2011, Chinese hackers targeted proprietary designs, formulas, and manufacturing processes of the chemical industry, including multiple Fortune 100 companies involved in the research and development of advanced materials.[91] Earlier in 2011, Chinese hackers targeted the networks of five international oil companies in an attempt to steal bid data.[92] In 2013, the PLA engaged in an extensive cyber-facilitated collection campaign against aerospace and defense firms, seeking information about drone technology.[93] This began with a widespread sweep of defense contractors prior to the hackers narrowing down their attacks to companies that specialized in drone technology.[94] Consistent with the earlier discussion, private industry—Symantec, McAfee, and FireEye, respectively—rather than the U.S. government identified these campaigns. In 2012, NASA acknowledged that it had experienced a series of attacks against its networks and that intruders had gained complete functional control over Jet Propulsion Laboratory networks.[95]

CONCLUSION

Foreign monetary and human capital, which pours into the United States, helps to keep commerce—a driver of innovation—moving. However, the channels established by the coursing of legitimate academic and business interactions also provide conduits that competitor and adversary governments can use to infiltrate intelligence collectors into the United States. Many of the activities discussed in this chapter boil down to individuals' decisions to cooperate with a foreign government—whether by engaging its representatives within the domestic setting or by clandestinely taking information abroad. These episodes provide indicators that may be used to better evaluate the risks to U.S. interests. Foreign students and researchers who express an interest in engaging U.S. institutions should be scrutinized for connections with foreign academic entities that have been linked with illicit activity (for example, Tianjin University). Furthermore, cultural affinity is a recurrent theme in collection on behalf of foreign entities. It is present in cases in which the individual remains in the United States and in those in which the individual attempts to permanently defect while in possession of proprietary information. It is not necessary or desirable to expect individuals to sever their ties to foreign cultures. However, participation in professional organizations organized around a shared cultural background should be of concern. This is even more the case if government entities sponsor or participate in these organizations, as in the case of the International Workshop on Innovation and Commercialization of Micro and Nanotechnology.

NOTES

1. *FBI Counterintelligence Visits to Libraries: Hearings before the Subcommittee on Civil and Constitutional Rights of the Committee on the Judiciary, House of Representatives*, 100th Cong. 266 (1988) (Testimony of James H. Geer, Assistant Director, Intelligence Division, Federal Bureau of Investigation).

2. Ibid.

3. Ibid., 262.

4. *Soviet Acquisition of Military Significant Western Technology: An Update*, 21.

5. Defense Security Service, *Targeting U.S. Technology: A Trend Analysis of Cleared Industry Reporting* (2014), 41.

6. Ibid.

7. Defense Security Service, *Targeting U.S. Technology: A Trend Analysis of Cleared Industry Reporting* (2013), 33.

8. National Counterintelligence Executive, *Annual Report to Congress on Foreign Economic Collection and Industrial Espionage: 1995*, 18–19.

9. Ibid.

10. Ibid.

11. Defense Security Service, *Targeting U.S. Technology: A Trend Analysis of Cleared Industry Reporting* (2013), 23–24.

12. U.S. Department of Justice, *Summary of Major U.S. Export Enforcement, Economic Espionage, Trade Secret and Embargo-Related Criminal Cases* (January 2009 to the Present: Updated August 12, 2015), 2015.

13. Ibid.

14. Ibid.

15. Defense Security Service, *Targeting U.S. Technology: A Trend Analysis of Cleared Industry Reporting* (2014), 41.

16. *PRC Acquisition of U.S. Technology*, 28.

17. *FBI Counterintelligence Visits to Libraries: Hearings before the Subcommittee on Civil and Constitutional Rights of the Committee on the Judiciary, House of Representatives*, 100th Cong. 171 (1988) (Testimony of James H. Geer, Assistant Director, Intelligence Division, Federal Bureau of Investigation).

18. Office of the National Counterintelligence Executive, *Annual Report to Congress on Foreign Economic Collection and Industrial Espionage, 2008* (Office of the National Counterintelligence Executive, 2009), 4.

19. *FBI Counterintelligence Visits to Libraries: Hearings before the Subcommittee on Civil and Constitutional Rights of the Committee on the Judiciary, House of Representatives*, 100th Cong. 116 (1988) (Testimony of James H. Geer, Assistant Director, Intelligence Division, Federal Bureau of Investigation).

20. Chun Han Wong, "Economic Espionage Charges Could Further Dent China-U.S. Ties," *Wall Street Journal*, May 22, 2015.

21. Ellen Nakashima, "Grand Jury Indicts Six Chinese Citizens in Alleged Plot to Steal Trade Secrets," *Washington Post*, May 20, 2015.

22. Ibid.

23. Andrew Grossman, "U.S. Charges Six Chinese with Economic Espionage," *Wall Street Journal*, May 20, 2015.

24. Ellen Nakashima, "U.S. Indicts 6 Chinese Citizens on Charges of Stealing Trade Secrets," *Washington Post*, May 19, 2015; Edward Wong, "Back Home, Chinese Scientists Indicted by U.S. Are Seen as Rising Stars," *New York Times*, May 12, 2015.

25. *United States of American v. Wei Pang, Hao Zhang, Huisui Zhang, Jinping Chen, Zhao Gang, and Chong Zhou.*

26. Ibid.

27. Ellen Nakashima, "Grand Jury Indicts Six Chinese Citizens in Alleged Plot to Steal Trade Secrets," *Washington Post*, May 20, 2015.

28. Ibid.

29. Andrew Grossman, "U.S. Charges Six Chinese with Economic Espionage," *Wall Street Journal*, May 20, 2015.

30. *United States of America v. Sixing Liu a.k.a. "Steve Liu" Criminal Complaint.* Magistrate No. 11-8022, 3.

31. "Former Employee of New Jersey Defense Contractor Sentenced to 70 Months in Prison for Exporting Sensitive Military Technology to China," March 25, 2013, www.fb.gov.

32. Ibid.

33. *United States of America v. Sixing Liu a.k.a. "Steve Liu" Criminal Complaint.* Magistrate No. 11-8022, 3.

34. Kathy Lynn Gray, "FBI Investigates China Ties of Ohio State Professor Who Resigned, Disappeared," *Columbus Dispatch*, September 8, 2015.

35. Benjamin Weiser, "3 N.Y.U. Scientists Accepted Bribes from China, U.S. Says," *New York Times*, May 20, 2013.

36. Ibid.

37. Edward Wong and Didi Kirsten Tatlow, "China Seen in Push to Gain Technology Insights," *New York Times*, June 5, 2013.

38. Koch-Weser and Ditz, *Chinese Investment in the United States*, 24.

39. *FBI Counterintelligence Visits to Libraries: Hearings before the Subcommittee on Civil and Constitutional Rights of the Committee on the Judiciary, House of Representatives*, 100th Cong. 263 (1988) (Testimony of James H. Geer, Assistant Director, Intelligence Division, Federal Bureau of Investigation).

40. Office of the National Counterintelligence Executive, *Annual Report to Congress on Foreign Economic Collection and Industrial Espionage: 2004*, 11.

41. "On Partnerships with Foreign Governments: The Case of Confucius Institutes," American Association of University Professors, June 2014.

42. Sari Horwitz, "Head of U.S.-Based Russian Cultural Center Being Investigated as Possible Spy," *Washington Post*, October 23, 2013.

43. Ibid.

44. Wise, *Tiger Trap*, 43–44.

45. *PRC Acquisition of U.S. Technology*, 28.

46. Ibid., 39.

47. Office of the National Counterintelligence Executive, *Annual Report to Congress on Foreign Economic Collection and Industrial Espionage 2001* (Office of the National Counterintelligence Executive, 2002), 3.

48. *PRC Acquisition of U.S. Technology*, 30.

49. Andrew Batson and Matthew Kamitsching, "China Plans System to Vet Foreign Deals for Security," *Wall Street Journal*, August 26, 2008.

50. Office of the National Counterintelligence Executive, *Annual Report to Congress on Foreign Economic Collection and Industrial Espionage 2001*, 3.

51. Fialka, *War by Other Means*, 92.

52. Ibid., 95–96.

53. U.S. Trade Representative, *2013 Special 301 Report*, 33.

54. Ibid.

55. *Meeting the Espionage Challenge: A Review of United State Counterintelligence and Security Programs. Report of the Select Committee on Intelligence. United States Senate*. Rep. No. 99-522. 99th Congress. At 112 (1986).

56. "Cybersnoops and Mincing Rascals: Chinese Spying," *Economist*, May 24, 2014.

57. Springut, Schlaikjeer, and Chen, *China's Program for Science and Technology Modernization*, 125.

58. Ibid., 107.

59. Ibid., 125.

60. "Suburban Chicago Woman Sentenced to Four Years in Prison for Stealing Motorola Trade Secrets before Boarding Plane to China," August 29, 2012, www.justice.gov; *United States of America v. Hanjuan Jin*. Appeal from the United States District Court for the Northern District of Ilinois Eastern Division No. 08 CR 192—Robert Castillo, Chief Judge. Argued September 9, 2013—Decided September 26, 2013.

61. U.S. Department of Justice, *Summary of Major U.S. Export Enforcement, Economic Espionage, Trade Secret and Embargo-Related Criminal Cases* (January 2008 to the Present: Updated March 26, 2014), 46.

62. *United States of America v. Evgeny Buryakov (a/k/a "Zhenya"), Igor Sporyshev, and Victor Podobnyy*.

63. Ibid.

64. Ibid.

65. Ibid.; Shane Harris, "The Russian News Agency Doubled as a Spy Machine," *Daily Beast*, January 27, 2015.

66. "The Insider Threat: An Introduction to Detecting and Deterring an Insider Spy," www.fbi.gov (accessed October 27, 2015).

67. Herbig, *Changes in Espionage in Americans: 1947–2007*.

68. *2009 Report to Congress of the U.S.-China Economy and Security Review Commission*, 155.

69. Ibid.

70. Herbig. *Changes in Espionage in Americans: 1947–2007*.

71. *2009 Report to Congress of the U.S.-China Economy and Security Review Commission*, 15.

72. *United States of America v. Dongfan "Greg" Chung*. October 2007. United States District Court, Central District of California, SA CR 08-0024; "Former Boeing Engineer Convicted of Economic Espionage in Theft of Space Shuttle Secrets for China," U.S. Department of Justice, July 16, 2009.

73. *2009 Report to Congress of the U.S.-China Economy and Security Review Commission*, 15.

74. Ibid.

75. Ibid.; *United States of America v. Dongfan "Greg" Chung*. October 2007. United States District Court, Central District of California, SA CR 08-0024.

76. *2009 Report to Congress of the U.S.-China Economy and Security Review Commission*, 15.

77. Ibid.

78. *United States of America v. Dongfan "Greg" Chung*. October 2007. United States District Court, Central District of California, SA CR 08-0024.

79. *2009 Report to Congress of the U.S.-China Economy and Security Review Commission*, 15; *United States of America v. Dongfan "Greg" Chung*. October 2007. United States District Court, Central District of California, SA CR 08-0024.

80. Ibid.

81. *2009 Report to Congress of the U.S.-China Economy and Security Review Commission*, 15; Richard A Serrano, "O.C. Man Is Accused of Being a Spy," *Los Angeles Times*, February 12, 2008; *United States of America v. Dongfan "Greg" Chung*. October 2007. United States District Court, Central District of California, SA CR 08-0024.

82. *United States of America v. Dongfan "Greg" Chung*. October 2007. United States District Court, Central District of California, SA CR 08-0024.

83. Richard A Serrano, "O.C. Man Is Accused of Being a Spy," *Los Angeles Times*, February 12, 2008.

84. *United States of America v. Dongfan "Greg" Chung*. October 2007. United States District Court, Central District of California, SA CR 08-0024.

85. Edward Pettersson, "Ex-Boeing Engineer Chung Guilty of Stealing Secrets (Update 3)," *Bloomberg*, July 16, 2009, www.bloomberg.com.

86. Tami Abdollah and Christopher Goffard, "Chinese Born Engineer Convicted Under Economic Espionage Act," *Los Angeles Times*, July 17, 2008.

87. *Soviet Acquisition of Military Significant Western Technology: An Update*, 16.

88. *PRC Acquisition of U.S. Technology*, 36.

89. *Venceremos Brigade Part 2: Hearings before the Committee on Internal Security, House of Representatives*, 96th Cong. 7825 (1972).

90. Calvin Sims, "Troubling Issues in a Silicon Valley Spy Case," *New York Times*, July 8, 1996.

91. Mark Claydon, "Report: Chinese Hackers Launched Summer Offensive on US Chemical Industry," *Christian Science Monitor*, November 1, 2011.

92. Ibid.

93. *2013 Report to Congress of the U.S. China Economic and Security Review Commission*, 223.

94. Edward Wong, "Hacking U.S. Secrets, China Pushes for Drones," *New York Times*, September 20, 2013.

95. *Cyber Espionage and the Theft of U.S. Intellectual Property and Technology before the House of Representatives. Committee on Energy and Commerce Subcommittee on Oversight and Investigations* (2013) (Testimony of Larry M. Wortzel).

Chapter Eight

The Evolving Relationship between the U.S. Government and Industry in Innovation and Implications for National Security

The U.S. government's relationship with industry and academia has become one of reliance since the end of the Cold War. Innovation in the shadow of the threat from the Soviet Union was geared toward answering specific problems. Breakthroughs then trickled down to improve civilian life. However, in the current paradigm, private industry drives innovation, with the U.S. government finding ways to benefit from technologies developed by the private sector (and in some instances providing the private sector with tools needed to excel at the process of innovation).

This current system creates two related problems. The first is that companies have different incentives than the government. Whereas the private sector is often willing to operate abroad in pursuit of new markets, this may not be the best development for U.S. interests as it puts new capabilities in the hands of competitors and adversaries. As discussed in the context of OSINT, information that is not currently controlled may later be deemed restricted. However, if a company has already disseminated technology or knowledge internationally, there is little hope for putting the genie back in the bottle. Additionally, government reliance on the private sector gives the private sector greater influence on policies, as it becomes a participant in defining how policy will impact its operations (for example, lobbying to prevent the introduction of an encryption standard in the mid-1990s, demanding government permission to release information about records requests, etc.).

THE RELATIONSHIP BETWEEN
GOVERNMENT, THE PRIVATE SECTOR,
AND ACADEMIA CONCERNING INNOVATION

The paradigm for U.S. innovation has become an increasingly complicated set of interactions between government, commercial, and academic entities. The Cold War model for innovation became the expected approach to developing and applying new knowledge. As a 2014 report by the Center for a New American Security noted, "The prevailing character of the military industrial environment remains heavily influenced by the middle and final years of the Cold War."[1] While the United States had certainly been an innovative country prior to the Second World War, it had been predominantly isolationist and did not have ongoing geopolitical competition as a driver for development of technology. It was not until the Cold War that the United States had to maintain a sustained international presence in peacetime.

The U.S. government's incorporation of industry into an innovation ecosystem was apparent with the establishment of the War Production Board in 1942 and became what Eisenhower would term "the military-industrial complex." By 1960, defense research accounted for 80 percent of federal research and development funds.[2] Mission-focused agencies—oriented toward achieving specific outcomes rather than "basic" research directed at scientific exploration—provided much of this Cold War–era funding.[3] Even sectors that now insist on their independence from government influence owe their existence to government investment. For instance, Silicon Valley dates to the 1940s with military-funded vacuum tube research at Stanford University. This in turn provided a basis for radar, radar jamming, and other signal intelligence developments.[4] The benefits from DoD-funded research to society writ large included GPS, magnetic random access memory, and the Internet.

TRANSITION FROM A GOVERNMENT-DRIVEN TO AN
INDUSTRY-DRIVEN INNOVATION ENVIRONMENT

With the end of the Cold War, profound changes took place in the defense industry that disengaged the U.S. government from innovators. The multifaceted corporations that had included defense components began to divest themselves of these units, which produced less than 20 percent of corporations' revenue.[5] Meanwhile, firms of a traditionally defense nature divested their commercial components.[6] This hard division between military and civilian missions made it difficult for defense technologies to be easily adapted for the civilian realm. Furthermore, it made it far more difficult to apply commercial breakthroughs to government agencies, including the defense sector.

The military-industrial complex continues to exist because the defense sector continues to lobby the federal government and win government contracts. The number of players who continue to operate in this context is impressive, with nearly 2,700 prime contracting companies.[7] However, the concept of defense mission–oriented technologies being spun off and modified for commercial application lengthens the research and development cycle to an uncompetitive level.[8] Because defense contractors are no longer capable of providing cutting-edge products for civilian purposes, a new set of players including start-ups has emerged to serve nondefense sector needs and in the process has developed technologies from which the U.S. government would benefit.

THE DEPARTMENT OF ENERGY
AND THE NATIONAL LABORATORY SYSTEM

The United States Department of Energy (DOE) national laboratories and technology centers comprise a network of facilities intended to advance science and technology to support DOE's mission. The network is overseen by the DOE and consists of seventeen national labs. Sixteen of the labs are known as Federally Funded Research and Development Centers (FFRDCs) that are public-private partnerships that conduct research for the U.S. government. The national labs are administered, managed, and staffed by private-sector entities operating under contract with DOE. This system of private and government has led to tremendous advances in science and technology and solving key national objectives.

The national laboratory system evolved from the massive scientific projects begun during World War II. New technologies such as radar, the computer, the proximity fuse, and the atomic bomb grew from this system. The laboratory establishment facilitates "big science" by enabling the undertaking of large-scale endeavors. The Manhattan Project is an early example. For the development of atomic weapons, multiple research laboratories containing large pieces of expensive equipment had to be established. The research and development of the atomic bomb took place in over thirty sites in the United States, employed 130,000 people, and cost USD $2 billion. The program left a network of national labs: Lawrence Berkeley National Laboratory, Los Alamos National Laboratory, Oak Ridge National Laboratory, Argonne National Laboratory, and Ames Laboratory. Two more were set up shortly after World War II: Sandia National Laboratory and Brookhaven National Laboratory. Originally, these labs were thought of as temporary facilities, intended for the specific purpose of atomic weapon development. However, after the success of the Manhattan Project, the newly created Atomic Energy Commission took over these laboratories and extended their lives for other projects. Additional funding and infrastructure were obtained to create other national laboratories for basic and classified research. Later, the Energy Research and Development Administration and currently the Department of Energy administer the laboratory system, which is the largest of its kind in the world.

An interesting feature of the national laboratories during the Manhattan Project is that the labs were set up with both competition and cooperation in mind. Often multiple laboratories with competing missions were created. For instance, Lawrence Livermore laboratory was designed to compete with Los Alamos in nuclear weapons design. It was hoped that competition over funding would create a culture of high-quality research. Other laboratories without overlapping missions were encouraged to cooperate with each other. Lawrence Livermore cooperated with Lawrence Berkeley Laboratory, for instance. With this market-driven paradigm as its foundation, it is interesting that the DOE's exchange programs permit individuals who represent direct geopolitical competitors to use its facilities because such activities decrease the United States' overall competitive edge.

The national laboratory system constitutes a partnership between military, academia, and industry. Most of these labs were staffed by local researchers but also allowed for visiting scientists to access the equipment. Today, the DOE provides more than 40 percent of the total national funding for physics, chemistry, materials science, and physical sciences. Some of the labs are managed by private companies while others are managed by academic institutions.

Because of its multifaceted missions and domestic partners, the DOE's laboratory system is arguably a tempting target for foreign governments seeking to enhance their countries' capacities for innovation. A cursory review of the Department's Office of International Affairs highlights multiple vulnerabilities. Perhaps the most significant of these is the U.S.–China Clean Energy Research Center. As discussed in previous chapters, U.S. clean energy technology has been an objective for acquisition by China. The opportunity to work with the DOE on this issue provides another conduit through which Beijing can obtain knowledge complementary to information gathered through other channels. Additionally, the DOE has a number of issue-specific arrangements with multiple countries of concern. As late as 2013, by which time Moscow had taken a decidedly anti-U.S. posture, DOE engaged in multiple new agreements with Russia. Showing similar questionable consideration for geopolitical realities, in 2015 Argonne Laboratory (that is, University of Chicago Argonne LLC) and China's Wuhan University agreed to a memorandum of understanding regarding cooperation on chemistry, catalysis, nanoscience, and nanotechnology. In 2014, areas of cooperation between DOE entities and China included a joint irradiation testing program, electric vehicle and industrial energy efficiency cooperation, and high-energy nuclear physics. These agreements were all concluded with countries that had demonstrated increasing hostility toward the United States—hostility that an innovative edge would bolster. Furthermore, the DOE's partnerships seemed to show little regard for the reality that these and other countries had attempted to illicitly obtain U.S. technology.

FEDERALLY FUNDED RESEARCH AND DEFENSE CENTERS

Federally Funded Research and Development Centers (FFRDCs) are public-private partnerships that conduct research for the U.S. government. They were created to be private entities that worked exclusively on complex government projects while remaining free of commercial conflicts of interest. They have helped maintain a stable workforce of highly skilled technical talent. There are currently forty-two U.S. government-sponsored FFRDCs. Both universities and corporations administer the centers.[9] The partnership of FFRDCs consists of three components: private commercial industry, academia (including nonprofit organizations), and government employees.[10] Each component has a different approach to research and can drive innovation in different ways. The purpose of these centers is to provide the U.S. government analysis and support but not to actually manufacture or market the technology.

Prior to World War II, the U.S. government funded very little scientific research.[11] The national security challenges of the war and subsequently the Cold War demanded larger-scale research projects and a mobilization of the U.S. research assets and personnel. The FFRDCs were instituted to advance the national security challenges of the day. The earliest ones were aimed at providing advanced R&D to the war effort. The complexity of the needs required resources not then available in the federal government. The first FFRDC was RAND, established in 1947 by the U.S. Air Force.

Government agencies are able to employ FFRDCs much as they can utilize general contractors for goods and services. Sponsoring governmental agencies must demonstrate that the FFRDC is being established to tackle long-term research and development that cannot be met as effectively by existing resources. They cannot be premised on short-term objectives. FFRDCs must operate in the public interest, provide disclosure to the sponsoring agency, and be free from organizational conflicts of interest.

The U.S. government does continue to drive certain R&D activities directed at addressing specific objectives that serve the national interest. The Department of Energy's National Incubator Initiative for Clean Energy was established to set up specialized business incubators focused on helping entrepreneurs commercialize clean energy technologies.[12] DOE Energy Innovation Hubs, an initiative that began in 2012, are intended to solve specific energy challenges.[13] Topics of focus include energy-efficient buildings, fuels from sunlight, and batteries and energy storage.[14] The National Institute of Standards and Technology's (NIST) Technology Innovation Program, created in 2008, was intended to support high-risk, high-reward research focused on areas where the government had a clear interest based on the magnitude of the problem and its importance for society.[15] All of these programs represented a realization that there was still a need to address the economic "problem of the commons" that could not be solved solely by relying on the private sector.

Furthermore, various agencies do continue to operate with the assumption that they will successfully spin off research. For instance, according to Robert Atkinson, president of the Information Technology and Innovation Foundation, DARPA has shifted toward a short-term, mission-oriented development approach.[16] Multiple federal agencies have attempted to create a culture of innovation by adopting an innovation lab concept.[17] The NSA's "Incubation Cell" is an example of such a lab. The objective is to create a venue for capturing the ideas of employees generated by their firsthand interaction with the workings of the agency. In another example of a government agency spinning off results of its R&D, NASA views its Space Technology program as developing and demonstrating technologies that not only serve future missions but also the broader aerospace field.[18]

Despite the aforementioned programs, the U.S. government is not positioned to lead innovation. The international nature of innovation creates difficulties for U.S. government entities—particularly those in the national security field—to operate like the private sector or academia. In 2012, a DoD task force recommended that DoD establish research entities abroad such as partnering with an existing DoD lab, creating a relationship with a university, or forming a government-to-government partnership. In addition, the task-force suggested that DoD lab directors increase the U.S. service laboratory locations where foreign entities could conduct basic research.[19] The task force's rationale for these recommendations was one of affording DoD greater access to the basic research being conducted outside of the United States, pointing out that "major corporations have approached the challenge [of identifying developments internationally] by establishing research entities in strategic locales populated by a mixture of U.S. citizens and local scientists."[20] However, foreign intelligence services and other threat actors will likely perceive that facilities and individuals operating abroad can be exploited as points of access. Furthermore, exporting research activities—and the outcomes of those activities—adds to foreign governments' baseline scientific capabilities. Exportation includes both the physical relocation of know-how to a location abroad (for example, collaboration at a foreign institution) and providing foreign researchers access to U.S. facilities. Unable to match the private sector and academic engines of innovation, the U.S. government will perpetually find itself lagging in many fields essential to national security.

INVESTMENTS WITHOUT REWARDS?

Government-driven innovation efforts have shifted from objective-oriented initiatives to investments in academia and industry that are not linked to addressing gaps in government capabilities. The National Science Foundation, the only federal agency dedicated to the support of basic research across all fields of science and engineering, has provided funding to universities for scientific research without apparent concern for whether the result might be commercialized and contribute to jobs in the United States.[21] The Obama administration has characterized federally funded research at universities as "creat[ing] a stream of new insights and technological breakthroughs" and "prepar[ing] the next generation of scientists and engineers, many of whom will pursue careers in private companies."[22] Funding university-based research risks subsidizing the education of foreign students and academics who, maliciously or otherwise, return the knowledge to their respective countries. In 2010, the director of the National Science Foundation provided testimony to the U.S. Senate about the desire to see "innovation ecosystem[s]"—including commercialization and start-ups—develop around universities.[23] Such investments can create complications. For instance, the National Institute for Allergy and Infectious Diseases funded research on the H5N1 virus. However, the Department of Health and Human Services deemed the research to be dual use in nature and requested researchers to refrain from publishing the results.[24]

Furthermore, the U.S. government may be losing control of its investments in research and development by encouraging commercialization as a primary objective, regardless of whether the government achieves a specific mission-oriented objective through its investment. The first step in this direction was the 1980 Bayh-Dole Act, which allowed universities, nonprofit organizations, and small businesses to pursue ownership of an invention that resulted from federally funded research. The White House, in a 2013 presidential memorandum, directed all federal research agencies to track concrete commercialization goals.[25] As of 2015, NSF, DOE, and NIH had expanded their efforts to encourage the formation of new companies based on university research.[26] In testimony before the U.S. Senate in 2010, the director of the National Science Foundation discussed efforts to increase the partnerships between academic and industrial communities that would provide avenues for accelerating innovation.[27] Furthermore, in 2011 the NSF launched its Innovation Corps, which provided entrepreneurship training to federally funded scientists by pairing them with business mentors to focus on discovering a demand-driven path from research to a marketable product.[28]

"Basic science," the pursuit of fundamental knowledge rather than an immediate application or product, remains an area where the government fills a unique niche. The agencies with greatest responsibility for this are Defense, Energy, and Health and Human Services. Although in 2012 the federal government funded only 31 percent of U.S. R&D, it funded 60 percent of U.S. basic research.[29] The private sector's much larger contribution to R&D is by contrast primarily directed at applied research. This trend has been the norm since the mid-1990s.[30] The DoD's nearly seventy service laboratory facilities conducted approximately a quarter of the department's basic research as of 2012.[31] The DOE's laboratories are an example of how shifting geopolitics impacted the focus of innovation. The labs, which were an outgrowth of the applied research of the Manhattan Project, became disaggregated in their foci after the Cold War.[32]

Multiple agencies also have specialized components responsible for pursuing innovative ideas. The most well known of these is the Department of Defense's Defense Advanced Research Projects Agency (DARPA), which the United States founded in the wake of the Soviet's 1957 launch of *Sputnik*. Its focus is on "transformational change" as opposed to "incremental advances."[33] Other agencies subsequently modeled entities on DARPA. In 2007, the Department of Energy received authorization to create an Advanced Research Projects Agency (ARPA-E). ARPA-E focuses on "transformational" energy technology projects. The Department of Homeland Security's Homeland Security Advanced Research Projects Agency (HSARPA) was established in 2002. Unlike DARPA or ARPA, HSARPA is more practical in its research. It conducts analysis to identify the operational gaps in the missions, systems, and processes of the twenty-two DHS components and finds areas where technologies would have the greatest impact. The Intelligence Advanced Research Projects Activity (IARPA), under the Office of the Director of National Intelligence, is an interagency iteration of this concept. It draws operational and R&D experience from across the intelligence community and facilitates the transition of research results to its customers for application.

A SUPPORTING ROLE TO
U.S. PRIVATE AND ACADEMIC SECTORS

In addition to funding research, the U.S. government is attempting to provide industry with tools that will increase their potential for innovation. The U.S. National Strategic Plan for Advanced Manufacturing included discussion of how the government could contribute to innovation that would benefit advanced manufacturing and bridge the gap between R&D activities and the deployment of practical application.[34] The National Institute of Standards and Technology in particular has supported efforts to capitalize on nanotechnology in manufacturing, facilitated rapid prototyping and manufacturing of multiple high-technology components, and supported the establishment of sustainable manufacturing processes.[35] NIST's Manufacturing Extension Partnership (MEP) program works through local MEP centers to support the adoption of innovative technologies by smaller U.S. manufacturers.[36] Furthermore, as of 2015 the government planned to create a network of forty-five Manufacturing Innovation Institutes.[37] These institutes were a joint project of the Department of Commerce, the Department of Energy, and the Department of Defense. They were envisioned as a way to bring together national labs, universities, and companies in regional clusters to develop and accelerate commercialization of new manufacturing technologies.[38]

Revitalizing U.S. manufacturing is an essential step to achieving end product innovation. Historical examples of how the feedback loop between research and production contributed to the development of new knowledge include Bell Labs, where engineers, co-located with technicians, developed and continually improved production processes for telecommunications equipment. Similarly, at DuPont, the partnership between design and production elements led to the affordable manufacture of Kevlar less than five years after it had been invented.[39] Interestingly, as of 2012 this item was still in such demand that the South Korean firm Kolon Industries Inc. was implicated in recruiting former and current DuPont employees in an attempt to acquire trade secrets related to Kevlar.[40]

Outsourcing of manufacturing, therefore, can contribute to the erosion of U.S. companies' innovative edge. An example is the personal computer industry in the United States. Beginning in the 1980s, the original equipment manufacturers (OEM) in the United States began to outsource the assembly of printed circuit boards to Asian contractors like South Korea, Taiwan, and China. The motivation was the proposed cost savings, premised on low labor costs and the economies of scale. At this point, the OEMs held the valuable intellectual property and design for the circuit boards. With time, many of the contractors encouraged the OEMs to allow them to contribute a greater share of the final product. Many of the components were also sourced from Asian suppliers, which eventually resulted in contractors controlling the supply chain. Gradually, the contractors took on more and more of the design work and engineering for the product. These contractors have ended up designing and manufacturing virtually all Windows personal computers. After a contractor has evolved and taken over the design, it may become a competitor to the OEM. This is what happened to television manufacturing where U.S. innovators such as RCA and Sylvania lost out to Asian companies like Sony.[41]

A related problem is U.S. manufacturers' offshoring technologies, which they believe have reached their apogee. For example, U.S. companies, thinking that battery and electronic manufacturing were mature industries, decided to offshore battery and electronics production to East Asian countries. The United States subsequently lost leadership in rechargeable battery manufacturing because the advancement of the technology that allowed more power to be packaged in smaller units only occurred after production facilities moved to Asia.[42] Only later did the world become interested in developing energy efficient vehicles using advanced electric batteries. The scenario of technology leaving the country is analogous to the previously discussed problem of unclassified research later being determined to have classified applications. The strong battery industry in Japan and South Korea gave those countries an advantage over U.S. companies in developing hybrid and electric vehicles. As a result, General Motors has had to outsource the battery for its Chevy Volt from a South Korean supplier. Now those countries have an advantage in developing vehicles with better rechargeable batteries.[43] Similarly, techniques, such as thin-film deposition for semiconductor production, have moved overseas. Thin-film deposition has turned out to be important for manufacturing solar panels.[44]

Therefore, moving an established base of knowledge out of the United States may be economical in the short run for individual U.S. companies, but in the longer term can place the United States as a country at a distinct disadvantage vis-à-vis competitors. Beyond simply leveling the playing field by bringing a foreign country's capabilities up to those of the United States, U.S. companies may actually cede the playing field. This practice allows U.S. expertise in various industries to wither, leaving the United States beholden to foreign providers. Efforts to reinvigorate manufacturing, such as those of NIST, are not only a useful counterbalance to foreign competition but also diminish the access that foreign state and nonstate actors have to U.S. proprietary information abroad. Encouraging the development of new knowledge within the United States creates a hostile operating environment for malicious state and nonstate intelligence collectors who must risk U.S. scrutiny to gather information and who, if caught, can be prosecuted under U.S. laws.

Maintaining capabilities is also the purpose of the Department of Defense's university-affiliated research centers (UARCs). The DoD established these to ensure that essential U.S. engineering and technology competencies were maintained.[45] The first UARC was the Applied Physics Laboratory at Johns Hopkins University, which dates to 1942.[46] Other UARCs include the Institute for Collaborative Biotechnologies at the University of California at Santa Barbara, the Institute for Creative Technologies at the University of Southern California, the Georgia Tech Research Institute at the Georgia Institute of Technology, the Institute for Soldier Nanotechnologies at MIT, the Institute for Advanced Technology at the University of Texas at Austin, Space Dynamics Laboratory at Utah State University, Applied Research Laboratory at Pennsylvania State University, the Applied Physics Laboratory at the University of Washington, the Applied Research Laboratory at the University of Hawaii at Manoa, and the Systems Engineering Research Center Stevens Institute of Technology.[47] Several of the establishments that play host to UARCs have been targeted or exploited by foreign intelligence collection activities. The University of Southern California, at which the Institute for Creative Technologies is located, provided a starting point for the three Chinese graduate students (recipients of DoD funding no less) who later stole U.S. private industry technology in conjunction with China's Tianjian University.

In addition to UARCs, federal agencies have established Centers of Excellence at U.S. universities. For instance, DHS's Science and Technology component had, as of 2013, nine university-based centers that represented consortia of more than 275 colleges and universities in forty-seven states.[48] Another example is the DHS Center for Visualization and Data Analytics, which develops technologies for analyzing large quantities of data to identify national security threats.

The U.S. government unintentionally subsidizes private sector innovation through the cultivation of its human capital. For instance, the National Security Agency, which requires cutting-edge skills, has stated that it trains rather than hires cyber security professionals, with 80 percent of NSA hires coming in at entry level.[49] However, developing experts from scratch may not be the most economical approach when dealing with a workforce that accepts movement through multiple careers as a norm. For instance, a former NSA Internet security architect founded VirTru—a firm that encrypts emails and prevents unauthorized viewers from intercepting messages.[50] The company's technology was derived from a trusted data format that the founder was working on at NSA.[51] The departure of skilled tech workers to private industry is an entrenched problem. As of 2000, cyber security experts who left government could expect a pay raise of anywhere between 25 percent and 400 percent.[52] The longevity of this problem suggests that the U.S. government can count on continuing to lose talent to private industry.

RELIANCE ON THE PRIVATE AND ACADEMIC SECTORS

It is increasingly difficult for the U.S. government to emulate and keep pace with the private sector in the area of innovation. Creation of market-based mechanisms has been a middle ground between government-driven and industry-driven innovation, with the government facilitating the interaction of private sector entities. As part of MEP, NIST created the National Innovation Marketplace—a web-based resource that helped manufacturers in using emerging technologies and finding market opportunities.[53] Similarly, the 2014 Quadrennial Homeland Security Review explicitly noted that DHS would continue to adopt "market-based solutions."

The current model leaves the U.S. government heavily reliant on private industry. Unlike the familiar military-industrial complex in which the U.S. government provided direction for programs that only subsequently spun off civilian applications, the government is attempting to identify existing technologies that it can adopt and adapt. This has created a number of issues that must be navigated. The first is that companies often have no incentives to cooperate with the government. Even in areas of cyber security, firms sometimes choose to avoid government engagement. Furthermore, because the most cutting-edge R&D is being done without government customers in mind, it may result in outcomes at odds with U.S. national security. Finally, companies that have the potential to impact U.S. elements of national power may actually engage in ventures that provide adversaries with access to sensitive knowledge and technology. This occurs despite the fact that many of the new high-tech start-ups are direct spin-offs of federally funded university research.[54]

Companies, because of short-term financial consideration and occasional ideological reasons, sometimes act on incentives that do not promote national security. For instance, as the National Counterintelligence Executive noted in a 2011 report, "Workers will tend to draw few distinctions between their home and work lives, and they will expect the access to any information they want—whether personal or professional—from any location."[55] The expectations of information access in any and all settings multiples the number of opportunities for information to be compromised. However, courting top talent may force companies to accede to these demands, opening up more opportunities for the compromise of information. Furthermore, companies that wish to maintain this culture may not prove to be viable partners for collaboration with government, even when they have unique and desired technology. Somewhere between profit and culture is public perception. As identified by a study by the Center for a New American Security, firms may be deterred from collaboration with the government due to the public relations implications of partnering with a military customer.[56] Another area of divergence is between small companies (for example, innovative start-ups) that do not see the need for contracting with the U.S. government.[57] Similarly, certain scientists are reluctant to cooperate with U.S. intelligence officers.[58] Scientific unwillingness to cooperate is primarily ideological—an unwillingness to sully their purely academic pursuits. Furthermore, the scientific community often welcomes transnational cooperation, which they may see as being at odds with the nation-state-centric function of intelligence collection.

Even when necessary, companies may be reluctant to engage the government to protect their own assets. Start-up companies are especially vulnerable to IP theft. Their existence is usually premised on cutting-edge ideas, but they often lack resources to deal with security and they are often staffed by graduate students or postdoctoral fellows who take proprietary information and transfer it to competitors when they inevitably leave the company.[59] However, according to a 2011 NCIX report, firms sometimes choose not to report thefts of sensitive information because a breach could tarnish a company's reputation and endanger its relationship with investors and customers.[60] This is not a new phenomenon. In 2000, a survey identified that only 32 percent of large companies and government agencies that were victims of hacking incidents reported the crimes to authorities.[61]

In addition to the fear of unwanted publicity resulting from a federal investigation, the high-tech sector has demonstrated a longstanding distrust of authorities. In 2000, tech firms refused to use an FBI-provided security program because they suspected that the software would give the Bureau access to their computer networks.[62] Following revelations in 2013 about NSA surveillance activities, a number of Silicon Valley entities signaled their displeasure. Among them was Google, which stopped attending cyber security meetings with the NSA.[63] Companies are also concerned that should an investigation be opened, the very trade secrets they were trying to protect may have to be revealed in court and in the media.

The hesitance to engage the government can also deprive agencies responsible for national security of necessary data. In early 2015, President Barack Obama and representatives of DHS (including the Secret Service) and the FBI met with tech sector leaders and requested that companies assist with combating future cyber attacks by sharing additional information with the government.[64] In an interesting double standard, while the federal government was pleading for data in 2015, Google had similarly demanded that the government permit it to release information about requests for data during the previous year.[65] Prior to the Snowden sabotage of NSA programs, there had at least been limited cooperation between the government and industry on security. For instance, in early 2010, Google secured assistance from the NSA to improve the defenses of Google's networks.[66]

Faced with the above obstacles, the U.S. government must approach many innovative companies as another customer or investor. For example, In-Q-Tel was founded in 1999 by the CIA as a private, nonprofit firm to provide venture capital for small companies developing technologies of interest to the U.S. intelligence community.[67] Rather than working through the standard government procurement process (which can dissuade companies from doing business with the government), In-Q-Tel uses private industry contractual terms. Its interactions with private sector companies are directed at adapting the technologies for the government's needs.[68] As of 2012, it had developed programs with more than 160 start-ups, which had yielded 297 pilot initiatives. The intelligence community has adopted and funded more than one hundred of the technologies funded by In-Q-Tel.[69]

Although it is a project of the CIA, In-Q-Tel serves a variety of U.S. government customers. As of 2012, the Defense Intelligence Agency ranked with the CIA as In-Q-Tel's two largest customers.[70] DHS has worked successfully with the company to identify innovative start-ups and invest in them to adapt their emerging commercial technologies.[71] The FBI has also used In-Q-Tel to review new technologies that have yet to be fully developed for the commercial market.[72] In-Q-Tel also contributes to the growth of the tech-oriented private sector through sales of its shares in ventures to companies that have included Google and IBM.[73]

Other government agencies have followed a similar path in their approach to the private sector: attempting to identify technology in development that could be of value. According to the Department of Homeland Security's Undersecretary for Science and Technology, DHS focuses on the late stages of R&D, seeking out technologies in which others have already invested.[74] DHS referred to this survey of public and private sector capabilities as "technology foraging."[75] In additional to its work through In-Q-Tel, the DHS S&T component manages the Broad Area Announcements and Small Business Innovative Research programs. Both of these initiatives are meant to attract small companies that have innovative concepts and make it more appealing to work with the U.S. government.[76] DoD also made a concerted effort to bypass the staid thinking of contractors when the Deputy Assistant Secretary of Defense for Systems Engineering visited a dozen Silicon Valley start-ups in late 2014.[77]

Both DoD and DHS established presences on the ground in Silicon Valley in order to give them greater proximity to and interaction with the technology industry. As of 2015, DHS established its office to recruit talent from the tech sector and to build relationships with industry.[78] DoD also set up its Defense Innovation Unit Experimental (DIUX), which will be staffed by reservists with responsibility for identifying emerging and breakthrough technologies and building relationships with DoD.[79] Additionally, DoD invested USD $75 million to develop the Flexible Hybrid Electronic Institute, a consortium of more than one hundred companies—including Apple (a company at odds with other elements of the U.S. government over encryption).[80]

IMPLICATIONS FOR U.S. CAPABILITIES TO ENSURE NATIONAL SECURITY

Industry's role as the incubator for innovation also means that while it is willing to work with the U.S. government, it can also take steps that run counter to U.S. government preferences. A clear area of controversy is the issue of encryption. The 2013 disclosures about the NSA from Edward Snowden drove the topic to the forefront for the technology community. Apple, with its mobile operating system for the iPhone 6, introduced encryption that even Apple could not unlock, allowing the company to claim that it was technically impossible to comply with government warrants.[81] (Prior to late 2014 Apple had been able to help law enforcement obtain data from iPhones.[82]) Apple was not the only company to effectively handcuff itself and swallow the key. In late 2014, WhatsApp, a Facebook-owned messaging service, announced that it would similarly encrypt, to the point of unretrievability, messages sent between Android phones.[83]

The encryption imbroglio also highlights the perils of ceding R&D to the private sector. To ensure that authorities could access information if necessary, the Obama administration found itself advocating for—rather than being able to introduce—a means of unlocking data. FBI director James Comey even advised tech sector representatives that "you should not look to the government for innovation. . . . Technological innovation is not our thing."[84] As a contrast to encryption, governance of satellite capabilities provides an example of how the U.S. government maintained control over technology, while still allowing it to be used for civilian purposes. According to a CIA document from the early 1970s, the National Photographic Interpretation Center was able to conduct reviews of satellite imagery from NASA to identify and withhold "sensitive" frames from public dissemination.[85] The National Imagery and Mapping Agency further demonstrated the value of possessing lesser resolution imagery when in 2001 it became the sole customer for photography of Afghanistan taken by the Space Imaging Company's IKONOS satellite. This commercially obtained imagery could be shared with other countries and the public without exposing classified U.S. capabilities.[86] Finally, the U.S. government in 2005 considered the possibility that the director of National Intelligence should develop the ability to provide imagery at 0.5-meter resolution (a capability available commercially)—at an unclassified level—to domestic customers.[87] Unlike satellite technology, encryption is out of the box. The U.S. government, rather than defining the market and spinning off useful but not compromising technology, is now in the unenviable position of supplicant to Silicon Valley

Another systemic factor that has put the U.S. government behind the curve on R&D is the dispersed nature of high-tech companies. As the head of the Information Technology and Innovation Foundation Robert Atkinson explained to Congress, "Washington is often far removed from the firms and other institutions that drive innovation. This is particularly true of small and mid-sized firms. In contrast, state and local government and metropolitan-level economic developers have a long track record of creating organizations that work more closely with firms."[88] Elsewhere, Atkinson noted that state and substate governments were "closer to the ground" and consequently possessed a better sense of which innovation clusters were important.[89] The National Science Foundation has also given greater prominence to the role of subfederal entities with its Partnerships for Innovation that include state and local governments.[90] Even more recently, the 2015 Strategy for American Innovation highlighted the federal government's supporting role to local and regional innovation ecosystems.[91] The increased importance of these entities is potentially problematic because, as discussed previously, they do not have the same concerns about national security and may consequently be less discerning gatekeepers.

U.S. companies have greater leeway to expand their operations internationally, tapping talent and markets they deem to be financially prudent. This is not a new phenomenon. General Electric, for instance, went aggressively global in the 1990s and, as of 2012, had research laboratories in India, China, Germany, and Brazil. IBM established a Swiss presence in 1956 and later established footprints in Israel (1972) and Japan (1982).[92] On the other end of the commercial spectrum from large multinational corporations are the small start-ups. These firms have limited resources and may not be able to obtain work permits for non-U.S. employees, but can use virtual workspaces to connect with employees regardless of time zone. The dispersion across time zones can actually be advantageous. By handing off projects across time zones, a small company can operate twenty-four hours per day.[93] The problem for both large and small companies is that global operations provide opportunities for foreign entities to exfiltrate proprietary knowledge and technology in an environment where they have a home field advantage.

The willingness of U.S. innovators to work with international partners also raises geopolitical concerns. As Ashley Tellis noted, "Fostering disruptive innovations remains the best way for the United States to maintain an advantage [vis-à-vis China]."[94] (Disruptive innovations are those advances that introduce entirely new concepts, rather than being gradual improvements on existing technologies.) However, U.S. corporations have continued to engage China on technology issues that could contribute to closing the gap between the two countries' capabilities. Microsoft, for instance, partnered with the China Electronics Technology Group Corporation, a government-owned defense company that oversees the research institutes that developed electronics for China's first nuclear bomb.[95] In 2015, Cisco planned to announce a partnership with China's Inspur Group, a server maker, in which the Chinese government has a controlling interest.[96] Among the objectives of the partnership was the joint development of hardware.[97] In addition, Intel's Chinese partner, Inspur, provided chips to four supercomputer sites in China that the U.S. government deemed to be involved in activities that were contrary to the national security and foreign policy interests of the United States.[98] The cozying up to state-owned enterprises is understandable from the perspective of gaining market access, but it also makes components of the U.S. private innovation sector beholden to an unfriendly government.

Citing their international customers, innovative U.S. companies have demonstrated a reluctance to adopt measures in furtherance of U.S. national security. The chief information security officer for Yahoo! suggested in 2015 that if the company was to build means for U.S. authorities to access data, then it could be argued that Yahoo should make similar concessions to the Chinese, Russian, Saudi Arabian, Israeli, and French governments.[99] The argument is not new. The technology industry expressed concern in 2000 about installing a "back door" into encryption technology that was to be shipped overseas because it was unlikely that foreign buyers would opt for equipment that they knew could be compromised.[100]

IMPLICATIONS OF GOVERNMENT
RELIANCE ON PRIVATE SECTOR INNOVATION

The balance between the federal government and private sector innovators is likely to shift toward even greater influence for the private sector. Reliance on industry to develop ideas and applications that the government can then use gives the private sector a greater role in the policymaking process. This was demonstrated in the mid-1990s with the tech sector's vocal pushback against the proposal for a national voice and data encryption standard designed by the NSA, which would permit law enforcement agencies to decode data when they possessed an appropriate warrant.[101] The subsequent Communications Assistance to Law Enforcement Act (CALEA) reflected the private sector's preference, permitting it to develop its own technology.[102] In 1999, lobbying by the private sector, which claimed it was losing market share to European rivals, resulted in a decision by the U.S. government to permit the export of encryption technology.[103] CALEA continues to be a concern, as it does not cover email, Internet messaging, social networking sites, or peer-to-peer activities because these technologies were not part of the communications landscape when the legislation became law. This deficiency has been highlighted by the U.S. Department of Justice because it has contributed to the phenomenon of "going dark"—the inability to collect intelligence. However, the tech sector has only increased its influence since the original CALEA was passed, calling into doubt the ability to develop an updated version of the law, even though such an update would be consistent with the spirit of the original intention of the legislation.

It is worth noting the contrast between historical problems of encryption and the current situation that has been created largely by industry opposition to assisting the U.S. government. During the 1940s, the U.S. government received copies of Soviet cable traffic that was supposed to have been unbreakable due the use of one-time pads (which uniquely enciphered each message). However, the inadvertent reuse of ciphers allowed the U.S. government to painstakingly decipher many of these communications, which provided insights about U.S. persons who were engaged in intelligence activities on behalf of Moscow. Communications companies cooperated with the U.S. government to acquire this cable traffic. Compare this with the present predicament, in which the U.S. government is again attempting to find threat actors, such as terrorists and criminals, who like the Soviet spies hid behind encryption. However, unlike the U.S. communications companies of the 1940s, U.S. tech companies are not only protecting the ciphered communications, they are also creating the capabilities for sending them.

Not only has the private sector contributed to shaping policies regarding technology, but it has also been vocal (and apparently effective) in circumscribing U.S. intelligence collection capabilities as those capabilities apply to technology. In 2014, the Obama administration conceded to technology companies' requests to disclose information about requests for information about Internet traffic that they received from the Foreign Intelligence Surveillance Court (FISC). This followed the filing of a lawsuit by Facebook, Microsoft, Google, Yahoo!, and LinkedIn.[104] Tech companies have also sought to protect their interests vis-à-vis the government on Capitol Hill. In 2013, Facebook, Google, Apple, Yahoo!, Microsoft, and AOL praised the sponsors of legislation that would end the NSA's bulk collection of phone records and create a privacy advocate within the FISC.[105] In addition to fighting against NSA collection, the tech industry also successfully assisted in derailing a summer

2015 bill that would have required social media companies to report instances of terrorist chatter to law enforcement.[106]

The tech industry has on occasion subsidized collection and enforcement activities to protect its intellectual property. Intel, Motorola, IBM, and Dell have all previously contributed funds to police departments. Intel also purchased a USD $10,000 body wire for the Sacramento County Sheriff's Department and Hewlett Packard used a corporate jet to fly law enforcement to Silicon Valley.[107] Additionally, companies may influence law enforcement activities through participation in joint investigations. Such an opportunity is illustrated by an Apple investigator's cooperation with the Santa Clara County District Attorney's Office Rapid Enforcement Allied Computer Team (REACT) on a case that involved an Apple employee who stole more than USD $100,000 worth of computers. The REACT task force leader acknowledged that it was not uncommon for the group to work with companies' security personnel on cases.[108]

CONCLUSION

The balance between the U.S. government and the private sector's leadership in innovation has fundamentally shifted since World War II, when the U.S. innovation ecosystem first had to consistently operate vis-à-vis the international environment. Throughout the Cold War, the U.S. government was the primary driver for the development of technology that ultimately benefited the civilian sector. It did this in combination with private industry, which played an essential role in providing the human capital and other resources for projects such as the development of the U-2. However, in the decades following the dissolution of the Soviet Union, the U.S. government took an increasingly secondary role to private industry. At present, the federal government seems to have adopted a role of providing the resources (for example, assistance with new manufacturing techniques and funding for basic science). Unlike the military-industrial complex of the Cold War, the relationship with industry is not linked to objectives that respond to government needs. Private industry and academia increasingly operate in an international environment. The U.S. government, because of national security considerations, cannot emulate this model. Furthermore, beyond logistics, private industry has become increasingly distant from collaboration with the U.S. government based on economic and ideological considerations.

This paradigm shift has made the United States less secure in several ways. The most obvious vulnerability is private industry's ability to shut out the government in terms of acquiring access to technologies, either for adoption and adaptation or for ensuring that they are not used to facilitate nefarious activity. While the hot-button issue is currently encryption and the "going dark" problem, the venture capital, scavenger-hunt approach of entities such as In-Q-Tel highlight the reliance of the government on the private sector. This is not only a potential problem in terms of companies not wishing to do business with Washington, but also in terms of companies not thinking about government customers and their unique needs as objectives toward which to orient R&D activities.

NOTES

1. Ben Fitzgerald and Kelly Sayler, *Creative Disruption: Technology, Strategy and the Future of the Global Defense Industry* (Washington, D.C.: Center for a New American Security, 2014), 7.

2. Atkinson, *Understanding the U.S. National Innovation System*, 6.

3. Ibid., 4.

4. Russ Mitchell, "Military Dollars Heading to Tech; Defense Secretary's Silicon Valley Visit Signals a New Cycle of Spending on Software," *Los Angeles Times*, April 24, 2015.

5. Ben Fitzgerald and Kelly Sayler, *Creative Disruption: Technology, Strategy and the Future of the Global Defense Industry* (Washington, D.C.: Center for a New American Security, 2014), 15.

6. Ibid.

7. Dan Steinbock, *The Challenges for America's Defense Innovation* (Washington, D.C.: Information Technology and Innovation Foundation, 2014), 14.

8. Gregory Tassey, *Beyond the Business Cycle: The Need for a Technology-Based Growth Strategy. Science and Public Policy* (Oxford: Oxford University Press, 2012).

9. "Master Government List of Federally Funded R&D Centers," *National Science Foundation*, June 2015.

10. *FFRDCs—A Primer: Federally Funded Research and Development Centers in the 21st Century* (Mitre Corporation).

11. Bruce C. Dale and Timothy D. Moy, *The Rise of Federally Funded Research and Development Centers* (Albuquerque, NM, and Livermore, CA: Sandia National Labs, 2000); *FFRDCs—A Primer*.

12. *A Strategy for American Innovation* (Washington, D.C.: National Economic Council and Office of Science Technology Policy, 2015).

13. *Subcommittee on Science and Space, Committee on Commerce, Science and Transportation, United States Senate, on Keeping America Competitive Through Investment in R&D* (2012) (Statement of Dr. John P. Holdren. Director, Office of Science and Technology Policy, Executive Office of the President of the United States).

14. U.S. Department of Energy, Office of Inspector General, *Audit Report: The Department of Energy's Energy Innovation Hubs* (Washington, D.C.: U.S. Department of Energy, 2013).

15. "Testimony of Patrick D. Gallagher, PhD, Director, National Institute of Standards and Technology, United States Department of Commerce, before the United States Senate, Committee on Commerce, Science and Transportation," March 10, 2010.

16. Dr. Robert D. Atkinson, President, Information Technology and Innovation Foundation. "Innovation in America: Opportunities and Obstacles before the Commerce, Science and Transportation Subcommittee on Competitiveness, Innovation, and Export Promotion. United States Senate," June 22, 2010.

17. *A Strategy for American Innovation.*

18. "Statement of Dr. Mason Peck, Chief Technologist, National Aeronautics and Space Administration before the Committee on Commerce, Science and Transportation, United States Senate."

19. U.S. Department of Defense, *Report of the Defense Science Board Task Force on Basic Research. Office of the Under Secretary of Defense, for Acquisition, Technology and Logistics* (Washington, D.C.: U.S. Department of Defense, 2012).

20. Ibid.

21. Dr. Robert D. Atkinson, President, Information Technology and Innovation Foundation. "Innovation in America: Opportunities and Obstacles before the Commerce, Science and Transportation Subcommittee on Competitiveness, Innovation, and Export Promotion. United States Senate," June 22, 2010.

22. *A Strategy for American Innovation.*

23. "Testimony of Dr. Areden L. Bement Jr. Director, National Science Foundation before the Senate Commerce, Science and Transportation Committee," March 10, 2010.

24. Frank Gottron and Dana A. Shea, *Publishing Scientific Papers with Potential Security Risks: Issues for Congress* (Washington, D.C.: Congressional Research Service, 2013).

25. *A Strategy for American Innovation.*

26. Ibid.

27. "Testimony of Dr. Areden L. Bement Jr. Director, National Science Foundation before the Senate Commerce, Science and Transportation Committee," March 10, 2010.

28. *A Strategy for American Innovation.*

29. Peter L. Singer, *Federally Supported Innovations: 22 Examples of Major Technology Advances That Stem from Federal Research Support* (Washington, D.C.: Information Technology and Innovation Foundation, 2014), 4.

30. Ibid., 6.

31. U.S. Department of Defense, *Basic Research. Report of the Defense Science Board Task Force on Basic Research. Office of the Under Secretary of Defense for Acquisition, Technology and Logistics 2012.*

32. American Academy of Arts and Sciences, *ARISE2: Advancing Research in Science and Engineering: Unleashing America's Research and Innovation Enterprise* (Cambridge, MA: American Academy of Arts and Sciences, 2013), 6.

33. www.darpa.mil (accessed January 2, 2016).

34. *An Overview of the Fiscal Year 2013 Budget for the National Institute of Standards and Technology before the United States Senate, Committee on Commerce, Science and Transportation, Subcommittee on Science and Space* (Patrick D. Gallagher, PhD, Under Secretary of Commerce for Standards and Technology, United States Department of Commerce).

35. "Testimony of Patrick D. Gallagher, PhD, Director, National Institute of Standards and Technology, United States Department of Commerce, before the United States Senate, Committee on Commerce, Science and Transportation," March 10, 2010.

36. Ibid.

37. *A Strategy for American Innovation.*

38. *Restoring American Energy Innovation Leadership: Report Card, Challenges, and Opportunities* (Washington, D.C.: Bipartisan Policy Center, 2015), 9.

39. "Testimony on the Role of Manufacturing Hubs in a 21st Century Innovation Economy by Secretary of Commerce Penny Pritzker, Committee on Commerce, Science, and Transportation, United States Senate," November 13, 2013.

40. United States Department of Justice, *PRO IP Act, Annual Report FY 2013*, 17.

41. Gary P. Pisano and Willy C. Shih, "Restoring American Competitiveness," *Harvard Business Review* (July–August 2009).

42. Ibid.

43. Stephen J. Ezell and Robert D. Atkinson, *The Case for a National Manufacturing Strategy* (Washington, D.C.: Information Technology and Innovation Foundation, 2011).

44. Ibid.

45. Dan Steinbock, *The Challenges for America's Defense Innovation*, 13; U.S. Department of Defense, *Report of the Defense Science Board Task Force on Basic Research. Office of the Under Secretary of Defense, for Acquisition, Technology and Logistics*, 18.

46. Steinbock, *The Challenges for America's Defense Innovation*, 13.

47. U.S. Department of Defense, *Report of the Defense Science Board Task Force on Basic Research*, 19.

48. "Testimony of the Honorable Tara O'Toole, MD, MPH, Under Secretary for Science and Technology, U.S. Department of Homeland Security, U.S. Senate, Homeland Security and Governmental Affairs Committee," July 17, 2013.

49. Martin C. Libicki, David Sentry, and Julia Pollak, *Hackers Wanted: An Examination of the Cybersecurity Labor Market* (Santa Monica, CA: Rand, 2014), 56–57.

50. Mohana Ravindranath, "NSA Work Inspires Cybersecurity Start-Ups," *Washington Post*, January 20, 2014.

51. Ibid.

52. Charles Piller, "High Tech's Distrust of FBI Could Impede Hacking Probe," *Los Angeles Times*, February 11, 2000.

53. *An Overview of the Fiscal Year 2013 Budget for the National Institute of Standards and Technology before the United States Senate, Committee on Commerce, Science and Transportation, Subcommittee on Science and Space* (Patrick D. Gallagher, PhD, Under Secretary of Commerce for Standards and Technology, United States of Commerce).

54. Singer, *Federally Supported Innovations*, 6.

55. Office of the National Counterintelligence Executive, *Foreign Spies Stealing US Economic Secrets in Cyberspace*, 7.

56. Fitzgerald and Sayler, *Creative Disruption*, 15.

57. U.S. Department of Defense, *Report of the Defense Science Board Task Force on Basic Research. Office of the Under Secretary of Defense for Acquisition, Technology and Logistics*.

58. Amos K. Wylie, "Unfair Exchange," *Studies in Intelligence* (Fall 1962).

59. "The IP Commission Report," 13.

60. Office of the National Counterintelligence Executive, *Foreign Spies Stealing US Economic Secrets in Cyberspace*, 3.

61. Charles Piller, "High Tech's Distrust of FBI Could Impede Hacking Probe," *Los Angeles Times*, February 11, 2000.

62. Ibid.

63. Damian Paletta and Danny Yadron, "White House to Create New Division to Streamline Cyberthreat Intelligence; Effort to Buttress Government, Corporate Defenses against Sophisticated Hackers," *Wall Street Journal*, February 11, 2015.

64. Damien Paletta, "White House Cybersecurity Event to Draw Top Tech, Wall Street Execs," *Wall Street Journal*, February 11, 2015.

65. Danny Yadron, "Tech Firms Criticize Policies on Security Requests; Google, Microsoft and Others Release Figures on Last Year," *Wall Street Journal*, February 3, 2014.

66. Ellen Nakashima, "Google to Enlist NSA to Ward off Attacks," *Washington Post*, February 4, 2010.

67. Dan Steinbock, *The Challenges for America's Defense Innovation*, 15.

68. U.S. Department of Defense, *Report of the Defense Science Board Task Force on Basic Research. Office of the Under Secretary of Defense, for Acquisition, Technology and Logistics*, 85.

69. Ibid.

70. Ibid.

71. "Testimony of the Honorable Tara O'Toole, MD, MPH, Under Secretary for Science and Technology, U.S. Department of Homeland Security, U.S. Senate, Homeland Security and Governmental Affairs Committee," July 17, 2013.

72. Jay Solomon, "Investing in Intelligence; Spy Agencies Seek Innovation through Venture-Capital Firm," *Wall Street Journal*, September 12, 2005.

73. Ibid.

74. "Testimony of the Honorable Tara O'Toole, MD, MPH, Under Secretary for Science and Technology, U.S. Department of Homeland Security, U.S. Senate, Homeland Security and Governmental Affairs Committee," July 17, 2013.

75. Ibid.

76. Daniel M. Gerstein, *Making DHS More Efficient: Industry Recommendations to Improve Homeland Security* (Santa Monica, CA: Rand, 2014).

77. John Markoff, "Pentagon Shops in Silicon Valley for Game Changers," *New York Times*, February 26, 2015.

78. Josh Hicks, "Homeland Security Is Laying Roots in Silicon Valley, and You Might Not Like Its Reasons," *Washington Post*, April 22, 2015.

79. Anna Mulrine, "Pentagon Cybersecurity Strategy Comes with Olive Branch to Silicon Valley," *Christian Science Monitor*, April 23, 2015.

80. W. J. Hennigan, "Pentagon Courts Tech Leaders," *Los Angeles Times*, August 29, 2015.

81. Sara Sorcher, "The Battle Between Washington and Silicon Valley Over Encryption," *Christian Science Monitor*, July 7, 2015.

82. Barrett Devlin, Danny Yadron, and Disuke Wakabayashi, "Apple and Others Encrypt Phones, Fueling Government Standoff," *Wall Street Journal*, November 18, 2014.

83. Ibid.

84. Cory Bennett, "FBI to Silicon Valley: Give us Access," *The Hill*, September 10, 2015.

85. Questionable NPIC Projects. May 8, 1973. Document 00200.

86. Mark Lowenthal, *Intelligence: From Secrets to Policy*, 2nd ed. (Washington, D.C.: Congressional Quarterly Press, 2003), 69.

87. Civil Applications Committee (CAC) Blue Ribbon Study. Independent Study Group Final Report, September 2005, 32.

88. Dr. Robert D. Atkinson, President, Information Technology and Innovation Foundation, "Innovation in America: Opportunities and Obstacles before the Commerce, Science and Transportation Subcommittee on Competitiveness, Innovation, and Export Promotion, United States Senate," June 22, 2010.

89. Atkinson, *Understanding the U.S. National Innovation System*, 17.

90. "Testimony of Dr. Areden L. Bement Jr. Director, National Science Foundation before the Senate Commerce, Science and Transportation Committee," March 10, 2010.

91. *A Strategy for American Innovation.*

92. U.S. Department of Defense, *Report of the Defense Science Board Task Force on Basic Research. Office of the Under Secretary of Defense for Acquisition, Technology and Logistics.*

93. Ibid.

94. Ashley J. Tellis, "Balancing without Containment: A U.S. Strategy for Confronting China's Rise," *Washington Quarterly* 36, no. 4 (2013): 109–24.

95. Paul Mozur and Jane Perlez, "U.S. Tech Giants May Blur National Security Boundaries in China Deals," *New York Times*, October 30, 2015.

96. Eva Dou and Don Clark, "Struggles in China Push Cisco to Strike a Deal," *Wall Street Journal*, September 23, 2015.

97. Ibid.

98. Paul Mozur and Jane Perlez, "U.S. Tech Giants May Blur National Security Boundaries in China Deals," *New York Times*, October 30, 2015.

99. Andrea Peterson, "NSA Director, Yahoo Executive Spar Over Cyber Spying," *Washington Post*, February 24, 2015.

100. Francine Kiefer and Laurent Belsie, "Cyber Attacks Knit Closer Ties between US, Industry Private Internet Firms, Long War of Government, Are Gathering at the White House Tomorrow," *Christian Science Monitor*, February 14, 2000.

101. John Markoff, "Technology; Wrestling Over the Key to the Codes," *New York Times*, May 9, 1993.

102. Darren E. Tromblay, *The U.S. Domestic Intelligence Enterprise: History, Development, and Operations* (Boca Raton, FL: Taylor and Francis/CRC Press, 2016).

103. George Gerstenzang, "Clinton Removes Export Limits on Encryption Technology," *Los Angeles Times*, September 17, 1999.

104. Barrett Devlin and Danny Yadron, "Government Reaches Deal with Tech Firms on Data Requests," *Wall Street Journal*, January 28, 2014.

105. Craig Timberg and Ellen Nakashima, "Amid NSA Spying Revelation, Tech Leaders Call for New Restraints on Agency," *Washington Post*, November 1, 2013.

106. Sara Sorcher, "Tech Firms Push Back on 'Reactionary' Politics Following Terror Attacks," *Christian Science Monitor*, December 17, 2015.

107. P. J. Huffstutter, "Tech Firms Pay Police Agencies to Fight Cyber Crime," *Los Angeles Times*, July 26, 1999.

108. David Sarno and Jessica Guynn, "Freeze, It's the iPolice," *Los Angeles Times*, May 5, 2010.

Chapter Nine

Impacts of Innovation Theft on U.S. National Security

When technology and innovation is stolen, the impacts can have far-reaching and unforeseen consequences for U.S. national security. Countries and non-state actors illicitly acquiring resources can put them to use in regional conflicts, such as India and Pakistan, which have both attempted to exfiltrate resources from the United States in furtherance of their subcontinental rivalry. China siphons unmanned aerial vehicle technology and may release this technology to regimes that engage in activities that contravene human rights.

Theft of innovation creates a Pandora's Box effect that introduces even greater uncertainty to international affairs. One of these effects is the ability to exercise international leadership. As the United States learned in the wake of the Soviets' launch of *Sputnik* in 1957, the ability to demonstrate a claim to cutting-edge technology was an attribute to which allies and others gave credence. Related to the concept of expectations in the international environment is the assessment of state and nonstate actors' abilities to achieve forward motion with innovation. Consequently, the acquisition of the tools of innovation—items to facilitate tests, modeling, and more—is an area of particular concern.

INTELLECTUAL PROPERTY THEFT IN SUPPORT OF MILITARY ELEMENTS OF NATIONAL POWER

Once information and technology has been exfiltrated from the United States, it has been repeatedly used to develop capabilities that are a military threat to the United States. Aspects of Chinese aerospace owe an unacknowledged debt to U.S. R&D. China's CFM-56 jet engine contains the same core section as the engine used in the B-1B bomber.[1] China's twin engine J-31 bears resemblance to the U.S. F-35.[2] This is hardly surprising because Chinese actors have repeatedly hacked the F-35's contractors, including Lockheed Martin in 2009 and Northrop Grumman in 2010. Furthermore, a Lockheed Martin official reportedly acknowledged that multiple F-35 subcontractors had been completely compromised.[3] The cockpit of China's J-20 aircraft bears a resemblance to the U.S. F-22 stealth fighter.[4] China's unmanned aerial vehicle sector is also characterized by indicators of theft-based design. Its Wing Loong drone bears a close resemblance to the U.S. MQ-9 Reaper.[5] China's design by deceit extends between aerospace. In 2007, Chinese cyber actors infiltrated the network of QinetiQ, a defense contractor. In 2012, when the PLA unveiled a bomb disposal robot, it had characteristics similar to one of the QinetiQ designs.[6]

Of course, the United States is not the only country that has seen its technology duplicated by other countries. China's Z-11 helicopter was reverse engineered from the French Aerospatiale AS-350 Ecureuil. Beijing's C-801 anti-ship cruise missile was believed to be a copy of the French Exocet missile.[7]

Russia similarly benefited from the theft of proprietary knowledge. Like Beijing, Moscow leveraged collection against the United States to bolster its aerospace assets. The Soviets copied their missile radar from blueprints of the F-14, F-15, and F-16.[8] Collection under the auspices of the Soviet VPK program contributed to a Soviet clone of the U.S. airborne radar system: the Blackjack bomber, which owed a debt to the BI-B.[9] In a tacit admission of defeat in the space race, the Soviet space shuttle design was based on purloined NASA documents.[10] Technology development premised on threat was not limited to the skies. The Kirov class destroyer and other weapons systems were launched sooner than the originals from which they were copied.[11] In addition to weaponry, underlying technological capabilities were the result of misappropriated intellectual property. For instance, the RYAD computer series was based on IBM computers, and integrated circuits relied on Texas Instruments products.[12]

Of course, basing developments on snatch-and-grab espionage has an inherent risk of not absorbing knowledge that will provide the basis for long-term development. For instance, Soviet engineers did not bother to conduct research on technologies such as cold-rolled steel armor because they had the U.S. formulas.[13] Such shortcuts could leave a threat actor vulnerable to getting more than they bargained for.

IMPLICATIONS FOR INTERNATIONAL RELATIONS

Compromising the capabilities for innovation can result in recipient countries using cutting-edge technologies to their financial or geopolitical benefit.

Even if such activities are not directed at the United States, the complications that they create may require a U.S. response. Two examples demonstrate the variants of this problem. The continued tension between India and Pakistan has taken on new dimensions because of both countries' nuclear programs. Both countries, however, have attempted to surreptitiously acquire items from the United States that would help them to maintain those programs. The second implication is apparent in the example of the Chinese acquisition of UAV technology that provides benefits on the global market.

India and Pakistan Nuclear Rivalry

The nuclear posturing on the Asian subcontinent has relied on the illicit acquisition of technology. Both countries have attempted to obtain testing equipment that could support the development of new capabilities. Megatech Engineering attempted to export high-technology testing equipment to the Indira Gandhi Center for Atomic Research as part of a conspiracy involving an Indian front company called Technology Options.[14] The U.S. Department of Commerce identified attempts by India to acquire electronic sensors and seismic test equipment in 2008 and 2009.[15] Seismic testing is consistent with measuring nuclear detonations—either in an attempt to develop one's own capabilities or to monitor an adversary's activities. In 2008, an Indian national and an Indian corporation were indicted for attempting to ship items to India's Vikram Sarabhai Space Center (part of the Indian government's Department of Space). The transactions involved complex electronic instruments used in high-performance testing and monitoring essential in the research and development of launching systems, including missile delivery systems.[16] Pakistan has also been identified as pursuing illicit acquisitions. As of 2013, Pakistan's Space and Upper Atmosphere Research Commission attempted to acquire an atmospheric testing device and associated antennae.[17] Previously, Pakistan attempted to obtain oscilloscopes from a company that had not acquired the proper U.S. license to provide these items.[18]

Both countries have endeavored to procure items that would bolster facilities related to their nuclear programs. Biospherical Instruments Inc. exported a profiling radiometer system to India's Space Application Center.[19] Magnetic Shield Corporation attempted to export magnetic shielding materials to the Indira Gandhi Center for Atomic Research.[20] India's Solid State Physics Lab attempted to obtain electronic components as of 2011. It had previously tried to acquire a bench-top muffle furnace.[21] The Bhabba Atomic Research Center in Mumbai, India, attempted to acquire presses and blades in 2007.[22] As of 2010, the Department of Commerce had identified an attempt to export items for use in the reactor and core of a nuclear power plant under construction in Islamabad, Pakistan.[23] Items exported included epoxy paint and paint thinner. Later that year, the Pakistan Atomic Energy Commission's (PAEC) Chashma Nuclear Power Plant attempted to obtain regulating and controlling instruments.[24] The PAEC attempted to acquire a calibrator and nuclear-related commodities according to the U.S. Department of Commerce.[25]

The outputs of research and development of nuclear facilities have limited use without delivery systems. Consequently, as of 2008 multiple individuals and an international electronics company were identified as having attempted to export five hundred controlled microprocessors and other electronic components to Indian government entities, including Vikram Sarabhai Space Center and Bharat Dynamics Ltd.[26] Items sought by these entities were intended for use in space launch vehicles and ballistic missile programs.[27] India's Defense Research Development Laboratory, which included the laboratory developing India's principal nuclear-capable ballistic missile, tried to acquire a control panel and a hot isostatic press, which would be used to produce carbon-carbon items.[28] This process reduces the porosity of metals and increases the density of other materials for the purposes of improving mechanical properties and workability.

Both countries' efforts to acquire items that will help them face off against each other on the subcontinent are complicated by their relationships with the United States. Pakistan is occasionally viewed as an ally in counterterrorism matters (although its credibility in this area is dubious considering the double game that its Inter-Services Intelligence Directorate seems to play[29]). India, meanwhile, was the beneficiary of a 2005 joint statement by President George W. Bush and Indian prime minister Manmohan Singh, which lifted a three-decade U.S. moratorium on nuclear trade with India.[30] Increased opportunities for legitimate transactions also provide cover for illicit interactions. According to a 2014 Brookings Institution publication, India is the third largest exporter of exchange students to the United States.[31] This academic avenue provides another way in which India may illicitly acquire cutting-edge knowledge relevant to the advancement of its nuclear program.

China and Unmanned Vehicle Technology

Unmanned vehicle technology is a cutting-edge sector with both military and civilian applications. It is applicable to war fighting and intelligence collection functions. Consequently, the technology, particularly its aerial vehicle application (UAVs), is a target of interest to foreign entities that have attempted to collect it. This collection is consistent with the concepts of "buying in" and "selling out" and with the previously discussed methodologies and tradecraft. Within the domestic setting, representatives of foreign entities have exploited various events to make contact with experts. Foreign governments have also employed cyber attacks from outside the United States. Such collection activities allow the competitor access to sensitive technology and may allow it to be transferred to third countries.

Collectors representing foreign entities have used trade shows as a venue to target unmanned vehicle technology. In 2012, two individuals associated with East Asia and Pacific government and commercial institutions approached an employee of a cleared contractor at an annual armed service–related convention and attempted to elicit information about micro air vehicles.[32] During a 2013 UAV conference, an individual affiliated with a Near East region company lost a three-page set of instructions that directed collectors to target specific companies and information. The documents directed the collector to attend relevant events, take photographs, obtain copies of specific presentations, and gather vendor marketing materials.[33]

Individuals in the United States have attempted to illicitly export unmanned vehicle technology to foreign clients. For instance, Harold Hanson, Nina Yaming Qi Hanson, and a Maryland-based company were indicted for the illegal export of miniature UAV autopilots to a company in China.[34] This incident focused on miniature UAV technology. Additionally, Yi-Lan Chen was arrested for attempting to illegally export P200 Turbine Engines, which could be used to operate UAVs and military target drones.[35] In 2015, Hui Sheng Shen and Huan Ling Chang attempted to acquire UAVs, including a hand-launched RQ-116, for clients they claimed were associated with the Chinese government and its intelligence service.[36] The Chinese-owned Ralls wind farm company expressed interest in owning facilities near the Naval Weapons Training Facility in Boardman, Oregon, which was a test site for UAVs.[37] Such a facility could create an opportunity for the Chinese to collect U.S. drone technology.

In addition, individuals in the United States have exported the underlying knowledge associated with unmanned vehicle technology. In March 2013, Sixing Liu was sentenced for stealing thousands of files, including UAV information, from his employer, L-3 Communications, with the intention of positioning himself for employment in China. Part of Liu's theft included traveling to China and presenting the stolen information at Chinese government–organized conferences, multiple Chinese universities, and the Chinese Academy of Sciences.[38] According to a September 2013 *New York Times* report, Liu's experience in China was not unique and China has obtained UAV information by debriefing multiple U.S. attendees at conferences and meetings in China.[39] Even when such interactions do not result in the disclosure of sensitive information, they still provide opportunities for foreign governments to fill gaps in their programs, bringing them closer to being able to compete with U.S. entities commercially or militarily.

China has also pursued UAV information through cyber channels. According to a 2013 report by the cyber defense firm FireEye, Chinese PLA-affiliated hackers focused on targeting defense-related firms for UAV technology.[40] According to the U.S.–China Economic and Security Review Commission, Chinese actors gathered information about the Global Hawk UAV and DoD technology about UAV video systems.[41]

All of these avenues of collection have bolstered China's UAV program. The country was a latecomer to the game, only unveiling its first concept UAVs in 2006.[42] Less than a decade later, China displayed an armed UAV, the Wing Loong, at an international defense exhibition.[43] The Wing Loong bore an uncanny resemblance to the U.S. MQ-9 Reaper.[44] The theft of U.S. UAV technology creates the problem of proliferation. As of 2014, U.S. intelligence community assessments determined that East Asia and Pacific countries could transfer UAV technology, including technology developed by reverse engineering, to third-country UAV customers.[45] As of 2013, six countries in Africa and Asia were negotiating to purchase the Wing Loong.[46] China's willingness to deal with international pariahs—as exemplified by its interactions with Sudan—suggests that its weapons sales may be indiscriminate, potentially arming problematic regimes.

China may also be attempting to directly challenge U.S. influence via the distribution of UAV technology. In December 2015, Iraqi forces used a Chinese-built Caihong-4 drone to strike an Islamic State position as part of the effort to retake Ramadi. (Caihong translates to "Rainbow"—perhaps an attempt to set China's brand apart from the U.S.-made "Reaper" and "Predator"?) China's sales are an encroachment on the Iraqi market, a province of the United States.[47] This would not be the first time China used ill-gotten technology to supplant the American originator. American Superconductor represents a dramatic example of such a situation.

IMPACT ON NONMILITARY ASPECTS OF NATIONAL POWER

Competition—sometimes relying on theft—has impacts on elements of national power beyond the military realm. In addition to the economic impacts tied to R&D and production, foreign governments' acquisition of capabilities to extract natural resources degrade the United States' ability to use economic sanctions. This makes it more difficult to curtail the behavior of regimes that engage in egregious activities, including the violation of human rights and fomentation of regional instability. Furthermore, a public race for technological superiority—such as that between the Soviet Union and the United States—can lead allies to question U.S. leadership if it appears to be lagging in comparison to competitors.

Economic

Some countries have used the theft or acquisition of technology to utilize its natural resources for its economic well-being. The acquisition of not otherwise available technological know-how permits a country to remain economically and financially viable through the exploitation of natural resources. As of 2008, the owners of a U.S. company pled guilty to conspiracy toward export of controlled engineering software for the design of an offshore oil and gas structure to Iran.[48] Cuba also obtained similar illicit assistance from a U.S. entity that provided specialized technical computer software and training. This provided the basis for modeling potential exploration and development of oil and gas within Cuban territorial waters.[49] Both countries were subject to sanctions intended to pressure totalitarian regimes to change their repugnant behaviors. Rather than acknowledging their violations of human rights, the regimes attempted to defeat the sanctions by improving their economic situation—using the technology of a country that supported those sanctions.

Diplomatic

The Soviet Union and its successor, the Russian Federation, have a lengthy history of using innovation as a tool to bolster their status in the international environment. The most notable Soviet episode was the 1957 launch of *Sputnik*, the earth-orbiting satellite. Prior to the launch, the CIA had assessed that the United States needed to beat the Soviets into space for psychological reasons. Although *Sputnik* had little functional significance, its launch did have significant implications for U.S. foreign policy. When the U.S. Information Agency conducted polling in five Western European countries, it discovered that there was a widespread impression that the Soviet Union was more scientifically advanced than the United States. The administration assessed that the apparent Soviet success was a blow to U.S. efforts at countering Soviet influence in neutral countries. The U.S. Department of State believed that for the Cold War neutrals, the Soviet success affirmed the wisdom of not aligning with either superpower. U.S. efforts to mitigate the damage from *Sputnik* included the establishment of NASA in 1958. Eisenhower established NASA to advance U.S. capabilities in space and catch up with the Soviets.[50] It is interesting that several decades later the Soviets would be collecting against the work of NASA, founded after the United States was caught off guard by a perceived Soviet innovation advantage in pursuit of information that would enhance Moscow's capabilities.

Russia's current space program, a descendant of the Soviet enterprise that produced *Sputnik*, serves a similar purpose of projecting influence. According to James Lewis of the Center for Strategic and International Studies, the "new focus of the Russian space program is prestige and national pride."[51] Amazingly, the United States has played into this bid for influence by agreeing in August 2015 to renew a contract with the Russian Federal Space Agency (Roscosmos) to transport American astronauts to the International Space Station.[52] This is particularly mindboggling because, between the mid-1970s and the early 1980s, NASA documents and NASA-funded contractor studies were the most important sources of unclassified material on aerospace issues for the Soviet Union.[53] The Senate Select Committee on Intelligence expressed concerns about the U.S. government's reliance on a Russian-made engine on the launch vehicles that put national security space satellites into orbit.[54]

In addition to its space exploits, Russia viewed its Skolkovo project as a centerpiece of its innovation capability. Moscow planned to display this accomplishment by hosting the summer 2014 G-8 summit.[55] However, due to Russian aggression in the Ukraine, it was suspended from the G-8 in early 2014, nullifying any chance that it would be showing off Skolkovo to one of the world's most exclusive geopolitical clubs.

China has also used its innovation (significant portions of which have been illicitly acquired from the United States) in the field of space exploration as a means to demonstrate its status as a significant power. The Chinese space program serves multiple foreign and domestic policy goals, with its primary purpose being political.[56] The program bolsters China's bid for regional leadership by demonstrating that it is more advanced than other Asian nations.[57] This is part of a broader strategy that includes the aggressive action of literally building new territory in the South China Sea.

TEXTBOX 9.1.   SABOTAGE

Competition over innovation and the capabilities it provides may manifest itself in sabotage of both physical and economic varieties. Penetration of high-technology infrastructure suggests the intent to decrease U.S. technical capabilities. Multiple states, including China, are infiltrating the networks of industrial control systems.[1] In 2009, reports surfaced that Russian and Chinese spies had penetrated the U.S. electric grid.[2] Attacking the U.S. power grid has apparently become a topic of academic study in China, as indicated by the work of researchers at the Institute of Systems Engineering of Dalian University of Technology. They published a paper on how an attack on a small U.S. power grid could lead to a cascading failure across the entire United States.[3]

Despite these signs that China is at least considering how to knock the United States offline, Washington and Beijing have established agreements to cooperate on developing strategies for grid modernization in both countries.[4]

Another indicator of how a foreign actor may destroy U.S. innovation is the 2014 hack of Sony Pictures Entertainment's servers and introduction of hard drive–erasing malware.[5] While this was apparently directed at entertainment industry intellectual property, it is well within the realm of possibility that similar actions could be directed at intellectual property in the field of technology, especially after a foreign entity had copied it. Economic disinformation has the potential to damage U.S. capabilities for innovation. As the National Counterintelligence and Security Center noted, foreign governments may use disinformation campaigns to frighten companies and clients from dealing with U.S. entities.[6] Themes of such campaigns may include the untrustworthiness and aggressiveness of external commercial entities.[7]

Multiple foreign governments have lengthy histories of perception management activities in the United States. These activities are normally focused on achieving preferred policy options without showing a foreign hand. They could also be turned on to U.S. companies to undermine public confidence in technology and to bolster the positive profile of technology. This situation is likely where a foreign government has sponsored the theft of technology from a U.S. entity, indigenized it, and then attempted to degrade the U.S. market share. Finally, SVR and Line ER officers Buryakov and Sporyshev, who were identified in early 2015, attempted to develop information about the New York Stock Exchange's use of exchange-traded funds and potential limits on the use of high-frequency automated trading systems.[8] Buryakov, according to national security journalist Shane Harris, was specifically interested in how exchange-traded funds might be used as a mechanism for destabilizing markets.[9]

NOTES

1. Siobhan Gorman, "NSA Director Warns of 'Dramatic' Cyberattack in Next Decade; U.S. Needs Better Preparations for Cyber Threats, Surveillance Chief Says," *Wall Street Journal*, November 21, 2014.

2. Siobhan Gorman, "U.S. News: Electricity Industry to Scan Grid for Spies," *Wall Street Journal*, June 18, 2009.

(continued)

3. John Markoff and David Barboza, "Academic Paper in China Sets Off Alarms in U.S.," *New York Times*, March 21, 2010.

4. *2014 Report to Congress of the U.S. China Economic and Security Review Commission*, 219.

5. James R. Clapper, Director of National Intelligence, "Statement for the Record. Worldwide Cyber Threats," September 10, 2015.

6. National Counterintelligence Center, *Annual Report to Congress on Foreign Economic Collection and Industrial Espionage: 1995*, 18.

7. Ibid.

8. *United States of America v. Evgeny Buryakov (a/k/a "Zhenya"), Igor Sporyshev, and Victor Podobnyy.*

9. Shane Harris, "The Russian News Agency Doubled as a Spy Machine," *Daily Beast*, January 27, 2015.

ILLICIT ACQUISITION OF S&T CAPABILITIES: THE GIFT THAT KEEPS ON GIVING

It is troubling enough when a state or nonstate actor acquires a piece of technology that can be reverse engineered to produce a finite amount of knowledge. It is even more troubling when a threat actor can tap the expertise of an individual, thereby gaining a resource that provides continuing input on problems of innovation. Perhaps most alarming is a threat actor's acquisition of R&D infrastructure, providing it a permanent platform to develop new capabilities. With its own laboratories, modeling software, and more, an adversary or competitor no longer needs to rely on an outside entity. Not only does this enhance its ability to catch up with the United States, but it also makes an actor less vulnerable to double-agent operations or other means of disruption by creating greater self-sufficiency and insularity.

Laboratory equipment has been a target of multiple state actors. For instance, China's Thirty-Third Institute and the Chinese Academy of Launch Vehicle Technology attempted to obtain vibration-testing equipment illegally from a U.S. company.[58] In another instance, China attempted to acquire design and testing technologies controlled on national security grounds from a U.S. entity.[59]

Iran has been another persistent pursuer of restricted technologies, a predilection that has included laboratory equipment. As of 2013, Iran attempted to obtain electronic test equipment.[60] In 2008, BIS identified an attempt to sell and export a United Computer Inclusive Hydraulic Floor Model Testing Machine to Iran.[61] Iran often attempts to ship items via third countries in an apparent attempt to obfuscate their ultimate destination. In 2009, BIS identified an individual attempting to ship laboratory equipment systems to Iran via the United Arab Emirates.[62] During the previous year, a U.S. person was sentenced for planning to export restricted test tube and microplate coating systems to Iran via the UAE.[63] Syria, a close ally of Iran, was also an intended recipient of equipment routed circuitously—apparently to avoid detection of its ultimate destination—which came to light as of 2010 when BIS identified an individual who had attempted to ship lab equipment from the United States to Syria via Indonesia.[64]

Multiple countries have sought to acquire modeling and simulation software that could help them develop new capabilities of concern for U.S. interests. The Beijing University of Aeronautics and Astronautics attempted to acquire flight simulation software as of 2011.[65] The Defense Security Service, in its 2014 report, stated that entities in the East Asia and Pacific region requested modeling and simulation software, especially as it applied to satellite applications, from U.S.-cleared defense contractors.[66] Iran is another country that has attempted to acquire high-tech computer-based systems. For instance, it was the intended recipient of engineering software shipped via the UAE in one instance and Brazil in another.[67]

PERILS OF WHOLESALE APPROPRIATION BY STATE ACTORS

There are threats from foreign entities indigenizing U.S. research and development from companies that have established a presence abroad, as has been previously discussed. However, governments may take a far less subtle approach by applying measures of coercion to appropriate capabilities. In a 2015 report, the U.S. Trade Representative noted that there was growing concern about the Chinese competition authorities increasing their scrutiny of companies that have intellectual property that Beijing deemed to be essential for implementing certain technological standards.[68] The Russian Federation has never been hesitant to appropriate enterprises that it viewed as a threat to individuals in power. In 2008, the FSB, Russia's internal security service and a successor to the KGB, raided the offices of BP and its Russian joint venture, TNK-BP.[69] A BP employee was detained and accused of collecting information on behalf of foreign petroleum companies.[70] Such strong-arm tactics could easily be deployed to gain control of R&D assets of companies that established a footprint in an authoritarian state such as China or Russia.

CONCLUSION

The ability to maintain a technological edge has implications for national security that extend beyond the immediate economic impacts felt by specific industries. During the Cold War and continuing today, state actors pursue scientific advancement (for example, space programs) as means to demonstrate power—this can produce diplomatic ramifications that damage the standing of the party on the losing end of the competition. When states piggyback off of purloined U.S. knowledge, they move closer to challenging U.S. interests. Furthermore, even when foreign governments do not use illicitly acquired technology to confront the United States, the results of applying this technology may result in or exacerbate existing conflicts, creating complications for U.S. attainment of policy objectives. Competition may result in scenarios in which foreign actors seek not only to acquire proprietary knowledge but also to obtain a monopoly on it by seizing assets of a company doing business in a country or by engaging in sabotage against a U.S. entity via a cyber attack.

NOTES

1. *PRC Acquisition of U.S. Technology*, 53.

2. Marcus Weisgerber, "China's Copycat Jet Raises Questions about F-35," September 23, 2015, www.defenseone.com.

3. *Report to Congress of the U.S. China Economic and Security Review Commission*, 112th Cong. 155 (2012).

4. Ibid., 129.

5. *2013 Report to Congress of the U.S. China Economic and Security Review Commission*, 223.

6. Testimony of Larry M. Wortzel, "Cyber Espionage and the Theft of U.S. Intellectual Property and Technology before the House of Representatives. Committee on Energy and Commerce Subcommittee on Oversight and Investigations," July 9, 2013.

7. *PRC Acquisition of U.S. Technology*, 53.

8. Fialka, *War by Other Means*, 9.

9. Andrew and Gordievsky, *KGB: The Inside Story*, 621–22.

10. Fialka, *War by Other Means*, 9.

11. Ibid., 88.

12. Andrew and Gordievsky, *KGB: The Inside Story*, 621–22.

13. Fialka, *War by Other Means*, 70.

14. U.S. Department of Commerce, *Don't Let This Happen to You: An Introduction to U.S. Export Control Law. Export Enforcement* (Washington, D.C.: U.S. Department of Commerce, 2008), 40.

15. U.S. Department of Commerce, Bureau of Industry and Security, *Annual Report to the Congress for Fiscal Year 2009* (Washington, D.C.: U.S. Department of Commerce 2009), 30; U.S. Department of Commerce, Bureau of Industry and Se-

curity, *Annual Report to the Congress for Fiscal Year 2008* (Washington, D.C.: U.S. Department of Commerce, 2008), 31.

16. U.S. Department of Justice, *Summary of Major U.S. Export Enforcement, Economic Espionage, Trade Secret and Embargo-Related Criminal Cases* (January 2008 to the Present: Updated March 26, 2014), 88.

17. U.S. Department of Commerce, Bureau of Industry and Security, *Annual Report to the Congress for Fiscal Year 2013* (Washington, D.C.: U.S. Department of Commerce, 2013), 39.

18. U.S. Department of Commerce, Bureau of Industry and Security, *Annual Report to the Congress for Fiscal Year 2010* (Washington, D.C.: U.S. Department of Commerce, 2010), 29.

19. U.S. Department of Commerce, *Don't Let This Happen to You*, 40.

20. Ibid., 41.

21. U.S. Department of Commerce, Bureau of Industry and Security, *Annual Report to the Congress for Fiscal Year 2011* (Washington, D.C.: U.S. Department of Commerce, 2011), 42; U.S. Department of Commerce, *Annual Report to the Congress for Fiscal Year 2010*, 37.

22. U.S. Department of Commerce, *Annual Report to the Congress for Fiscal Year 2008*, 34.

23. U.S. Department of Commerce, *Annual Report to the Congress for Fiscal Year 2011*, 34.

24. U.S. Department of Commerce, *Annual Report to the Congress for Fiscal Year 2010*, 34.

25. U.S. Department of Commerce, *Annual Report to the Congress for Fiscal Year 2013*, 37; U.S. Department of Commerce, Bureau of Industry and Security, *Annual Report to the Congress for Fiscal Year 2012* (Washington, D.C.: U.S. Department of Commerce, 2012), 26.

26. U.S. Department of Justice, *Summary of Major U.S. Export Enforcement, Economic Espionage, Trade Secret and Embargo-Related Criminal Cases* (January 2008 to the Present: Updated March 26, 2014, 89.

27. U.S. Department of Commerce, *Don't Let This Happen to You*, 39.

28. Ibid., 41.

29. Mark J. Roberts, "Pakistan's Inter-Services Intelligence Directorate: A State within a State?" *Joint Forces Quarterly* 1, no. 48 (2008), 108–9.

30. "The US.-India Nuclear Deal," November 5, 2010, www.cfr.org.

31. "The Geography of Foreign Students in U.S. Higher Education: Origins and Destinations," August 29, 2014, Brookings Institution.

32. Defense Security Service, *Targeting U.S. Technology: A Trend Analysis of Cleared Industry Reporting* (2013), 28.

33. Defense Security Service, *Targeting U.S. Technology: A Trend Analysis of Cleared Industry Reporting* (2014), 46.

34. "Testimony by Kevin J. Wolf, Assistant Secretary for Export Administration, Bureau of Industry and Security, U.S. Department of Commerce before the National Security and Foreign Affairs Subcommittee of the Committee on Oversight and Reform," March 23, 2010.

35. Ibid.

36. U.S. Department of Justice, *Summary of Major U.S. Export Enforcement, Economic Espionage, Trade Secret and Embargo-Related Criminal Cases* (January 2009 to the Present: Updated August 12, 2015).

37. Damian Paletta, Keith Johnson, and Sudeep Reddy, "Obama Blocks Chinese Firm from Wind-Farm Projects," *Wall Street Journal*, September 29, 2012.

38. United States Department of Justice, *PRO IP Act, Annual Report FY 2013*, 17.

39. Edward Wong, "Hacking U.S. Secrets, China Pushes for Drones," *New York Times*, September 20, 2013.

40. Ibid.; *2013 Report to Congress of the U.S. China Economic and Security Review Commission*, 113th Cong. First Session, November 2013, 223.

41. *2014 Report to Congress of the U.S. China Economic and Security Review Commission*, 113th Cong. Second Session, November 2014, 295.

42. "China's New Drones Raise Eyebrows," *Wall Street Journal*, November 18, 2010.

43. *2013 Report to Congress of the U.S. China Economic and Security Review Commission*, 223.

44. Ibid.

45. Defense Security Service, *Targeting U.S. Technology: A Trend Analysis of Cleared Industry Reporting* (2014), 33.

46. *2013 Report to Congress of the U.S. China Economic and Security Review Commission*, 223.

47. Patrick Boehler and Gerry Doyle, "Use by Iraqi Military May be a Boon for China-Made Drones," *New York Times*, December 17, 2015.

48. U.S. Department of Justice, *Summary of Major U.S. Export Enforcement, Economic Espionage, Trade Secret and Embargo-Related Criminal Cases* (January 2008 to the Present: Updated March 26, 2014), 89.

49. Ibid., 90.

50. Kenneth Osgood, *Total Cold War: Eisenhower's Secret Propaganda Battle at Home and Abroad* (Wichita: University Press of Kansas, 2006), 330, 337, 338, and 349.

51. James Andrew Lewis, *Space Exploration in a Changing International Environment* (Washington, D.C.: Center for Strategic and International Studies, 2014), 13.

52. "NASA Notifies Congress about Space Station Contract Modification with Russia," www.nasa.gov.

53. *FBI Counterintelligence Visits to Libraries: Hearings before the Subcommittee on Civil and Constitutional Rights of the Committee on the Judiciary, House of Representatives*, 100th Cong., 275 (1988) (Testimony of James H. Geer, Assistant Director, Intelligence Division, Federal Bureau of Investigation).

54. *Report of the Select Committee on Intelligence: United States Senate, Covering the Period January 3, 2013 to January 5, 2015*. Rep. 114-8, at 18 (2015).

55. "Can Russia Create a New Silicon Valley? Innovation in Russia," *Economist*, July 14, 2012.

56. Lewis, *Space Exploration in a Changing International Environment*, 7.

57. Ibid.

58. U.S. Department of Commerce, *Don't Let This Happen to You*, 40.

59. U.S. Department of Commerce, *Annual Report to the Congress for Fiscal Year 2012*, 38.

60. U.S. Department of Commerce, *Annual Report to the Congress for Fiscal Year 2013*, 32.

61. U.S. Department of Commerce, *Annual Report to the Congress for Fiscal Year 2008*, 38.

62. U.S. Department of Commerce, *Annual Report to the Congress for Fiscal Year 2009*, 28; U.S. Department of Commerce, *Annual Report to the Congress for Fiscal Year 2012*, 37.

63. U.S. Department of Justice, *Summary of Major U.S. Export Enforcement, Economic Espionage, Trade Secret and Embargo-Related Criminal Cases* (January 2008 to the Present: Updated March 26, 2014), 93.

64. U.S. Department of Commerce, *Annual Report to the Congress for Fiscal Year 2010*, 32.

65. U.S. Department of Commerce, *Annual Report to the Congress for Fiscal Year 2012*, 31.

66. Defense Security Service, *Targeting U.S. Technology: A Trend Analysis of Cleared Industry Reporting* (2014), 37.

67. U.S. Department of Commerce, *Annual Report to the Congress for Fiscal Year 2008*, 40; U.S. Department of Commerce, *Annual Report to the Congress for Fiscal Year 2009*, 36.

68. U.S. Trade Representative, *2015 Special 301 Report* (Washington, D.C.: U.S. Trade Representative, 2015), 42.

69. Andrew E. Kramer, "Russia Arrests 2 Tied to BP Joint Venture," *New York Times*, March 21, 2008.

70. Ibid.

Chapter Ten

Defending Against and Disrupting Threats to Innovation

Multiple U.S. government agencies have established programs to help private sector entities effectively protect their knowledge and technology. This is not a simple task for several reasons. First, as the FBI has noted, foreign intelligence services have increasingly shifted their collection from defense contractors to entities not as well versed in protecting their assets.[1] This is consistent with the idea that the work, which drives innovation, is increasingly being done outside of the government. It is more difficult to keep track of developments that may eventually support classified applications, especially when the U.S. government is increasingly relying on the private sector to develop concepts that the government can then adopt and adapt. The second problem—a lack of institutional knowledge in bureaucracies—is not unique to navigating the intersection of intelligence and innovation, but is certainly relevant to the issue. In 2012, Frank Figluzzi, the FBI's assistant director for counterintelligence, claimed, "We need to make the general public aware of the threat from economic espionage. Clearly it is time to do something new and outside the box."[2] Figluzzi's comment seemed to reflect ignorance about a succession of FBI programs that looked like the reinvention of the wheel.

THE FBI COUNTERINTELLIGENCE PUBLIC SECTOR OUTREACH

The FBI plays a key role in protecting innovation and maintaining national security in the United States, as evidenced by its long history of outreach with the public sector. As mentioned previously, the FBI's structure and culture has traditionally emphasized the investigative, reactive functions of its mission. Proactive intelligence collection and counterintelligence activities have been a more challenging endeavor. Nevertheless, most Bureau investigations in the past and present have been predicated by information derived from the public in some way, be it informants, tips from the public, or referrals from other government or law enforcement agencies. The Bureau excels at cultivating relationships with the public. Indeed, its decentralized structure of fifty-six field offices and multitude of resident agencies promotes the localized domain-driven information gathering that is essential for initiating and pursuing investigations. In recent times, the Bureau has recognized the importance of establishing dialogue and partnerships with industry and academia to facilitate investigations and establish tripwires to warn against emerging threats. Current programs like the Strategic Partnership Program, InfraGard, and the Key Partnership Engagement Program aim to foster closer ties between the Bureau and the public sector. Although sometimes haphazardly implemented and sporadically supported depending upon the whims of the current field office special agent in charge, these programs are meant to mitigate threats to U.S. security and protect U.S. innovation and accrued knowledge.

FBI Plant Survey Program

The FBI first recognized the need to interface with the public sector in the 1930s and 1940s with its Plant Survey Program. Although primarily a reactive law enforcement agency, with this program the Bureau implemented preemptive measures to counter the threats to essential wartime industries. This program and the associated clandestine collection activities directed at identifying espionage and sabotage were the early precursors of its modern counterintelligence, counterterrorism, and infrastructure protection responsibilities. Through its activities in plant protection, the Bureau was able to develop and exploit foreign intelligence collection abroad.

The United States had learned from experience that even if it did not involve itself directly in conflict it could still be a target. For instance, in 1916, prior to the U.S. entry into World War I, German saboteurs had set off an explosion at a munitions stockpile on Black Tom Island in New York Harbor. Later, as hostilities in Europe intensified, the FBI initiated a Plant Survey Program, which was operational by the fall of 1939.[3] With this program, the FBI prepared a guide to instruct plant managers on topics including the duties of employees, the role of the FBI in plant protection, the importance of reporting irregularities, protecting the scene of a crime, developing informants, and recognizing espionage and sabotage techniques.[4] The FBI's approach to plant protection was twofold. First, special agents inspected sites, identified vulnerabilities, and provided recommendations on how to mitigate threats.[5] The inspections afforded the agents with the opportunity to obtain suggestions from plant protection officials.[6] The results from these plant surveys were then passed to the Office of Naval Intelligence or the Military Intelligence Division, depending on which service a relationship with the facility.[7]

In addition to the plant inspections, the FBI also implemented longer-term efforts to engage plant management in maintaining awareness of potential threats. The FBI at least initially helped organize schools for plant protection officers, assisted in teaching selected subjects, and provided speaking engagements with plant personnel. The FBI relationship with plant managers were of a distinctly liaison nature, rather than an informant relationship.[8] By late 1942, the FBI was no longer conducting plant surveys.

Development of Espionage, Counterintelligence, and Counterterrorism Awareness (DECA)

The FBI's Development of Espionage, Counterintelligence, and Counterterrorism Awareness (DECA) was a successor to the Plant Security Program. It was established in the early 1980s as an avenue to engage the corporate community and educate it on what to expect from Soviet and other intelligence services. With the program, the FBI's resources were linked with the security measures employed by U.S. defense contractors and focused on the targets of foreign intelligence service activity.[9] As described by an FBI official to Congress in 1988, DECA "seeks to heighten the awareness of corporate executives and their employees to the hostile intelligence services threat."[10]

DECA broadened its mission during its existence. For instance, the FBI realized that much of the sensitive information of value to foreign entities was not always classified defense information. Much information of interest to adversaries was unclassified and frequently publicly available. The FBI began to focus more on emerging technologies such as genetic engineering.[11] As the program went on, the FBI also focused less on interacting with the facility security officers of U.S. companies and more directly with the rank-and-file employees, especially those that had direct contact with foreign agents.[12] This interaction with employees allowed for the opportunity for a true give-and-take relationship between the FBI and the public entity. The FBI was able to educate companies and their employees about threats as well as receive information and investigative leads concerning foreign governments' attempts to illicitly collect economic and technological information.[13]

DECA employed resources from both FBI headquarters and all its field offices. In 1990, the FBI appointed a national DECA coordinator and established a national DECA advisory committee.[14] At the field level, DECA coordinators in each of the FBI's field offices had regular liaisons with companies within the field offices territory. Each DECA coordinator aimed to assist the private sector in understanding and recognizing foreign economic and espionage threats as well as the tradecraft that the foreign governments employed to collect intelligence.[15]

DECA became a platform from which multiple agencies could contribute to counterintelligence. For instance, the National Counterintelligence Center (NACIC) worked with the FBI through the DECA program.[16] Additionally, the Central Intelligence Agency (CIA) provided information to the FBI by way of the DECA program.[17]

Awareness of National Security Issues and Response (ANSIR)

The FBI's Awareness of National Security Issues and Response (ANSIR) program was the successor to DECA. ANSIR was a response to the changing dynamics of a post–Cold War environment. According to the deputy assistant director responsible for the program, these factors included foreign intelligence services' expansion of targeting to include unclassified private sector proprietary economic information, the escalated threat of a terrorist attack on American interests, and the problems of computer intrusion and viruses.[18] The focus of ANSIR tended to be on violations of the Economic Espionage Act.[19] The program represented the first effort by the U.S. government to provide national security threat information to individual U.S. corporations with critical technologies or sensitive economic information that foreign governments or organizations may target.[20]

ANSIR had an ambitious agenda that was not matched by the limited resources that the FBI assigned to cover it. Up to forty thousand U.S corporate security directors and executives, law enforcement personnel, and other government agencies received warning information through this program.[21] However, as of 2001 the entire program was overseen by a single Supervisory Special Agent (the lowest rung of FBI management) in the National Security Division at FBI headquarters.[22] Each of the FBI's fifty-six field offices had a special agent who coordinated the ANSIR program locally. However, this function was an ancillary duty that was not supposed to take more than 10 percent of the agent's time.[23] It was mandatory that a special agent fill the role as, according to the deputy assistant director in charge of the program, "decades of experience with the ANSIR audience has shown that the private sector prefers discussing national security issues with an individual who has operational experience."[24] This seemed to be a holdover of the attitude, indicated by the "war stories" remark, that characterized DECA.

TEXTBOX 10.1.   LIBRARY AWARENESS PROGRAM

Foreign intelligence services can get a head start on U.S. efforts to disrupt their targeting of American interests by collection of open-source materials that provide a basis for more incisive targeting of sensitive information. Commercial databases, trade and scientific journals, corporate publications, and openly available U.S. government data can all provide data on new R&D, competitors' strengths and weaknesses, and personality profile data. For instance, during the 1980s, the FBI identified that the Soviet Union KGB's Line X, which was responsible for the collection of scientific and technical issues, had a great interest in developing sources and contacts among librarians in the greater New York area.[1] This information, in its own right, is often of value to collectors and may also provide leads to focus clandestine collection and to identify targets that possess information of interest.[2] Soviet intelligence initiated background investigations on individuals whom they identified through research and spotting conducted in the libraries.[3] Foreign entities' perception of this information's value is evident in their efforts to acquire it. According to the U.S. government, traditional intelligence services may resort to clandestine collection to acquire publicly available materials. Measures include the use of false names when accessing open-source databases and requests that a legal and open relationship be kept confidential.[4] According to an FBI official's congressional testimony, "the information available to the Soviet intelligence service in the specialized and technical libraries is not classified, restricted or unlawful to collect and maintain, Soviet intelligence tactics and methodology employed to collect such information have illustrated a blatant disregard for American laws and the personal rights of American citizens. Soviet intelligence officers have stolen, or caused to be stolen by their agents, hundreds of thousands of items of microfiche from these libraries. Soviet intelligence officers have initiated background investigations on individuals whom they have identified through research and spotting conducted in the libraries."[5]

The FBI's New York field office initiated a program in the 1980s to address these early stages of collection. The Library Awareness Program was modeled after the FBI's national DECA initiative.[6] The Library Awareness Program's objectives were to inform selected librarians that they and their libraries were and had historically been significant Soviet intelligence targets for intelligence activities, including recruitment. Most of these librarians were affiliated with academic

(continued)

institutions, as opposed to public libraries.[7] Furthermore, the program's emphasis on intelligence activities on the milieu provided opportunities to identify intelligence officers, identify agents of foreign intelligence, assess Soviet tradecraft and methodology, and determine Soviet intelligence objectives.[8] As an FBI official testified to Congress, "This is part of what we put together to decide where we are going to focus the resources that we have."[9] Furthermore, awareness of Soviets' interests could help decision making by other government entities beyond the Bureau. As the same Bureau official noted, some of the information was positive intelligence that could be of value to other parts of the U.S. government. The information might also inform strategic mitigation by identifying targets, which the Bureau might suggest, should become classified.[10] The New York program began in 1985 and had been preceded by a 1973–1976 initiative.[11] It used only a few agents who did not work full time on the program.[12] By the late 1980s, it had become public and had become the subject of controversy and a 1988 lawsuit.[13] In 1988, FBI director William Sessions agreed to curtail some of the program's more controversial aspects.[14]

While these Bureau programs encountered public criticism in the media, in Congress, and in the courtroom, foreign intelligence collectors continued to exploit publicly available information for knowledge or as a means to incisively target proprietary items. The Office of the National Counterintelligence Executive (ONCIX)—predecessor to the current National Counterintelligence and Security Center—repeatedly highlighted that foreign intelligence collectors viewed conferences, conventions, and trade shows as opportunities to develop information of interest.[15] These events arguably reduce the need to sift through copious open-source information by aggregating experts in their respective fields into one setting, providing foreign intelligence the opportunity to shoot the proverbial fish in the barrel. Additionally, the ONCIX has continued to emphasize foreign entities' interest in open-source information. As it described in a 2011 report, "Foreign collectors are aware that much US economic and technological information is available in professional journals, social networking and other public websites, and the media."[16] The increasing availability of information online means that intelligence services and other foreign entities no longer have to risk exposure by making physical appearances to gather open-source information. The concept common to both scenarios is that foreign collectors are increasingly finding ways to decrease their exposure, making them less vulnerable to traditional counterintelligence.

NOTES

1. *FBI Counterintelligence Visits to Libraries: Hearings before the Subcommittee on Civil and Constitutional Rights of the Committee on the Judiciary, House of Representatives*, 100th Cong. 306 (1988) (Testimony of James H. Geer, Assistant Director, Intelligence Division, Federal Bureau of Investigation).

2. National Counterintelligence Center, *Annual Report to Congress on Foreign Economic Collection and Industrial Espionage: 1995*, 20.

3. *FBI Counterintelligence Visits to Libraries: Hearings before the Subcommittee on Civil and Constitutional Rights of the Committee on the Judiciary, House of Representatives*, 100th Cong. 112 (1988) (Testimony of James H. Geer, Assistant Director, Intelligence Division, Federal Bureau of Investigation).

4. National Counterintelligence Center, *Annual Report to Congress on Foreign Economic Collection and Industrial Espionage: 1995*, 20.

5. *FBI Counterintelligence Visits to Libraries: Hearings before the Subcommittee on Civil and Constitutional Rights of the Committee on the Judiciary, House of Representatives*, 100th Cong. 112 (1988) (Testimony of James H. Geer, Assistant Director, Intelligence Division, Federal Bureau of Investigation).

6. Ibid., 111.

7. Robert McFadden, "F.B.I. in New York Asks Librarians' Aid in Reporting on Spies," *New York Times*, September 18, 1987.

8. *FBI Counterintelligence Visits to Libraries: Hearings before the Subcommittee on Civil and Constitutional Rights of the Committee on the Judiciary, House of Representatives*, 100th Cong. 111 (1988) (Testimony of James H. Geer, Assistant Director, Intelligence Division, Federal Bureau of Investigation).

9. Ibid., 123.

10. Ibid., 144.

11. Ibid., 125.

12. Robert McFadden, "F.B.I. in New York Asks Librarians' Aid in Reporting on Spies," *New York Times*, September 18, 1987.

13. David Johnston, "Documents Disclose F.B.I. Investigations of Some Librarians," *New York Times*, November 7, 1989; Bill McAllister, "Stalking Spies in Libraries Triggers Suit against FBI; Details of Controversial Program Sought," *Washington Post*, June 3, 1988.

14. Bill McAllister, "FBI to Limit Probes of Library Users; Program to Detect Foreign Agents Is Altered to Guard Patron Privacy," *Washington Post*, November 15, 1988.

15. Office of the National Counterintelligence Executive, *Foreign Economic Collection and Industrial Espionage FY07* (Office of the National

(continued)

Counterintelligence Executive, 2008); Office of the National Counterintelligence Executive, *Foreign Spies Stealing US Economic Secrets in Cyberattacks*, 2.

16. Office of the National Counterintelligence Executive, *Foreign Spies Stealing US Economic Secrets in Cyberattacks*.

Strategic Partnerships Program

The FBI's current counterintelligence-based public outreach program is known as the Strategic Partnership Program (SPP). The SPP is a loose partnership between a regional FBI field office and the businesses, academic institutions, think tanks, and trade organizations operating within the field office area of responsibility. As of 2014, it had more than fifteen thousand contacts in these sectors.[25] The program consists of approximately eighty special agents who are well versed in counterintelligence.[26] It is designed to foster dialogue for the mutual benefit of the FBI and the outside organization. Each of the fifty-six FBI offices has designated at least one and sometimes multiple Agents that specialize in conducting outreach activities regarding counterintelligence and counterespionage matters. These agents routinely provide security awareness training and deal with threats and concerns from the outside partner. This close relationship can be beneficial for both the FBI and for the partner. The SPP program also provides a platform for interagency collaboration on shared areas of concern. One example was the creation of a DSS/FBI Strategic Partnership Task Force at the Washington Field Office, "established to include CI outreach to industry and create opportunities for the two entities to work together in countering the threat to cleared industry through information sharing and joint support efforts."[27]

The partnerships can facilitate information gathering in support of ongoing FBI investigations. It is much easier to garner the cooperation and trust of an organization if personal relationships and mutual understanding have already been established. Many investigations involve the use of advanced techniques like surveillance and sting operations that require intimate collaboration with the victim organization. The earlier the victim organization notifies and begins working the FBI, the greater likelihood of a successful investigation and eventual prosecution. For instance, if a company has concerns about an employee displaying insider threat indicators, a typical reaction of the company would be to simply terminate the employee and to remove the problem. However, this simple knee-jerk reaction does not allow for an investigation into the true nature of the threat, the potential damage to the organization, or any possibility of a criminal prosecution. If the FBI is notified at an early stage, the Bureau may initiate an investigation that preserves evidence and may catch the putative spy in the act of economic espionage.

Second, the SPP enables the FBI to gain a more detailed understanding of the threat facing a particular industry or organization by engaging with the organization. This knowledge assists the FBI in recognizing widespread threats and trends that might not otherwise be apparent. In an organization that does not always promote subject matter expertise, these partnerships can be a valuable learning tool enabling the establishment of threat tripwires to alert the Bureau when threats emerge.

A third benefit of the FBI Strategic Partnership concerns the prevention of crime through training and promoting greater awareness. Regular security awareness training provided by strategic partnership coordinators reminds employees, executives, and students alike about the need for securing innovation and the threats facing them both as an individual and as an organization.

The SPP has made progress in promoting security awareness, particularly regarding economic espionage issues to a variety of industries. Previous outreach efforts have emphasized the cleared defense industry as a target for economic espionage, and the SPP has expanded the Bureau's outreach to industries that are unaccustomed to thinking about foreign adversaries and had typically little interaction with the FBI. The agriculture and seed industry, for instance, was caught off guard in 2012 when the FBI arrested several Chinese individuals for digging up corn seeds from a test plot in Iowa.[28] The culprits were apprehended on a plane to China with seeds hidden in their luggage in packages disguised to look like popcorn. News of these cases shocked the industry and created a desire to interface more closely with the FBI. The SPP is perfectly poised to partner with this industry to help "harden the target," as FBI agents are fond of saying. Other industries such as oil and gas, nanotechnology, and microelectronics are in a similar position of being targeted by foreign adversaries.

From an economic espionage vantage point, academia has largely been neglected from counterintelligence outreach. Academia in general has traditionally been more difficult for the FBI to partner with. The academic culture is based on maintaining openness and promotes extensive collaboration with the scientific community. This culture is frequently viewed at odds with the FBI's counterintelligence mission of thwarting foreign actors' collection efforts. But as more and more research and development occurs at U.S. universities and as these universities collaborate more and more with foreign entities, the security risks increase and need for the FBI to interface effectively grows. Universities, long resistant to cooperation with the FBI and reluctant to do anything perceived as curtailing the free exchange of information, are now more vulnerable than ever. In 2005, FBI director Robert Muller announced the formation of the National Security Higher Education Advisory Board (NSHEAB), consisting of presidents and chancellors of several prominent U.S. universities. It is designed to foster outreach and to promote understanding between the academic community and the FBI.[29]

The mission of the SPP becomes all the more critical as the problem of economic espionage continues to increase year by year. The current FBI director, James Comey, has stated that economic espionage is now the second highest priority in the FBI, just behind fighting terrorism.[30]

The SPP has adopted outreach strategies that are designed to interface with the public in new ways and reach new audiences with its security awareness message. As a law enforcement organization, it has not been known for creative approaches or "outside the box" thinking. An example of a novel approach is the production of several videos (*Betrayed*, *Game of Pawns*, and *The Company Man*) dramatizing real espionage cases. These videos have high production value and allow the audience to better appreciate the subtle and insidious threat espionage poses to the United States, its institutions, and citizens. The FBI took the unusual step of presenting the video *Game of Pawns* to the media in 2013 and making it available publicly on the Internet. This video was also unusual in that its target audience was U.S. study abroad students, a group at risk of targeting and recruitment by foreign intelligence services and one that has been largely ignored by the U.S. intelligence community. Although occasionally in the mainstream press by pundits and reporters, the videos have been effective at reaching new audiences with the FBI's security messages and driving home the threats facing the United States.

The FBI has also looked to the private sector to develop approaches mitigating the threat from entities targeting innovation. In 2011, it created an Intellectual Property Threat Small Working Group, which consisted of corporate security officers from Fortune 100 companies to focus on bolstering relationships of trust between law enforcement agencies and industry and improving information sharing regarding intellectual property theft. The objective of this effort was to generate lateral liaison among industry peers and to generate high-profile intellectual property cases.[31] However, the Bureau has still not figured out the most effective way to work with private industry. According to the CEO of the National Cyber Forensics and Training Alliance, the FBI would accept unclassified information from the private sector and then classify it, which prevented the Bureau from then sharing it with other entities in the private sector.[32]

InfraGard

The FBI supports another initiative between the law enforcement public and private sector known as InfraGard. InfraGard is a member-based rather than organization-based program intended to support the protection of critical U.S. infrastructure and promote information sharing. The program aims to bring together subject matter experts who can communicate through federal law enforcement and government agencies through local InfraGard chapters.[33] The program began in 1996 as collaboration between the FBI's Cleveland field office and subject matter experts from local industry and academia and was intended to focus on cyber and physical security matters. The program quickly expanded to the other fifty-six FBI field offices. As of April 2014, there are 25,863 active members including business executives, academics, and state and local law enforcement.[34] There is a least one InfraGard chapter in the territory of each of the FBI's fifty-six field offices. Members are determined by the FBI after applicant record checks are completed. The regional chapter meetings promote trusted discussions of member vulnerabilities as well as the needs of the FBI. The program consists of seventeen infrastructure categories including agriculture and food, energy, and defense.[35] InfraGard allows subject matter experts from these sectors to exchange information and discuss vulnerabilities among themselves and with the U.S. intelligence community. The FBI Cyber Division's National Industry Partnership Unit uses the InfraGard network to facilitate the transfer of information between the public and private sectors.[36]

Key Partnership Engagement Unit (KPEU)

With increasing reliance on electronic record keeping and communication, it is no surprise that adversaries are employing various cyber techniques to steal sensitive information from U.S. organizations. These organizations are often unsure how to adequately safeguard their computer systems. In addition, they are often reluctant to share information about cyber attacks for fear of damaging public image, shareholder confidence, and losing sales. In an effort to address this problem, the FBI has recently established the Key Partnership Engagement Unit (KPEU).[37] This program is targeted at senior executives of key private sector corporations. The KPEU is intended to promote the FBI's government and industry collaboration to cyber security through the exchange of information. It is unclear just how effective such a program will be.

DEPARTMENT OF HOMELAND SECURITY PROGRAMS

DHS has its own outreach program under the auspices of Immigration and Customs Enforcement (ICE). "Project Shield America" is an ICE initiative that engages industry and academia. It includes presentations for U.S. manufacturers and exporters of arms and sensitive technology. These include information about export laws, licensing issues, and "red flag" indicators associated with illegal procurement and best practices for compliance with government agencies. One Project Shield America success occurred in 2009, when an industry outreach event identified a dual Canadian/Iranian citizen who was attempting to acquire pressure transducers from a U.S. company.[38] Another success occurred when Homeland Security Investigations (an ICE component) learned of an online illegal purveyor of export-restricted software products during a private industry outreach meeting.[39] DHS inherited an outreach concept from at least one component agency. Prior to absorption into DHS, the U.S. Customs Service, under the Department of the Treasury, initiated Project GEMINI, which advised U.S. businesses export requirements and encourage their reporting of attempts to illegally acquire or export sensitive military equipment or technologies.[40]

DEFENSE SECURITY SERVICE PROGRAMS

The Department of Defense's Defense Security Service (DSS) has implemented multiple measures to protect sensitive industries from compromise by foreign entities. It created a course on foreign ownership and control issues (FOCI) and hosted conferences on these issues.[41] Furthermore, DSS provides tailored assessments, known as "Gray Torch," which are meant to strengthen the company's understanding of the nature of the foreign intelligence threat and to identify and recognize unlawful attempts to acquire U.S. technology developed or produced in the facilities operating under the National Industrial Security Program.[42] DSS has also gone so far as to exchange personnel with companies under its purview. In 2009, it initiated its Partnership with Industry Program, which involved the exchange of security personnel for a week to improve communications and give the private sector a better understanding of DSS's mission.[43] The Counterintelligence Partnership with Cleared Industry Program, which began in 2012, gives companies the opportunity to work directly with the DSS Counterintelligence Directorate. Participants provide value to DSS through discussion of pitfalls, successes, best practices, and lessons learned in a nonattribution environment. Companies benefit from access to DSS information systems that they can use to analyze threat information relevant to their activities.[44]

DEPARTMENT OF COMMERCE PROGRAMS

The Bureau of Industry and Security (BIS) engages in a variety of outreach activities. Its Project GUARDIAN contacts U.S. manufacturers and exporters that handle technologies and goods that specific proliferation networks are targeting. It apprises them of the acquisition threat and solicits cooperation in identifying and responding to suspicious purchase requests.[45] In 2014, BIS initiated 103 Project GUARDIAN outreach contacts and developed 206 leads.[46] BIS also conducts multiple seminars throughout the United States that focus on high-tech communities that are most affected by commerce regulations.[47] BIS also reaches representatives of technology firms through its Annual Export Control Forum.[48] As noted previously, academia has expressed concern about deemed exports due to the impact that these regulations would have on foreign students' research. Consequently, BIS has been working with nonprofit organizations associated with university research programs to explain deemed export regulations.[49]

U.S. INTELLIGENCE COLLECTION ON ECONOMIC MATTERS

The United States' experience with intelligence collection to support innovation has been complicated by multiple factors. First, as a leading innovator, it is more likely to be the target than the recipient of collection. Its interest in foreign innovation is a policy problem, the net assessment of a country's capabilities, or a counterintelligence issue, identifying whether and how a foreign competitor or adversary obtained proprietary information. Second, intelligence collection in support of innovation is a politically charged issue. The U.S. government is not in the business of picking national champions, meaning that intelligence would have to be made equally available to all users. Political figures have been far more eager to push for collection oriented to economics and innovation than intelligence community officials have. Finally, the softer issues such as economics have tended to be of interest only when the United States was not engaged in conflict. Thus, the heyday of debate about the role of the intelligence community in collection of economic information was the middle of the so-called peace dividend of the 1990s.

INSTANCES OF GOVERNMENT PROVISION
OF COLLECTION TO PRIVATE INDUSTRY

Although the United States does not have a tradition of the private sector reporting intelligence activities (unlike France and Japan), there were short-lived programs that involved the intelligence community providing intelligence to U.S. companies. During the Carter administration, the CIA briefed selected corporate presidents about industrial and economic intelligence collected from countries in which those executives' companies did business.[50] The CIA selected companies based on those companies' willingness to allow the Agency to debrief employees who traveled abroad.[51] This debriefing program was likely a predecessor to what is now the CIA's National Resources Division. Another Carter-era program of sharing with the private sector involved U.S. companies receiving declassified CIA intelligence via Commerce Department briefings.[52] Private industry continues to receive assistance from the intelligence community but with identifying threats, rather than identifying opportunities for promotion of interests. (It is interesting to note that U.S. presidents beloved by people who do not favor intelligence gathering sometimes make the most interesting use of that very intelligence.)

Even after the Carter administration and its associated programs came to a close, the topic of U.S. government intelligence support to private industry remained a topic of debate. Multiple chairmen of the Senate Select Committee on Intelligence (SSCI) expressed beliefs that companies should receive information collected by the CIA that might affect them.[53] Another member of Congress favored using the intelligence community to collect information that could be provided to industry (providing it to a single company would be an unfair advantage).[54] However, there was no suggestion that the private sector should help set the intelligence community's agenda. As General William Odom, who had headed the NSA, observed, it was impractical for the IC to engage in collection for the private sector as it would be impossible to obtain the guidance that would make such collection effective.[55] Intelligence community officials saw no place for collection in furtherance of private sector innovation. Former director of Central Intelligence Robert Gates felt the role of U.S. intelligence should be defensive in nature and used to identify violations of trade agreements and ferret out moles.[56] Similarly, former FBI director Louis Freeh stated that he was opposed to the use of U.S. government resources to collect against foreign companies.[57]

The U.S. has collected on policy issues that impact its commercial and economic interests. It has not collected on individual companies. This can be viewed in two broad categories of information. The first is economic intelligence that supports negotiations on trade issues. For instance, in the 1990s, the U.S. trade representative Mickey Kantor used information collected by the CIA and the NSA in negotiations with Japan.[58] Information included conversations among Japanese bureaucrats and executives from Toyota and Nissan.[59] Kantor received analyses of the limits to which his Japanese counterparts could be pressured.[60] More recently, the *New York Times* reported that the U.S. Department of Agriculture had used NSA reporting to support negotiations.[61] The second element of economic collection is the development of negative intelligence, the information about how foreign actors are seeking to compromise U.S. commercial activities. Under the category of negative intelligence is the identification of inappropriate activities that foreign entities may employ to gain an unfair advantage against U.S. entities doing business abroad. In 1993, the Clinton administration asked the CIA to track illegal tactics that foreign entities used to win business.[62] The Agency gathered information about improper French commission payments to Brazilian officials.[63] A second subcategory of negative intelligence is counterintelligence (the identification of foreign entities' efforts to target U.S. information) and counterespionage (the disruption, through criminal prosecution, of the individuals who implement foreign entities' intentions).

Unfortunately, the United States has suffered several embarrassments operationally and analytically in the field of economic intelligence gathering. In 1995, the French counterintelligence service unraveled a U.S. operation, which resulted in five U.S. intelligence operatives being expelled from the country.[64] Four of the operatives were of CIA officers under diplomatic cover at the U.S. embassy, and one operative was under nonofficial cover. The female nonofficial cover officer, masquerading as a public relations officer for a save-the-rainforest foundation, courted an aide to Prime Minister Balladur.[65] CIA officers queried the aide on the French position concerning the General Agreements on Tariffs and Trade (GATT) talks and also attempted to obtain GATT-related information from a communications ministry official.[66] The French were so incensed by this episode that they suspended intelligence coordination with the United States on multiple topics including terrorism and arms trafficking and would not permit the United States to conduct intelligence operations against non-French targets in France.[67] U.S. operations in Germany were also detected by that country's intelligence resources. As of 1997, a CIA operative under diplomatic cover attempted to obtain data from a high-ranking official of Germany's economics ministry who had access to information about companies that exported high-technology items to Iran.[68] Then in 1999, Germany identified three U.S. persons working for the CIA and forced the United States to recall them.[69]

The United States clearly does not currently engage in activities directed at providing specific U.S. entities a distinct advantage. Edward Snowden put the issue back in the headlines with his 2013 divulgences about supposed U.S. spying on the Brazilian energy company Petrobras.[70] A more recent reminder of economically oriented collection was the mid-2015 revelation of the German BND's cooperation with the NSA since 2008 to develop intelligence about European entities, including what is now known as the Airbus Group.[71]

However, in the context of collection that serves strategic, rather than proprietary, interests, such targets make sense. Petrobras can reasonably be expected to have an impact on global energy markets of interest to the U.S. government. Airbus, which has customers worldwide, has the potential to impact the balance of forces through sales to countries hostile to U.S. interests.

The issue is not whether U.S. collection on economic matters is legitimate, but whether it is worthwhile. As noted previously, the U.S. intelligence community is not necessarily poised to keep pace with specific developments in innovation that impact economic and other concerns. It is also unclear that the intelligence community knows what to collect. Following the 1995 episode in Paris, U.S. ambassador Pamela Harriman expressed her consternation that the CIA had damaged bilateral relations by clandestinely collecting information that could have been gleaned from the local press.[72] Furthermore, even if the intelligence community could successfully collect data on economic matters, including drivers of innovation that could impact the economic setting, there have been doubts that the intelligence community was capable of effectively analyzing it.[73] The skill sets necessary to bridge the gap between economic and innovation issues seems to remain the stuff of the venture capital world, just as the private sector cyber security industry seems to be outpacing the U.S. government's capabilities.

DISRUPTION

The above programs are adjuncts to intelligence collection. They enlist leads from industry and academia to more clearly understand the threat. However, once a threat is identified, it must be disrupted. The United States often takes overt steps to halt or impede illicit activity. This may be as simple as an arrest and prosecution or, as in the 2014 case of the five Chinese hackers, an indictment that serves as a shot across the bow. If a state sponsor is clearly involved, the United States may impose sanctions against the offending government. However, the United States may choose to keep its response covert, using its identification of attempts to surreptitiously acquire technology as a channel to derail an adversary's attempts to acquire high-tech capabilities.

One example of how a channel can be manipulated to mislead an adversary was an operation, code-named SHOCKER, run by the FBI and the Department of Defense. SHOCKER provided information to the Soviet Union via a double agent over a number of years. Information intended to mislead Moscow included research about U.S. WMD capabilities. In 1959, the Bureau initiated the operation to ferret out the Soviet intelligence presence in Washington through the use of a dangle (that is, maneuvering an individual into a position that elicits a foreign intelligence service's recruitment pitch). For several years, the Bureau continued this essentially defensive operation (disrupting the element of Moscow's intelligence apparatus that was present within the United States). However, in 1965, the Bureau partnered with the Department of Defense to use the by then established dangle as a channel through which the U.S. government could push the Soviets tantalizing but useless information about military developments pertaining to weapons of mass destruction.[74]

A later operation developed around a Soviet source that the French had took the Soviets' technology shopping list and helped them to the checkout, albeit with items tailored to U.S. specification. The KGB's First Chief Directorate had established its Directorate T to collect against Western countries' research and development programs through its operational arm, known as Line X.[75] The French recruited a member of Directorate T, Vladimir Ippolotovich Vetrov, code-named FAREWELL.[76] Vetrov furnished reports from Directorate T on goals, achievements, and not-yet-reached objectives. Using this knowledge of the Soviets' playbook, the CIA decided in 1982 to feed the KGB the objects that it was attempting to acquire. These would come through U.S. sources and, according to Gus W. Weiss, who served as a White House policy advisor, "would have been 'improved,' that is, designed so that on arrival in the Soviet Union they would appear genuine but would later fail." The domestic environment was crucial to the success of this operation, as it was the technology that was a product of uniquely American firms that the Soviets were trying to collect. Various U.S. companies assisted in preparing items for Line X. The FBI handled the domestic aspects of the operation.[77] As a result, the Soviets received defective computer chips, which they installed in military equipment; incorrect plans disrupted factory outputs; and compromised pipeline software resulted in pipeline pressure that produced a three-kiloton explosion in June 1982 (which occurred in an unpopulated region of Siberia).[78]

CONCLUSION

The majority of U.S. programs to protect innovation are defensive in nature. At best, they prevent compromise by threat actors, but any lapse is an adversary's gain. This is arguably the legacy of law enforcement as the basis of the United States' most significant counterintelligence agency—the FBI. There is a cultural aversion to competing with a threat and instead an unrealistic assumption that the threat can be stopped—whether through prosecution or expulsion of a spy form the United States—and consequently a reliance on measures that are meant to bring those threats to light. However, U.S. intelligence, including the FBI, has occasionally taken a more proactive approach, meant to set back an adversary or to help U.S. institutions to operate with greater savvy vis-à-vis competitors. The proliferation of private sector cyber firms that are inclined toward more aggressive measures suggests that there is public support for approaches to illicit exfiltration than have been the norm.

NOTES

1. Evan Perez, "FBI's New Campaign Targets Corporate Espionage," *Wall Street Journal*, May 11, 2012.
2. Ibid.
3. Raymon Batvinis, *The Origins of FBI Counterintelligence* (Wichita: University Press of Kansas, 2007), 83.
4. Memorandum for the Director, Federal Bureau of Investigation, November 15, 1939, declassified July 13, 1990.
5. Batvinis, *The Origins of FBI Counterintelligence*, 83.
6. Memorandum for the Director, Federal Bureau of Investigation, November 15, 1939, declassified July 13, 1990.
7. Batvinis, *The Origins of FBI Counterintelligence*, 83.
8. Memorandum for the Director, Federal Bureau of Investigation, November 15, 1939, declassified July 13, 1990.
9. Freddie L. Capps Jr., "Espionage Awareness Programs," *FBI Law Enforcement Bulletin* 60, no. 9 (September 1991).
10. *FBI Counterintelligence Visits to Libraries: Hearings before the Subcommittee on Civil and Constitutional Rights of the Committee on the Judiciary, House of Representatives*, 100th Cong. 111 (1988) (Testimony of James H. Geer, Assistant Director, Intelligence Division, Federal Bureau of Investigation).
11. Gregory M. Lamb, "Leaks Flow East—and West; US Industry and High-Tech Spies," *Christian Science Monitor*, December 28, 1982; *FBI Counterintelligence Visits to Libraries: Hearings before the Subcommittee on Civil and Constitutional Rights of the Committee on the Judiciary, House of Representatives*, 100th Cong. 176-177 (1988) (Testimony of James H. Geer, Assistant Director, Intelligence Division, Federal Bureau of Investigation).
12. Gregory M. Lamb, "Leaks Flow East—and West; US Industry and High-Tech Spies," *Christian Science Monitor*, December 28, 1982.
13. National Counterintelligence Center, *Annual Report to Congress on Foreign Economic Collection and Industrial Espionage: 1995*, 4.
14. Freddie L. Capps Jr., "Espionage Awareness Programs," *FBI Law Enforcement Bulletin* 60, no. 9 (September 1991).
15. National Counterintelligence Center, *Annual Report to Congress on Foreign Economic Collection and Industrial Espionage: 1995*, 6.

16. National Industrial Security Program Policy Advisory Committee Minutes of the Meeting, September 27, 1995.

17. National Counterintelligence Center, *Annual Report to Congress on Foreign Economic Collection and Industrial Espionage: 1995*, 7.

18. Ibid.

19. www.fas.org; Thomas R. Stutler, "Stealing Secrets Solved: Examining the Economic Espionage Act of 1996," *FBI Law Enforcement Bulletin* 69, no. 11 (November 2000).

20. John F. Lewis Jr., "Fighting Terrorism in the 21st Century," *FBI Law Enforcement Bulletin* (March 1999).

21. Ibid.

22. "Michael J Waguespack, Deputy Assistant Director, National Security Division, FBI, before the House Committee on Government Reform, Subcommittee on National Security, Veterans Affairs and International Relations," April 3, 2001.

23. Ibid.

24. Ibid.

25. *Committee on the Judiciary, Subcommittee on Crime and Terrorism, United States Senate, at a Hearing Entitled "Economic Espionage and Trade Secret Theft: Are Our Laws Adequate for Today's Threats?"* (2014) (Statement of Randall C. Coleman, Assistant Director, Counterintelligence Division, Federal Bureau of Investigation).

26. Ibid.

27. *DSS Access* 2, no. 2 (Summer 2013).

28. Department of Justice Press release December 12, 2013.

29. FBI National Press Office, September 15, 2005.

30. "Economic Espionage. Protecting America's Trade Secrets," www.fbi.gov.

31. *Committee on Judiciary, United States Senate, Entitled Oversight of Intellectual Property Law Enforcement Efforts* (2011) (Statement of Gordon M. Snow, Assistant Director, Cyber Division Federal Bureau of Investigation), June 22, 2011.

32. U.S. Department of Justice, Office of the Inspector General, *Audit of the Federal Bureau of Investigation's Implementation of Its Next Generation Cyber Initiative* (Washington, D.C.: U.S. Department of Justice, 2015), 20.

33. "InfraGard: A Collaboration for National Infrastructure Protection," www.infragard.net.

34. Private sector outreach section, www.fbi.gov.

35. "InfraGard: A Collaboration for National Infrastructure Protection," www.infragard.net.

36. U.S. Department of Justice, *Audit of the Federal Bureau of Investigation's Implementation of Its Next Generation Cyber Initiative*, 18.

37. "Statement Before the House Homeland Security Committee, Subcommittee on Cyber Security, Infrastructure Protection, and Security Technologies; Washington, D.C. April 16, 2014," www.fbi.gov.

38. "Statement for the Record, U.S. Immigration and Customs Enforcement, before the U.S. House of Representatives Committee on Homeland Security, Subcommittee on Oversight, Investigation and Management on 'Homeland Security

Investigations: Examining DHS's Efforts to Protect American Jobs and Secure the Homeland,'" July 28, 2011.

39. "Written Testimony of ICE Homeland Security Investigations Executive Associate Director Peter Edge for a Senate Committee on Appropriations Subcommittee on Homeland Security hearing titled 'Investing in Cybersecurity: Understanding Risks and Building Capabilities for the Future,'" May 7, 2014.

40. Department of the Treasury Efforts to Prevent Illicit Transfers of U.S. Military Technologies, March 23, 2000, 14.

41. Defense Security Service, *Stakeholder Report, 2012*, 7.

42. Ibid., 11.

43. Ibid., 4.

44. "DSS Counterintelligence Partners with Industry to Mitigate Foreign Intelligence Threats," *Access: Official Magazine of the Defense Security Service* 3, no. 4 (Winter 2014).

45. U.S. Department of Commerce, *Annual Report to the Congress for Fiscal Year 2011*, 13.

46. U.S. Department of Commerce, *Annual Report to the Congress for Fiscal Year 2014*, 15.

47. U.S. Department of Commerce, *Annual Report to the Congress for Fiscal Year 2011*, 12.

48. Ibid.

49. Ibid., 13.

50. Walter Pincus, "CIA Targets Overseas Firms but Draws a Line," *Washington Post*, March 5, 1995.

51. Ibid.

52. Ibid.

53. Ibid.

54. Kenneth J. Cooper, "Intelligence Goes Public in the House; Panel's New Chairman Opens Hearing Today," *Washington Post*, March 9, 1993.

55. Ronald J. Ostrow and Paul Richter, "Economic Espionage Poses Major Peril to U.S. Interests Spying," *Los Angeles Times*, September 28, 1991.

56. George Lardner Jr. and Walter Pincus, "CIA's Gates Opposed to 'Commercial Spying': Unconventional Arms Seen as Greatest Danger," *Washington Post*, December 12, 1991; Ronald J. Ostrow and Paul Richter, "Economic Espionage Poses Major Peril to U.S. Interests Spying," *Los Angeles Times*, September 28, 1991.

57. Frank Swoboda, "Economic Espionage Rising," *Washington Post*, February 29, 1996.

58. David E. Sanger and Tim Weiner, "Emerging Role for the CIA: Economic Spy," *New York Times*, October 15, 1995.

59. Ibid.

60. Ibid.

61. James Risen and Laura Poitras, "Spying by N.S.A. Ally Entangled U.S. Law Firm," *New York Times*, February 16, 2014.

62. David E. Sanger and Tim Weiner, "Emerging Role for the CIA: Economic Spy," *New York Times*, October 15, 1995.

63. David Ignatius, "The French, the CIA and the Man Who Sued Too Much," *Washington Post*, January 8, 1996.

64. James Risen, "Downplayed by CIA, Paris Incident Has Wide Impact," *Los Angeles Times*, October 11, 1995; William Drozdiak, "Bonn Expels U.S. Official for Spying," *Washington Post*, March 9, 1997.

65. David E. Sanger and Tim Weiner, "Emerging Role for the CIA: Economic Spy," *New York Times*, October 15, 1995.

66. Ibid.

67. William Drozdiak, "Bonn Expels U.S. Official for Spying," *Washington Post*, March 9, 1997; James Risen, "Downplayed by CIA, Paris Incident Has Wide Impact," *Los Angeles Times*, October 11, 1995.

68. William Drozdiak, "Bonn Expels U.S. Official for Spying," *Washington Post*, March 9, 1997; Alan Cowell, "Bonn Said to Expel U.S. Envoy Accused of Economic Spying," *New York Times*, March 10, 1997.

69. William Drozdiak, "Germans Force U.S. to Recall 3 CIA Agents in Spy Case," *Washington Post*, September 30, 1999.

70. John Lyons, "New Spying Allegations Add to Brazil Rift," *Wall Street Journal*, September 8, 2013.

71. Alison Smale, "Germany, Too, Is Accused of Spying on Its European Allies," *New York Times*, May 5, 2015.

72. William Drozdiak, "Bonn Expels U.S. Official for Spying," *Washington Post*, March 9, 1997.

73. David E. Sanger and Tim Weiner, "Emerging Role for the CIA: Economic Spy," *New York Times*, October 15, 1995.

74. David Wise, *Cassidy's Run: The Secret Spy War over Nerve Gas* (New York: Random House, 2000).

75. Gus W. Weiss, "Duping the Soviets: The Farewell Dossier," *Studies in Intelligence* 39 (1996): 5.

76. Andrew and Gordievsky, *KGB: The Inside Story*, 622.

77. Gus W. Weiss, "Duping the Soviets: The Farewell Dossier," *Studies in Intelligence* 39 (1996): 5.

78. William Safire, "The Farewell Dossier," *New York Times*, February 2, 2004.

Conclusion

Innovation and accrued knowledge are essential to sustaining multiple elements of national power. The ability of the United States to remain secure and maintain or project its self-interest in the world depends on the ability to innovate and reap the benefits of such innovation. Loss of this innovation through licit and illicit means has a profound deleterious effect on national security. However, this impact is not always fully appreciated by the U.S. government, the private sector, or the American people if their attitudes and actions are any indication. Once knowledge has left the country, it is gone for good. Legitimate transfers of knowledge are, of course, not always a net negative because there are attendant benefits such as the creation of new markets. It is nonetheless a point of no return, and decisions regarding the accessibility of innovation should take this Rubicon into consideration.

Throughout much of the last century, the U.S. government was a driving force behind innovation, as technological evolution and breakthroughs were essential to national security—both in terms of military power and the broader ability to demonstrate leadership. Protecting this information was largely the responsibility of the U.S. government security and intelligence services. This paradigm has shifted in recent decades. More and more, the private and academic sectors serve as the prime sources of innovation with much of the significant advances being made in smaller start-up companies rather than government-sponsored laboratories. This is further complicated by the trend in recent years of certain sectors of private industry demonstrating reticence to work with the U.S. government. The role and methods needed to protect U.S. innovation must also change to keep pace with new realities.

The private sector and academia are prime drivers of innovation and thus targets of adversaries wishing to acquire their knowledge. No longer can these entities remain blissfully ignorant of the threats that are stalking their progress. As the creators of new knowledge—and no longer working under the aegis of U.S. government security—they are in the crosshairs of state and nonstate actors that now throw formidable resources at companies and academia that cannot easily match this onslaught. No longer can the private sector and academia simply rely on the U.S. government for its sole source of protection. More and more, the U.S. government, private industry, and academia must work together and cooperate to disrupt a common threat.

This is no simple task, as it is complicated by cross-cutting corporate cultures. The traditional entrepreneurial "can do" culture of industry has become increasingly at odds with U.S. national security. The private sector and academia have pursued markets abroad with seemingly little concern for how their actions might contribute to competitors' and adversaries' capabilities in the longer term. (They also set themselves up for the loss of proprietary information that they did not intend to transfer.) Furthermore, the attitude of self-reliance has in some quarters curdled into open hostility toward government involvement, as illustrated by the contretemps surrounding the issue of encryption. Meanwhile, the U.S. government has not been able to keep pace with the evolving security landscape, as indicated by the emergence of private sector cyber security firms that even the government has had to leverage for assistance.

Regardless of their views on engagement with the government, each company and academic institution must take steps—if only for their own good—to clearly identify the unique, proprietary, and valuable knowledge within the organization. This inventory will provide the basis for internal assessment and amelioration of vulnerabilities and will also help U.S. authorities to understand what threat actors may target.

State and nonstate actors identify contacts through which they can obtain knowledge. Ultimately, this boils down to the human factor. One does not have to be a business executive, a college dean, or a technology wunderkind to be targeted by a foreign intelligence service or company. With so much personal information readily available in electronic form, from social media sites and electronic communications, it is quite easy for an adversary to target an individual employee or even a college student. Indeed, the compromise of personnel records of twenty-one million U.S. citizens in the OPM cyber breach should serve as a frightening reminder of how vulnerable every American is to exploitation.

A recruited individual may provide a competitor or adversary with surreptitious access to proprietary information or may function as walking intellectual property by taking knowledge with them to another company or another country. The introduction of the cyber operating environment has created new variations on old problems. The threat to proprietary information still, in the simplest form, resolves to the individual: the disgruntled or avaricious employee who downloads information and turns it over to a competitor, the unwitting worker who opens a link in a socially engineered spear-phishing email, or the system administrator who forgets to roll out the newest software patch.

Securing innovation in the global environment requires calculated risks and perpetual analysis of the costs and benefits of decisions. The U.S. government, private industry, and academia cannot, nor should they, avoid an international presence. Rather, they must take into account their exposure to the potential loss of intellectual capital when making their decisions. Risk-versus-reward choices must continually be made each time a U.S. entity contemplates a partnership with a foreign entity (whether abroad or on American soil). The totality of the circumstances should dictate when or if the transaction should proceed.

U.S. entities must be willing to conduct the due diligence needed to create a fair assessment of the risks. It is important that new avenues open up to facilitate this analysis. This process must entail more than simply reviewing the balance sheets. It also needs to incorporate an understanding of a foreign government's technology acquisition objectives and the institutions (for example, intelligence services, state-controlled firms, etc.) that the government may use to reach its objectives. Finally, any assessment should take into account specific issues of methodology and tradecraft (for example, do they use social engineering such as "honey traps" to gain access to individuals with knowledge of value?). Of course, analysis is useless if it does not provide the basis for decision making. Shareholders and other stakeholders should insist that those assessments become the basis for developing a set of measures to reduce identified vulnerabilities that a threat actor might otherwise exploit for illicit acquisition. Furthermore, this should not be a one-time process. Rather, any joint venture or international expansion should be subject to ongoing analysis as part of determining the viability of the project. Criteria and channels for reporting of suspicious activities should be established, with periodic reviews conducted to determine whether new vulnerabilities might be emerging.

The need for greater awareness is not limited to the private sector and academia. The U.S. government must approach global engagement with equally stringent security. U.S. government entities, such as CFIUS, also need to take a more holistic approach when assessing proposed foreign transactions. National security extends beyond direct impacts on the military and defense industry. Cutting-edge fields like clean energy are equally important to preserving elements of national power as cleared defense contractors. It is important to periodically review the benefit of relationships that do exist between the U.S. and its foreign partners because these can change with time. For instance, when the United States entered into agreements with China in 1979 regarding scientific collaboration, the U.S. objective was diplomatic engagement. However, while China has continued to benefit from these arrangements in sensitive fields, it has become increasingly hostile to the U.S. geopolitical interests. A reevaluation of the U.S. relationship with China is long overdue.

In addition to thinking about how factors beyond an immediate transaction may impact the integrity of proprietary information, the private sector, academia, and U.S. government entities must also look inward to ensure their decision making is not being influenced by mirror imaging. The United States must realize that other nations and other cultures do not view the world in the same way as Americans do. By projecting U.S. values and morals on other nations, the United States runs the risk of being perpetually caught off guard by a world that plays by a different set of rules. Just as other cultures view human rights issues in different terms, so too do the attitudes of economic espionage vary greatly among nation-states. While there is a broad willingness to call out the former violations, there is not nearly such loud vocalizing against the latter problem. There is, instead, often an attitude that all is acceptable. Even the so-called allies of the United States have engaged in the theft of proprietary business information from American entities and there is no reason to expect that they have suddenly reformed and refrained from this practice. Another area in which the United States is susceptible to mirror imaging is in its belief that their counterparts are equally independent institutions. However, an authoritarian state—like China—exerts influence over all aspects of society and coopts them as it sees fit. (China even extends this view to the ethnic Chinese population, regardless of location, which it views as beholden to Beijing's interests.)

Although foreign governments utilize intelligence resources to acquire U.S. proprietary information, the U.S. government has abstained from state-sponsored economic espionage, although it has collected on geopolitically significant macroeconomic issues. U.S. entities would arguably stand to gain through economic espionage activities similar to those from which their competitors benefit. Foreign companies do innovate and lead in certain technology sectors. A U.S. company wishing to gain advantage could save time and money by stealing the technology. In addition to innovation, there is much to gain from acquiring proprietary business information. Sales figures, marketing strategies, promotional plans, customer lists, and pricing information can be of tremendous advantage to any company, whether domestic or foreign. In addition, collection against U.S. competitors would potentially be useful for counterintelligence purposes with the objective of determining and disrupting those foreign entities' exploitation of U.S. interests. The United States must make a determination about the ethics of engaging economic espionage activity. Such choices are more complicated and nuanced than the media or U.S. politicians make them out to be. Without an informed populace that truly understands the current state of affairs, protection and advancement of U.S. interests is unlikely to occur.

However, although the question of U.S.-sponsored economic espionage has periodically reemerged as an item for consideration, the realities of implementing such a program make government sponsorship unrealistic. Washington is unable to use private companies and academia with the same impunity as an authoritarian state or a country with state-owned enterprises that can be directed. Even if intelligence collection was feasible, it would be impossible to disseminate the results in a meaningful manner. In order to avoid showing favoritism to any one company, information would need to be made equally accessible, negating its value as a means to obtain a competitive edge. Furthermore, such broad dissemination would likely compromise the sources and methods that had been used to obtain the information in the first place. A more viable approach would involve revising the Foreign Corrupt Practices Act so that U.S. firms could independently engage in parochial intelligence collection against foreign competitors without repercussions from the U.S. judicial system.

If the United States cannot employ economic espionage to its gain, then Washington should bear it in mind as a way to induce an adversary's loss. As previously discussed, more than one U.S. intelligence operation used knowledge of what a foreign government wanted as the basis for instigating technological setbacks. In the current era, disinformation can be posted by U.S. entities—with innovation to protect—so when the next cyber intrusion occurs, the adversary may not know if the stolen information is genuine or not. The risks of stealing and relying upon faulty information can cost an adversary time and money. An adversary can be led astray and spend years pursuing dead ends in terms of product development. Penetration of an adversary's research and development—via clandestine intelligence collection—to assess progress facilitates incisive compromises as well as helps the U.S. private sector without showing favoritism to any specific company.

Disruption through judicial channels is currently unsatisfactory. Current penalties for theft of innovation are often not commensurate with the damage caused by the theft. The monetary fines are such that many adversaries can treat them as costs of doing business. One of the obstacles to prosecuting an economic espionage case involves the difficulty in proving the direct connection between the crime and the foreign entity. Even when anyone with common sense can see the foreign nexus, the U.S. legal system presents so many roadblocks that it is nearly impossible to secure a conviction.

The threat to innovation cannot be handled merely as a judicial problem—it is often for the benefit of nation-states that operate with impunity. Governments need to be aware that they are accountable for the criminal acts their businesses and citizens commit. A simple denial that the government was unaware of what a private citizen is doing should not be a free pass to avoid blame. It is bitterly funny that a totalitarian government can suddenly claim to have no knowledge about its citizens' activities at the exact moment when the obliviousness is convenient. Treating a national security crisis as a diplomatic matter complete with all the typical political posturing does little to effectively mitigate the problem. Thus far, diplomatic efforts have not done much to stem the flow of innovation and intellectual property from U.S. businesses. The nadir of such mishandling was the 2015 meeting of Chinese president Xi Jinping with President Obama. At this exchange between two heads of state, a new cyber agreement was announced that supposedly put the issue of cyber attacks to rest. Both sides agreed "neither country's government will conduct or knowingly support cyber-enabled theft of intellectual property, including secrets or other confidential business information, with the intent of providing competitive advantages to companies or commercial sectors." Problem solved? Well, not really. Cyber attacks emanating from China took place the very next day. In reality, the two sides agreed to nothing. Although President Obama hailed the deal as "creating architecture to govern behavior in cyberspace that is enforceable and clear," it actually accomplished little. In fact, Xi Jinping always insisted that his government "does not engage in theft of commercial secrets in any form" or encourage Chinese companies to do so. He considers China to be the *victim* of cyber espionage rather than the perpetrator. No wonder nothing was done to stem the cyber attacks.

However, there is little incentive for a more aggressive policy against the state and nonstate actors that are pillaging U.S. knowledge because current public opinion is more oriented toward blaming the victims. When a cyber breach occurs, the media immediately goes on the attack and implies that the target of the attack was somehow irresponsible and allowed the attack to occur through negligence. Businesses—like Blue Cross—act in their own best interest, and it is hardly in their best interest to allow customer or proprietary business information to be stolen. Blaming the victim provides a double win for the adversary, especially in a competitive sector. Not only do they abscond with the proprietary information, but they also force their victim to spend valuable time and resources compensating customers and trying to improve their public image. All these resources are diverted from the true objectives of the business to innovate and produce products and services (while their competitor continues to push forward, unimpeded—possibly with the newfound benefit of purloined knowledge).

The inappropriate and hostile attitude the media has shown toward victims encourages the victims not to come forward and report the attacks. Many companies do not want to play the public relations game and run the risk of losing customers and shareholders. There is additional fear that if they do come forward, the sensitive information would have to be revealed in court and the media and consequently become public. They often feel it is best to keep quiet. However, a majority of economic espionage cases are predicated in some fashion on a member of the public coming forward. Victims who feel obligated to remain silent not only harm their own interests but also deprive the U.S. government of greater awareness of how the country is being targeted by competitors and adversaries.

There is an acute need for a new approach to securing innovation. Because it is no longer the driver or even the primary customer for many cutting-edge technologies, the U.S. government must start thinking as an actor operating within a market-driven setting and consider what incentives and disincentives it can use to obtain desired outcomes. Rather than approaching private industry as a naysayer, Washington will need to find a way to focus collaboration on shared values and outcomes. The private sector must incorporate strategic intelligence awareness into its operations. Short-term gains such as market access can become liabilities rather than assets if foreign actors find a way to exploit inherent vulnerabilities. Furthermore, private industry cannot fight state-sponsored intelligence services singlehandedly. It is in their best interest to engage Washington on shared objectives of disrupting exploitation by state and nonstate actors that are attempting to degrade the U.S. advantage via theft of proprietary information. Finally, the U.S. government must be more circumspect in its participation in bilateral and multilateral ventures to ensure that it is a net beneficiary of the arrangement, specifically in the area of academic research. Grants provided by federal funding agencies like the National Science Foundation or the National Institute of Health need to have security stipulations and corresponding money allocations. The days when academic research labs can pay no concern to security and share absolutely everything with the world is coming to an end. If federal funding is accepted, some assurance that the United States will be the primary beneficiary must be made.

Selected Bibliography

2004 Report to Congress of the U.S. China Economic and Security Review Commission, 108th Cong. 185 (2004).

2007 Report to Congress of the U.S. China Economic and Security Review Commission, 110th Cong. 132 (2007).

2010 Report to Congress of the U.S. China Economic and Security Review Commission, 111th Cong. 237-239 (2010).

2013 Report to Congress of the U.S. China Economic and Security Review Commission, 113th Cong. 108 (2013).

2014 Report to Congress of the U.S. China Economic and Security Review Commission. 113th Cong. 293 (2014).

Abdollah, Tami, and Christopher Goffard. "Chinese Born Engineer Convicted Under Economic Espionage Act." *Los Angeles Times*, July 17, 2008.

Ablon, Lillian, Martin C. Libicki, and Andrea A. Golay. *Hacker's Bazaar Markets for Cybercrime Tools and Stolen Data*. Santa Monica, CA: Rand, 2014.

Aguayo, Terry. "National Briefing: South Florida Couple Pleads Not Guilty to Spying." *New York Times*, January 20, 2006.

American Academy of Arts and Sciences. *ARISE2: Advancing Research in Science and Engineering: Unleashing America's Research and Innovation Enterprise.* Cambridge, MA: American Academy of Arts and Sciences, 2013.

American Association of University Professors. "On Partnerships with Foreign Governments: The Case of Confucius Institutes." American Association of University Professors, June 2014.

Andrew, Christopher, and Oleg Gordievsky. *KGB: The Inside Story*. New York: HarperCollins, 1990.

Annual Open Hearing on Current and Projected National Security Threats to the United States: Hearings before the Select Committee on Intelligence of the United States Senate, 113th Cong. 3 (2014).

Ante, Spencer E. "IBM, Lenovo Wrestle Security Worries." *Wall Street Journal*, June 26, 2014.

Ante, Spencer, and William Mauldin. "IBM, Lenovo Deal Likely to Spark Security Review." *Wall Street Journal*, January 24, 2014.

Assessing China's Efforts to Become an "Innovation Society": A Progress Report. Hearing before the U.S. China Economic and Security Review Commission, 112th Cong. 156 (2012).

Atkinson, Robert D. *Enough Is Enough: Confronting Chinese Innovation Mercantilism.* Washington, D.C.: Information Technology and Innovation Foundation, 2012.

———. "Innovation in America: Opportunities and Obstacles before the Commerce, Science and Transportation Subcommittee on Competitiveness, Innovation, and Export Promotion. United States Senate," June 22, 2010.

———. *Understanding the U.S. National Innovation System.* Washington, D.C.: Information Technology and Innovation Foundation, 2014.

Bamford, James. "Frozen Assets: The Newest Front in Global Espionage Is One of the Least Habitable Locales on Earth—the Arctic." *Foreign Policy* (May 2015).

Barron, John. *Operation SOLO: The FBI's Man in the Kremlin.* Washington, D.C.: Regnery Publishing, 1994.

Batson, Andrew, and Matthew Kamitsching. "China Plans System to Vet Foreign Deals for Security." *Wall Street Journal*, August 26, 2008.

Batvinis, Raymond. *The Origins of FBI Counterintelligence.* Lawrence: University Press of Kansas, 2007.

Bement, Areden L. "Testimony of Dr. Areden L. Bement Jr. Director, National Science Foundation before the Senate Commerce, Science and Transportation Committee," March 10, 2010.

Bennett, Cory. "FBI to Silicon Valley: Give us Access." *The Hill*, September 10, 2015.

Berteau, David J., Scott Miller, Bryan Crotty, and Paul Nadeau. *Leveraging Global Value Chains for a Federated Approach to Defense.* Washington, D.C.: Center for Strategic and International Studies, 2014.

Bipartisan Policy Center, American Energy Innovation Council. *Restoring American Energy Innovation Leadership: Report Card, Challenges, and Opportunities.* Washington, D.C.: Bipartisan Policy Center, 2015.

Bland, Will. "Innovation on Demand: Russia Is Trying to Build Its Very Own Version of Silicon Valley." *Wall Street Journal*, June 16, 2010.

Blustein, Paul. "France and Israel Alleged to Spy on U.S. Firms." *Washington Post*, August 16, 1996.

Boehler, Patrick, and Gerry Doyle. "Use by Iraqi Military May be a Boon for China-Made Drones." *New York Times*, December 17, 2015.

Brenner, Susan W., and Anthony C. Crescenze. "State-Sponsored Crime: The Futility of the Economic Espionage Act." *Houston Journal of International Law* 28 (2006), 389–465.

Budget-in-Brief Fiscal Year 2016, Homeland Security.

Burgess, John, and John Mintz. "CIA FBI Chiefs Warn Panel Over Economic Espionage; U.S. Advanced Technology Is a Target." *Washington Post*, April 30, 1992.

"Can Russia Create a New Silicon Valley? Innovation in Russia." *Economist*, July 14, 2012.

Capps, Freddie L. "Espionage Awareness Programs." *FBI Law Enforcement Bulletin* 60, no. 9 (September 1991), 17–19.

Center for Strategic and International Studies. *CSIS Commission on Smart Power.* Washington, D.C.: Center for Strategic and International Studies, 2007.

Central Intelligence Agency. *Report to Congress on Chinese Espionage Activities Against the United States.* www.cia.gov. Accessed October 14, 2015.

Cha, Ariana Eunjung. "Even Spies Embrace China's Free Market." *Washington Post,* February 15, 2008.

Chemova, Yuliya. "Russia's Tech Startup Scene Retreats Amid Ukraine Conflict." *Wall Street Journal,* September 8, 2014.

Chen, Kathy. "White House Asks FBI to Curb Warnings on Foreign Ownership of Telecom Firms." *Wall Street Journal,* September 8, 2000.

"China's New Drones Raise Eyebrows." *Wall Street Journal,* November 18, 2010.

China's Propaganda and Influence Operations, Its Intelligence Activities That Target the United States, and the Resulting Impacts on U.S. National Security. Hearing before the U.S.–China Economic and Security Review Commission, 111th Cong. 133 (2009).

"China Throws Open Its Seaboard." *Economist,* March 12, 1988.

Civil Applications Committee (CAC) Blue Ribbon Study. Independent Study Group Final Report. September 2005.

Clapper, James R. "Statement for the Record. Worldwide Cyber Threats." House Permanent Select Committee on Intelligence. September 10, 2015.

Clark, Don. "Medvedev's Silicon Valley Visit Yields Deal with Cisco." *Wall Street Journal,* June 24, 2010.

Claydon, Mark. "Report: Chinese Hackers Launched Summer Offensive on US Chemical Industry." *Christian Science Monitor,* November 1, 2011.

Collins, Catherine. "Senators Take a Fresh Look at Rules for Lobbyists and Foreign Agents." *Los Angeles Times,* July 14, 1991.

Comey, James. "Statement of James B. Comey, Director of the Federal Bureau of Investigation, before the United States Senate Committee on the Judiciary," May 21, 2014.

The Commission on the Theft of American Intellectual Property. *The IP Commission Report.* Washington, D.C.: National Bureau of Asian Research, 2013.

Committee on the Judiciary, Subcommittee on Crime and Terrorism, United States Senate, at a Hearing Entitled "Economic Espionage and Trade Secret Theft: Are Our Laws Adequate for Today's Threats?" (2014). Statement of Randall C. Coleman, Assistant Director, Counterintelligence Division, Federal Bureau of Investigation.

Committee on Judiciary, United States Senate, Entitled Oversight of Intellectual Property Law Enforcement Efforts (2011). Statement of Gordon M. Snow, Assistant Director, Cyber Division Federal Bureau of Investigation, June 22, 2011.

Cooper, Kenneth J. "Intelligence Goes Public in the House; Panel's New Chairman Opens Hearing Today." *Washington Post,* March 9, 1993.

Cowell, Alan. "Bonn Said to Expel U.S. Envoy Accused of Economic Spying." *New York Times,* March 10, 1997.

Cumming, Alfred, and Todd Masse. *FBI Intelligence Reform Since September 11, 2001: Issues and Options for Congress.* Washington, D.C.: Congressional Research Service, 2004.

Cyber Espionage and the Theft of U.S. Intellectual Property and Technology before the House of Representatives. Committee on Energy and Commerce Subcommittee on Oversight and Investigations (2013). Testimony of Larry M. Wortzel.

"Cybersnoops and Mincing Rascals: Chinese Spying." *Economist*, May 24, 2014.

Dahlburg, John-Thor. "The Nation: Florida Couple Indicted as Cuban Agents." *Los Angeles Times*, January 10, 2006.

Dailey, Brian D., and Patrick J. Parker, eds. *Soviet Strategic Deception.* Lexington, MA: Lexington Books, 1987.

Davidson, Joe. "Lack of Digital Talent Adds to Cybersecurity Problems." *Washington Post*, July 19, 2015.

De La Merced, Michael J., and Peter Lattiman. "Appeals Court Limits Federal Law Used in Goldman Programmer Case." *New York Times*, April 12, 2012.

Defense Group Inc. *Open Power, Hidden Dangers: IBM Partnerships in China.* Vienna, VA: Defense Group Inc., 2015.

Defense Security Service. *Stakeholder Report*, 2012.

———. *Strategic Plan 2020.*

———. *Targeting U.S. Technology: A Trend Analysis of Cleared Industry Reporting.* Defense Security Service, 2013.

———. *Targeting U.S. Technology: A Trend Analysis of Cleared Industry Reporting.* Defense Security Service, 2014.

Devlin, Barrett. "Russian Spy Ring Aim to Make Children Agents." *Wall Street Journal*, July 26, 2012.

———. "U.S. News: FBI to Use Spy Law to Battle Trade Theft." *Wall Street Journal*, July 24, 2015.

Devlin, Barrett, and Danny Yadron. "Government Reaches Deal with Tech Firms on Data Requests." *Wall Street Journal*, January 28, 2014.

Devlin, Barrett, Danny Yadron, and Disuke Wakabayashi. "Apple and Others Encrypt Phones, Fueling Government Standoff." *Wall Street Journal*, November 18, 2014.

Dilanian, Ken. "Cyber Security Gets Confrontational." *Los Angeles Times*, December 4, 2012.

Dotson, John. *The Confucian Revival in Propaganda Narratives of the Chinese Government. U.S. China Economic and Security Review Commission Staff Research Paper*, July 20, 2011.

Dou, Eva, and Don Clark. "Struggles in China Push Cisco to Strike a Deal." *Wall Street Journal*, September 23, 2015.

Drew, Christopher. "New Spy Game." *New York Times*, October 18, 2010.

Drinkhall, Jim. "Security Loophole: East Bloc Businessmen Freely Come and Go in U.S. Defense Areas." *Wall Street Journal*, January 23, 1984.

Drogin, Bob. "Yearlong Hacker Attack Nets Sensitive U.S. Data Technology." *Los Angeles Times*, October 7, 1999.

Drozdiak, William. "Bonn Expels U.S. Official for Spying." *Washington Post*, March 9, 1997.

———. "Germans Force U.S. to Recall 3 CIA Agents in Spy Case." *Washington Post*, September 30, 1999.

"DSS Counterintelligence Partners with Industry to Mitigate Foreign Intelligence Threats." *Access: Official Magazine of the Defense Security Service* 3, no. 4 (Winter 2014), 16–17.

Earley, Pete. *Comrade J: The Untold Secrets of Russia's Master Spy in America After the End of the Cold War.* New York: Penguin, 2007.

Economic Espionage: A Foreign Intelligence Threat to American Jobs and Homeland Security before the Subcommittee on Counterterrorism and Intelligence, Committee on Homeland Security, 112th Cong. (2012). Statement of C. Frank Figluzzi, Assistant Director, Counterintelligence Division, Federal Bureau of Investigation.

Edge, Peter. "Written Testimony of ICE Homeland Security Investigations Executive Associate Director Peter Edge for a Senate Committee on Appropriations Subcommittee on Homeland Security Hearing Titled 'Investing in Cybersecurity: Understanding Risks and Building Capabilities for the Future.'" May 7, 2014.

Eftimiades, Nicholas. "Statement by Nicholas Eftimiades, Author, 'Chinese Intelligence Operations' before the Joint Economic Committee, United States Congress, Wednesday, May 20, 1998."

Eligon, John, and Patrick Zuo. "Designer Seed Thought to Be Latest Target by Chinese." *New York Times*, February 5, 2014.

Engleman, Eric, and Jonathan D. Salant. "Chinese Firm Beefs up Its Lobbying Amid National Security Probe on Hill." *Washington Post*, August 27, 2012.

Englund, Will. "Russia's Fading Scientific Prospects." *Washington Post*, December 22, 2011.

Faturechi, Robert. "Chinese Accused of Email Hacking Scam." *Los Angeles Times*, May 21, 2014.

FBI Counterintelligence Visits to Libraries: Hearings before the Subcommittee on Civil and Constitutional Rights of the Committee on the Judiciary, House of Representatives, 100th Cong. 115 (1988). Testimony of James H. Geer, Assistant Director, Intelligence Division, Federal Bureau of Investigation.

FBI FY2014 Budget Justification.

FBI FY2015 Budget Justification.

The FBI and CISPES, S. Prt. 101-46, (1989).

FBI Counterintelligence National Strategy: A Blueprint for Protecting U.S. Secrets, Federal Bureau of Investigation. November 4, 2011. http://www.fbi.gov/news/stories/2011/november/counterintelligence_110411.

Federal Bureau of Investigation. "Former Dow Research Scientist Convicted of Stealing Trade Secrets and Perjury." February 7, 2011. www.fbi.gov.

———. "Former DuPont Scientist Pleads Guilty to Economic Espionage: Admits He Provided Trade Secrets to Companies Controlled by Chinese Government. U.S. Attorney's Office. Northern District of California. March 2, 2012." www.fbi.gov.

———. "Former Employee of New Jersey Defense Contractor Sentenced to 70 Months in Prison for Exporting Sensitive Military Technology to China." March 25, 2013. www.fb.gov.

———. "Russian Agent and Other Members of Procurement Network of Russian Military and Intelligence Operating in the U.S. and Russia. U.S. Attorneys Office. October 3, 2012." www.fbi.gov.

———. "Statement Before the House Homeland Security Committee, Subcommittee on Cyber Security, Infrastructure Protection, and Security Technologies; Washington, D.C. April 16, 2014." www.fbi.gov.

———. "Walter Liew Sentenced to 15 Years in Prison for Economic Espionage: Court Orders Lengthy Prison Term, $27.8 Million Forfeiture, and $511,000 in Restitution After First Ever Jury Trial for Economic Espionage. U.S. Attorney's Office. July 11, 2014." www.fbi.gov.

The Federal Lobbying Disclosure Laws: Hearings before the Subcommittee on Oversight of Government Management of the Committee on Governmental Affairs, 102nd Cong. 38 (1991).

Fialka, John. *War by Other Means: Economic Espionage in America*. New York: W. W. Norton, 1999.

"Firewalls and Firefights; Business and Cyber Crime." *Economist*, August 10, 2013.

Fiscal Year 2016 Budget of the U.S. Government.

Fitzgerald, Ben, and Kelly Sayler. *Creative Disruption: Technology, Strategy and the Future of the Global Defense Industry*. Washington, D.C.: Center for a New American Security, 2014.

Fletcher, Owen. "Alibaba's Interest Poses Tests." *Wall Street Journal*, October 4, 2011.

"Former Boeing Engineer Convicted of Economic Espionage in Theft of Space Shuttle Secrets for China." *U.S. Department of Justice*, July 16, 2009.

Freeland, Chrystina. "The Next Russian Revolution." *Atlantic*, October 2011.

Gallagher, Patrick D. "Testimony of Patrick D. Gallagher, PhD., Director, National Institute of Standards and Technology, United States Department of Commerce, before the United States Senate, Committee on Commerce, Science and Transportation." March 10, 2010.

"The Geography of Foreign Students in U.S. Higher Education: Origins and Destinations." August 29, 2014. Brookings Institution.

Gerstein, Daniel M. *Making DHS More Efficient: Industry Recommendations to Improve Homeland Security*. Santa Monica, CA: Rand, 2014.

Gerstenzang, George. "Clinton Removes Export Limits on Encryption Technology." *Los Angeles Times*, September 17, 1999.

Gillis, Justin. "Scientists Accused of Theft; Espionage Alleged against Japanese." *Washington Post*, May 10, 2001.

Goel, Vindu. "Narendra Modi, Indian Premier, Courts Silicon Valley to Try to Ease Nation's Poverty." *New York Times*, September 27, 2015.

"Gone but Not Forgotten: Diasporas." *Economist*, June 27, 2015.

Gorman, Siobhan, "China Singled Out for Cyberspying." *Wall Street Journal*, November 4, 2011.

———. "NSA Director Warns of 'Dramatic' Cyberattack in Next Decade; U.S. Needs Better Preparations for Cyber Threats, Surveillance Chief Says." *Wall Street Journal*, November 21, 2014.

———. "U.S. News: Electricity Industry to Scan Grid for Spies." *Wall Street Journal*, June 18, 2009.

Gottron, Frank, and Dana A. Shea. *Publishing Scientific Papers with Potential Security Risks: Issues for Congress*. Washington, D.C.: Congressional Research Service, 2013.

Gray, Kathy Lynn. "FBI Investigates China Ties of Ohio State Professor Who Resigned, Disappeared." *Columbus Dispatch*, September 8, 2015.

Grossman, Andrew. "U.S. Charges Six Chinese with Economic Espionage." *Wall Street Journal*, May 20, 2015.

Hanemann, Thilo, and Daniel H. Rosen. *High Tech: The Next Wave of Chinese Investment in America*. The Asia Society, 2014; 2010 Report to Congress of the U.S.–China Economic and Security Review Commission, 111th Cong. Second Session, November 2010.

Harris, Shane. "The Russian News Agency Doubled as a Spy Machine." *Daily Beast*, January 27, 2015.

Hennigan, W. J. "Pentagon Courts Tech Leaders." *Los Angeles Times*, August 29, 2015.

Herbig, Katherine L. *Changes in Espionage in Americans: 1947–2007*. U.S. Department of Defense, Defense Personnel Security Research Center, 2008.

Hiatt, Fred. "Soviets Shift to Commercial Spying; Primakov Says Traditional Espionage Against U.S. Has Declined." *Washington Post*, December 13, 1991.

Hicks, Josh. "Homeland Security Is Laying Roots in Silicon Valley, and You Might Not Like Its Reasons." *Washington Post*, April 22, 2015.

Hoffman, Bruce, Edwin Meese III, and Timothy J. Roemer. *The FBI: Protecting the Homeland in the 21st Century.* 9/11 Review Commission, 2015.

Homeland Security Investigations: Examining DHS's Efforts to Protect American Jobs and Secure the Homeland before the U.S. House of Representatives Committee on Homeland Security, Subcommittee on Oversight, Investigation and Management. Statement for the Record, U.S. Immigration and Customs Enforcement, July 28, 2011.

Horwitz, Sari. "Head of U.S.-Based Russian Cultural Center Being Investigated as Possible Spy." *Washington Post*, October 23, 2013.

Huffstutter, P. J. "Tech Firms Pay Police Agencies to Fight Cyber Crime." *Los Angeles Times*, July 26, 1999.

Ignatius, David. "The French, the CIA and the Man Who Sued Too Much." *Washington Post*, January 8, 1996.

Impact of Attorney General's Guidelines for Domestic Security Investigations (The Levi Guidelines), S. Rep 98-134 (1984) (November 1983).

"Intelligence Team Given National Honor." *Los Alamos National Laboratory*, www.lanl.gov, February 28, 2011.

Investigative Report on the U.S. National Security Issues Posed by Chinese Telecommunications Companies Huawei and ZTE: A Report by Chairman Mike Rogers and Ranking Member C.A. Dutch Ruppersberger of the Permanent Select Committee on Intelligence. U.S. House of Representatives, 112th Cong 13-14 (2012).

Jackson, James K. *The Committee on Foreign Investment in the United States.* Washington, D.C.: Congressional Research Service, 2014.

———. *The Exon-Florio National Security Test for Foreign Investment.* Washington, D.C.: Congressional Research Service, 2013.

Jenkins, Brian Michael, Sorrel Wildhorn, and Marvin M. Lavin. *Intelligence Constraints of the 1970s and Domestic Terrorism: Executive Summary.* Santa Monica, CA: Rand Corporation, 1982.

Johnson, Jeh Charles. "Prepared Testimony on 'Worldwide Threats and Homeland Security Challenges' Secretary of Homeland Security Jeh Charles Johnson, House Committee on Homeland Security," October 21, 2015.

Johnston, David. "Documents Disclose F.B.I. Investigations of Some Librarians." *New York Times*, November 7, 1989.

Kaplan, Karen. "Army, USC Join Forces for Virtual Research Technology: Effort Could Provide More Realistic Military Training Simulations—and Better Hollywood Special Effects." *Los Angeles Times*, August 18, 1999.

"Keep Your T-Bonds, We'll Take the Bank, Sovereign Wealth Funds." *Economist*, July 28, 2007.

Kennedy, David M. *Over Here: The First World War and American Society.* Oxford: Oxford University Press, 2004.

Kiefer, Francine, and Laurent Belsie. "Cyber Attacks Knit Closer Ties between US, Industry Private Internet Firms, Long War of Government, Are Gathering at the White House Tomorrow." *Christian Science Monitor*, February 14, 2000.

Koch-Weser, Iacob, and Garland Ditz. *Chinese Investment in the United States: Recent Trends in Real Estate, Industry, and Investment Promotion.* Washington, D.C.: U.S. China Economic and Security Review Commission, 2015.

Korn, Melissa. "Microsoft Brings U.S. and China Universities Together." *Wall Street Journal*, June 19, 2015.

Kramer, Andrew E. "Innovation, By Order of the Kremlin." *New York Times*, April 11, 2010.

———. "Russia Arrests 2 Tied to BP Joint Venture." *New York Times*, March 21, 2008.

Krekel, Bryan, Patton Adams, and George Bakos. *Occupying the Information High Ground: Chinese Capabilities for Computer Network Operations and Cyber Espionage.* Washington, D.C.: U.S. China Economic and Security Review Commission, 2012.

LaFraniere, Sharon. "FBI Reassigns 300 Counterspies to Crime-Fighting." *Washington Post*, January 9, 1992.

Lake, Eli. "FBI Took Long Look at AIPAC Activities: Probe Targeted Suspected Spies." *Washington Times*, January 18, 2011.

Lally, Kathy. "Medvedev, iPad in Hand, Tries to Stress High-Tech at News Conference." *Washington Post*, May 19, 2011.

Lamb, Gregory M. "Leaks Flow East and West; US Industry and High-Tech Spies." *Christian Science Monitor*, December 28, 1982.

Lardner, George, and Walter Pincus. "CIA's Gates Opposed to 'Commercial Spying': Unconventional Arms Seen as Greatest Danger." *Washington Post*, December 12, 1991.

Lee, Gary. "Rep. Glickman Introduces Lobbying Bill; Foreign Agents Would Have to File Reports." *Washington Post*, April 12, 1991.

Lew, Chris. *Chinese Motivations for Corporate Espionage—a Historical Perspective.* New York: FireEye, 2013.

Lewis, James Andrew. *Space Exploration in a Changing International Environment.* Washington, D.C.: Center for Strategic and International Studies, 2014.

Lewis, John F. "Fighting Terrorism in the 21st Century." *FBI Law Enforcement Bulletin*, March 1999.

Libicki, Martin C., David Sentry, and Julia Pollak. *Hackers Wanted: An Examination of the Cybersecurity Labor Market.* Santa Monica, CA: Rand, 2014.

Loiko, Sergei. "Russian Leader Fetes Schwarzenegger; Medvedev, Seeking Economic and Tech Ties, Take Him to a Silicon Valley-Type Hub He's Planning." *Los Angeles Times*, October 12, 2010.

Lowenthal, Mark. *Intelligence: from Secrets to Policy.* 2nd ed. Washington, D.C.: Congressional Quarterly Press, 2003.

"Lurching into the Fast Lane: Industry in Russia." *Economist*, July 14, 2012.

Lute, Jane Hall. Statement for the Record, "DHS Cybersecurity: Roles and Responsibilities to Protect the Nation's Critical Infrastructure," Deputy Secretary Jane Hall Lute, U.S. Department of Homeland Security, before the House Committee on Homeland Security, March 13, 2013.

Lyons, John. "New Spying Allegations Add to Brazil Rift." *Wall Street Journal*, September 8, 2013.

Malackowski, James E. "The Intellectual Property Marketplace: Past, Present and Future." *John Marshall Journal of Intellectual Property Law* 5 (2006), 605–16.

Mandia, Kevin. "Written Testimony before the Subcommittee on Crime and Terrorism, Judiciary Committee, United States Senate. May 8, 2013."

Mandiant Intelligence Center Report. "APT1: Exposing One of China's Cyber Espionage Units." http://intelreport.mandiant.com/.

Markoff, John. "Pentagon Shops in Silicon Valley for Game Changers." *New York Times*, February 26, 2015.

———. "Technology; Wrestling Over the Key to the Codes." *New York Times*, May 9, 1993.

Markoff, John, and David Barboza. "Academic Paper in China Sets Off Alarms in U.S." *New York Times*, March 21, 2010.

Markon, Jerry, and Philip Rucker. "The Suspects in a Russian Spy Ring Lived All-American Lives." *Washington Post*, June 30, 2010.

Maskell, Jack. *Legal and Congressional Ethics Standards of Relevance to Those Who Lobby Congress.* Washington, D.C.: Congressional Research Service, 1996.

———. *Lobbying Congress: An Overview of Legal Provisions and Congressional Ethics Rules.* Washington, D.C.: Congressional Research Service, 2010.

Masse, Todd, and William Krouse. *The FBI: Past, Present, and Future.* Washington, D.C.: Congressional Research Service, 2003.

Mauldin, William, and Brent Kendall. "Court Backs Chinese Firm over White House—Ruling Says Company's Rights Were Violated in National Security Review of Purchase of Wind Projects Near Naval Facility." *Wall Street Journal*, July 16, 2014.

McAllister, Bill. "FBI to Limit Probes of Library Users; Program to Detect Foreign Agents Is Altered to Guard Patron Privacy." *Washington Post*, November 15, 1988.

———. "Stalking Spies in Libraries Triggers Suit against FBI; Details of Controversial Program Sought." *Washington Post*, June 3, 1988.

McFadden, Robert. "F.B.I. in New York Asks Librarians' Aid in Reporting on Spies." *New York Times*, September 18, 1987.

"Medvedev Ups the Tempo of Change; the Russian President Wants His Country to Attain Greater Heights." *Wall Street Journal*, June 16, 2010.

"Meeting the Espionage Challenge: A Review of United State Counterintelligence and Security Programs." Report of the Select Committee on Intelligence. United States Senate. Report No. 99-522, at 26 (1986).

Meier, Barry. "Lawmakers Seek to Close Foreign Lobbyist Loopholes." *New York Times*, June 12, 2008.

Mitchell, Russ. "Military Dollars Heading to Tech; Defense Secretary's Silicon Valley Visit Signals a New Cycle of Spending on Software." *Los Angeles Times*, April 24, 2015.

"Mixed Bag, Pros and Cons: SOE's Are Good at Infrastructure Projects, Not So Good at Innovation." *Economist*, January 21, 2012.

Memorandum for the Director. Federal Bureau of Investigation. November 15, 1939. Declassified July 13, 1990.

———. Federal Bureau of Investigation. November 2, 1940. Declassified July 16, 1990.

Modification of the Foreign Agents Registration Act of 1938: Hearings before the Subcommittee on Administrative Law and Governmental Relations of the Committee on the Judiciary House of Representatives, 102nd Cong. 33 (1991).

Morain, Dan. "Spies Never Came in from the Cold." *Los Angeles Times*, September 24, 1990.

Morton, John. "Testimony of John Morton, Director, U.S. Immigration and Customs Enforcement, Before the U.S. House of Representatives Committee on the Judiciary, Subcommittee on Intellectual Property, Competition and the Internet on 'Promoting Investment and Protecting Commerce Online: Legitimate Sites v Parasites, Part II." April 5, 2011.

Mozur, Paul, and Jane Perlez. "U.S. Tech Giants May Blur National Security Boundaries in China Deals." *New York Times*, October 30, 2015.

Mueller, Robert S. "Statement of Robert S. Mueller, Director, Federal Bureau of Investigation, before the Committee on Judiciary, United States Senate, Regarding Oversight of the Federal Bureau of Investigation." December 14, 2011.

Mulrine, Anna. "Pentagon Cybersecurity Strategy Comes with Olive Branch to Silicon Valley." *Christian Science Monitor*, April 23, 2015.

Muro, Mark, Jonathan Rothwell, Scott Andes, Kenan Fikri, and Siodharth Kulkarni. *America's Advanced Industries: What They Are, Where They Are, and Why They Matter.* Washington, D.C.: Brookings, 2015.

Nakashima, Ellen. "Fierce Fight for Expert Workers." *Washington Post*, November 13, 2012.

——. "Google to Enlist NSA to Ward Off Attacks." *Washington Post*, February 4, 2010.

——. "Grand Jury Indicts Six Chinese Citizens in Alleged Plot to Steal Trade Secrets." *Washington Post*, May 20, 2015.

——. "U.S. Indicts 6 Chinese Citizens on Charges of Stealing Trade Secrets." *Washington Post*, May 19, 2015.

Nakashima, Ellen, and Brian Krebs. "As Cyberattacks Increase, U.S. Faces Shortage of Security Talent." *Washington Post*, December 23, 2009.

National Counterintelligence Center. *Annual Report to Congress on Foreign Economic Collection and Industrial Espionage: 1995*. National Counterintelligence Center, 1996.

——. *Annual Report to Congress on Foreign Economic Collection and Industrial Espionage: 1996*. National Counterintelligence Center, 1997.

——. *Annual Report to Congress on Foreign Economic Collection and Industrial Espionage: 1997*. National Counterintelligence Center, 1998.

——. *Annual Report to Congress on Foreign Economic Collection and Industrial Espionage: 1999*. National Counterintelligence Center, 2000.

National Industrial Security Program Policy Advisory Committee Minutes of the Meeting, September 27, 1995.

National Security Strategy of the United States 2015.

Nelson, Jack. "Spies Took $300 Billion Toll on U.S. Firms in '97." *Los Angeles Times*, January 12, 1998.

New Neighbors: Chinese Investment in the United States by Congressional District. A Report by the National Committee on U.S.–China Relations and the Rhodium Group. New York: Rhodium Group, 2015.

Nondiplomatic Activities of Representatives of Foreign Governments: A Preliminary Study Prepared by the Staff of the Committee on Foreign Relations. Washington, D.C.: U.S. Government Printing Office, 1962.

Office of the National Counterintelligence Executive. *Annual Report to Congress on Foreign Economic Collection and Industrial Espionage, 2001*. Office of the National Counterintelligence Executive, 2002.

——. *Annual Report to Congress on Foreign Economic Collection and Industrial Espionage: 2002*. Office of the National Counterintelligence Executive, 2003.

——. *Annual Report to Congress on Foreign Economic Collection and Industrial Espionage: 2003*. Office of the National Counterintelligence Executive, 2004.

——. *Annual Report to Congress on Foreign Economic Collection and Industrial Espionage: 2004*. Office of the National Counterintelligence Executive, 2005.

——. *Annual Report to Congress on Foreign Economic Collection and Industrial Espionage: 2005*. National Counterintelligence Executive, 2006.

——. *Annual Report to Congress on Foreign Economic Collection and Industrial Espionage: 2008*. Office of the National Counterintelligence Executive, 2009.

——. *Foreign Spies Stealing US Economic Secrets in Cyberspace, Report to Congress on Foreign Economic Collection and Industrial Espionage, 2009–2011*. Office of the National Counterintelligence Executive, 2011.

———. *National Counterintelligence Strategy.* National Counterintelligence Executive, 2007.

Office of the Director of National Intelligence. *National Intelligence Strategy.* Washington, D.C.: Office of the Director of National Intelligence, 2014.

Omestad, Thomas. "Cloak and Dagger as R&D. The French Do It. The Brits Do It. But Corporate Spying May Not Be for Us." *Washington Post,* June 27, 1993.

Osgood, Kenneth. *Total Cold War: Eisenhower's Secret Propaganda Battle at Home and Abroad.* Wichita: University Press of Kansas, 2006.

Ostrow, Ronald J., and Paul Richter. "Economic Espionage Poses Major Peril to U.S. Interests Spying." *Los Angeles Times,* September 28, 1991.

O'Toole, Tara. "Testimony of the Honorable Tara O'Toole, MD, MPH, Under Secretary for Science and Technology, U.S. Department of Homeland Security, U.S. Senate, Homeland Security and Governmental Affairs Committee," July 17, 2013.

An Overview of the Fiscal Year 2013 Budget for the National Institute of Standards and Technology before the United States Senate, Committee on Commerce, Science and Transportation, Subcommittee on Science and Space. Patrick D. Gallagher, PhD, Under Secretary of Commerce for Standards and Technology, United States Department of Commerce.

Paletta, Damian. "Cybersecurity Firm Says It Found Spyware on Government Network in April." *Wall Street Journal,* June 15, 2015.

———. "White House Cybersecurity Event to Draw Top Tech, Wall Street Execs." *Wall Street Journal,* February 11, 2015.

Paletta, Damian, Keith Johnson, and Sudeep Reddy. "Obama Blocks Chinese Firm from Wind-Farm Projects." *Wall Street Journal,* September 29, 2012.

Paletta, Damian, and Danny Yadron. "White House to Create New Division to Streamline Cyberthreat Intelligence; Effort to Buttress Government, Corporate Defenses against Sophisticated Hackers." *Wall Street Journal,* February 11, 2015.

"Panel Chairman Seeks Study of FBI Reorganization; Rep Wolf Cites Concerns on Impact of Shifting Agents to Counterterrorism Effort." *Washington Post,* June 5, 2002.

Partnership for Public Service. *Cyber In-Security II: Closing the Federal Talent Gap.* Washington, D.C.: Partnership for Public Service, 2015.

Pasternak, Judy, and Robert C. Paddock. "Possible Espionage Probed at NASA Research Center." *Los Angeles Times,* November 19, 1992.

Peck, Mason. "Statement of Dr. Mason Peck, Chief Technologist, National Aeronautics and Space Administration before the Committee on Commerce, Science and Transportation, United States Senate."

Perez, Evan. "FBI's New Campaign Targets Corporate Espionage." *Wall Street Journal,* May 11, 2012.

Peterson, Andrea. "NSA Director, Yahoo Executive Spar Over Cyber Spying." *Washington Post,* February 24, 2015.

Pettersson, Edward. "Ex-Boeing Engineer Chung Guilty of Stealing Secrets (Update 3)." *Bloomberg,* July 16, 2009, www.bloomberg.com.

Piller, Charles. "High Tech's Distrust of FBI Could Impede Hacking Probe." *Los Angeles Times,* February 11, 2000.

Pimentel, Stanley A. Society of Former Special Agents. "Interview of Former Special Agent Richard A. Marquise." Unpublished interview, April 11, 2008.

Pincus, Walter. "CIA Targets Overseas Firms but Draws a Line." *Washington Post*, March 5, 1995.

———. "Russian Spies on Rise Here; Administration Worried about 'Aggressive' Economic Espionage." *Washington Post*, September 21, 1999.

Pisano, Gary P., and Willy C. Shih. "Restoring American Competitiveness." *Harvard Business Review* (July–August 2009).

"Political Priority, Economic Gamble: Special Economic Zones." *Economist*, April 4, 2015.

Powers, Richard Gid. *Broken: The Troubled Past and Uncertain Future of the FBI*. New York: Free Press, 2004.

"Premier FBI Cybersquad in Pittsburgh to Add Agents." *New York Times*, August 17, 2014.

Pritzker, Penny. "Testimony on the Role of Manufacturing Hubs in a 21st Century Innovation Economy by Secretary of Commerce Penny Pritzker, Committee on Commerce, Science, and Transportation, United States Senate," November 13, 2013.

A Progress Report: Hearing before the U.S. China Economic and Security Review Commission, 112th Cong. 90 (2012).

Questionable NPIC Projects. May 8, 1973. Document 00200 (part of the CIA's "Family Jewels" documents).

Ragsdale, Daniel. "Written Testimony of ICE Deputy Director Daniel Ragsdale for a House Committee on Appropriations Subcommittee on Homeland Security hearing on ICE's FY 2015 Budget Request," March 13, 2014.

Raice, Shayndi. "China's Huawei Draws Scrutiny for Deal to Buy Small U.S. Tech Firm." *Wall Street Journal*, November 19, 2010.

———. "U.S. Panel Poised to Recommend Against Huawei Deal." *Wall Street Journal*, February 11, 2011.

Ravindranath, Mohana. "NSA Work Inspires Cybersecurity Start-Ups." *Washington Post*, January 20, 2014.

Rein, Lisa. "Millennials Working in Government Are at Their Lowest Levels in Five Years, New Report Finds." *Washington Post*, August 24, 2015.

Report to Congress of the U.S. China Economic and Security Review Commission, 110th Cong. 127 (2007).

Report to Congress of the U.S. China Economic and Security Review Commission, 112th Cong. 407 (2012).

Report to Congress of the U.S. China Economic and Security Review Commission, 113th Cong. 165 (2014).

Report of the Select Committee on Intelligence: United States Senate, Covering the Period January 3, 2013 to January 5, 2015. Rep. 114-8, at 18 (2015).

Report of the Select Committee on U.S. National Security and Military/Commercial Concerns with the People's Republic of China, 105th Cong. (1999).

Respault, Robin, and Rory Carroll. "China May Have Edge in Race to Build California's Bullet Train." *Reuters*, May 21, 2015.

Restoring American Energy Innovation Leadership: Report Card, Challenges, and Opportunities. Washington, D.C.: Bipartisan Policy Center, 2015.

Richards, Evelyn. "Americans Conducting 'Computer Diplomacy'; Goal Is to Liberate Soviets, Promote Peace." *Washington Post*, August 28, 1989.

Riebling. Mark. *Wedge: The Secret War between the FBI and the CIA.* New York: Alfred A. Knopf, 1994.

Richelson, Jeffrey T. *The US Intelligence Community.* 6th ed. Boulder, CO: Westview Press, 2011.

Riley, Naomi Schaefer. "Young, Jewish and Going to Israel; Taglit-Birthright Has Given Away 300,000 10-Day Trips, Hoping to Stir an Appreciation of Jewish Heritage." *Wall Street Journal*, November 1, 2012.

Risen, James. "Downplayed by CIA, Paris Incident Has Wide Impact." *Los Angeles Times*, October 11, 1995.

Risen, James, and Laura Poitras. "Spying by N.S.A. Ally Entangled U.S. Law Firm." *New York Times*, February 16, 2014.

Roberts, Mark J. "Pakistan's Inter-Services Intelligence Directorate: A State within a State?" *Joint Forces Quarterly* 1, no. 48 (2008).

Safire, William. "The Farewell Dossier." *New York Times*, February 2, 2004.

Salidjanova, Nargiza. *Going Out: An Overview of China's Outward Foreign Direct Investment.* Washington, D.C.: U.S. China Economic and Security Review Commission, 2011.

Sanger, David E., and Tim Weiner. "Emerging Role for the CIA: Economic Spy." *New York Times*, October 15, 1995.

Sarno, David, and Jessica Guynn. "Freeze, It's the iPolice." *Los Angeles Times*, May 5, 2010.

Schneider, Keith. "U.S. Confiscating A-Plant Wiretaps." *New York Times*, August 2, 1991.

Schwirtz, Michael. "Russia Asks Schwarzenegger to Help in a Tough Task." *New York Times*, October 12, 2010.

Semansky, Patrick. "In Fierce Battle for Cyber Talent, Even NSA Struggles to Keep Elites on Staff." *Nextgov.com*, April 14, 2015.

Shea, Dennis C. "The Impact of International Technology Transfer on American Research and Development before the Committee on Science, Space, and Technology Subcommittee on Investigations and Oversight, United States House of Representatives," December 5, 2012.

Shpiro, Shlomo. "Soviet Espionage in Israel, 1973–1991." *Intelligence and National Security* 30, no. 4 (2015): 486–507.

Sims, Calvin. "Troubling Issues in a Silicon Valley Spy Case." *New York Times*, July 8, 1996.

Singer, Peter L. *Federally Supported Innovations: 22 Examples of Major Technology Advances That Stem from Federal Research Support.* Washington, D.C.: Information Technology and Innovation Foundation, 2014.

Sipress, Alan. "Computer System Under Attack: Commerce Department Targeted; Hackers Traced to China." *Washington Post*, October 6, 2006.

"Six Now Expelled in Belgian Espionage." *New York Times*, August 23, 1983.

Smale, Alison. "Germany, Too, Is Accused of Spying on Its European Allies." *New York Times*, May 5, 2015.

Solomon, Jay. "Investing in Intelligence; Spy Agencies Seek Innovation through Venture-Capital Firm." *Wall Street Journal*, September 12, 2005.

———. "Phantom Menace, FBI Sees Big Threat from Chinese Spies." *Wall Street Journal*, August 10, 2005.

Sorcher, Sara. "The Battle Between Washington and Silicon Valley Over Encryption." *Christian Science Monitor*, July 7, 2015.

———. "Tech Firms Push Back on 'Reactionary' Politics Following Terror Attacks." *Christian Science Monitor*, December 17, 2015.

"The South China Miracle: A Great Leap Forward." *Economist*, 1991.

Springut, Micah, Stephen Schlaikjeer, and David Chen. *China's Program for Science and Technology Modernization: Implications for American Competitiveness.* Arlington, VA: Centra Technology Inc., 2011.

Staley, Oliver. "For MIT the Launch of a Russian Satellite." *Washington Post*, May 12, 2013.

"Start-Ups Join Microsoft Accelerator." *Washington Post*, August 18, 2014.

Steinbock, Dan. *The Challenges for America's Defense Innovation.* Washington, D.C.: Information Technology and Innovation Foundation, 2014.

A Strategy for American Innovation. Washington, D.C.: National Economic Council and Office of Science Technology Policy, 2015.

Stutler, Thomas R. "Stealing Secrets Solved: Examining the Economic Espionage Act of 1996." *FBI Law Enforcement Bulletin* 69, no. 11 (November 2000), 11–16.

Subcommittee on Science and Space, Committee on Commerce, Science and Transportation, United States Senate, on Keeping America Competitive Through Investment in R&D (2012). Statement of Dr. John P. Holdren. Director, Office of Science and Technology Policy, Executive Office of the President of the United States.

"The Surveillance State and Its Discontents." *Foreign Policy*, December 2013.

Suttmeier, Richard P. *Trends in U.S. China Science and Cooperation: Collaborative Knowledge Production for the Twenty-First Century?* Washington, D.C.: U.S. China Economic and Security Review Commission, 2014.

Swoboda, Frank. "Economic Espionage Rising." *Washington Post*, February 29, 1996.

Szamossegi, Andrew. *An Analysis of Chinese Investments in the U.S. Economy.* Washington, D.C.: U.S. China Economic and Security Review Commission, 2012.

Tadena, Nathalie. "Engineer Gets 4 Years In Motorola Secrets Case." *Wall Street Journal*, August 30, 2012.

Tasssey, Gregory. *Beyond the Business Cycle: The Need for a Technology-Based Growth Strategy. Science and Public Policy.* Oxford: Oxford University Press, 2012.

Tellis, Ashley J. "Balancing without Containment: A U.S. Strategy for Confronting China's Rise." *The Washington Quarterly* 36, no. 4 (2013): 109–24.

"Ten Years After: The Bureau Since 9/11." *Federal Bureau of Investigation*, http://www.fbi.gov/about-us/ten-years-after-the-fbi-since-9-11. Accessed July 20, 2014.

"Three Indicted in Lucent Trade-Secret Case." *New York Times*, June 1, 2001.

Timberg, Craig, and Ellen Nakashima. "Amid NSA Spying Revelation, Tech Leaders Call for New Restraints on Agency." *Washington Post*, November 1, 2013.

Today's Rising Terrorist Threat and the Danger to the United States: Reflections on the Tenth Anniversary of the 9/11 Commission Report. Washington, D.C.: Bipartisan Policy Center, 2014.

Trends and Implications of Chinese Investment in the United States: Hearing before the U.S. China Economic and Security Review Commission, 113th Cong. (2013).

Treverton, Gregory F., and Seth G. Jones. *Measuring National Power*. Santa Monica, CA: Rand, 2005.

Tromblay, Darren E. *The U.S. Domestic Intelligence Enterprise: History, Development, and Operations*. Boca Raton, FL: Taylor and Francis/CRC Press, 2016.

"Two Engineers Indicted in Economic Espionage." *Los Angeles Times*, September 27, 2007.

U.S. Cybersecurity and Policy: Senate Armed Services Committee (September 29, 2015). Statement for the Record, U.S. Cybersecurity and Policy, Senate Armed Services Committee, James R. Clapper, Director of National Intelligence.

U.S. Department of Commerce, Bureau of Industry and Security. *Annual Report to the Congress for Fiscal Year 2008*. Washington, D.C.: U.S. Department of Commerce, 2008.

———. *Annual Report to the Congress for Fiscal Year 2009*. Washington, D.C.: U.S. Department of Commerce, 2009.

———. *Annual Report to the Congress for Fiscal Year 2010*. Washington, D.C.: U.S. Department of Commerce, 2010.

———. *Annual Report to the Congress for Fiscal Year 2011*. Washington, D.C.: U.S. Department of Commerce, 2012.

———. *Annual Report to the Congress for Fiscal Year 2012*. Washington, D.C.: U.S. Department of Commerce, 2013.

———. *Annual Report to the Congress for Fiscal Year 2013* Washington, D.C.: U.S. Department of Commerce, 2014.

———. *Annual Report to the Congress for Fiscal Year 2014*. Washington, D.C.: U.S. Department of Commerce, 2015.

———. *Don't Let This Happen to You: An Introduction to U.S. Export Control Law. Export Enforcement*. Washington, D.C.: U.S. Department of Commerce, 2008.

U.S. Department of Defense. *Report of the Defense Science Board Task Force on Basic Research. Office of the Under Secretary of Defense, for Acquisition, Technology and Logistics*. Washington, D.C.: U.S. Department of Defense, 2012.

———. *Soviet Acquisition of Military Significant Western Technology: An Update*. Washington, D.C.: Office of the Secretary of Defense, 1985.

U.S. Department of Energy. *Letter Report on Selected Aspects of the Department of Energy's Activities Involving the Foreign Intelligence Surveillance Act*. Washington, D.C.: U.S. Department of Energy, 2009.

U.S. Department of Energy, Office of Inspector General. *Audit Report: The Department of Energy's Energy Innovation Hubs*. Washington, D.C.: U.S. Department of Energy, 2013.

———. *Inspection Report: Follow-On Review of the Status of the U.S. Department of Energy's Counterintelligence Implementation Plan.* Washington, D.C.: U.S. Department of Energy, 2000.

U.S. Department of Energy, Office of Inspector General, Office of Audit Service. *Audit Report: Review of the Status of the U.S. Department of Defense's Counterintelligence Implementation Plan.* Washington: D.C.: U.S. Department of Energy, 1999.

U.S. Department of Energy, Office of Inspector General, Office of Audits and Inspections. *Inspection Report: Continuity of Operations Planning and Intelligence Readiness.* Washington, D.C.: U.S. Department of Energy, 2012.

U.S. Department of Energy, Office of Inspector General, Office of Inspections and Special Inquiries. *Inspection Report: The Consolidated Terrorism Watchlist Nomination Process at the Department of Energy.* Washington, D.C.: U.S. Department of Energy, 2007.

———. *Inspection Report: Internal Controls Over Computer Property at the Department's Counterintelligence Directorate.* Washington, D.C.: U.S. Department of Energy, 2007.

———. *Inspection Report: Internal Controls Over Sensitive Compartmented Information Access for Selected Field Intelligence Elements.* Washington, D.C.: U.S. Department of Energy, 2008.

U.S. Department of Homeland Security, Immigration and Customs Enforcement. "Statement for the Record, U.S. Immigration and Customs Enforcement, before the U.S. House of Representatives Committee on Homeland Security, Subcommittee on Oversight, Investigation and Management on 'Homeland Security Investigations': Examining DHS's Efforts to Protect American Jobs and Secure the Homeland," July 28, 2011.

U.S. Department of Homeland Security, Immigration and Customs Enforcement, Homeland Security Investigations. "Written Testimony of ICE Homeland Security Investigations Executive Associate Director Peter Edge for a Senate Committee on Appropriations Subcommittee on Homeland Security Hearing Titled 'Investing in Cybersecurity: Understanding Risks and Building Capabilities for the Future,'" May 7, 2014.

U.S. Department of Justice. *Chinese National Charged with Economic Espionage Involving Theft of Trade Secrets from Leading Agricultural Company Based in Indianapolis.* Washington, D.C., U.S. Department of Justice, 2010.

———. *Federal Bureau of Investigation. FY2015 Budget at a Glance.* Washington, D.C.: U.S. Department of Justice, 2014.

———. *Former Boeing Engineer Convicted of Economic Espionage in Theft of Space Shuttle Secrets for China.* Washington, D.C.: U.S. Department of Justice, 2009.

———. *New Indictment Expands Charges against Former Lucent Scientists Accused of Passing Trade Secrets to Chinese Company.* April 11, 2002. www.justice.gov.

———. *Pair from Cupertino and San Jose, California, Indicted for Economic Espionage and Theft of Trade Secrets from Silicon Valley Companies.* December 4, 2002. www.justice.gov.

——. *PRO IP Act, First Annual Report 2008–2009.* Washington, D.C., U.S. Department of Justice, 2009. 14.

——. *PRO IP Act, Annual Report FY 2011.* Washington, D.C.: U.S. Department of Justice, 2011.

——. *PRO IP Act, Annual Report FY 2012.* Washington, D.C.: U.S. Department of Justice, 2012.

——. *PRO IP Act, Annual Report FY 2013.* Washington, D.C., U.S. Department of Justice, 2013.

——. *Sinovel Corporation and Three Individuals Charged in Wisconsin with Theft of Amsc Trade Secrets.* Justice News, Department of Justice Office of Public Affairs, June 27, 2013.

——. "Suburban Chicago Woman Sentenced to Four Years in Prison for Stealing Motorola Trade Secrets before Boarding Plane to China." August 29, 2012, www.justice.gov.

——. *Summary of Major U.S. Export Enforcement, Economic Espionage, Trade Secret and Embargo-Related Criminal Cases* (January 2008 to the Present: Updated March 26, 2014). Washington, D.C.: U.S. Department of Justice, 2014.

——. *Summary of Major U.S. Export Enforcement, Economic Espionage, Trade Secret and Embargo-Related Criminal Cases* (January 2009 to the Present: Updated August 12, 2015). Washington, D.C.: U.S. Department of Justice, 2015.

——. "Two Bay Area Men Indicted on Charges of Economic Espionage." September 26, 2007, www.justice.gov.

U.S. Department of Justice, Office of the Inspector General. *Audit of the Federal Bureau of Investigation's Implementation of Its Next Generation Cyber Initiative.* Washington, D.C.: U.S. Department of Justice, 2015.

——. *The Federal Bureau of Investigation's Efforts to Hire, Train, and Retain Intelligence Analysts.* Washington, D.C.: U.S. Department of Justice, Office of the Inspector General, 2005.

——. *The Federal Bureau of Investigation's Efforts to Improve the Sharing of Intelligence and Other Information.* Washington, D.C.: U.S. Department of Justice, Office of the Inspector General, Audit Division, 2003.

——. *Review of the FBI's Handling of Intelligence Information Related to the September 11 Attacks.* Washington, D.C.: U.S. Department of Justice, Office of the Inspector General, 2006.

U.S. Government Accountability Office. *Export Controls: Improvements to Commerce's Dual Use System Needed to Ensure Protection of U.S. Interest in the Post-9/11 Environment.* Washington, D.C.: Government Accountability Office, 2006.

U.S. Intellectual Property Enforcement Coordinator. *2013 Joint Strategic Plan on Intellectual Property Enforcement.* Washington, D.C.: U.S. Intellectual Property Enforcement Coordinator, 2013.

Office of the U.S. Trade Representative. *2011 Special 301 Report.* Washington, D.C.: Office of the U.S. Trade Representative.

——. *2013 Special 301 Report.* Washington, D.C.: Office of the U.S. Trade Representative, 2013.

———. *014 Report to Congress on China's WTO Compliance.* Washington, D.C.: Office of the U.S. Trade Representative, 2014.

———. *2015 Special 301 Report.* Washington, D.C.: Office of the U.S. Trade Representative, 2015.

United States of America v. Dongfan "Greg" Chung. October 2007. United States District Court, Central District of California, SA CR 08-0024.

United States of America v. Evgeny Buryakov (a/k/a "Zhenya"), Igor Sporyshev, and Victor Podobnyy.

United States of America v. Hanjuan Jin. Appeal from the United States District Court for the Northern District of Illinois Eastern Division No. 08 CR 192. Robert Castillo, Chief Judge. Argued September 9, 2013–Decided September 26, 2013.

United States of America v. Sixing Liu a.k.a. "Steve Liu" Criminal Complaint. Magistrate No. 11-8022.

Venceremos Brigade Part 2: Hearings before the Committee on Internal Security, House of Representatives, 96th Cong. 7825 (1972).

Vise, David A., and Lorraine Adams. "FBI to Restructure, Adding Emphasis on Crime Prevention." *Washington Post,* November 11, 1999.

Waguespack, Michael J. "Michael J Waguespack, Deputy Assistant Director, National Security Division, FBI, before the House Committee on Government Reform, Subcommittee on National Security, Veterans Affairs and International Relations," April 3, 2001.

Weinstein, Allen, and Alexander Vassiliev. *The Haunted Wood.* New York: Random House, 1999.

Weisgerber, Marcus. "China's Copycat Jet Raises Questions about F-35." September 23, 2015, www.defenseone.com.

Weise, Elizabeth. "FireEye Has Become Go-To Company for Breaches." *USA Today,* May 21, 2015.

Weiser, Benjamin. "3 N.Y.U. Scientists Accepted Bribes from China, U.S. Says." *New York Times,* May 20, 2013.

Weiss, Gus W. "The Farewell Dossier: Duping the Soviets." *Studies in Intelligence* 39, no. 5 (1996), 121–26.

Wildavsky, Ben. *The Great Brain Race: How Global Universities Are Reshaping the World.* Princeton, NJ: Princeton University Press, 2010.

Wilke, John R. "Two Silicon Valley Cases Raise Fears of Chinese Espionage." *Wall Street Journal,* January 15, 2003.

Winkler, Rolfe. "Google Sells Handset Business to Lenovo; the Nearly $3 Billion Deal Comes Two Years after Google Bought Motorola for $12.5 Billion." *Wall Street Journal,* January 29, 2014.

Wise, David. *Cassidy's Run: The Secret Spy War over Nerve Gas.* New York: Random House, 2000.

———. *Tiger Trap: America's Secret Spy War with China.* New York: Houghton Mifflin Hartcourt, 2011.

Wolf, Kevin J. "Testimony by Kevin J. Wolf, Assistant Secretary for Export Administration, Bureau of Industry and Security, U.S. Department of Commerce before the National Security and Foreign Affairs Subcommittee of the Committee on Oversight and Reform," March 23, 2010.

Wong, Chun Han. "Economic Espionage Charges Could Further Dent China–U.S. Ties." *Wall Street Journal*, May 22, 2015.

Wong, Edward. "Back Home, Chinese Scientists Indicted by U.S. Are Seen as Rising Stars." *New York Times*, May 12, 2015.

———. "Hacking U.S. Secrets, China Pushes for Drones." *New York Times*, September 20, 2013.

Wong, Edward, and Didi Kirsten Tatlow. "China Seen in Push to Gain Technology Insights." *New York Times*, June 5, 2013.

Wood, John. "Written Testimony of U.S. Immigration and Customs Enforcement Homeland Security Investigation Assistant Director John Wood for a House Committee on Homeland Security Subcommittee on Counterterrorism and Intelligence Hearing Titled 'Economic Espionage: A Foreign Intelligence Threat to American Jobs and Homeland Security,'" June 27, 2012.

Wortzel, Larry M. "Testimony of Larry M Wortzel. Cyber Espionage and the Theft of U.S. Intellectual Property and Technology before the House of Representatives. Committee on Energy and Commerce Subcommittee on Oversight and Investigations," July 9, 2013.

Wright, Robin. "France Accuses U.S. Diplomats of Espionage." *Los Angeles Times*, February 23, 1995.

Wylie, Amos K. "Unfair Exchange." *Studies in Intelligence* (Fall 1962), 9–15.

Yadron, Danny. "Cybersecurity Firm's Strategy Raises Eyebrows." *Wall Street Journal*, September 9, 2015.

———. "Latest Cyber Deal Shows Security Is Hot Sector." *Wall Street Journal*, January 3, 2014.

———. "Tech Firms Criticize Policies on Security Requests; Google, Microsoft and Others Release Figures on Last Year." *Wall Street Journal*, February 3, 2014.

Yadron, Danny, James T. Areddy, and Paul Mozur. "China Hacking Deep, Diverse—Internet Spies Stretch Beyond Government Offering Beijing Cover, Experts Say." *Wall Street Journal*, May 30, 2014.

Zhang, Yajun, and Eliot Gao. "China Criticizes U.S. Review of Sensitive Deals." *Wall Street Journal*, February 18, 2011.

Index

academia: for CERC, 110–11; China and, 108, 110, 113, 123; cultural ties of, 167; in economic espionage, 229–30; elicitation influence on, 81–82; innovation by, 243–44; intelligence collection by, xv, 173; investment for, 185; U.S. government influenced by, 184–85; world leader of, 162
accrued knowledge. *See* knowledge
active defense, 56
Advanced Research Projects Agency (ARPA-E), 186
Advanced Resistant Threat One (APT1), 53
aerospace, 120, 165
agricultural innovation, 121–22
agriculture research, 121
AIPAC. *See* American Israeli Political Affairs Committee
Airbus Group, 235–36
Alexander, Keith, xvi
amendment, 7, 9. *See also* Byrd Amendment; Exon-Florio Amendment
American Israeli Political Affairs Committee (AIPAC), 72
American Superconductor Inc. (AMSC), 157

ANSIR. *See* Awareness of National Security Issues and Response
APT1. *See* Advanced Resistant Threat One
ARPA-E. *See* Advanced Research Projects Agency
assessing, 78
atomic bomb, 22
Atomic Energy Commission, 37
Awareness of National Security Issues and Response (ANSIR), 224

basic science, 186
BIS. *See* Bureau of Industry and Security
bullet train, 104–5
Bureau of Industry and Security (BIS): agency of, 19; analytical duties of, 42; China against, 42; cyber attack on, 42; on EAR, 41; end-user check by, 41; export license by, 40, 41; function of, 40, 52; partners of, 40; Project GUARDIAN by, 233; for technology, 39
Buryakov, Evgeny, 10–11
buying in: engagement by, xiii; by foreign government, 161; intelligence collection by, 161; international, xviii

cooperation with, 38–39; FIEs by, 37; function of, 52; innovation by, 36–37; interagency analytic assistance by, 39; 1998 CI Implementation Plan by, 37–38; private sector influence on, 181; subject matter expertise by, 38

Department of Homeland Security (DHS): function of, 51; HSI by, 31–32; ICE by, 31–32; Project Shield America by, 232; for Silicon Valley, 192–93

developing, 78

development collection, 155

Development of Espionage, Counterintelligence, and Counterterrorism Awareness (DECA), 223–24

DHS. *See* Department of Homeland Security

diplomacy, 172, 248

direct investment, 100–1

DIS. *See* Defense Investigative Service

DISP. *See* Defense Industrial Security Program

disruption, of threat, 236–37

DNI. *See* Director of National Intelligence

DoD. *See* Department of Defense, U.S.

DOE. *See* Department of Energy

Dongfan Chung, 170–71

Dow Chemical company, 136–37

DSS. *See* Defense Security Service

DSS/FBI Strategic Partnership Task Force, 228

DuPont Corporation, 123, 136

EAR. *See* Export Administration Regulations

economic espionage: academia in, 229–30; adversary influenced by, 247; ANSIR for, 224; by China, 66; cultural ties influence on, 74–75; by French intelligence services, 71; front companies for, 88; by GRU, 70–71; by Kexue, 121; knowledge from, 5; penalties for, *14*, 14–15; sponsorship of, 247; SPP for, 229–30; by U.S. government, 246–47; volunteering for, 79; by Xiaodong, 121. *See also* espionage

Economic Espionage Act of 1996, 13–15

economic intelligence collection, 65, 66, 235–36

economic viability, 11

ego, 82

863 Program, 66, 108

elements of national power (ENPs), 4; tools of, 1–2

elicitation, 86; academia influenced by, 81–82

encryption, xi, 193, 196

end-user check, 41–42

energy, 155–56

energy generation, 156

energy storage, 156

energy technology, 186

ENPs. *See* elements of national power

entertainment industry, 153–54

espionage: by Chi, 172; by China, 105–6; by Israel, 72; knowledge by, 206; proprietary information by, 73–74; shared ideology influence on, 75; by Soviet Union, 8

Espionage Act of 1917, 6–7

Exon-Florio Amendment, 43–44

export, 209. *See also* deemed export; re-export

Export Administration Regulations (EAR), 41

export license, 40–41

facility information, 87

FARA. *See* Foreign Agents Registration Act

FDI. *See* foreign direct investment

About the Authors

Darren E. Tromblay has served as an intelligence analyst with the Federal Bureau of Investigation for more than a decade. He holds an MA from George Washington University's Elliott School of International Affairs and an MS from the National Defense Intelligence College. He earned his BA from the University of California. Mr. Tromblay is the author of *U.S. Domestic Intelligence Enterprise: History, Development, and Operations* (2016). His articles have been published in *Intelligence and National Security*, *Small Wars Journal*, and the *International Journal of Intelligence Ethics*.

Robert Spelbrink currently serves as a special agent at the Federal Bureau of Investigation, where he has worked counterintelligence and counterespionage cases for twelve years. He currently supervises the FBI's National Strategic Partnership Program that provides security outreach to the private sector and government agencies. Prior to joining the FBI, he earned a PhD in cellular biology from the University of Missouri in Columbia and did postdoctoral research at the Danforth Plant Science Center in St. Louis, Missouri. He also has a BS in biology and a BS in business administration from the University of Missouri in St. Louis.

Made in the USA
Middletown, DE
27 August 2019